Prentice-Hall Computer Applications in Electrical Engineering Series

FRANKLIN F. KUO, *Editor*

ABRAMSON AND KUO   *Computer-Communication Networks*
BOWERS AND SEDORE   *SCEPTRE:*
  A Computer Program for Circuit and Systems Analysis
CADZOW   *Discrete-Time Systems: An Introduction with Interdisciplinary Applications*
CADZOW AND MARTENS   *Discrete-Time and Computer Control Systems*
DAVIS   *Computer Data Displays*
FRIEDMAN AND MENON   *Fault Detection In Digital Circuits*
HUELSMAN   *Basic Circuit Theory*
JENSEN AND LIEBERMAN   *IBM Circuit Analysis Program:*
  Techniques and Applications
JENSEN AND WATKINS   *Network Analysis: Theory and Computer Methods*
KOCHENBURGER   *Computer Simulation of Dynamic Systems*
KUO AND MAGNUSON   *Computer Oriented Circuit Design*
LIN   *An Introduction to Error-Correcting Codes*
NAGLE, CARROLL, AND IRWIN   *An Introduction to Computer Logic*
RHYNE   *Fundamentals of Digital Systems Design*
SIFFERLEN AND VARTANIAN   *Digital Electronics with Engineering Applications*
STAUDHAMMER   *Circuit Analysis by Digital Computer*
STOUTEMYER   *PL/1 Programming for Engineering and Science*

An Introduction to Computer Logic

H. TROY NAGLE, Jr.

Alumni Associate Professor

B. D. CARROLL

Associate Professor

J. DAVID IRWIN

Associate Professor and Head

Department of Electrical Engineering

Auburn University

PRENTICE-HALL, INC.

Englewood Cliffs, New Jersey

Library of Congress Cataloging in Publication Data

NAGLE, H. TROY
    An introduction to computer logic

    Includes bibliographies.
      1. Logic circuits. 2. Electronic digital
computers—Circuits. I. Carroll, B. D.,
joint author. II. Irwin, J. David, joint
author. III. Title.
TK7888.4.N33   621.3819′58′2   74-5419
ISBN 0-13-480012-5

© 1975 by Prentice-Hall, Inc.
Englewood Cliffs, N.J.

10 9 8 7 6 5 4 3 2

Printed in the United States of America

PRENTICE-HALL INTERNATIONAL, INC., *London*
PRENTICE-HALL OF AUSTRALIA, PTY. LTD., *Sydney*
PRENTICE-HALL OF CANADA, LTD., *Toronto*
PRENTICE-HALL OF INDIA PRIVATE LIMITED, *New Delhi*
PRENTICE-HALL OF JAPAN, INC., *Tokyo*

Contents

Preface

This book is intended to be used primarily as a text for introductory courses in computer logic or digital systems design. The book can also be used for self-instruction or for purposes of review or clarification by practicing engineers and computer scientists who are not intimately familiar with the subject. To this end the presentation of the subject material has been simplified by carefully blending theoretical concepts with practical applications.

The content of the text has been judiciously selected. Coverage is divided into four major areas: an introduction including number systems and computer codes; fundamentals of combinational logic circuits; fundamentals of sequential logic circuits; and special topics including fault diagnosis, computer-aided design, and many others.

Introductory material is presented in Chapters 0 and 1. The topics covered are a history of digital computers, their organization, and the number systems and codes commonly employed by them.

Four chapters are devoted to the study of combinational logic circuits. Chapter 2 discusses Boolean algebra and switching functions; Chapter 3, switching function minimization. Computer-aided design of combinational logic is introduced in Chapter 4 while a series of special topics including NAND/NOR synthesis, threshold logic and multivalued logic are examined in Chapter 5.

Five chapters are devoted to the study of sequential circuits. Chapter 6 gives an in-depth introduction to models, flip-flops, and various sequential circuit types. Emphasis is placed on sequential circuit analysis. A lengthy presentation of the synthesis of both completely and incompletely specified synchronous sequential circuits appears in Chapter 7. Chapter 8 describes both pulse mode and fundamental mode asynchronous sequential circuits. Computer-aided design of synchronous sequential circuits is discussed in Chapter 9 while several special topics including input sequences, decomposition, and linear sequential machines are highlighted in Chapter 10.

Chapter 11 emphasizes practical applications of both combinational logic and sequential circuits. A series of digital subsystems is presented followed by a number of independent case studies.

The final chapter of the book is devoted to fault diagnosis and reliability of logic circuits. Chapter 12 covers the detection and location of faults in combinational logic circuits including test generation and application. This chapter is also concerned with fault diagnosis of sequential circuits.

In developing our presentation of the subject matter we assume no prerequisite topics, and hence the material may be taught to beginning students. The material corresponds closely to that recommended for a course in switching theory and logic design by the COSINE committee report[†] for computer engineering students. In addition, the text may be used for course I6 of the computer science curriculum recommended by the ACM report.[‡] A text of this nature is rapidly becoming standard for use in both electrical engineering and computer science curricula.

The material is well suited for coverage in quarter-oriented or semester-oriented courses. The book has evolved from a set of notes used in a three-quarter sequence of introductory courses (of three credit hours each) at Auburn University and was developed over a period of several years. We cover Chapters 0, 1, 2, and 3 with portions of Chapter 5 in a three-quarter hour course entitled "Combinational Logic Circuits." Chapters 6, 7, 8, and portions of Chapter 10 are studied in a second course entitled "Sequential Machines." A third course entitled "Fault Diagnosis of Digital Systems" is founded on Chapter 12. Chapters 4 and 9 serve as reference material and describe computer-aided design programs. These programs are used in the later stages of the first two courses to introduce the student to the practical solution of large design problems. Needless to say, the courses form a prerequisite chain which can be truncated at any point.

For schools on the semester system we recommend the following two plans for courses. For those who want a one-semester survey in digital

[†]C. L. Coates et al., "An Undergraduate Computer Engineering Option for Electrical Engineering," *Proceedings of the IEEE*, Vol. 59, June, 1971, pp. 854–860.

[‡]————, "Curriculum '68," *Communications of the ACM*, Vol. 11, March 1968, pp. 151–197.

systems design the following outline can be implemented in a three-semester hour course. The course should cover Chapter 1, omitting complementary arithmetic and computer codes, then progress through Chapters 2, 3, 6, 7, 8, and 11, omitting the discussion of the state assignment problem in Chapter 7. This survey coverage emphasizes the fundamental topics in the book and should fully use the computer-aided design programs if possible.

For those schools on the semester system desiring full coverage of the material, two three-semester hour courses can be organized as follows. Course one should examine Chapters 0, 1, 2, 3, parts of Chapters 5 and 12. Chapter 4 is reserved for last if there is time remaining. The second course should begin with Chapter 6 and proceed through Chapters 7, 8, 10, 11, and finish Chapter 12. If time permits, the discussion of prime compatibles in Chapter 9 should be emphasized. The computer-aided design programs should be liberally employed in both courses.

To further assist the user of this book we have developed an instructor's manual containing problem solutions, sample quizzes, and possible course syllabi.

We feel compelled at this point to state that each author has contributed equally to the contents of the text. Hence the ordering of the author's names does not signify the level of contributions.

Also, we must acknowledge that many of our colleagues, graduate and undergraduate students helped develop the material in this book. We are especially indebted to Professor Martial A. Honnell for his meticulous screening of the final manuscript. We would also like to thank Dr. Chester C. Carroll, Vice President for Research at Auburn University, for encouraging us to write this book. Others who made contributions in a variety of ways are: Kay Black, W. H. Bolt, D. B. Bradley, J. R. Heath, Kathy Hornsby, T. A. Irving, Dewanda Johnson, Gary Johnson, Venelia Turner, H. P. Parrish, C. L. Rogers, and S. G. Shiva.

Finally, the authors wish to thank our wives, Fran, Deirdre, and Edie, for their continued interest, encouragement, and assistance throughout the development of the book.

H. TROY NAGLE, JR.
B. D. CARROLL
J. DAVID IRWIN

Auburn, Alabama

0

Introduction

In recent years the digital computer has become an important data processing tool which is continuously gaining popularity with scientists, engineers, educators, and businessmen around the world. Digital computers may be found in laboratories monitoring and controlling experiments, in industrial production lines, in business accounting and inventory systems, and in scientific data processing centers and will perhaps soon appear in the average citizen's home. Before we examine the subject matter of this text, computer logic, let us introduce some general background information and jargon in order to provide the reader with the proper perspective.

History

The first computer was probably the abacus, which has been used in the Orient for over 3,000 years. This device, still in use today, had little competition until the 1600's when John Napier used logarithms as the basis for a device which multiplied numbers. His work led to the invention of the slide rule. Then in 1642, Blaise Pascal built an adding machine which had geared wheels much like the modern odometer.

In 1820 Charles Babbage built the first device which used the principles of modern computers. His machine evaluated polynomials by a difference technique. He also conceived a mechanical machine which resembled modern-day computers with a *store* and arithmetic unit. However, the precision required for constructing the mechanical gears was beyond capabilities of the craftsmen of his time.

The first real progress toward electronic digital computers came in the late 1930's when Howard Aiken of Harvard University and George Slibitz of Bell Telephone Laboratories developed an automatic calculator using relay networks. Other relay machines were developed during World War II for artillery ballistic calculations. Although these machines were relatively slow and comparatively large, they demonstrated the versatility of the electronic computer. Then in the early 1940's, John Mauchly and J. Presper Eckert Jr. of the University of Pennsylvania designed and built a vacuum tube computer which they called the Electronic Numerical Integrator and Computer (ENIAC); it was completed in 1945 and installed at Aberdeen Proving Ground, Maryland. ENIAC used 18,000 electron tubes, which required tremendous amounts of power; its failure rate was high and it was difficult to program because a plugboard was required.

Three very important discoveries were then made which began the rapid evolution toward today's digital computer. First, John von Neumann proposed that the program reside in the computer's memory where it could be changed at will, solving the programming difficulties of ENIAC; second, in 1947 the transistor was invented, which drastically reduced the size and power requirements by replacing the electron vacuum tube; and, third, J. W. Forrester and his associates at MIT developed the magnetic core memory which made large amounts of storage feasible.

ENIAC and other vacuum tube computers of the late 1940's and early 1950's have been labeled as the first generation of digital computers. The advent of transistors brought about the second generation of machines, which where smaller in size, were faster, and featured increased capabilities over their ancestors. In the late 1950's and early 1960's, the third generation of machines appeared. These machines are characterized by their use of integrated circuits consisting of subminiature packages of multiple transistor circuits which provided still another drastic reduction in size. Improvements in packaging and memory technology also contributed to the improved third-generation machines.

In the late 1960's still another breed of computer appeared, the minicomputer. In addition to their large complex machines, many manufacturers offered these small, limited-capability, general-purpose computers on the market. These minicomputers, which derive their name from their size and cost, have been used in many diverse applications and their popularity is still increasing at a remarkable rate. We have seen three generations of digital computers in about 30 years. It is interesting to speculate on what new discoveries will usher in the fourth.

With this brief historical background, let us now explain some of the modern computer jargon.

Digital Computers

What is a digital computer? A digital computer is an electronic device whose components may be classified as input/output equipment, memory elements, arithmetic units, or control functions. The interaction of these elements is shown in Fig. 0.1. The memory elements contain the data plus a stored list of instructions. The control unit takes, or fetches, these instructions from memory in sequential order unless it encounters a special kind of instruction called synonymously a branch, jump, skip, or transfer. The branch instructions allow looping and decision-making programs to be generated. An important feature of the stored-program computer is its ability to fetch any given instruction from the program list as directed by another instruction in the list, place the given instruction in the arithmetic unit, alter it as desired, and return it to the program list in memory. Much of the power of the stored-program computer is derived from this ability of a program to change itself.

The arithmetic and control units of a digital computer are usually constructed using semiconductor logical elements packaged in a wide variety of schemes. Older models of the second generation have transistors, resistors, diodes, etc., mounted on printed circuit boards, while later models of the third generation use integrated circuits. The memory units in digital computers are sometimes constructed using high-speed semiconductor elements; however, magnetic devices are the predominant elements used in memories. The spectrum of magnetic memory devices include magnetic core, the standard computer memory element; magnetic disk, tape, and drum, which are auxiliary memory devices for bulk or mass storage of programs and data; and plated wire, which is a replacement for magnetic core in some high-speed applications. Memory units are divided into cells called words, and each cell is known by its physical location, or memory address. Memory units may be

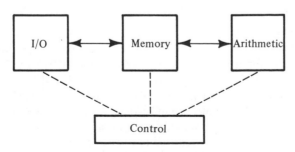

Fig. 0.1   The digital computer.

characterized by their cycle time, where memory cycle time may be defined as the interval of time required to extract (read) a word from memory and then return it to its original location in the memory unit.

The concept of a memory address for a memory cell is equivalent to a mailing address for a mailbox. For example, every post office has rows of mailboxes, each identified by a unique numbered position. Similarly, each memory cell resides in a unique numbered position, the number being the memory address.

Now, let us further examine the interaction of the computer's components as shown in Fig. 0.1. Programs are stored in the computer's memory as discussed previously. However, the programs are inserted into memory by the control unit in conjunction with the input/output (I/O) equipment, sometimes called peripheral devices. Programs are usually given to the computer in the form of punched paper tape or cards. The I/O equipment processes these media as will be shown later.

The computer may output data on several types of peripherals; a typewriter or a line printer is typical. Cathode-ray tubes (CRT's) are also available to display the results of a program's calculations. Analog-to-digital converters, digital-to-analog converters, plotters, paper-tape readers and punches, card readers and punches, magnetic reading and recording devices, and typewriters are the most commonly used input/output equipment.

In summary, the memory unit holds the data and instructions for a particular program. The control unit follows the stored list of instructions, directing the activities of the arithmetic unit and I/O devices until the program has run to completion. Each unit performs its tasks under the synchronizing influence of the control unit.

Computer Codes

Arithmetic Codes

We have briefly discussed the instructions and data stored in the digital computer's memory unit, but no mention was made of the form of these items. Numbers are stored in the computer's memory in the binary (base 2) number system. Binary numbers are written much like decimal numbers except with only two possible binary digits (bits), 1 and 0.

For example, 129 in decimal means $1 \times 10^2 + 2 \times 10^1 + 9 \times 10^0$, or each digit's position represents a weighted power of 10. Note that the 10 digits are 0 through $10 - 1 = 9$. Each digit in a binary number, say 1011, is represented by a weighted power of 2, or $1 \times 2^3 + 0 \times 2^2 + 1 \times 2^1 + 1 \times 2^0$. To convert the binary number to decimal, the weighted sum above is determined as

$$(1011)_2 = 1 \times 8 + 0 \times 4 + 1 \times 2 + 1 \times 1 = (11)_{10}$$

or one-zero-one-one in binary equals eleven in decimal.

Data in the form of binary numbers are stored in registers in the computer and are represented as follows:

1	0	1	1	0	0	0	1	1	1

This is a 10-bit register which might reside in the arithmetic or memory unit. In memory the data in the register are called a word (the word length is 10 bits in this example). Patterns of ones and zeroes are the only information that can be stored in a computer's registers or memory. The assignment of a meaning to the bit patterns is called coding, and the codes used in most computers for data are simply variations of the binary weighting scheme just presented.

Input/Output Codes

Although the computer employs binary data, users prefer alphabetic and numeric data representations, for example, records of sales, lists of names, and test grades. The set of alphanumeric symbols allowed for many computers is called the character set and has a special binary-like code called the American Standard Code for Information Interchange (ASCII). In this code the alphanumeric and other special characters (punctuation, algebraic operators, etc.) are coded with eight bits each; a partial listing of this code is given in Chapter 1. Suppose we wanted to give the digital computer a message "ADD 1". This message has five characters, the fourth one being a space or blank. In the ASCII code, our message becomes

Symbol	ASCII Code
A	01000001
D	01000100
D	01000100
	10100000
1	10110001

After our message is sent to the computer, a program in the computer's memory accepts it and acts accordingly.

Instruction Codes

The computer's instructions always reside in the main memory, usually a core system, and therefore, by definition, are also represented by patterns of ones and zeroes. The instructions are generally broken down into subfields which are coded separately. These subfields are the operation code (op code) and the memory address. These codes are illustrated in the next section.

Computer Instructions

As the control unit of a digital computer fetches instructions from memory for execution, several types of operations may result. (1) *Arithmetic instructions* cause the binary data to be added, subtracted, multiplied, or divided as specified by the computer programmer in his program. (2) *Test and compare operations* are available and determine the relation (greater than, less than, equal to, etc.) of two pieces of binary data. (3) *Branch or skip instructions* may be employed which alter the sequential nature of program execution, based on the results of a test or compare. This type of function adds considerable flexibility to programs. (4) *Input and output commands* are included for reading messages into the computer, writing messages from the computer, and controlling peripheral devices. (5) *Logical and shifting operations* provide the computer with the ability to translate and interpret all the different codes it uses. These instructions allow *bit* manipulation to be accomplished under program control. All instructions for any digital computer may be grouped into one of these five categories.

Application Programming

Programming the digital computer is the art of compiling a list of instructions for the computer so that it can efficiently perform a specified task. As indicated earlier, the digital computer's instructions must be coded in patterns of ones and zeroes before the computer can interpret them. If all programs had to be written in this form, the digital computer would be of very limited use. These patterns of ones and zeroes are called machine language instructions and very few programmers ever attempt to write programs in this manner. Programmers do use higher-level, more reasonable, symbolic languages in which to program their problems, and consequently these languages must be translated into machine language for the computer. The question now arises, who shall perform this laborious translation chore? The most efficient translator is not the programmer, but the digital computer itself. Any job done by a computer is done under program control; therefore the program which translates higher-level languages into machine language has been given a special name, the *compiler*. By using compiler languages such as FORTRAN, COBOL, ALGOL, or PL/1, the programmer has at his discretion a wide range of machine language instructions in a form which he can easily understand and efficiently use. Of course the full flexibility of machine language is difficult to incorporate into compiler languages but a magnificent amount has been retained.

System Programming

At this time let us contemplate the manner in which a given digital computer might be operated. In particular three different operating systems will be discussed: user control, batch processing, and time sharing.

If a machine is operated by each user as he executes his program, the machine is dedicated to his program and no one else may use the computer until the current user is finished. The computer is then dependent on human commands during the time between programs and hence much time can be spent idling. This operating system is convenient for the user if the computer is available when he needs it, for once he is "on the machine" he may modify his programs or execute several successive ones before he turns the machine over to the next user.

The batch operating system eliminates most of the computer idle time by establishing one operator who collects all the user programs and feeds them to the computer continuously. A special program called the operating system handles the routine tasks needed to change from one user's program to the next. This special program falls into a category of programs called *system software*. The operating system program resides in the memory unit, and the memory locations it uses are protected from each user. Thus, although idle time is reduced, the available memory storage for the user is also reduced. In addition, the user must wait for the operator to return his program, which is always a source of irritation and confrontation.

A more advanced operating system called time sharing allows multiple users to execute their programs almost simultaneously. Remote terminals consisting of limited input/output devices are connected to the digital computer and each terminal is assigned to a single user. The users are relatively slow while the computer is extremely fast. This speed differential allows the computer to skip around between users, or time share, in such a manner as to convince each user that he has the machine all to himself. Although this operating system seems very attractive, it has disadvantages, the first of which is cost. The addition of the remote terminals is expensive. Also the time-sharing system program is complicated and long, which means it uses a lot of memory space and computer time. In addition, since each user's program is stored in memory simultaneously, each user's available portion of memory is very limited. Therefore, time sharing usually requires the maximum number of memory elements that a particular computer can accommodate.

Computer Hardware

Earlier we discussed the evolution of computer hardware from mechanical devices to relays, electron tubes, transistors, and integrated circuits. Figure 0.2 illustrates several of these devices. Modern computers are built of integrated circuits which are arranged to realize the registers and control circuits

(a) Abacus

(b) Relays

(c) Electron tubes

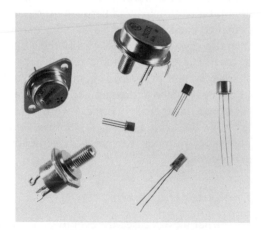

(d) Transistors

Fig. 0.2 Photographs of computer hardware.

(e) Integrated circuits

Small-scale integration

Medium-scale integration

Large-scale integration

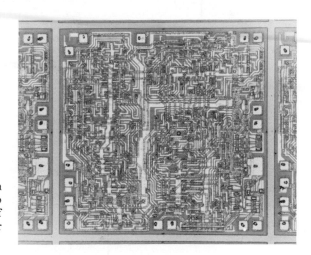

(f) Internal view of an integrated-circuit chip (MC74450). (Courtesy of Motorola Semiconductor Products, Inc.)

Fig. 0.2—*Cont.*

necessary to implement the computer's instruction set. The smallest unit of computer hardware is called a gate. Gates are the basic building blocks for all the internal parts of the computer except the core memory. Gates may be interconnected to form combinational logic networks, as illustrated in Fig. 0.3. Note that the network has six gates. The inputs in this example are labeled $x_1, \ldots, x_5$, and the output $f(x_1, \ldots, x_5)$ is a function only of the present value of the input signals. Hence, a distinguishing feature of the combinational logic circuit is that it possesses no memory of previous input signals. The subjects of analysis, synthesis, and fault diagnosis of combinational logic networks consume a major portion of this text.

All digital computers contain computer registers which serve to hold information. These registers and certain parts of the control unit belong to a class of digital computer components called sequential circuits. A sequential circuit is, in general, a combinational logic circuit with memory as modeled in Fig. 0.4. Sequential circuit analysis, synthesis, and fault diagnosis comprise

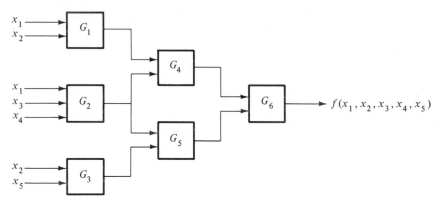

Fig. 0.3   Combinational logic network.

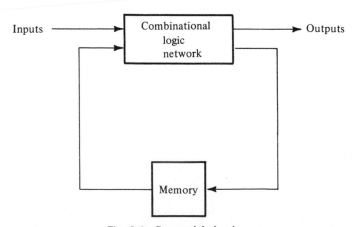

Fig. 0.4   Sequential circuit.

the second focal point of this text. Only after the reader has mastered the fundamentals of combinational and sequential circuits can he proceed with the design and construction of digital computer hardware.

Summary

In this introductory chapter we have tried to provide motivation for the material which follows. We have briefly explained what a computer is, how it is organized, the codes it employs, the manner in which it is programmed, and the hardware of which it is composed. The material contained in the remaining chapters is prerequisite to any hardware design or implementation for digital computers or other complex digital systems.

REFERENCES

1. BOOTH, A. D., and K. H. V. BOOTH, *Automatic Digital Calculators* (2nd ed.). New York: Academic Press, Inc., 1956.

2. GEAR, C. W., *Computer Organization and Programming*. New York: McGraw-Hill Book Company, 1969.

3. PHISFER, M., *Logical Design of Digital Computers*. New York: John Wiley & Sons, Inc., 1958.

4. RICHARDS, R. K., *Arithmetic Operations in Digital Computers*. New York: Van Nostrand Reinhold Company, 1955.

5. TRUXAL, J. G., and E. E. DAVID, directors, *The Man-Made World*. New York: McGraw-Hill Book Company, 1971.

1

Number Systems and Computer Codes

The basis for most information interchange is a coded symbolic representation for ideas, quantities, models, etc. The symbolic representation is structured around a set of symbols with rigid rules which govern the use of symbols in the set. Examples are readily observed in printed text, algebra, mathematics, and a student's report card or even his bank account. Symbolic representation of information within the digital computer may be analyzed in two parts: number systems and computer codes. In this chapter we shall examine each in moderate detail.

Number Systems

A number system consists of an ordered set of symbols, called digits, with relations defined for addition ($+$), subtraction ($-$), multiplication ($\times$), and division ($\div$). The *radix*, or *base*, of the number system is the total number of digits allowed in the number system. Table 1.1 lists several common radix systems. Any number in the system is said to have both an integer and a fractional part which are separated by the radix point ($.$). In some cases the integer or fractional part is absent.

We shall now examine two ways of writing a number in a number system: the juxtapositional notation and the polynomial representation.

TABLE 1.1. Number Systems

Radix, r	Name
2	Binary
3	Ternary
4	Quaternary
8	Octal
10	Decimal
16	Hexadecimal

Juxtapositional Notation

Suppose you borrow one hundred twenty-three dollars and thirty-five cents from your local banker. The check he gives you then indicates the amount 123.35. In writing this number we have used the juxtapositional notation. The check may be swapped for 1 one hundred dollar bill, 2 ten dollar bills, 3 one dollar bills, 3 dimes, and 5 pennies. Therefore, the position of each digit tells us its relative weight or importance.

In general, a number N in the juxtapositional notation is written as follows:

$$N = (a_{n-1}a_{n-2} \cdots a_1 a_0.a_{-1} \cdots a_{-m})_r \qquad (1\text{-}1)$$

where r = base or radix
  a_i = digits
  n = number of integer digits
  m = number of fractional digits
  a_{n-1} = most significant digit
  a_{-m} = least significant digit
Since the total number of digits used in the number system is equal to the number system base r,

$$0 \leq a_i \leq r - 1 \qquad (1\text{-}2)$$

where $-m \leq i \leq n - 1$.

Polynomial Representation

The $(123.35)_{10}$ dollar loan can be written in polynomial notation as

$$N = (123.35)_{10} = 1 \times 100 + 2 \times 10 + 3 \times 1 + 3 \times .1 + 5 \times .01$$
$$= 1 \times 10^2 + 2 \times 10^1 + 3 \times 10^0 + 3 \times 10^{-1} + 5 \times 10^{-2}$$

Note that each digit resides in a weighted position and that the weight of each position is a power of the radix 10.

In general, any number N may be written as a polynomial in the form

$$N = \sum_{i=-m}^{n-1} a_i r^i \tag{1-3}$$

where each symbol is defined above. For our loan, $r = 10$ and

$$a_i = 0, \quad i \geq 3$$
$$a_2 = 1$$
$$a_1 = 2$$
$$a_0 = 3$$
$$a_{-1} = 3$$
$$a_{-2} = 5$$
$$a_i = 0, \quad i \leq -3$$

Number Systems Table

A comparison of the number systems listed in Table 1.1 is summarized in Table 1.2. Note, for example, that

$$N = (14)_{10} = (1110)_2 = (112)_3 = (32)_4 = (16)_8 = (E)_{16}$$

All the numbers in the table are written in juxtapositional notation. For the hexadecimal system we had to have 16 digits which were chosen to be 0, 1, 2, 3, 4, 5, 6, 7, 8, 9, A, B, C, D, E, and F, and which are standard in the literature. A table such as Table 1.2 could be used for base conversion, that is, to convert numbers given in one base to some other base. However, we shall present simple methods later in this chapter which will eliminate the need for any table look-up procedure.

The binary number system ($r = 2$) requires only two bits, 0 and 1. This system is ideally suited for use in digital computers which are constructed of two-state devices which in general are either on or off. One of the states is labeled *one* and the other *zero*. By connecting a series of these two-state devices together we form what is called a register, as shown in Fig. 1.1. The 5-bit register shown there contains the number

$$(10110)_2 = (22)_{10}$$

1	0	1	1	0

Fig. 1.1.   A five-bit register.

as determined from Table 1.2. Computer registers range in size from 1 to 64 bits and are sometimes even longer.

TABLE 1.2.　Number Systems Table

$r = 10$	$r = 2$	$r = 3$	$r = 4$	$r = 8$	$r = 16$
0	0	0	0	0	0
1	1	1	1	1	1
2	10	2	2	2	2
3	11	10	3	3	3
4	100	11	10	4	4
5	101	12	11	5	5
6	110	20	12	6	6
7	111	21	13	7	7
8	1000	22	20	10	8
9	1001	100	21	11	9
10	1010	101	22	12	A
11	1011	102	23	13	B
12	1100	110	30	14	C
13	1101	111	31	15	D
14	1110	112	32	16	E
15	1111	120	33	17	F
16	10000	121	100	20	10
17	10001	122	101	21	11
18	10010	200	102	22	12
19	10011	201	103	23	13
20	10100	202	110	24	14
21	10101	210	111	25	15
22	10110	211	112	26	16

Signed-Magnitude Numbers

Digital computers use binary numbers when performing the calculations prescribed by the programmer. To differentiate between positive and negative data the machine employs a special sign convention in addition to the binary number system shown previously; see Table 1.3. The form for these signed-magnitude numbers is summarized below. The signed-magnitude number N may be written in either of the following notations:

$$\text{Juxtaposition:}\quad N = \pm(a_{n-1} \cdots a_0.a_{-1} \cdots a_{-m})_r \qquad (1\text{-}4)$$

$$\text{Signed magnitude:}\quad N = (sa_{n-1} \cdots a_0.a_{-1} \cdots a_{-m})_{rsm} \qquad (1\text{-}5)$$

where s is 0 if N is positive and $r - 1$ if N is negative.

Example.

$$N = -(13)_{10}$$
$$= -(1101)_2 \quad \text{(see Table 1.2)}$$
$$= (11101)_{2sm} \quad \text{(see Table 1.3)}$$

The subscript sm indicates use of the signed-magnitude binary number system.

TABLE 1.3. *Signed-Magnitude Binary Numbers*

Signed Decimal	Signed Binary	Signed Decimal	Signed Binary
+0	0 0 0 0 0	−0	1 0 0 0 0
+1	0 0 0 0 1	−1	1 0 0 0 1
+2	0 0 0 1 0	−2	1 0 0 1 0
+3	0 0 0 1 1	−3	1 0 0 1 1
+4	0 0 1 0 0	−4	1 0 1 0 0
+5	0 0 1 0 1	−5	1 0 1 0 1
+6	0 0 1 1 0	−6	1 0 1 1 0
+7	0 0 1 1 1	−7	1 0 1 1 1
+8	0 1 0 0 0	−8	1 1 0 0 0
+9	0 1 0 0 1	−9	1 1 0 0 1
+10	0 1 0 1 0	−10	1 1 0 1 0
+11	0 1 0 1 1	−11	1 1 0 1 1
+12	0 1 1 0 0	−12	1 1 1 0 0
+13	0 1 1 0 1	−13	1 1 1 0 1
+14	0 1 1 1 0	−14	1 1 1 1 0
+15	0 1 1 1 1	−15	1 1 1 1 1

Few digital computers actually use this signed-magnitude number system. Some of the other more common systems will be presented throughout this chapter.

Floating Point Numbers

Engineers and scientists frequently do their mathematical computation in the "scientific" or floating point notation. For example, one million six hundred and fifty thousand is written as

$$N = 1,650,000.$$
$$= .165 \times 10^7$$

In a more complete notation

$$N = (1,650,000.)_{10}$$
$$= (.165)_{10} \times 10^{(7.)_{10}}$$

In floating point notation all numbers are written as a fraction times the base raised to a power. In general, if

$$N = \pm(a_{n-1} \cdots a_0.a_{-1} \cdots a_{-m})_r$$

then N can be written in a more compact form as

$$N = F \times r^E \qquad (1\text{-}6)$$

where

$$F = \pm(.a_{n-1} \cdots a_{-m})_r \qquad (1\text{-}7)$$

and

$$E = \pm(b_{k-1} \cdots b_0.)_r \qquad (1\text{-}8)$$

In other words, the fractional part F is multiplied by the base r raised to the exponent E. If we let S_F be the sign symbol for F and S_E the sign symbol for E, then a reduced floating point notation results:

$$N = (S_F S_E, b_{k-1} \cdots b_0, a_{n-1} \cdots a_{-m})_r \qquad (1\text{-}9)$$

where S_F and S_E are either 0 for plus or 1 for minus.

Example.

Suppose we are to write

$$N = (1{,}650{,}000.)_{10}$$

in floating point notation with $n + m = 5$ and $k = 3$. Under these conditions F and E become

$$F = +(.16500)_{10}$$
$$E = +(007.)_{10}$$

and thus N can be written as

$$N = (00{,}007{,}16500)_{10}$$

which is floating point notation.

Example.

Now let us write

$$N = -(101101.101)_2$$

in floating point if $n + m = 10$ and $k = 6$. Then

$$F = -(.1011011010)_2$$
$$E = +(6.)_{10} = +(000110)_2 \quad (\text{see Table 1.2})$$

and hence,

$$N = (10{,}000110{,}1011011010)_2.$$

Arithmetic

Every child learns the rudiments of mathematics by memorizing addition and multiplication tables for the base 10 as shown in Table 1.4. Using the table for addition in reverse we may subtract. In a similar manner the process of long division uses trial and error multiplication and subtraction to obtain the quotient. In this section we shall practice our arithmetic in the base 2. Binary arithmetic is easier than decimal arithmetic because there are only two allowable digits, 0 and 1. Hence the addition and multiplication tables are quite short; see Table 1.5.

TABLE 1.4.   *Decimal Addition and Multiplication*

+	0	1	2	3	4	5	6	7	8	9
0	0	1	2	3	4	5	6	7	8	9
1	1	2	3	4	5	6	7	8	9	10
2	2	3	4	5	6	7	8	9	10	11
3	3	4	5	6	7	8	9	10	11	12
4	4	5	6	7	8	9	10	11	12	13
5	5	6	7	8	9	10	11	12	13	14
6	6	7	8	9	10	11	12	13	14	15
7	7	8	9	10	11	12	13	14	15	16
8	8	9	10	11	12	13	14	15	16	17
9	9	10	11	12	13	14	15	16	17	18

×	0	1	2	3	4	5	6	7	8	9
0	0	0	0	0	0	0	0	0	0	0
1	0	1	2	3	4	5	6	7	8	9
2	0	2	4	6	8	10	12	14	16	18
3	0	3	6	9	12	15	18	21	24	27
4	0	4	8	12	16	20	24	28	32	36
5	0	5	10	15	20	25	30	35	40	45
6	0	6	12	18	24	30	36	42	48	54
7	0	7	14	21	28	35	42	49	56	63
8	0	8	16	24	32	40	48	56	64	72
9	0	9	18	27	36	45	54	63	72	81

TABLE 1.5.   *Binary Addition and Multiplication*

+	0	1		×	0	1
0	0	1		0	0	0
1	1	10		1	0	1

Binary Addition

Table 1.5 is employed to add the binary digits, or bits, of two numbers together. Note that as we perform the addition $1 + 1$ we get a sum digit of 0 and a carry of 1. The carry must be added into the next column of bits as we add in the normal pattern from right to left. Two examples of binary addition are given below.

Example.

```
  1     1 1   Carries
     1 0 0 1   Augend
 +   1 0 1 1   Addend
   1 0 1 0 0   Sum
```

Example.

$$
\begin{array}{r}
1\ 1\ 1\ 1\ 1\ 1 \\
1\ 1\ 1\ 1\ 0\ 1 \\
+\qquad\ 1\ 1\ 1 \\
\hline
1\ 0\ 0\ 0\ 1\ 0\ 0
\end{array}
$$

In the second example we encountered a column which had two 1 bits and a carry 1 bit which had to be totaled. This addition was performed as follows:

$$
\begin{aligned}
1 + 1 + 1 &= (1 + 1) + 1 \\
&= (10)_2 + (01)_2 \\
&= 11
\end{aligned}
$$

Thus the sum bit was 1 *and* the carry bit was 1.

If a long column of binary numbers must be added together, the addition is more easily performed by adding them in pairs, as demonstrated in the following example.

Example.

The procedure for adding a column of binary numbers is illustrated below.

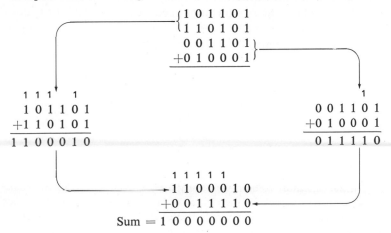

Binary Subtraction

Subtraction in binary may be thought of as the inverse of addition. The rules for subtraction follow directly from Table 1.5 and are summarized as

$$
\begin{aligned}
1 - 0 &= 1 \\
1 - 1 &= 0 \\
0 - 0 &= 0 \\
10 - 1 &= 1 \quad \text{or} \quad 0 - 1 = 1 \text{ borrow } 1
\end{aligned}
$$

If we attempt to subtract a 1 bit from a 0 bit in a given column, a 1 must be borrowed from the next more significant column.

Example. Method 1

```
    1 10   1 10        Borrows
  1 0̸ 1  0̸ 0̸  1 1     Minuend
−     1  0 1  0 1     Subtrahend
  ─────────────────
  1 1  1 1  1 0       Difference
```

In this example we first encounter a borrow in the third column from the right. The borrow must come from the 1 located two columns to the left. The appropriate borrows are written over the minuend terms in the third and fourth columns from the right. Note that the sum of the borrows yields the original 1 in the fifth column from the right. The reader who is still unsure about this borrow procedure is invited to verify it by subtracting 1 from 4 in binary as a simple example.

In the last example we encountered a certain amount of difficulty in keeping a record of the required borrows. A second method is sometimes employed which "pays back" borrows by adding them into the subtrahend before the next bit subtraction takes place. This technique, referred to here as method 2, simplifies the borrowing procedure and, in fact, provides the illusion that borrows are really never made at all. The trivial example of subtracting 1 from 2 in binary will serve to illustrate the technique.

Example.

We want to subtract 1 from 2 in binary:

```
                10          10
   1 0        1 0̸         1 0̸
               −1          −1
 −0 1        −0 1        −0 1
 ─────       ─────       ─────
                           0 1
```

In the rightmost column we immediately encounter a borrow. Hence, we in essence borrow a 1 for the rightmost column and pay it back by adding a 1 to the subtrahend in the next left column. In practice we subtract 1 from the minuend in the next left column. It is important to note that this operation leaves the relative magnitude of the numbers unchanged. Then the subtraction can be easily performed.

The next two examples are further illustrations of the technique.

Example. Method 2

```
   10 11 10 10         Borrows
  1 0̸ 1 0̸ 0̸  1 1      Minuend
 −1 1  1 1            Payback
 −      1 0 1  0 1    Subtrahend
 ──────────────────
  0 1  1 1  1 1  1 0  Difference
```

Example. Method 2

```
      11 10   10
     1 1̸ 0̸ 1 0̸
    −1 1    1
    −  1  1 0 1
    ─────────────
      0 1  1 0 1
```

Binary Multiplication

Binary multiplication is performed in the same fashion as decimal multiplication with the exception that multiplicative binary operations are much simpler, as is demonstrated in Table 1.5. Care must be exercised, however, when adding the partial product columns.

Example.

```
    1 0 1 1   Multiplicand
  ×   1 0 1   Multiplier
  ─────────
    1 0 1 1   Partial product
  0 0 0 0     Partial product
1 0 1 1       Partial product
─────────────
1 1 0 1 1 1   Product
```

Example.

```
      1 0 1 1 1
  ×     1 0 1 0
  ───────────────
      0 0 0 0 0
    1 0 1 1 1
  0 0 0 0 0
1 0 1 1 1
───────────────
1 1 1 0 0 1 1 0
```

Note that there is one partial product for every multiplier bit. This procedure can be performed more efficiently by merely shifting one unit to the left rather than listing a partial product for a multiplier bit of zero. One can see from the two examples above how easily this procedure can be accomplished.

Binary Division

Binary division is performed using the same trial and error procedure as decimal division. However, the procedure is easy since there are only two values to try. Copies of the divisor terms are subtracted from the dividend, yielding positive intermediate remainder terms.

Example.

In this example the binary division of $(117)_{10}$ by $(9)_{10}$ is performed:

$$
\begin{array}{r}
1\ 1\ 0\ 1 \\
1\ 0\ 0\ 1\overline{)1\ 1\ 1\ 0\ 1\ 0\ 1} \\
1\ 0\ 0\ 1 \\
\hline
1\ 0\ 1\ 1 \\
1\ 0\ 0\ 1 \\
\hline
1\ 0\ 0\ 1 \\
1\ 0\ 0\ 1 \\
\hline
\end{array}
$$

The quotient is $(1101)_2 = (13)_{10}$.

Example.

The division of $(117)_{10}$ by $(7)_{10}$ is illustrated below:

$$
\begin{array}{r}
1\ 0\ 0\ 0\ 0 \\
1\ 1\ 1\overline{)1\ 1\ 1\ 0\ 1\ 0\ 1} \\
1\ 1\ 1 \\
\hline
0\ 1\ 0\ 1 \\
\end{array}
$$

The answer is $(10000)_2 = (16)_{10}$ with a remainder of $(0101)_2 = (5)_{10}$.

Number Base Conversions

Table 1.2 graphically demonstrates the need for algorithmic approaches for conversions between number systems of different bases. Two techniques which are usually employed for base conversion are the series substitution method and the radix divide/multiply technique.

Conversion Formulas

Series substitution. The series substitution method is suggested by equation (1-3). That is, any number in the base r can be written as

$$
N = \sum_{i=-m}^{n-1} a_i r^i
$$
$$
= a_{n-1}r^{n-1} + \cdots + a_0 r^0 + a_{-1}r^{-1} + \cdots + a_{-m}r^{-m} \qquad (1\text{-}10a)
$$

The use of (1-10a) in number base conversions is referred to as the series substitution method. In practice, the terms of the series are expressed in one base, say base $r = \alpha$; then each factor of each term is converted to another base, say base $r = \beta$, and then the series is evaluated using base β arithmetic. The following examples demonstrate this technique.

Example.

Convert $(14)_{16}$ to base 2. By (1-10a)

$$(14)_{16} = (1)_{16} \times (10)_{16}^1 + (4)_{16} \times (10)_{16}^0$$

But from Table 1.2

$$(1)_{16} = (1)_2$$
$$(4)_{16} = (100)_2$$
$$(10)_{16} = (10000)_2$$

Therefore,

$$(14)_{16} = (1)_2 \times (10000)_2 + (100)_2 \times (1)_2$$
$$= (10000)_2 + (100)_2$$
$$= (10100)_2$$

It is important to remember that the above multiplication and addition were performed in base 2 arithmetic.

Example.

Convert $(14)_{16}$ to base 10. Using (1-10a),

$$(14)_{16} = (1)_{16} \times (10)_{16}^1 + (4)_{16} \times (10)_{16}^0$$

But

$$(1)_{16} = (1)_{10}$$
$$(10)_{16} = (16)_{10}$$
$$(4)_{16} = (4)_{10}$$

Then

$$(14)_{16} = (1)_{10} \times (16)_{10}^1 + (4)_{10} \times (16)_{10}^0$$
$$= (16)_{10} + (4)_{10}$$
$$= (20)_{10}$$

Example.

Convert $(24)_8$ to base 10. Employing equation (1-10a) and remembering that the multiplication and addition must be performed in base 10 arithmetic,

$$N = (2)(8)^1 + (4)(8)^0 = 16 + 4 = (20)_{10}$$

Example.

Convert $(24)_8$ to base 2. The conversion process is

$$N = (10)(1000) + (100)(1) = (10100)_2$$

Example.

Convert $(10100)_2$ to base 10.

$$N = (1)(2)^4 + (1)(2)^2 = 16 + 4 = (20)_{10}$$

The reader can use Table 1.2 to check the above examples. The remaining two examples illustrate conversions with numbers containing a fractional part.

Example.

Convert $(AF3.15)_{16}$ to base 10.

$$(A)_{16} = (10)_{10}$$
$$(F)_{16} = (15)_{10}$$
$$(3)_{16} = (3)_{10}$$
$$(1)_{16} = (1)_{10}$$
$$(5)_{16} = (5)_{10}$$
$$(10)_{16} = (16)_{10}$$

$N = (10)(16)^2 + (15)(16)^1 + (3)(16)^0 + (1)(16)^{-1} + (5)(16)^{-2}$
$= 2560 + 240 + 3 + .0625 + .01953125$
$= (2803.08203125)_{10}$

Example.

Convert $(1603.51)_7$ to base 10.

$N = (1)(7)^3 + (6)(7)^2 + (1)(7)^0 + (5)(7)^{-1} + (1)(7)^{-2}$
$= 343 + 294 + 3 + \underline{.142857}$
$\qquad + .02040816326530661224\ldots$

The line under the fraction .142857 indicates that the sequence repeats, i.e., .142857142857 . . . . If only four significant digits are retained in the fractional part ($m = 4$), then

$$N = (640.1633)_{10}$$

A second method for evaluating the series in equation (1-10a) when N is an integer is shown below:

$$N = (\cdots((a_{n-1}r + a_{n-2})r + a_{n-3})r + \cdots + a_1)r + a_0 \qquad (1\text{-}10b)$$

This equation indicates that the evaluation of the series may be accomplished by multiplying the most significant digit by the radix, adding the next most significant digit, then multiplying by the radix again, etc.

Example.

Convert $(AF3)_{16}$ to base 10 using (1-10b). From Table 1.2,

$$r = (16)_{10}$$
$$(A)_{16} = (10)_{10}$$
$$(F)_{16} = (15)_{10}$$
$$(3)_{16} = (3)_{10}$$

For this example

$$N = (a_2 r + a_1)r + a_0$$
$$= ((10)(16) + 15)16 + 3$$

Performing the indicated arithmetic yields

$$N = (2803)_{10}$$

A similar algorithm can be used for fractional conversions.

Radix divide/multiply. Another method for number base conversion referred to as the radix divide/multiply method may be used for number base conversion. This method converts a number from base $r = \alpha$ to base $r = \beta$ by using arithmetic in base $r = \alpha$. Conversion of integer numbers $(N_I)_\alpha$ is accomplished by repeated divisions of the number by the radix $(\beta)_\alpha$. Conversion of fractional numbers $(N_F)_\alpha$ is accomplished by repeated multiplication of the number by the radix $(\beta)_\alpha$.

To demonstrate the conversion procedure a number $(N)_\alpha$ is written as

$$(N)_\alpha = (N_I)_\alpha + (N_F)_\alpha \tag{1-11}$$

where $(N_I)_\alpha$ represents the integer part and $(N_F)_\alpha$ the fractional part. Then

$$(N_I)_\alpha = a_{n-1}\beta^{n-1} + \cdots + a_1\beta^1 + a_0\beta^0 \tag{1-12}$$

$$(N_F)_\alpha = a_{-1}\beta^{-1} + \cdots + a_{-m}\beta^{-m} \tag{1-13}$$

Given $(N_I)_\alpha$ and $(N_F)_\alpha$ the procedure now allows us to express the digits a_i of each in base α and for eventual conversion on an individual basis to base β. Hereafter the numbers are all assumed to be expressed in base α. If we divide the integer part N_I by the radix β, then the result can be written as

$$\underbrace{\frac{N_I}{\beta} = a_{n-1}\beta^{n-2} + \cdots + a_1\beta^0}_{\text{Quotient}} + \underbrace{\frac{a_0}{\beta}}_{\text{Remainder}}$$

In juxtapositional notation

$$\frac{N_I}{\beta} = \underbrace{(a_{n-1} \cdots a_1.)_\beta}_{\text{Quotient}} + \underbrace{\frac{a_0}{\beta}}_{\text{Remainder}}$$

or

$$
\begin{array}{r}
a_{n-1} \cdots a_1 \quad \text{Quotient} \\
\beta\sqrt{N_I} \qquad\qquad \\
\cdot \qquad\qquad\quad \\
\cdot \qquad\qquad\quad \\
\hline
a_0 \quad \text{Remainder}
\end{array}
$$

In other words, one division of the integer part $(N_I)_\alpha$ by the radix $(\beta)_\alpha$ yields $(a_0)_\alpha$ as a remainder. Successive divisions will yield $a_1, a_2, \ldots, a_{n-1}$ as remainders. Once a division produces a zero quotient, the conversion is complete. Then each digit $(a_i)_\alpha$ may be converted to base β.

Example.

Convert $N = (234.)_{10}$ to base 8. The successive divisions are

$$
\begin{array}{ccc}
29 & 3 & 0 \\
8\overline{\smash{)}234} & 8\overline{\smash{)}29} & 8\overline{\smash{)}3} \\
16 & 24 & 0 \\
\overline{74} & \overline{5} = a_1 & \overline{3} = a_2 \\
72 \\
\overline{2} = a_0
\end{array}
$$

$$N = (a_2 a_1 a_0)_8 = (352)_8$$

This example took three divisions to produce a zero quotient. A shorthand notation is normally used in this method as shown below:

$$
\begin{array}{ll}
8 \mid 234 \\
8 \mid 29 & 2 = a_0 \\
8 \mid 3 & 5 = a_1 \\
 0 & 3 = a_2 \\
& \text{Remainders} \\
N = (352)_8 \\
& \text{Quotients}
\end{array}
$$

A quick check will show that the above answer is correct, i.e.,

$$N_{10} = (3)(8)^2 + 5(8)^1 + 2(8)^0$$
$$= (234)_{10}$$

Example.

Convert $(1024)_{10}$ to base 5.

$$
\begin{array}{ll}
5 \mid 1024 \\
5 \mid 204 & 4 \\
5 \mid 40 & 4 \\
5 \mid 8 & 0 \\
5 \mid 1 & 3 \\
 0 & 1
\end{array}
$$

$$N = (13044)_5$$

The preceding two examples illustrate the technique for integer conversion. Note that all arithmetic in the previous examples has been performed in base 10.

The fractional part of the number N in equation (1-13) is multiplied by the radix β to generate the digits of N for the base β, i.e.,

$$(\beta)(N_F) = a_{-1} + a_{-2}\beta^{-1} + \cdots + a_{-m}\beta^{-m+1}$$

or

$$\begin{array}{r} N_F \\ \times \quad \beta \\ \hline a_{-1}.\,a_{-2}\,\cdots\,a_{-m} \end{array}$$

$$\underbrace{\quad}_{\substack{\text{Integer} \\ \text{part}}} \underbrace{\qquad}_{\substack{\text{Fractional} \\ \text{part}}}$$

The integer part of the product is the digit a_{-1} for the new base β. If we again multiply the fractional part of the above product (i.e., $a_{-2} \cdots a_{-m}$) by β, we shall obtain a_{-2}. Multiplications of the fractional part by the radix β are continued until either the fractional part of the product becomes zero or enough digits in the new base have been generated.

Example.

Convert the fraction $N = (.1285)_{10}$ to base 4.

$$\begin{array}{ccc}
.1285 & .5140 & .0560 \\
\times \quad 4 & \times \quad 4 & \times \quad 4 \\
\hline
0.5140 & 2.0560 & 0.2240 \\
\;\rule{0pt}{1em}\llcorner\; a_{-1} & \;\llcorner\; a_{-2} & \;\llcorner\; a_{-3}
\end{array}$$

$$\begin{array}{ccc}
.2240 & .8960 & .5480 \\
\times \quad 4 & \times \quad 4 & \times \quad 4 \\
\hline
0.8960 & 3.5480 & 2.3360 \\
\;\llcorner\; a_{-4} & \;\llcorner\; a_{-5} & \;\llcorner\; a_{-6}
\end{array}$$

$$N = (.a_{-1} \cdots a_{-6} \cdots)_4$$
$$= (.020032\cdots)_4$$

This same example is now repeated in another shorthand version:

$$N = (.1285)_{10} = (?)_4$$

$$\left|\begin{array}{l}
.1285 \times 4 \\
0.5140 \times 4 \\
2.0560 \times 4 \\
0.2240 \times 4 \\
0.8960 \times 4 \\
3.5840 \times 4 \\
2.3360
\end{array}\right.$$

$$\vdots$$

$$N = (.020032\ldots)_4$$

Each step of the technique multiplies the new base 4 by the fractional part of the previous product. The integer parts of each product are copied in the order indicated by the arrow to produce the desired result. No digit conversion is needed because 0, 2, and 3 have the same representation in base 10 and base 4.

Example.

Convert $(.6)_{10}$ to base 8.

$$
\begin{array}{l}
.6 \times 8 \\
4.8 \times 8 \\
6.4 \times 8 \\
3.2 \times 8 \quad \text{Sequence repeats} \\
1.6 \times 8 \\
4.8 \times 8
\end{array}
$$

$$N = (.\overline{4631})_8$$

Once again the bar under the fraction indicates that the sequence repeats itself.

Generation of the integer and fractional parts may be combined into one unified technique as shown in the following example.

Example.

$$N = (39.125)_{10} = (?)_4$$

Radix
point

$$
\begin{array}{ll}
4 \;\rfloor\, 39 & .125 \times 4 \\
4 \;\rfloor\, 9 \quad 3 & 0.500 \times 4 \\
4 \;\rfloor\, 2 \quad 1 & 2.000 \\
0 \quad 2
\end{array}
$$

$$N = (213.02)_4$$

General Conversion Algorithm

The many examples presented above demonstrate the base conversion techniques. To make the procedure more explicit a generalized conversion algorithm is stated below.

Algorithm 1-1.

To convert a number N from base α to base β we may use either

(a) The series substitution method and arithmetic in base β, *or*

(b) The radix divide/multiply technique and arithmetic in base α.

In general, conversion between any two bases α and β is possible, as indicated by Algorithm 1-1. However, the conversions that are the easiest to perform are those in which only decimal arithmetic is used. Hence, the procedure which is perhaps most convenient for base conversion is stated in the following algorithm.

Algorithm 1-2.

To convert a number N from base α to base β we may use

(a) The series substitution method and decimal arithmetic to convert N from base α to base 10, *and*

(b) The radix divide/multiply technique and decimal arithmetic to convert N from base 10 to base β.

Algorithm 1-2 in general requires more steps than Algorithm 1-1; however, the former is much easier and often faster because all arithmetic is performed in decimal.

Practice in Base Conversions

In this section a series of examples is presented which employs Algorithm 1-2 in the conversion process.

Example.

Convert $(1025.25)_{10}$ to base 2.

```
2 | 1025                              .25 × 2
2 | 512   1              .           0.50 × 2
2 | 256   0                          1.00 × 2
2 | 128   0
2 |  64   0
2 |  32   0
2 |  16   0
2 |   8   0
2 |   4   0
2 |   2   0
2 |   1   0
      0   1
```

Hence the number in binary is

$$N = (10000000001.01)_2$$

Example.

Convert $(1110101)_2$ to base 8. The first step is to convert the number to decimal using the series substitution method:

$$N = (1)(2)^6 + (1)(2)^5 + (1)(2)^4 + (1)(2)^2 + (1)(2)^0$$
$$= 64 + 32 + 16 + 4 + 1$$
$$= (117)_{10}$$

The next step is to use the radix divide/multiply technique to convert from decimal to octal:

```
8 | 117
8 |  14   5
8 |   1   6
      0   1
```

Hence,

$$N = (165)_8$$

Example.

Perform the conversion from quaternary to quinary indicated below:

$$N = (1023.231)_4 = (?)_5$$

Following the procedure illustrated in the previous example yields

$$N = (1)(4)^3 + (2)(4)^1 + (3)(4)^0 + (2)(4)^{-1} + (3)(4)^{-2} + (1)(4)^{-3}$$
$$= 64 + 8 + 3 + .5 + .1875 + .015625$$
$$= (75.703125)_{10}$$

Then

5	75		.703125 × 5
5	15	0	3.515625 × 5
5	3	0	2.578125 × 5
	0	3	2.890625 × 5
			4.453125 × 5

Hence,

$$N = (1023.231)_4 = (300.3224\ldots)_5$$

Example.

This example is concerned with finding a number in base 9 that is the product of $(125)_6$ and $(40)_7$ in which the multiplication is performed in decimal, i.e.,

$$N = (125)_6 \times_{10} (40)_7 = (?)_9$$

First the two terms in the product are converted to decimal:

$$(125)_6 = (1)(6)^2 + (2)(6)^1 + 5(6)^0$$
$$= (53)_{10}$$

Likewise

$$(40)_7 = (4)(7)^1 + (0)(7)^0$$
$$= (28)_{10}$$

Performing the decimal multiplication,

$$
\begin{array}{r}
53 \\
\times 28 \\
\hline
424 \\
106 \\
\hline
1484
\end{array}
$$

The problem now reduces to the following:

$$N = (1484)_{10} = (?)_9$$

Hence,

$$
\begin{array}{r|ll}
9 & 1484 \\
9 & 164 & 8 \\
9 & 18 & 2 \\
9 & 2 & 0 \\
& 0 & 2
\end{array}
$$

Therefore,

$$N = (2028)_9 = (125)_6 \times_{10} (40)_7$$

Note that this example has made repeated use of Algorithm 1-2. Although many conversions were required, they were straightforward because only decimal arithmetic was used.

Base 2^k Conversions

In the last section we found that

$$N = (1025.25)_{10} = (10000000001.01)_2$$

Suppose that one needs to find $N = (?)_8$.

If we start with N in binary, group the bits in units of three in both directions from the binary point, and then convert each group to octal using Table 1.2, we obtain the following:

$$N = \underbrace{010}\,\underbrace{000}\,\underbrace{000}\,\underbrace{001}.\underbrace{010}$$
$$\quad\; 2 \quad\; 0 \quad\; 0 \quad\; 1 \;.\; 2$$

$$(2001.2)_8$$

A quick check using the series substitution method will show that $(2001.2)_8$ is equivalent to $(1025.25)_{10}$. This simple conversion was possible because the bases are related by the expression $8 = 2^3$. It is the exponent that suggests the grouping of 3 bits. The following algorithm generalizes this technique for conversion between any two bases in which one is an integer power of the other.

Algorithm 1-3.

(a) To convert a number N from base α to base β when $\beta = \alpha^k$ and k is an integer, group the digits of the number N in base α into units of k digits in both directions from the radix point, and then convert each group of k digits to base β.

(b) To convert a number N from base β to base α when $\beta = \alpha^k$ and k is an integer, merely convert each digit in base β to k digits in base α.

The following examples illustrate the power and speed of this approach:

Example.

Perform the indicated conversion:

$$N = (1011011.1010111)_2 = (?)_8$$

The conversion is from base 2 to base 8 where $8 = 2^3$. Hence Algorithm 1-3(a) should be employed with $k = 3$. Grouping the bits in units of $k = 3$ and using Table 1.2 we obtain

001011011.101011100

1 3 3 . 5 3 4

$$N = (133.534)_8$$

Note that extra zeroes may be added at each end of the number if needed.

Example.

Convert $(AF.16C)_{16}$ to base 2. The indicated conversion is from base 16 to base 2 where $16 = 2^4$. Hence employing Algorithm 1-3(b) and Table 1.2 yields

A   F . 1   6   C
$$N = (10101111.000101101100)_2$$

Example.

Convert $(AF.16C)_{16}$ to base 8. Note in this example that 16 is not a power of 8. However, $16 = 2^4$ and $8 = 2^3$. Therefore we can solve this problem by using a double conversion, first from base 16 to base 2 and then from base 2 to base 8. The first conversion was performed in the previous example and resulted in

$$N = (10101111.000101101100)_2$$

The second base conversion employs Algorithm 1-3(a) and yields

$$N = 010101111.000101101100$$

2   5   7 . 0   5   5   4

$$N = (257.0554)_8$$

Complementary Arithmetic

Complementary arithmetic is a powerful yet simple technique which facilitates many mathematical operations. The following material will serve to explain and demonstrate the usefulness of this important subject.

In the operation of subtraction, the subtraction of a number B from a number A, written as $A - B$, may be considered as the addition of a number $C = -B$ and the number A, or in other words

$$A - B = A + (-B)$$
$$= A + C \tag{1-14}$$

If we allow A and C to be either positive or negative numbers, then any subtraction operation may be written as an addition. The negative numbers, as in (1-14), will be written in complementary form and, as will be demonstrated in subsequent paragraphs, the sign of the resultant difference will always be correct.

The ability to subtract numbers by the addition of complements is an important characteristic of the digital computer. The digital hardware for addition can then perform subtraction as well, which results in a significant reduction in electronic circuitry. Since multiplication and division are also based on addition and subtraction, the adder circuits of the digital computer can be adapted to provide all the necessary arithmetic operations for mathematical computations.

Complementary notation is defined for integer numbers of the form

$$(N)_r = a_{n-1}r^{n-1} + a_{n-2}r^{n-2} + \cdots + a_1 r + a_0 \qquad (1\text{-}15)$$

where n is the number of digits and r is the base. Let us now examine these complementary numbers in more detail.

Radix Complement

The *radix complement* for a number N as defined in (1-15) is

$$[N]_r = r^n - (N)_r$$

where n is the number of digits in N.

Let us now examine the effect of this radix complement on (1-14):

$$(A)_r - (B)_r = (A)_r - (B)_r + r^n - r^n$$
$$= (A)_r + (r^n - (B)_r) - r^n$$
$$= (A)_r + [B]_r - r^n \qquad (1\text{-}16)$$

Therefore, to subtract two numbers A and B in radix r, we may add the radix complement of B to A and subtract the radix raised to the nth power. If A and B have n digits then the term r^n will have $n + 1$ digits. The subtraction of this term r^n is especially easy to handle because the most significant digit is a 1, and all others are 0, as will be shown by example later.

Note that

$$(N)_r = r^n - [N]_r$$

Radix Complement Number System

Here we shall examine a radix complement number system which allows us to accomplish all cases of

$$N = A + B$$

where A and B may be either positive or negative numbers. Each number in an $(n + 1)$-digit radix complement number system (*rcns*) may be expressed as

$$N = (sa_{n-1} \ldots a_0)_{rcns}$$

where for positive N

$$s = 0$$
$$(a_{n-1} \ldots a_0) = (N)_r \qquad (1\text{-}17a)$$

and for negative N

$$s = r - 1$$
$$(a_{n-1} \ldots a_0) = [N]_r \qquad (1\text{-}17b)$$

In other words, positive numbers are written in a signed-magnitude form, while negative numbers are expressed in signed radix complement notation. When numbers are expressed in the radix complement number system, the sign digit is appended to the magnitude digits and the resulting numbers are simply added, regardless of the sign of the result. Sign digits are handled as if they were data digits. Examples of arithmetic in the radix complement number system follow.

The radix complement number system with $r = 2$ is frequently used in digital computers. All numbers in the computer's memory remain in the two's complement number system throughout all sequences of arithmetic calculations. Number system conversions take place when data numbers are transmitted to and from input-output devices.

Two's Complement

The radix complement for binary numbers is

$$[N]_2 = 2^n - (N)_2 \qquad (1\text{-}18)$$

where n is the number of bits in N.

Example.

Determine the two's complement of $N = (10111010100)_2$. From (1-18),

$$[N]_2 = 2^{11} - (10111010100)_2$$

Performing the indicated subtraction yields

```
    1 1 1 1 1 1 1 1 10        Borrows
  1 0 0 0 0 0 0 0 0 0 0 0     2¹¹
    1 0 1 1 1 0 1 0 1 0 0     N in binary
    0 1 0 0 0 1 0 1 1 0 0     Two's complement of N
```

Therefore,

$$[N]_2 = (01000101100)_2$$

The procedure for determining the two's complement illustrated above is simplified by applying the following algorithm.

Algorithm 1-4.

To determine the two's complement of a binary number, copy down the digits beginning at the least significant bit and proceed toward the most significant bit until the first 1 has been copied. After copying down a single 1, then copy down the opposite of each of the remaining bits as you proceed toward the most significant bit.

Example.

$$(N)_2 = (10111010100)_2$$

$$[N]_2 = (?)_2$$

Applying Algorithm 1-4,

$$N = 1011101010\overset{\downarrow}{0}0$$
$$[N]_2 = (0100010\overline{1100})_2$$

The arrow indicates the first 1.

The two's complement notation may be employed in subtraction in the manner described below. To calculate the difference between two n-bit numbers

$$N = (A)_2 - (B)_2$$

1. Add $(A)_2 + [B]_2$.
2. If a carry bit was produced for the $n + 1$ position, the result is

$$+((A)_2 + [B]_2)_2$$

3. If no carry bit was produced for the $n + 1$ position, the result is

$$-[(A)_2 + [B]_2]_2$$

We may demonstrate the procedure by example.

Example.

$$N = (10110)_2 - (01011)_2$$

Here $n = 5$ and

$$(A)_2 + [B]_2 = (10110)_2 + [01011]_2$$
$$= 10110 + 10101$$
$$= 101011$$

Carry bit ignored

Therefore,

$$N = +((A)_2 + [B]_2)_2$$
$$= +(01011)_2$$

Example.

$$N = (0000111)_2 - (1110110)_2$$

For this example $n = 7$ and

$$(A)_2 + [B]_2 = (0000111)_2 + [1110110]_2$$
$$= 0000111 + 0001010$$
$$= 00010001$$

└─────────────────────────────── No carry bit

Therefore,

$$N = -[(A)_2 + [B]_2]_2 = -[0010001]_2$$
$$= -(1101111)_2$$

Let us now consider a simple desk calculator which uses the two's complement number system in which the sign of the result is automatically determined by adding the sign bits and always ignoring end carries.

Two's Complement Calculator

Suppose that the desk calculator is designed to operate in the two's complement number system of Table 1.6. The calculator is to have the

TABLE 1.6.   Two's Complement Number System

Signed Decimal	Two's Complement N. S.	Signed Decimal	Two's Complement N. S.
+15	01111	−1	11111
+14	01110	−2	11110
+13	01101	−3	11101
+12	01100	−4	11100
+11	01011	−5	11011
+10	01010	−6	11010
+9	01001	−7	11001
+8	01000	−8	11000
+7	00111	−9	10111
+6	00110	−10	10110
+5	00101	−11	10101
+4	00100	−12	10100
+3	00011	−13	10011
+2	00010	−14	10010
+1	00001	−15	10001
+0	00000	−16	10000

following features:

1. All numbers must be represented by 5 bits, i.e., $n = 4$,

$$-16 \leq N \leq 15$$

$$-2^{n-1} \leq N \leq 2^{n-1} - 1 \tag{1-19}$$

2. The most significant bit represents the sign of the number, 0 for positive and 1 for negative.
3. The magnitude of all negative numbers is represented in two's complement notation.
4. All positive numbers are in signed-magnitude form.

Once again, the only operation performed by the calculator is addition. Numbers expressed in the above notation are said to be written in the 5-bit two's complement number system.

Example.

Use the desk calculator to perform the following subtraction:

$$N = (15)_{10} - (13)_{10}$$

From Table 1.6 the number conversion is

Decimal		Two's Complement Number System
+15	$\longrightarrow$	01111
−13	$\longrightarrow$	10011

$$N = 01111 + 10011$$
$$= 100010$$

Sign

Ignored

Using Table 1.6, the answer is

$$N = +(2)_{10}$$

Example.

Use the calculator to determine

$$N = -(5)_{10} - (13)_{10}$$

Decimal		Two's Complement Number System
−5	$\longrightarrow$	11011
−13	$\longrightarrow$	10011

$$N = 11011 + 10011$$
$$= 101110$$

Sign

Ignored

At this point it is obvious that something very peculiar has happened in this example. The addition of two negative numbers yielded a positive result. The proper explanation for this phenomenon is that the answer was too large to be held by the calculator in 5 bits. Therefore the size of the calculator must be increased or the size of the numbers decreased.

In our last example we encountered a problem which frequently arises in digital computers. The computer has a special circuit which checks all additions to see if the result is of the wrong sign; if the sign is in error, then the program which produced the error is either warned or terminated. This error is called *overflow*.

One last point should be mentioned about Table 1.6. In the table,

$$-(16)_{10} \triangleq (10000)_{2\text{cns}}$$

This is a definition. Negative full scale in an $(n + 1)$-digit radix complement number system is always given by

$$-(2^n) \triangleq (100 \ldots 00)_{r\text{cns}}$$

Negative full scale may be added to any positive number and may be the correct result for the addition of two negative numbers.

Two's Complement Arithmetic

Most digital computers today use a two's complement number system, like the one in Table 1.6, for integer arithmetic. The number of bits in the number system matches the computer's word length.

By using a complementary number system, the computer need have only adder and complementing circuits to perform addition and subtraction. The resulting savings in hardware complexity has made complementary number systems very popular in digital computers.

We have seen that if numbers are expressed in a two's complement number system, addition may be used to accomplish subtraction. Let us examine a two's complement number system for a small 16-bit digital computer.

Numbers for the computer are expressed as

$$N = (sa_{14}a_{13}a_{12} \cdots a_1a_0)_{2\text{cns}}$$

where, for N positive

$$s = 0$$
$$(a_{14} \cdots a_0)_2 = (N)_2$$

and for N negative

$$s = 1$$
$$(a_{14} \cdots a_0) = [N]_2$$

Numbers written in this format are said to be in a 16-bit two's complement number system.

Example.

Show how a 16-bit computer would perform

$$N = (1,863)_{10} - (23,020)_{10}$$

The solution follows the outline below.

1. Convert the numbers $(1,863)_{10}$ and $(23,020)_{10}$ to binary signed magnitude.
2. Write the binary numbers in the 16-bit two's complement number system.
3. Add the two numbers.
4. Convert the answer to binary signed magnitude.
5. Convert the answer to decimal.

Solution.

STEP 1.

```
8 | 1,863              8 | 23,020
8 |  232   7           8 |  2,877   4
8 |   29   0           8 |    359   5
8 |    3   5           8 |     44   7
       0   3           8 |      5   4
                              0   5
```

$$N = (3,507)_8 - (54,754)_8$$

$$N = (0,011101000111)_{2sm} + (1,101100111101100)_{2sm}$$

STEP 2.

$$N = (0,011101000111)_{2cns} + (1,010011000010100)_{2cns}$$

STEP 3.

$$
\begin{array}{r}
0,000011101000111 \\
+1,010011000010100 \\
\hline
1,010110101011011 = N
\end{array}
$$

$$N = (1,010110101011011)_{2cns}$$

STEP 4.

$$N = (1,101001010100101)_{2sm}$$

STEP 5.

$$N = -(51,245)_8$$
$$= -(5 \times 8^4 + 8^3 + 2 \times 8^2 + 4 \times 8^1 + 5 \times 8^0)_{10}$$
$$= -(5 \times 4,096 + 512 + 2 \times 64 + 4 \times 8 + 5 \times 1)_{10}$$
$$= -(20,480 + 512 + 128 + 32 + 5)_{10}$$
$$N = -(21,157)_{10}$$

The reader should check this answer using decimal arithmetic. Before the reader becomes discouraged from all the work the computer must do to perform this simple task, we must remember that the computer adds two numbers in about 1 microsecond. Therefore, even if the computer does have to do a few conversions, it will still beat the mathematician by a factor of 10,000 or so.

Diminished Radix Complement

The diminished radix complement is defined by the equation

$$[N]_{r-1} = [N]_r - 1$$
$$= r^n - (N)_r - 1 \tag{1-20}$$

where n is the number of digits in N, and the subscript $r - 1$ represents the diminished radix.

Let us examine the effect of the diminished radix complement on the subtraction operation

$$N = (A)_r - (B)_r$$

The equation may be rewritten as

$$N = (A)_r - (B)_r + r^n - r^n + 1 - 1$$
$$= (A)_r + (r^n - (B)_r - 1) - r^n + 1$$
$$= (A)_r + [B]_{r-1} - r^n + 1 \tag{1-21a}$$

If A and B are each n digits in length, r^n will contain $n + 1$ digits and hence will cancel any carry bit from the most significant column in the sum $(A)_r + [B]_{r-1}$. Whenever the difference is positive, there will be such a carry. Therefore we may ignore the term $-r^n$, but the term $+1$ will have to be included. This is accomplished in practice by letting the carry generated by the most significant bits of $(A)_r$ and $[B]_{r-1}$ propagate around to the least significant bit position. This procedure is called *end-around carry*, and the answer obtained is in the proper form.

When the difference is negative there is no carry bit generated from the most significant column of $(A)_r$ and $[B]_{r-1}$, and

$$N = -(r^n - 1 - (A)_r - [B]_{r-1})$$
$$= -[(A)_r + [B]_{r-1}]_{r-1} \tag{1-21b}$$

In other words, if we add $(A)_r$ and $[B]_{r-1}$ and no end-around carry is generated, then the result is the negative diminished radix complement of the sum.

One's Complement

The diminished radix complement for binary numbers is called one's complement and is written as

$$[N]_{2-1} = 2^n - (N)_2 - 1 \tag{1-22}$$

Example.

Find the one's complement of N where

$$N = (10111010100)_2$$

Subtracting each digit from the radix less 1 is equivalent to interchanging 1's for 0's and 0's for 1's. Hence,

$$[N]_{2-1} = (01000101011)_2$$

Finally, let us employ the one's complement to perform subtraction via equation (1-21a).

Example.

$$N = (1110110)_2 - (111)_2$$

The conversion is

Binary

$$
\begin{array}{ccc}
1110110 & \xrightarrow{\text{One's comp.}} & 1110110 \\
-0000111 & \xrightarrow{\phantom{\text{One's comp.}}} & 1111000
\end{array}
$$

Performing the addition,

$$
\begin{array}{l}
1110110 \\
\underline{1111000} \\
11101110 \\
\quad\lfloor\!\!\longrightarrow\ 1 \quad \text{End-around carry} \\
\underline{1101111}
\end{array}
$$

Therefore,

$$N = +(1101111)_2$$

Example.

Evaluate the difference

$$N = (11011)_2 - (1101111)_2$$

Following equation (1-21b), the code conversion is

Binary

$$
\begin{array}{ccc}
+(11011)_2 & \xrightarrow{\text{One's comp.}} & 0011011 \\
-(1101111)_2 & \xrightarrow{\phantom{\text{One's comp.}}} & 0010000
\end{array}
$$

The addition produces

$$
\begin{array}{l}
0011011 \\
\underline{0010000} \\
00101011 \\
\quad\lfloor\!\!\longrightarrow\ 0 \quad \text{No end-around carry} \\
\underline{0101011}
\end{array}
$$

The absence of the carry means that

$$N = -[0101011]_{2-1}$$
$$= -(1010100)_2$$

Computer Codes

Before beginning our discussion of various codes it would be helpful to clarify in a simple sense what is meant by the word *coding*. Although we rarely think about it, we encounter coding many times in our everyday lives. Driving down the street we approach a traffic light in which a red signal "stands for" stop, a green signal stands for go, and a yellow signal stands for caution. In other words the code is

Red light: Stop
Yellow light: Caution
Green light: Go

At a local baseball game the umpire raises his arms with two fingers showing on his right hand and three fingers showing on his left. We automatically interpret this code to mean that the count on the current batter is two strikes and three balls. These simple examples illustrate the basic idea and no doubt the reader can think of many more.

We cannot communicate directly with the computer through speech or written language (not yet, at any rate) and hence we code to facilitate the normal flow of information within and among computational and data-handling equipment.

Our presentation of codes is limited to the listing of several useful ones. Binary coded decimal codes, Gray codes, and the alphanumeric codes are perhaps the most important ones for computer usages. However, we shall list several others which find applications in the design of digital systems.

Binary Coded Decimal

Perhaps the most common code is called *binary coded decimal*. This code, simply referred to as BCD, is so common that it is often thought of as uncoded. The code consists of 4 bit positions, each of which is assigned a *weight* which is a power of 2. The least significant (rightmost) bit has a weight of 2^0, the next significant bit has a weight of 2^1, etc. Hence, the decimal digits can be represented by 4 bits such that

0:	0000	5:	0101
1:	0001	6:	0110
2:	0010	7:	0111
3:	0011	8:	1000
4:	0100	9:	1001

This code is thus a weighted code in which the weight is (8421) or, equivalently, $(2^3 2^2 2^1 2^0)$. This code is commonly used in digital computers with digit-organized memories. However, note that this code is somewhat inefficient since 4 bits, which are capable of representing 16 items, are used in BCD to represent only 10.

Example.

Encode the decimal number $N = (9750)_{10}$ in BCD code.

$$9: \quad 1001$$
$$7: \quad 0111$$
$$5: \quad 0101$$
$$0: \quad 0000$$

Therefore,

$$N = (1001\ 0111\ 0101\ 0000)_{BCD}$$

4221 Code

The 4221 code is another weighted code in which the bit positions are assigned the weights (4221). Hence, the digit 9 that is represented by 1001 in BCD is assigned the code 1111 in 4221 code. The decimal digits are represented as

0:	0000	5:	0111
1:	0001	6:	1100
2:	0010	7:	1101
3:	0011	8:	1110
4:	1000	9:	1111

This code is used in many computer-type operations, and much of its usefulness stems from the fact that it is a self-complementing code—as are all other codes whose weights add up to 9. A *self-complementing* code may be defined as one for which the nine's complement of a number represented in the code is found by simply taking the one's complement of the coded representation.

Example.

Encode the decimal number $N = (9750)_{10}$ in 4221 code.

$$9: \quad 1111$$
$$7: \quad 1101$$
$$5: \quad 0111$$
$$0: \quad 0000$$

Therefore,

$$N = (1111110101110000)_{4221}$$

Example.

Show that the nine's complement of a number in decimal may be found by taking the one's complement of the number's 4221 representation. Given the number

$$N = (9750)_{10}$$

we recall that

$$[N]_{10-1} = (0249)_{10}$$

Also, from the previous example,

$$N = (1111110101110000)_{4221}$$

and therefore

$$[N]_{2-1} = (0000\ 0010\ 1000\ 1111)_{4221}$$
$$= (0249)_{10}$$

Hence,

$$[N]_{10-1} = [N]_{2-1}$$

The Gray Code

A cyclic code may be defined as any code in which, for every code word, an end-around shift operation yields another code word. For example, if 001 is a code word, then so are 100 and 010. The advantage enjoyed by this type of code is the obvious ease with which the codes can be generated and manipulated.

The Gray code is one of the most common types of cyclic codes. It has the characteristic that only 1 bit position will change at a time as the digits represented by the code are advanced from one number to the next. As an example consider the 4-bit Gray code shown below:

0:	0000	8:	1100
1:	0001	9:	1101
2:	0011	10:	1111
3:	0010	11:	1110
4:	0110	12:	1010
5:	0111	13:	1011
6:	0101	14:	1001
7:	0100	15:	1000

Note that since only 1 bit at a time changes in progressing from one number to the next as in a counter, a false output caused by multiple bit changes which do not occur at exactly the same instant will never be generated.

Example.

Consider the rotating coded disk shown in Fig. 1.2. The shaded areas on the disk are metal conductors. As the disk rotates, the metal conductors along

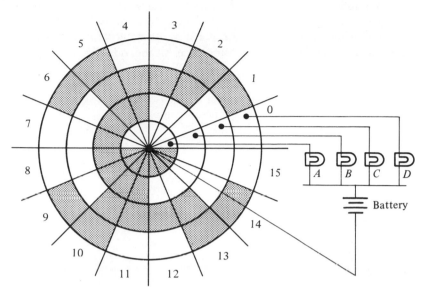

Fig. 1.2　Gray coded disk.

the four tracks encounter sliding contacts. This connection between the sliding contacts and metal conductors energizes the lights.

Each sector on the disk has a code 0, 1, . . . , 15. Therefore, by observing the lights we may determine the position of the disk to within one sector or 22.5°.

Suppose we examine the lights and find that A is on, B is off, C is flickering on and off, and D is on; i.e., the code is

$$A\ \ B\ \ C\ \ D$$
$$1\ \ 0\ \ f\ \ 1$$

Examination of Fig. 1.2 indicates that the disk is on the sector boundary between sectors 14 and 13 since the codes for these sectors are

$$14 \longrightarrow 1001$$
$$13 \longrightarrow 1011$$

EXCESS-3

EXCESS-3 is a special code produced by adding decimal 3 (binary 0011) to the corresponding BCD code. Hence, the decimal digits are represented as shown below:

0:	0011	5:	1000
1:	0100	6:	1001
2:	0101	7:	1010
3:	0110	8:	1011
4:	0111	9:	1100

This code is particularly useful in instances where it is desired to perform arithmetic using complements. This code, like the 4221 code, is called a self-complementing code because the nine's complement of a decimal digit may be obtained by complementing each bit individually.

Example.

Encode the decimal number $N = (9750)_{10}$ in EXCESS-3 and use the one's complement to find the nine's complement.

Coding in EXCESS-3 yields

$$9 \longrightarrow 1100$$
$$7 \longrightarrow 1010$$
$$5 \longrightarrow 1000$$
$$0 \longrightarrow 0011$$

and therefore

$$N = (1100\ 1010\ 1000\ 0011)_{\text{EXCESS-3}}$$

Then

$$[N]_{2-1} = (0011010101111100)_{\text{EXCESS-3}}$$

$$[N]_{10-1} = [N]_{2-1} = (0011\ 0101\ 0111\ 1100)_{\text{EXCESS-3}}$$

$$[N]_{10-1} = (0249)_{10}$$

A Simple Parity Code

In contrast to the above codes, a parity code is used to detect and some-times correct errors in information which is being processed in computational equipment. For example, when information is written into a computer memory or on magnetic tape, a *parity bit* is added to the information and used to detect errors. Consider, for example, the strip of magnetic tape shown in Fig. 1.3. The tape consists of nine tracks, eight of which are used for information and one which is used for parity check. The parity bit is used to establish either even or odd parity over the entire coded word. Suppose, as shown in the figure, that even parity is to be established and that the information bits are

01011000

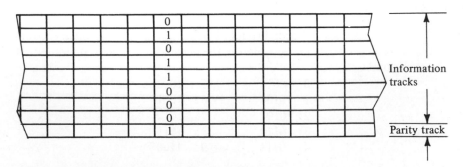

Fig. 1.3   An illustration of parity coding on magnetic tape.

Then the complete coded word, obtained by adding a parity bit to the end of the information bits, is

$$010110001$$

Since even parity is to be established, one need only ensure that the total number of 1's in the complete coded word is even. Note that if an odd number of errors should occur in the coded word, they would be easily detected since even parity would then no longer exist. In general, to detect more errors or be able to correct any errors, more parity bits are required.

Two-out-of-Five Code

The two-out-of-five code is a multibit code basically designed for ease of error detection in various types of computational and register-shifting operations. Five bits are used to represent the digits 0 through 9. As the name implies, 2 and only 2 of the 5 bits are 1's. as shown below:

0:	11000	5:	01010
1:	00011	6:	01100
2:	00101	7:	10001
3:	00110	8:	10010
4:	01001	9:	10100

This structure allows for relatively simple detection of errors should they occur due to malfunctions in equipment since the number of 1's in each word must be exactly 2.

Example.

Encode the decimal number $N = (237)_{10}$ in the two-out-of-five code.
From the listing above

$$2 \longrightarrow 00101$$
$$3 \longrightarrow 00110$$
$$7 \longrightarrow 10001$$

Hence,

$$N = (001010011010001)_{\text{two-out-of-five}}$$

Since the number of digits in decimal is 3, there must be $2 \times 3 = 6$ "one" bits in the two-out-of-five representation.

Biquinary Code

The biquinary code is listed below:

0:	01 00001	5.	10 00001
1:	01 00010	6:	10 00010
2:	01 00100	7:	10 00100
3:	01 01000	8:	10 01000
4:	01 10000	9:	10 10000

Note that each code word is 7 bits long, containing exactly two 1's and five 0's. This arrangement permits simple detection of single errors and a large number of multiple errors. Because the code consists of 7 bits, it is capable of representing $2^7 = 128$ items. Hence, like the two-out-of-five code, the biquinary code wastes more bit positions than many other error detection digital arithmetic codes.

Alphanumeric Codes

Alphanumeric codes are used when information processing equipment must handle letters and special symbols as well as decimal digits. These codes are typically 6 to 8 bits in length. Table 1.7 shows one version of two typical and important alphanumeric codes: the ASCII code, pronounced "askey," which stands for American Standard Code for Information Interchange,

TABLE 1.7. Alphanumeric Codes

Character	EBCDIC Code	ASCII Code	Character	EBCDIC Code	ASCII Code
blank	0100 0000	P010 0000	A	1100 0001	P100 0001
.	0100 1011	P010 1110	B	1100 0010	P100 0010
(	0100 1101	P010 1000	C	1100 0011	P100 0011
+	0100 1110	P010 1011	D	1100 0100	P100 0100
$	0101 1011	P010 0100	E	1100 0101	P100 0101
*	0101 1100	P010 1010	F	1100 0110	P100 0110
)	0101 1101	P010 1001	G	1100 0111	P100 0111
—	0110 0000	P010 1101	H	1100 1000	P100 1000
/	0110 0001	P010 1111	I	1100 1001	P100 1001
,	0110 1011	P010 1100	J	1101 0001	P100 1010
'	0111 1101	P010 0111	K	1101 0010	P100 1011
=	0111 1110	P011 1101	L	1101 0011	P100 1100
			M	1101 0100	P100 1101
0	1111 0000	P011 0000	N	1101 0101	P100 1110
1	1111 0001	P011 0001	O	1101 0110	P100 1111
2	1111 0010	P011 0010	P	1101 0111	P101 0000
3	1111 0011	P011 0011	Q	1101 1000	P101 0001
4	1111 0100	P011 0100	R	1101 1001	P101 0010
5	1111 0101	P011 0101	S	1110 0010	P101 0011
6	1111 0110	P011 0110	T	1110 0011	P101 0100
7	1111 0111	P011 0111	U	1110 0100	P101 0101
8	1111 1000	P011 1000	V	1110 0101	P101 0110
9	1111 1001	P011 1001	W	1110 0110	P101 0111
			X	1110 0111	P101 1000
			Y	1110 1000	P101 1001
			Z	1110 1001	P101 1010

Note: P = parity bit.

and the EBCDIC code, which is the Extended BCD Interchange Code. The latter code is the one used in the IBM System/360 and 370 machines.

Example.

Encode the special message CATCH 22 in ASCII code with even parity and group the coded word into 16-bit segments.

$$
\begin{array}{cc}
\text{C} & \text{A} \\
\text{Segment 1:} \quad (1100\ 0011\ 0100\ 0001)_{\text{ASCII}} \\
\end{array}
$$

Segment 1:   C   A
(1100 0011 0100 0001)$_{\text{ASCII}}$

Segment 2:   T   C
(1101 0100 1100 0011)$_{\text{ASCII}}$

Segment 3:   H   BLANK
(0100 1000 1010 0000)$_{\text{ASCII}}$

Segment 4:   2   2
(1011 0010 1011 0010)$_{\text{ASCII}}$

Note that this message can be stored in four memory registers of a 16-bit computer as

Register 1:   1100 0011 0100 0001
Register 2:   1101 0100 1100 0011
Register 3:   0100 1000 1010 0000
Register 4:   1011 0010 1011 0010

Summary

In this chapter we have presented and explored the number systems commonly used in modern computer equipment. Simple base conversion algorithms have been presented which allow the reader the mobility to move quickly and efficiently between various number systems. The most important schemes employed in practice for performing computer arithmetic have also been examined. In addition, the useful codes normally encountered in computer equipment have been discussed.

REFERENCES

1. BARTEE, T. C., *Digital Computer Fundamentals*. New York: McGraw-Hill Book Company, 1960, 1966, and 1972.

2. CHU, Y., *Digital Computer Design Fundamentals*. New York: McGraw-Hill Book Company, 1962.

3. FLORES, I., *The Logic of Computer Arithmetic*. Englewood Cliffs, N.J.: Prentice-Hall, Inc., 1963.

4. GSCHWIND, H. W., *Design of Digital Computers*. Berlin: Springer-Verlag, 1967.

5. HILL, F. J., and G. R. PETERSON, *Introduction to Switching Theory and Logical Design*. New York: John Wiley & Sons, Inc., 1968.

6. PETERSON, W. W., *Error-Correcting Codes*. Cambridge, Mass.: The M.I.T. Press, 1961.

7. RICHARDS, R. K., *Arithmetic Operations in Digital Computers*. New York: Van Nostrand Reinhold Company, 1955.

PROBLEMS

1.1. Write the numbers below in the reduced floating point notation for the specified values of m, n, and k:
(a) $N = -(167801)_{10}$, $m + n = 7$, $k = 2$.
(b) $N = (10110.01)_2$, $m + n = 9$, $k = 3$.
(c) $N = (547543261.13)_8$, $m + n = 12$, $k = 2$.

1.2. Given the binary numbers below, determine $A + B$, $A - B$, $C \times D$, and C/D:

$$A = 1011010$$
$$B = 101111$$
$$C = 1010101$$
$$D = 110$$

1.3. Perform the following indicated operations:

(a)   1101
          0101
        +1101
        ———

(c) $111\sqrt{110}$

(b)   10110110
        −01011011

(d)   1011
        × 101

1.4. Given the octal numbers below, calculate $A + B$, $A \times B$, and A/B:

$$A = 165$$
$$B = 24$$

1.5. Calculate the product of the two hexadecimal numbers 2CF3 and 2B.

1.6. Use Algorithm 1-2 to perform the following number base conversions:
(a) $(250)_8 \rightarrow (?)_{10}$.
(b) $(250)_8 \rightarrow (?)_{16}$.
(c) $(250)_8 \rightarrow (?)_2$.

1.7. Given $N = (174.25)_{10}$, use the radix divide/multiply technique to determine N_8 and N_2.

1.8. Work problems 1.6(b) and 1.6(c) using the base 2^k conversion method.

1.9. Convert $(256.2)_8$ to base 16 using base 2^k conversion.

1.10. Perform the calculation indicated below:

$$(1011011)_2 \times_{10} (42)_{16} = (?)_8$$

1.11. Perform the base conversions indicated below:
(a) $N = (182.25)_{10} = (?)_8$.
(b) $N = (1023)_4 = (?)_5$.

1.12. Determine the product of A and B and give the answer in base 5 where

$$A - (101011)_2$$
$$B = (110001)_2$$

1.13. Perform the indicated multiplication:

$$(102)_8 \times_2 (22)_4 = (?)_8$$

1.14. Convert $N = (263.5625)_{10}$ to base 2. Then convert this answer in base 2 directly to base 4.

1.15. Use the two's complement arithmetic to perform the following subtractions:
(a) $N = 622 - 408$.
(b) $N = 380 - 520$.

1.16. Using two's complement arithmetic, perform the following subtractions:
(a) $N = (1101011)_2 - (1010)_2$.
(b) $N = (1010101)_2 - (0101010)_2$.

1.17. Use any method to determine the product $N = A \times B$ where

$$A = (0, 1010)_{2cns}$$
$$B = (1, 1001)_{2cns}$$

1.18. Perform the following subtraction in the one's complement number system:

$$N = (907)_{10} - (555)_{10}$$

1.19. Use one's complement arithmetic to perform the following subtraction:

$$N = (1011)_2 - (101011)_2$$

1.20. (a) Name two binary codes in which the nine's complement of a decimal digit may be obtained by complementing each code bit individually.
(b) Excluding parity, name two codes primarily used for error detection.
(c) Name two alphanumeric codes. How many bits does each code employ?
(d) An information word is coded into 8 bits as 10111010. Assign a parity bit to the end of this word to establish even parity over the entire code word.

1.21. Convert the following numbers to the radix complement number system:

$$A = +(AF3)_{16}$$
$$B = -(13C)_{16}$$
$$C = -(085)_{16}$$
$$D = +(9B4)_{16}$$

when
(a) $r = 10, n = 5$.
(b) $r = 8, n = 5$.
(c) $r = 2, n = 12$.

1.22. Perform the following operations on the numbers $A, B, C,$ and D defined in Problem 1.21:

$$N_1 = A + B$$
$$N_2 = A + C$$
$$N_3 = A + D$$
$$N_4 = B + C$$
$$N_5 = B + D$$
$$N_6 = C + D$$

using the
(a) Ten's complement number system.
(b) Eight's complement number system.
(c) Two's complement number system.

1.23. Perform the following calculations using a four-digit ten's complement number system:
(a) $+(395)_{10} + (632)_{10} = (?)_{10}$.
(b) $+(395)_{10} - (632)_{10} = (?)_{10}$.
(c) $-(395)_{10} + (632)_{10} = (?)_{10}$.
(d) $-(395)_{10} - (632)_{10} = (?)_{10}$.
Explain any unusual results.

1.24. Perform the following calculations using the two's complement calculator presented in this chapter:
(a) $+(5)_{10} + (11)_{10} = (?)_{10}$.
(b) $+(5)_{10} - (16)_{10} = (?)_{10}$.
(c) $-(4)_{10} - (12)_{10} = (?)_{10}$.
(d) $+(12)_{10} - (8)_{10} = (?)_{10}$.
Explain any unusual results.

1.25. Perform the following operations using binary arithmetic. The numbers are in binary signed-magnitude notation with the most significant bit being the sign bit. Check your answers by converting the numbers to decimal and performing the operations in base 10.

(a) $\begin{array}{r} 00101.110 \\ +10010.001 \\ \hline \end{array}$ (b) $\begin{array}{r} 01011.0101 \\ -00110.1100 \\ \hline \end{array}$

(c) $\begin{array}{r} 0101.010 \\ \times 1011.100 \\ \hline \end{array}$ (d) $\begin{array}{r} 101101 \\ \times 001110 \\ \hline \end{array}$

1.26. Assume that the numbers in Problem 1.25(a) and (b) are in the radix complement number system with $r = 2$. Perform the indicated operations. Check your answers using decimal arithmetic.

1.27. Convert the following numbers:
(a) $+(025)_{10} = (?)_{10\text{cns}}$.
(b) $-(025)_{10} = (?)_{10\text{cns}}$.
(c) $[025]_{10} = (?)_{10}$.
(d) $[025]_{10-1} = (?)_{10}$.

1.28. Convert the following numbers:
(a) $(965)_{10\text{cns}} = (?)_{2\text{cns}}$.
(b) $(065)_{10\text{cns}} = (?)_{2\text{cns}}$.

(c) $(9025)_{10cns} = (?)_{2cns}$.

(d) $(0925)_{10cns} = (?)_{2cns}$.

Choose a sufficient number of bits in each conversion to ensure no loss of accuracy in the numbers.

1.29. Show how a 16-bit computer, using the two's complement number system, would calculate

(a) $(16,850)_{10} - (2,925)_{10} = (?)_{10}$.

(b) $(16,850)_{10} + (2,925)_{10} = (?)_{10}$.

(c) $(2,925)_{10} - (16,850)_{10} = (?)_{10}$.

1.30. Show how a 16-bit computer would calculate the following numbers in two's complement arithmetic:

(a) $[+(16,850)_{10}] + [+(33)_{10}] = (?)_{10}$.

(b) $[+(16,850)_{10}] + [-(33)_{10}] = (?)_{10}$.

1.31. Perform the following subtractions using diminished radix complement arithmetic:

(a) $(85,432)_{10} - (36,842)_{10} = (?)_{10}$.

(b) $(36,842)_{10} - (85,432)_{10} = (?)_{10}$.

(c) $(10111010)_2 - (11010)_2 = (?)_2$.

(d) $(11010)_2 - (10111010)_2 = (?)_2$.

1.32. Perform the following code conversions:

(a) $(1011001111001001)_{EXCESS-3} = (?)_{BCD}$.

(b) $(1011001111001001)_{EXCESS-3} = (?)_{10}$.

(c) $[(1011001111001001)_{EXCESS-3}]_{10-1} = (?)_{10}$.

(d) $(0011100001111100)_{EXCESS-3} = (?)_{4221}$.

1.33. Perform the following conversions:

(a) $(AO)_{16} = (?)_{ASCII}$.

(b) $(1C)_{16} = (?)_{ASCII}$.

(c) $(1011001001001000)_{ASCII} = (?)_{EBCDIC}$.

(d) $(0100000111010100)_{ASCII} = (?)_{EBCDIC}$.

1.34. Examine the Gray-coded disk of Fig. 1.2. Suppose the display lights give the following indications: A is off, B is on, C is on, and D is flickering on and off. Locate the position of the disk by sector numbers.

1.35. For the nine-track magnetic tape of Fig. 1.3, the following 8-bit messages are to be recorded. Determine the parity bit to establish odd parity for each message.

(a) 10111010P.

(b) 00111000P.

(c) 10011001P.

(d) 01011010P.

2

Algebra
of
Switching
Functions

In this chapter we begin the analysis and synthesis of combinational logic networks. To analyze and synthesize logic networks, several different techniques may be employed to arrive at the same result. For example, in addressing any one given combinational logic design task, one might employ truth tables, logical expressions, Karnaugh maps, logic diagrams, tabular procedures, timing diagrams, or computer-aided design programs. In this chapter we shall define truth tables, logical expressions, and logic and timing diagrams; the other techniques will be addressed later.

The analysis and synthesis tools presented in this chapter are based on the fundamental concepts of Boolean algebra, and hence this topic will be examined first.

Boolean Algebra

In 1849, George Boole presented an algebraic formulation of the processes of logical thought and reason [1]. This formulation has come to be known as Boolean algebra, a brief summary of which follows.

The basic description of the Boolean algebra formulation is set forth in a number of premises or postulates. We present here a set of seven postulates which provide the basis for building the Boolean algebra. Although only six are needed, we have added the seventh to simplify the proofs of our theorems.

Postulate 1. Definition

A Boolean algebra is a closed algebraic system containing a set K of two or more elements and the two operators $\cdot$ and $+$; alternatively, for every a and b in set K, $a \cdot b$ belongs to K and $a + b$ belongs to K. ($+$ is called OR and $\cdot$ is called AND.)

Postulate 2. Law of Substitution

In the closed algebraic system two expressions are said to be equal ($=$) if one can be replaced by the other.

Postulate 3. Existence of 1 and 0

There exist unique elements 1 (one) and 0 (zero) in set K such that for every a in K

(a) $a + 0 = a$.
(b) $a \cdot 1 = a$.

Postulate 4. Commutativity

For every a and b in K

(a) $a + b = b + a$.
(b) $a \cdot b = b \cdot a$.

Postulate 5. Associativity

For every a and b in K

(a) $a + (b + c) = (a + b) + c$.
(b) $a \cdot (b \cdot c) = (a \cdot b) \cdot c$.

Postulate 6. Distributivity

For every a and b in K

(a) $a + (b \cdot c) = (a + b) \cdot (a + c)$.
(b) $a \cdot (b + c) = (a \cdot b) + (a \cdot c)$.

Postulate 7. Existence of the Complement

For every a in K there exists a unique element called $\bar{a}$ (complement of a) in K such that

(a) $a + \bar{a} = 1$.
(b) $a \cdot \bar{a} = 0$.

Upon this set of premises we may now develop other useful relationships which we shall call theorems. Before proceeding to the theorem development, let us examine the postulates more closely to understand exactly what they mean.

Venn Diagrams for Postulates [2]

The postulates may be graphically presented in the form of Venn diagrams. This graphical description is possible since the algebra of sets is a Boolean algebra with sets corresponding to elements, intersection corresponding to $\cdot$, and union corresponding to $+$. On the Venn diagram, sets are shown as closed contours (squares, circles, elipses, etc.). Let us demonstrate the Venn diagram in Fig. 2.1. Shown in this figure are the sets a, b, $a \cdot b$, and $a + b$. Alternative notation sometimes used for $a + b$ is $a \vee b$ or $a \cup b$, and for $a \cdot b$, ab or $a \wedge b$ or $a \cap b$. Now we can test the postulates.

Postulates 1 and 2 are fundamental statements of fact and will not be shown as Venn diagrams. Postulate 3 defines the properties of 1, called the universal set because it contains all other sets, and 0, called the null set because it contains no other sets. Postulate 3 is illustrated in Fig. 2.2. Notice that in Fig. 2.2(a) set $a \cdot 1$, the intersection of set a and set 1, is identical to the original set a; in Fig. 2.2(b), the union of the null set, 0, and set a results in

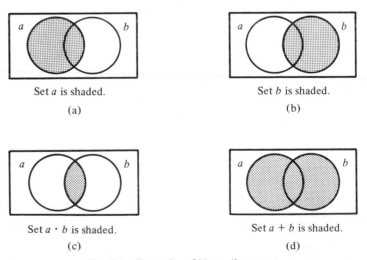

Set a is shaded.

(a)

Set b is shaded.

(b)

Set $a \cdot b$ is shaded.

(c)

Set $a + b$ is shaded.

(d)

Fig. 2.1   Examples of Venn diagrams.

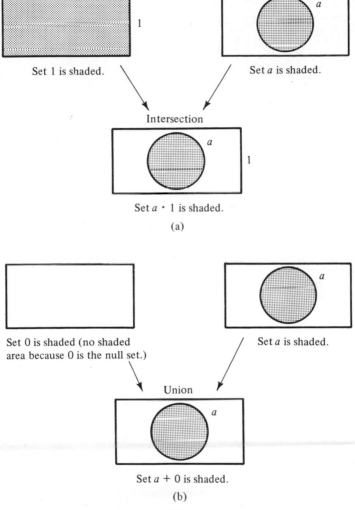

Fig. 2.2 Venn diagram (a) for Postulate 3b, and (b) for Postulate 3a.

the set $a + 0$, which is again identical to set a. Now, we are beginning to see the relationship between Venn diagrams and Boolean algebra. Postulates 4 and 5 are intuitively obvious on Venn diagrams and will be omitted.

Postulate 6 has significant meaning when viewed on a Venn diagram; see Fig. 2.3. From the figure it is quite evident that the set $a + bc$ and the set $(a + b)(a + c)$ are two representations of the same shaded area and hence $a + bc$ is equal to $(a + b)(a + c)$. The Venn diagram for Postulate 6(b) is left as an exercise for the reader.

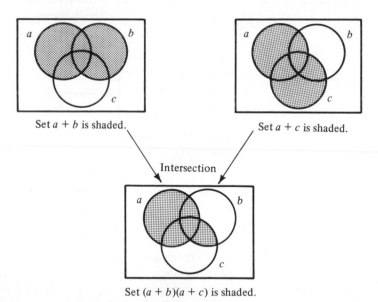

Set $b \cdot c$ is shaded.   Set a is shaded.

Union

Set $a + bc$ is shaded.

Set $a + b$ is shaded.   Set $a + c$ is shaded.

Intersection

Set $(a + b)(a + c)$ is shaded.

Fig. 2.3   Venn diagrams for Postulate 6a.

Postulate 7 refers to the complement of a. If a is the shaded set shown in Fig. 2.4, the complement of a, $\bar{a}$, is that area outside a in the universal set. In other words both a and $\bar{a}$ are mutually exclusive and lie inside the universal

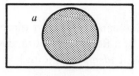

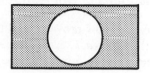

Set a is shaded.   Set $\bar{a}$ is shaded.

Fig. 2.4   Venn diagram for $\bar{a}$.

set as shown in the figure. Since they are mutually exclusive, they contain no area in common and hence their interesection is the null set, or $a \cdot \bar{a} = 0$. The union of a and $\bar{a}$ is by definition the universal set, or $a + \bar{a} = 1$.

At this point let us ask the question, What is the complement of 1? The universal set, 1, contains all other sets; hence its complement must be the null set, 0. Another important point is that the complement of $\bar{a}$ is just the set a. The results of this discussion are listed below:

$$\bar{1} = 0$$
$$\bar{0} = 1$$
$$\bar{\bar{a}} = a$$

The property $\bar{\bar{a}} = a$ is sometimes called *involution*. This concludes our discussion of the postulates; now we are ready to develop several very useful theorems in Boolean algebra.

Duality

The principle of duality is a very important concept in Boolean algebra. Briefly stated, the *principle of duality* pronounces that given an expression which is always valid in Boolean algebra, the dual expression is also always valid. The dual expression is found by replacing all $+$ operators with $\cdot$, all $\cdot$ operators with $+$, all 1's with 0's, and all 0's with 1's. An example is shown below. Given this expression

$$a + (bc) = (a + b)(a + c)$$

the dual of this expression is

$$a(b + c) = ab + ac.$$

Please note that these expressions are the (a) and (b) parts of Postulate 6. In fact, Postulates 3 through 7 are all listed as dual expressions.

The principle of duality will be used extensively in proving Boolean algebra theorems. We shall prove that one expression is valid using the postulates and previously proven theorems. Once the expression is proved valid, by duality its *dual* is also valid. In other words, we prove one expression and get another one "free."

Theorems of Boolean Algebra

We shall now prove several theorems in Boolean algebra. In these theorems, the letters a, b, c, etc., represent elements of a Boolean algebra. The first theorem we shall prove describes the property of *idempotency* and is stated below.

Theorem 8. Idempotency

   (a) $a + a = a$.
   (b) $a \cdot a = a$.

Proof. We may prove either the (a) or (b) part of this theorem. Suppose we prove the (a) part:

$$
\begin{aligned}
a + a &= a + a \\
&= (a + a)1 & \text{[P3(b)]} \\
&= (a + a)(a + \bar{a}) & \text{[P7(a)]} \\
&= a + a\bar{a} & \text{[P6(a)]} \\
&= a + 0 & \text{[P7(b)]} \\
&= a & \text{[P3(a)]}
\end{aligned}
$$

This form of proof will be used for all the theorems. Each step consists of employing Postulate 2, the law of substitution, in conjunction with other postulates (and later theorems as they are developed). The postulates used in a particular step are listed to the right. An important point to remember is that symbols on opposing sides of equals may be used interchangeably; for example, Theorem 8 tells us that a may be substituted for $a \cdot a$ and also that $a \cdot a$ may be substituted for a.

The next theorem emphasizes further the properties of the unique elements 1 and 0.

Theorem 9.

   (a) $a + 1 = 1$.
   (b) $a \cdot 0 = 0$.

Proof. Let us again prove the (a) part of this theorem:

$$
\begin{aligned}
a + 1 &= a + 1 \\
&= (a + 1) \cdot 1 & \text{[P3(b)]} \\
&= 1 \cdot (a + 1) & \text{[P4(b)]} \\
&= (a + \bar{a})(a + 1) & \text{[P7(a)]} \\
&= a + \bar{a} \cdot 1 & \text{[P6(a)]} \\
&= a + \bar{a} & \text{[P3(b)]} \\
&= 1 & \text{[P7(a)]}
\end{aligned}
$$

Thus the (a) part of this theorem is valid; therefore the (b) part is valid by the principle of duality.

At this point let us summarize all the properties of the unique elements 1 and 0 which we have presented thus far:

$$a + 0 = a \qquad a + 1 = 1$$
$$a \cdot 0 = 0 \qquad a \cdot 1 = a$$
$$\bar{0} = 1 \qquad \bar{1} = 0$$

The · (AND) properties of 1 and 0 remind us of the fundamental properties of multiplication in standard mathematics; however, the + (OR) properties quickly remind us that we are *not* dealing with mathematics we previously have studied, and none of the mathematical properties which we employed there can be assumed for use in Boolean algebra. We may use only the postulates and theorems we are developing in Boolean algebra, for this is a completely new and different system in which we are now working.

The Boolean algebra property of *absorption* is now proved in the next theorem. Absorption has no counterpart in standard mathematics.

Theorem 10. Absorption

   (a) $a + ab = a$.
   (b) $a(a + b) = a$.

Proof. Proving the (a) part,

$$\begin{aligned} a + ab &= a + ab \\ &= a \cdot 1 + ab && \text{[P3(b)]} \\ &= a(1 + b) && \text{[P6(b)]} \\ &= a(b + 1) && \text{[P4(a)]} \\ &= a \cdot 1 && \text{[T9(a)]} \\ &= a && \text{[P3(b)]} \end{aligned}$$

In proving this theorem we employed the concept that the element name, a, in Theorem 9(a) may be changed at will without affecting the validity of the expression. For example,

$$a + 1 = 1$$
$$b + 1 = 1$$
$$X + 1 = 1$$
$$Q_3 + 1 = 1$$
$$\bar{z} + 1 = 1$$

are several ways in which Theorem 9(a) may be expressed. We shall make liberal use of this concept in what follows.

The next theorem demonstrates the elimination of an extra element from a Boolean expression.

Theorem 11.

(a) $a + \bar{a}b = a + b$.

(b) $a(\bar{a} + b) = ab$.

Proof. For this theorem we shall switch and prove the (b) part:

$$
\begin{aligned}
a(\bar{a} + b) &= a(\bar{a} + b) \\
&= a\bar{a} + ab && [\text{P6(b)}] \\
&= 0 + ab && [\text{P7(b)}] \\
&= ab + 0 && [\text{P4(a)}] \\
&= ab && [\text{P3(a)}]
\end{aligned}
$$

The correct manner for using this theorem is to find an element and its complement in an expression which matches the form of the theorem. The following examples demonstrate the manner in which the theorem can be used to simplify Boolean expressions.

Example.

$$XY + \overline{XY}Z = XY + Z \quad [\text{T11(a)}]$$

Example.

$$
\begin{aligned}
\bar{X} + YX &= \bar{X} + XY && [\text{P4(b)}] \\
&= \bar{X} + Y && [\text{T11(a)}]
\end{aligned}
$$

Example.

$$X(\bar{X} + Z)(P + A) = XZ(P + A) \quad [\text{T11(b)}]$$

Example.

$$
\begin{aligned}
\bar{X}(X + Z) + \bar{A} + AZ &= \bar{X}Z + \bar{A} + AZ && [\text{T11(b)}] \\
&= \bar{X}Z + \bar{A} + Z && [\text{T11(a)}] \\
&= \bar{A} + Z + \bar{X}Z && [\text{P4(a)}] \\
&= \bar{A} + Z + Z\bar{X} && [\text{P4(b)}] \\
&= \bar{A} + Z && [\text{T10(a)}]
\end{aligned}
$$

The idea of complement is now extended from an element to an expression by De Morgan's theorem.

Theorem 12. De Morgan's Theorem

(a) $\overline{a + b} = \bar{a}\bar{b}$.

(b) $\overline{ab} = \bar{a} + \bar{b}$.

Proof. Let us prove the (a) part. If

$$X = a + b$$

then $\bar{X} = \overline{a + b}$. By Postulate 7

$$X \cdot \bar{X} = 0 \quad \text{and} \quad X + \bar{X} = 1$$

If $X \cdot Y = 0$ and $X + Y = 1$, then $Y = \bar{X}$ because the complement of X is unique. Therefore we let $Y = \bar{a}\bar{b}$ and test $X \cdot Y$ and $X + Y$:

$$
\begin{aligned}
X \cdot Y &= (a + b)(\bar{a}\bar{b}) & \text{(P2)} \\
&= (\bar{a}\bar{b})(a + b) & \text{[P4(b)]} \\
&= (\bar{a}\bar{b})a + (\bar{a}\bar{b})b & \text{[P6(b)]} \\
&= a(\bar{a}\bar{b}) + (\bar{a}\bar{b})b & \text{[P4(b)]} \\
&= (a\bar{a})b + \bar{a}(\bar{b}b) & \text{[P5(b)]} \\
&= 0 \cdot b + \bar{a}(b \cdot \bar{b}) & \text{[P7(b), 4(b)]} \\
&= b \cdot 0 + \bar{a} \cdot 0 & \text{[P4(b), 7(b)]} \\
&= 0 + 0 & \text{[T9(b)]} \\
&= 0 & \text{[P3(a)]}
\end{aligned}
$$

$$
\begin{aligned}
X + Y &= (a + b) + \bar{a}\bar{b} & \text{(P2)} \\
&= (b + a) + \bar{a}\bar{b} & \text{[P4(a)]} \\
&= b + (a + \bar{a}\bar{b}) & \text{[P5(a)]} \\
&= b + (a + \bar{b}) & \text{[T11(a)]} \\
&= (a + \bar{b}) + b & \text{[P4(a)]} \\
&= a + (\bar{b} + b) & \text{[P5(a)]} \\
&= a + (b + \bar{b}) & \text{[P4(a)]} \\
&= a + 1 & \text{[P7(a)]} \\
&= 1 & \text{[T9(a)]}
\end{aligned}
$$

Therefore, by uniqueness of $\bar{X}$

$$Y = \bar{X}$$
$$\bar{a}\bar{b} = \overline{a + b}$$

Theorem 12 may be generalized to include longer expressions as shown below:

(a) $\overline{a + b + \cdots + z} = \bar{a}\bar{b} \cdots \bar{z}$.
(b) $\overline{ab \cdots z} = \bar{a} + \bar{b} + \cdots + \bar{z}$.

The rule to follow when complementing an expression is to use relation (a) or (b) above by replacing $+$ (OR) by $\cdot$ (AND) and vice versa and to replace each variable with its complement. Further examples of the use of Theorem 12 are illustrated below.

Example.

$$
\begin{aligned}
\overline{X + \bar{Y}} &= \bar{X}\bar{\bar{Y}} & \text{[T12(a)]} \\
&= \bar{X}Y & \text{(Involution)}
\end{aligned}
$$

Example.

$$\overline{\overline{X}\overline{Z}} = \overline{\overline{X}} + \overline{\overline{Z}} \quad [\text{T12(b)}]$$
$$= X + \overline{Z} \quad (\text{Involution})$$

Example.

$$\overline{a + a\overline{c} + yz} = \overline{a} \cdot \overline{a\overline{c}} \cdot \overline{yz} \quad\quad [\text{T12(a)}]$$
$$= \overline{a}(\overline{a} + \overline{\overline{c}})(\overline{y} + \overline{z}) \quad [\text{T12(b)}]$$
$$= \overline{a}(\overline{a} + c)(\overline{y} + \overline{z}) \quad (\text{Involution})$$
$$= \overline{a}(\overline{y} + \overline{z}) \quad\quad [\text{T10(b)}]$$

Example.

$$\overline{a(b + z(x + \overline{a}))} = \overline{a} + \overline{(b + z(x + \overline{a}))} \quad [\text{T12(b)}]$$
$$= \overline{a} + \overline{b}(\overline{z(x + \overline{a})}) \quad\quad [\text{T12(a)}]$$
$$= \overline{a} + \overline{b}(\overline{z} + \overline{(x + \overline{a})}) \quad [\text{T12(b)}]$$
$$= \overline{a} + \overline{b}(\overline{z} + \overline{x}\overline{\overline{a}}) \quad\quad [\text{T12(a)}]$$
$$= \overline{a} + \overline{b}(\overline{z} + \overline{x}a) \quad\quad (\text{Involution})$$
$$= \overline{a} + \overline{b}(\overline{z} + \overline{x}) \quad\quad [\text{T11(a)}]$$

De Morgan's theorem presents the general technique to be used for complementing Boolean expressions.

A common mistake made in using Boolean algebra will now be shown:

$$AB + \overline{AB} = 1 \quad [\text{P7(a)}]$$
$$AB + \overline{A} + \overline{B} = 1 \quad [\text{T12(b)}]$$

are valid expressions, but

$$AB + \overline{A}\overline{B} \neq 1$$

With this point, De Morgan's theorem is now complete. Let us next consider the *consensus* theorem.

Theorem 13. Consensus

(a) $ab + \overline{a}c + bc = ab + \overline{a}c$.
(b) $(a + b)(\overline{a} + c)(b + c) = (a + b)(\overline{a} + c)$.

Proof. Henceforth, Postulates 4 and 5 will be used without reference.

$$ab + \overline{a}c + bc = ab + \overline{a}c + bc$$
$$= ab + \overline{a}c + 1 \cdot bc \quad\quad [\text{P3(b)}]$$
$$= ab + \overline{a}c + (a + \overline{a})bc \quad [\text{P7(a)}]$$
$$= ab + \overline{a}c + abc + \overline{a}bc \quad [\text{P6(b)}]$$
$$= (ab + abc) + (\overline{a}c + \overline{a}cb)$$
$$= ab + \overline{a}c \quad\quad [\text{T10(a)}]$$

The key to using this theorem is to find an element and its complement, note the associated terms, and eliminate the included term. Several examples follow.

Example.

$$AB + \bar{A}CD + BCD = AB + \bar{A}CD \quad [\text{T13(a)}]$$

Example.

$$\bar{a}X + a(Z + W) + X(Z + W) = \bar{a}X + a(Z + W) \quad [\text{T13(a)}]$$

Example.

$$(a + \bar{b})(\bar{a} + c)(\bar{b} + c) = (a + \bar{b})(\bar{a} + c) \quad [\text{T13(b)}]$$

Example.

$$(X + Y)Z + \bar{X}\bar{Y}W + ZW = (X + Y)\dot{Z} + \overline{(X + Y)}W + ZW \quad [\text{T12(a)}]$$
$$= (X + Y)Z + \overline{(X + Y)}W \qquad\qquad [\text{T13(a)}]$$

In each of the preceding examples, an element or expression and its complement offer the key to reducing the expression.

Now several useful theorems will be presented in rapid order.

Theorem 14.

(a) $ab + a\bar{b} = a$.
(b) $(a + b)(a + \bar{b}) = a$.

Proof. This theorem is another form of Postulate 7. It occurs so often in practice that we call it a new theorem.

$$ab + a\bar{b} = ab + a\bar{b}$$
$$= a(b + \bar{b}) \quad [\text{P6(b)}]$$
$$= a\cdot 1 \qquad [\text{P7(a)}]$$
$$= a \qquad\quad [\text{P3(b)}]$$

Theorem 15.

(a) $ab + a\bar{b}c = ab + ac$.
(b) $(a + b)(a + \bar{b} + c) = (a + b)(a + c)$.

Proof. This theorem is another form of Theorem 11.

$$ab + a\bar{b}c = ab + a\bar{b}c$$
$$= a(b + \bar{b}c) \quad [\text{P6(b)}]$$
$$= a(b + c) \qquad [\text{T11(a)}]$$
$$= ab + ac \qquad [\text{P6(b)}]$$

Theorem 16.

(a) $ab + \bar{a}c = (a + c)(\bar{a} + b)$.
(b) $(a + b)(\bar{a} + c) = ac + \bar{a}b$.

Proof. This theorem is very useful for changing the form of Boolean expressions.

$$ab + \bar{a}c = ab + \bar{a}c$$
$$= (ab + \bar{a})(ab + c) \qquad \text{[P6(a)]}$$
$$= (a + \bar{a})(b + \bar{a})(a + c)(b + c) \qquad \text{[P6(a)]}$$
$$= 1 \cdot (\bar{a} + b)(a + c)(b + c) \qquad \text{[P7(a)]}$$
$$= (\bar{a} + b)(a + c)(b + c) \qquad \text{[P3(b)]}$$
$$= (\bar{a} + b)(a + c) \qquad \text{[T13(b)]}$$

The following examples illustrate the usefulness of the last three theorems.

Example.
$$\bar{A}BC + \bar{A}B\bar{C} = \bar{A}B \quad \text{[T14(a)]}$$

Example.
$$\bar{A}BC + \bar{A}\bar{B}C = \bar{A}C \quad \text{[T14(a)]}$$

Example.
$$(P + \bar{Q})(P + Q + Z) = (P + \bar{Q})(P + Z) \quad \text{[T15(b)]}$$
$$= P + \bar{Q}Z \quad \text{[P6(a)]}$$

Example.
$$\bar{X}\bar{Z} + X\bar{Z}W + ZW = \bar{X}\bar{Z} + \bar{Z}W + ZW \quad \text{[T15(a)]}$$
$$= \bar{X}\bar{Z} + W \quad \text{[T14(a)]}$$
$$= (\bar{X} + W)(W + \bar{Z}) \quad \text{[P6(a)]}$$

Example.
$$(\bar{X}Y + XZ)(X + \bar{Y}) = (\bar{X} + Z)(X + Y)(X + \bar{Y}) \quad \text{[T16(a)]}$$
$$= (\bar{X} + Z)X \quad \text{[T14(b)]}$$
$$= ZX \quad \text{[T11(b)]}$$

For quick reference a listing of all the postulates and theorems is given at the end of this section in Table 2.2.

One final example is given which demonstrates the use of many of the previous theorems.

Example.
$$(A + B)(A + \bar{B}\bar{A})C + \overline{\bar{A}(B + \bar{C})} + \bar{A}B + ABC$$
$$= (A + B)(A + \bar{B})C + \overline{\bar{A}(B + \bar{C})} + \bar{A}B + ABC \quad \text{[T11(a)]}$$
$$= AC + \overline{\bar{A}(B + \bar{C})} + \bar{A}B + ABC \quad \text{[T14(b)]}$$
$$= AC + \overline{\bar{A}(B + \bar{C})} + \bar{A}B + BC \quad \text{[T15(a)]}$$
$$= AC + \bar{A}B + \overline{\bar{A}(B + \bar{C})} \quad \text{[T13(a)]}$$
$$= AC + \bar{A}B + A + \overline{B + \bar{C}} \quad \text{[T12(b)]}$$
$$= AC + \bar{A}B + A + \bar{B}C \quad \text{[T12(a)]}$$
$$= \bar{A}B + A + \bar{B}C \quad \text{[T10(a)]}$$
$$= B + A + \bar{B}C \quad \text{[T11(a)]}$$
$$= B + A + C \quad \text{[T11(a)]}$$

The reader must remember that very few individuals will attack these examples in precisely the same manner. The speed with which these Boolean expressions can be simplified via algebra is dependent on the readers familiarity with the theorems. The reader who knows the theorems well will be able to spot their applications immediately and thus can simplify many expressions by inspection.

Venn Diagrams Revisited

Earlier we examined the postulates using the Venn diagram; here we shall do likewise for selected theorems. Figure 2.5 displays Theorem 13(a) in Venn diagrams. The set $ab + \bar{a}c$ is identical to the set $ab + \bar{a}c + bc$. The set bc is included in $\bar{a}b + ac$.

Theorem 16(b) is presented again in Fig. 2.6. First we find the sets $a + b$ and $\bar{a} + c$, and then we interesect these two areas to find $(a + b)(\bar{a} + c)$.

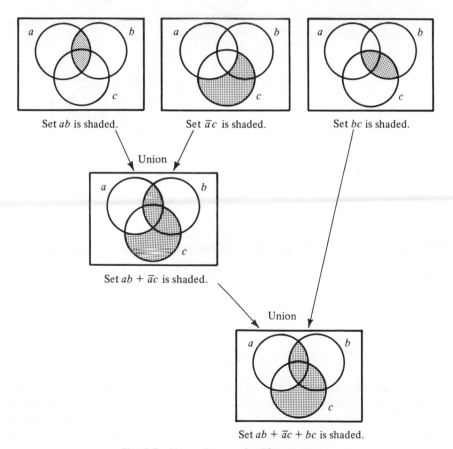

Set ab is shaded.   Set $\bar{a}c$ is shaded.   Set bc is shaded.

Union

Set $ab + \bar{a}c$ is shaded.

Union

Set $ab + \bar{a}c + bc$ is shaded.

Fig. 2.5 Venn diagram for Theorem 13a.

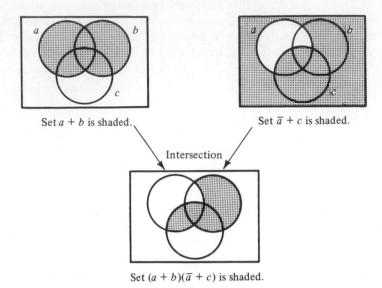

Set $(a + b)(\bar{a} + c)$ is shaded.

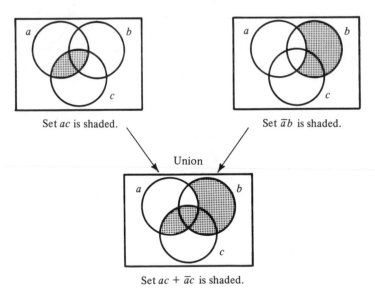

Set $ac + \bar{a}c$ is shaded.

Fig. 2.6   Venn diagrams for Theorem 16b.

Last, we find the sets ac and $\bar{a}b$, and then we "union" them to obtain $ac + \bar{a}b$. The sets $(a + b)(\bar{a} + c)$ and $ac + \bar{a}b$ are indeed identical. It is important to note that the theorems which have been presented are either immediately obvious or can be quickly demonstrated via Venn diagrams. Hence, the reader is encouraged to use this graphical picture to aid him in remembering these important theorems.

Boolean Functions

The postulates and theorems of Boolean algebra presented above are given in general terms without the elements of the set K being specified. Hence, the results are valid for any Boolean algebra. In the discussions that follow, emphasis will focus on the Boolean algebra where $K = \{0, 1\}$. This formulation is often referred to as *switching algebra*.

The concept of a function is well known to those familiar with ordinary algebra. *Boolean functions* represent the corresponding concept for Boolean algebra and can be defined as follows. Let $X_1, X_2, \ldots, X_n$ be symbols called *variables*, each of which represent either the element 0 or 1 of a Boolean algebra (0 or 1 is said to be the *value* of the variable), and let $f(X_1, X_2, \ldots, X_n)$ represent a Boolean function of $X_1, X_2, \ldots, X_n$. The function f represents the value 0 or the value 1 depending on the set of values assigned to $X_1, X_2, \ldots, X_n$. A Boolean function can be described by a Boolean expression as follows:

$$f(A, B, C) = AB + \bar{A}C + A\bar{C}$$

If $A = 1, B = C = 0$, then $f = 1$ as verified below:

$$
\begin{aligned}
f(1, 0, 0) &= 1 \cdot 0 + \bar{1} \cdot 0 + 1 \cdot \bar{0} \\
&= 1 \cdot 0 + 0 \cdot 0 + 1 \cdot 1 \quad (\bar{1} = 0, \bar{0} = 1) \\
&= 0 + 0 + 1 \cdot 1 \qquad \text{[T9(b)]} \\
&= 1 \cdot 1 \qquad\qquad\quad \text{[P3(a)]} \\
&= 1 \qquad\qquad\qquad \text{[P3(b)]}
\end{aligned}
$$

When $A = 0, B = 1$, and $C = 0$, it can be seen that $f = 0$.

An alternative description of a Boolean function can be given by a truth table. A *truth table* displays all possible combinations of values of $X_1, \ldots, X_n$ and the corresponding value of f.

It is helpful at this time to summarize all the Boolean properties of 1 and 0:

$$
\begin{array}{lll}
\bar{1} = 0 & \bar{0} = 1 & \\
0 + 0 = 0 & 1 \cdot 1 = 1 & \text{(P3)} \\
0 + 1 = 1 & 1 \cdot 0 = 0 & \text{(T9)} \\
1 + 0 = 1 & 0 \cdot 1 = 0 & \text{(T9)} \\
1 + 1 = 1 & 0 \cdot 0 = 0 & \text{(T9)}
\end{array}
\qquad (2\text{-}1)
$$

If we evaluate the function $f(A, B, C)$ for all possible input combinations, we find

$$f(0, 0, 0) = 0$$
$$f(0, 0, 1) = 1$$
$$f(0, 1, 0) = 0$$
$$f(0, 1, 1) = 1$$
$$f(1, 0, 0) = 1$$
$$f(1, 0, 1) = 0$$
$$f(1, 1, 0) = 1$$
$$f(1, 1, 1) = 1$$

If these values are listed in a tabular form, we obtain the truth table shown as Table 2.1. Replacing all 0's in the table with F's (false) and all 1's with T's

TABLE 2.1. Truth Table for f(A, B, C)

A	B	C	$f(A, B, C)$
0	0	0	0
0	0	1	1
0	1	0	0
0	1	1	1
1	0	0	1
1	0	1	0
1	1	0	1
1	1	1	1

(true) yields another form of the truth table and also demonstrates part of the one-to-one correspondence which exists between the Boolean algebra and the truth-functional calculus [3]. The truth table for $f(X_1, X_2, \ldots, X_n)$ is shown below:

X_1	X_2	$\ldots$	X_n	$f(X_1, X_2, \ldots, X_n)$
0	0	$\ldots$	0	a_0
0	0	$\ldots$	1	a_1
		$\cdot$		$\cdot$
		$\cdot$		$\cdot$
		$\cdot$		$\cdot$
1	1	$\ldots$	0	a_{2^n-2}
1	1	$\ldots$	1	a_{2^n-1}

Since there are n variables and each variable has two possible values, there are 2^n ways of assigning these values to the n variables; hence, the truth table has 2^n rows. Note that for any combination of values for the variables, $X_1, \ldots,$

X_n, there are two possible values for the general function $f(X_1, X_2, \ldots, X_n)$; hence, we could write down 2^N different truth tables for n variables where $N = 2^n$ is the number of rows. Therefore, there are 2^{2^n} different Boolean functions of n variables. Even for a small number of variables, the possible number of different Boolean functions is staggering, as shown below:

n	2^n	2^{2^n}
0	1	2
1	2	4
2	4	16
3	8	256
4	16	65,536
.	.	.
.	.	.
.	.	.

The Boolean functions for zero, one, and two variables are listed below:

$$n = 0: \quad f_1 = 0$$
$$f_2 = 1$$

$$n = 1: \quad f_1(A) = 0$$
$$f_2(A) = \bar{A}$$
$$f_3(A) = A$$
$$f_4(A) = 1$$

$$n = 2: \quad f_1(A, B) = 0$$
$$f_2(A, B) = \bar{A}\bar{B}$$
$$f_3(A, B) = \bar{A}B$$
$$f_4(A, B) = A\bar{B}$$
$$f_5(A, B) = AB$$
$$f_6(A, B) = \bar{A}\bar{B} + \bar{A}B = \bar{A}$$
$$f_7(A, B) = \bar{A}\bar{B} + A\bar{B} = \bar{B}$$
$$f_8(A, B) = \bar{A}\bar{B} + AB$$
$$f_9(A, B) = \bar{A}B + A\bar{B}$$
$$f_{10}(A, B) = \bar{A}B + AB = B$$
$$f_{11}(A, B) = A\bar{B} + AB = A$$
$$f_{12}(A, B) = \bar{A}\bar{B} + \bar{A}B + A\bar{B} = \bar{A} + \bar{B}$$
$$f_{13}(A, B) = \bar{A}\bar{B} + \bar{A}B + AB = \bar{A} + B$$
$$f_{14}(A, B) = \bar{A}\bar{B} + A\bar{B} + AB = A + \bar{B}$$
$$f_{15}(A, B) = \bar{A}B + A\bar{B} + AB = A + B$$
$$f_{16}(A, B) = \bar{A}\bar{B} + \bar{A}B + A\bar{B} + AB = 1$$

These functions are shown below in truth table form:

$$n = 0:$$

f_1	f_2
0	1

$$n = 1:$$

A	$f_1(A)$	$f_2(A)$	$f_3(A)$	$f_4(A)$
0	0	1	0	1
1	0	0	1	1

$$n = 2:$$

A	B	f_1	f_2	f_3	f_4	f_5	f_6	f_7	f_8	f_9	f_{10}	f_{11}	f_{12}	f_{13}	f_{14}	f_{15}	f_{16}
0	0	0	1	0	0	0	1	1	1	0	0	0	1	1	1	0	1
0	1	0	0	1	0	0	1	0	0	1	1	0	1	1	0	1	1
1	0	0	0	0	1	0	0	1	0	1	0	1	1	0	1	1	1
1	1	0	0	0	0	1	0	0	1	0	1	1	0	1	1	1	1

Earlier in this section, we saw how one can evaluate a Boolean function using Boolean algebra and the properties of 1 and 0. A variation of the same technique may be employed to make the paper work more convenient. This technique performs the Boolean algebra immediately on the truth table. For example, consider our previous function

$$f(A, B, C) = AB + \bar{A}C + A\bar{C}$$

The truth table may be obtained as follows:

A	B	C	AB	$\bar{A}$	$\bar{A}C$	$AB + \bar{A}C$
0	0	0	$0 \cdot 0 = 0$	$\bar{0} = 1$	$1 \cdot 0 = 0$	$0 + 0 = 0$
0	0	1	$0 \cdot 0 = 0$	$\bar{0} = 1$	$1 \cdot 1 = 1$	$0 + 1 = 1$
0	1	0	$0 \cdot 1 = 0$	$\bar{0} = 1$	$1 \cdot 0 = 0$	$0 + 0 = 0$
0	1	1	$0 \cdot 1 = 0$	$\bar{0} = 1$	$1 \cdot 1 = 1$	$0 + 1 = 1$
1	0	0	$1 \cdot 0 = 0$	$\bar{1} = 0$	$0 \cdot 0 = 0$	$0 + 0 = 0$
1	0	1	$1 \cdot 0 = 0$	$\bar{1} = 0$	$0 \cdot 1 = 0$	$0 + 0 = 0$
1	1	0	$1 \cdot 1 = 1$	$\bar{1} = 0$	$0 \cdot 0 = 0$	$1 + 0 = 1$
1	1	1	$1 \cdot 1 = 1$	$\bar{1} = 0$	$0 \cdot 1 = 0$	$1 + 0 = 1$

$\bar{C}$	$A\bar{C}$	$(AB + \bar{A}C) + A\bar{C}$	$f(A, B, C)$
$\bar{0} = 1$	$0 \cdot 1 = 0$	$0 + 0 = 0$	0
$\bar{1} = 0$	$0 \cdot 0 = 0$	$1 + 0 = 1$	1
$\bar{0} = 1$	$0 \cdot 1 = 0$	$0 + 0 = 0$	0
$\bar{1} = 0$	$0 \cdot 0 = 0$	$1 + 0 = 1$	1
$\bar{0} = 1$	$1 \cdot 1 = 1$	$0 + 1 = 1$	1
$\bar{1} = 0$	$1 \cdot 0 = 0$	$0 + 0 = 0$	0
$\bar{0} = 1$	$1 \cdot 1 = 1$	$1 + 1 = 1$	1
$\bar{1} = 0$	$1 \cdot 0 = 0$	$1 + 0 = 1$	1

After some practice, only the result need be entered into each column. Thus far, we have defined the meaning of a Boolean function and have presented a method for obtaining the corresponding truth table. Having discussed the many facets of the Boolean functional notation, we now address the problem of simplifying or reducing these functions.

Simplification of Boolean Functions

For any given Boolean function we may attempt to reduce or simplify the function to obtain some desired goal or to satisfy some criteria. A common goal to seek is the reduction of the number of literals in the expression representing a Boolean function. A *literal* is defined as each occurrence of a variable or complemented variable in a Boolean expression. The concept of a literal is best described by example.

1. $f(X, Y, Z) = \bar{X}Y(Z + \bar{Y}X) + \bar{Y}Z$. This function has seven literals.
2. $g(A, B, C) = A\bar{B} + \bar{A}B + AC$. This function has six literals.

We may apply the postulates and theorems of Boolean algebra to these functions to try to eliminate literal occurrences.

Example.

$$
\begin{aligned}
f(X, Y, Z) &= \bar{X}Y(Z + \bar{Y}X) + \bar{Y}Z \\
&= \bar{X}YZ + \bar{X}Y\bar{Y}X + \bar{Y}Z && \text{[P6(b)]} \\
&= \bar{X}YZ + 0 + \bar{Y}Z && \text{[P7(b)]} \\
&= \bar{X}YZ + \bar{Y}Z && \text{[P3(a)]} \\
&= \bar{X}Z + \bar{Y}Z && \text{[T15(a)]} \\
&= (\bar{X} + \bar{Y})Z && \text{[P6(b)]} \\
&= \overline{XY}Z && \text{[T12(b)]}
\end{aligned}
$$

Either of the last two forms has three literals, the minimum number possible.

Notice in the last example that the Boolean function $f(X, Y, Z)$ was written as seven different Boolean expressions. In general, any Boolean function may be written an infinite number of ways; however, each function has one and only one truth table. This important point will be discussed in more detail later.

Example.

Consider now a function of four variables with 13 literals:

$$
\begin{aligned}
f(A, B, C, D) &= ABC + AB\underline{D} + \bar{A}B\bar{C} + CD + B\bar{D} \\
&= ABC + A\underline{B} + \bar{A}B\bar{C} + CD + B\bar{D} && \text{[T15(a)]} \\
&= \underline{ABC} + \underline{AB} + B\bar{C} + CD + B\bar{D} && \text{[T15(a)]} \\
&= AB + B\bar{C} + CD + B\bar{D} && \text{[T10(a)]} \\
&= AB + CD + B(\bar{C} + \bar{D}) && \text{[P6(b)]} \\
&= AB + \underline{CD} + B\overline{CD} && \text{[T12(b)]} \\
&= AB + \underline{CD} + B && \text{[T11(a)]} \\
&= B + CD && \text{[T10(a)]}
\end{aligned}
$$

In this example we have reduced the number of literals from 13 to 3.

One last point of importance to be presented is that we sometimes use the theorems in "reverse" in order to initially expand the function or add literals at some intermediate point in the algebraic process so that we can later achieve an overall reduction in literals. An example of this is shown below.

Example.

$$
\begin{aligned}
f(A, B, C, D, E) &= \underline{AB} + \bar{A}C\bar{D}E + \bar{B}C\bar{D} \\
&= AB + \bar{A}C\bar{D}E + \underline{BC\bar{D}E} + \bar{B}C\bar{D} \quad \text{[T13(a)]} \\
&= AB + \bar{A}C\bar{D}E + C\bar{D}E + \bar{B}C\bar{D} \quad \text{[T15(a)]} \\
&= AB + C\bar{D}E + \bar{B}C\bar{D} \quad \text{[T10(a)]}
\end{aligned}
$$

In the last example we began with 9 literals, expanded to 13, and finally reduced the answer to 8 literals.

As a final example of expansion to achieve literal reduction, consider the following:

Example.

$$
\begin{aligned}
f(A, B, C, D, E) &= (\bar{A} + B + \bar{C})(\bar{A} + B + D + E)(C + D) \\
&= (\bar{A} + B + \bar{C})(\bar{A} + B + \underline{C + D + E})(\underline{C + D}) \quad \text{[T15(b)]} \\
&= (\bar{A} + B + \bar{C})(C + D) \quad \text{[T10(b)]}
\end{aligned}
$$

In this example Theorem 15(b) is used to insert the variable C into the second term, which allows it to be absorbed by the last term.

Functional Theorems of Boolean Algebra

Three additional Boolean algebra theorems will now be presented, which are given in the functional notation without proof.

Theorem 17. Dual

$$
f^D(x_1, x_2, \ldots, x_n) = \bar{f}(\bar{x}_1, \bar{x}_2, \ldots, \bar{x}_n)
$$

This theorem states that the dual of a function may be found by finding the complement of the function and then complementing all the variables.

Theorem 18.

(a) $x_1 + f(x_1, x_2, \ldots, x_n) = x_1 + f(0, x_2, \ldots, x_n)$.

(b) $x_1 \cdot f(x_1, x_2, \ldots, x_n) = x_1 \cdot f(1, x_2, \ldots, x_n)$.

The foundation for this theorem is Postulate 3 and Theorem 8. Since $x_1 = x_1 + x_1 = x_1 + 0$, the x_1 inside the function in the (a) part of Theorem 18 may be replaced by 0.

Theorem 19.

(a) $f(x_1, x_2, \ldots, x_n) = x_1 f(1, x_2, \ldots, x_n) + \bar{x}_1 f(0, x_2, \ldots, x_n)$.

(b) $f(x_1, x_2, \ldots, x_n) = [x_1 + f(0, x_2, \ldots, x_n)] \cdot [\bar{x}_1 + f(1, x_2, \ldots, x_n)]$.

The proof of this theorem is left as an exercise for the reader. *Hint:* Use P3(b), P7(a), and T18.

Theorem 19 is used to expand functions or to add literals.

Example.

$$
\begin{aligned}
f(A, B, C) &= AB + A\bar{C} + \bar{A}C \\
&= A(1 \cdot B + 1 \cdot \bar{C} + \bar{1} \cdot C) + \bar{A}(0 \cdot B + 0 \cdot \bar{C} + \bar{0} \cdot C) \quad \text{[T19(a)]} \\
&= A(B + \bar{C}) + \bar{A}C \\
&= B[A(1 + \bar{C}) + \bar{A}C] + \bar{B}[A(0 + \bar{C}) + \bar{A}C] \quad \text{[T19(a)]} \\
&= B[A + \bar{A}C] + \bar{B}[A\bar{C} + \bar{A}C] \\
&= AB + \bar{A}BC + A\bar{B}\bar{C} + \bar{A}\bar{B}C \\
&= C[AB + \bar{A}B \cdot 1 + A\bar{B} \cdot \bar{1} + \bar{A}\bar{B} \cdot 1] \\
&\quad + \bar{C}[AB + \bar{A}B \cdot 0 + A\bar{B} \cdot \bar{0} + \bar{A}\bar{B} \cdot 0] \quad \text{[T19(a)]} \\
&= ABC + \bar{A}BC + \bar{A}\bar{B}C + AB\bar{C} + A\bar{B}\bar{C}
\end{aligned}
$$

We have used Theorem 19(a) about A, B, and C to expand this function from 6 literals to 15 literals. Notice that the expression with 15 literals is of a special form. This is called a canonical form and will be discussed in great depth later.

This completes our discussion of Boolean algebra. Table 2.2 contains a

TABLE 2.2. Boolean Algebra Postulates and Theorems

Expression	Dual
P3(a): $a + 0 = a$	P3(b): $a \cdot 1 = a$
P4(a): $a + b = b + a$	P4(b): $ab = ba$
P5(a): $a + (b + c) = (a + b) + c$	P5(b): $a(bc) = (ab)c$
P6(a): $a + bc = (a + b)(a + c)$	P6(b): $a(b + c) = ab + ac$
P7(a): $a + \bar{a} = 1$	P7(b): $a \cdot \bar{a} = 0$
T8(a): $a + a = a$	T8(b): $a \cdot a = a$
T9(a): $a + 1 = 1$	T9(b): $a \cdot 0 = 0$
T10(a): $a + ab = a$	T10(b): $a(a + b) = a$
T11(a): $a + \bar{a}b = a + b$	T11(b): $a(\bar{a} + b) = ab$
T12(a): $\overline{a + b} = \bar{a}\bar{b}$	T12(b): $\overline{ab} = \bar{a} + \bar{b}$
T13(a): $ab + \bar{a}c + bc = ab + \bar{a}c$	T13(b): $(a + b)(\bar{a} + c)(b + c)$ $= (a + b)(\bar{a} + c)$
T14(a): $ab + a\bar{b} = a$	T14(b): $(a + b)(a + \bar{b}) = a$
T15(a): $ab + a\bar{b}c = ab + ac$	T15(b): $(a + b)(a + \bar{b} + c)$ $= (a + b)(a + c)$
T16(a): $ab + \bar{a}c = (a + c)(\bar{a} + b)$	T16(b): $(a + b)(\bar{a} + c) = ac + \bar{a}b$
T17: $f^D(x_1, x_2, \ldots, x_n) = \bar{f}(\bar{x}_1, \bar{x}_2, \ldots, \bar{x}_n)$	
T18(a): $x_1 + f(x_1, x_2, \ldots, x_n) = x_1 + f(0, x_2, \ldots, x_n)$	
T18(b): $x_1 f(x_1, x_2, \ldots, x_n) = x_1 f(1, x_2, \ldots, x_n)$	
T19(a): $f(x_1, x_2, \ldots, x_n) = x_1 f(1, x_2, \ldots, x_n) + \bar{x}_1 f(0, x_2, \ldots, x_n)$	
T19(b): $f(x_1, x_2, \ldots, x_n) = [x_1 + f(0, x_2, \ldots, x_n)][\bar{x}_1 + f(1, x_2, \ldots, x_n)]$	

complete summary of all the Boolean algebra postulates and theorems we have developed. This table provides a convenient source of information to which we shall refer in later chapters whenever we need to use Boolean algebra.

Switching Circuits

Digital computers and other devices are constructed of large numbers of digital switching circuits, which may be categorized as either combinational or sequential logic circuits. Here we shall examine only the first category. The physical devices may be described mathematically by Boolean functions. The internal signals in the computer are symbolized as Boolean variables, and the switching devices themselves are symbolized as Boolean operators. A sample of the common switching devices is represented in symbolic form in Table 2.3. Symbol set 1 will be used in this text because it has been adopted as the military standard in MIL SPEC 806B. Symbol set 2 is very commonly used, as are other sets which are not presented. Switching devices are commonly called *gates*, a term we shall use henceforth.

The study of the use of Boolean algebra for the analysis and design of switching circuits is called *switching theory*. Many terms are used synonymously in the language of switching theory and need clarification. In particular, the terms *switching* and *logic* are often interchanged. Hence, terms such as *switching circuit* and *logic circuit* have the same meaning. The terms *switching function* or *logic function* are often used when referring to a Boolean function which describes a switching circuit.

Symbols and Operations

To understand computer logic one must master completely the operators in Table 2.3. Each operator, or gate, will now be examined.

AND. The truth table for the AND operator may be determined from Boolean algebra. Referring to equation (2-1),

a	b	$f(a, b)$
0	0	0
0	1	0
1	0	0
1	1	1

$$f(a, b) = ab$$

This truth table for the AND gate illustrates that the output of the gate is 1 if and only if both of its inputs are 1 simultaneously.

TABLE 2.3.   *Symbols for Switching Devices*

Operator	Symbol Set 1	Symbol Set 2
AND	a b ⟶ $f(a, b) = ab$	a b ⟶ $f(a, b) = ab$
OR	a b ⟶ $f(a, b) = a + b$	a b ⟶ $f(a, b) = a + b$
NOT	a ⟶ $f(a) = \bar{a}$	a ⟶ $f(a) = \bar{a}$
NAND	a b ⟶ $f(a, b) = \overline{ab}$	a b ⟶ $f(a, b) = \overline{ab}$
NOR	a b ⟶ $f(a, b) = \overline{a + b}$	a b ⟶ $f(a, b) = \overline{a + b}$
EXCLUSIVE OR	a b ⟶ $f(a, b) = a \oplus b$	a b ⟶ $f(a, b) = a \oplus b$

OR. The OR operator is identical to the OR operator in Boolean algebra and has also been completely specified in equation (2-1).

a	b	$f(a, b)$
0	0	0
0	1	1
1	0	1
1	1	1

$$f(a, b) = a + b$$

This truth table shows us the key to the OR gate; the output of an OR gate is 0 if and only if both of its inputs are 0.

NOT. A NOT gate always has only one input and serves to complement a variable. The NOT gate is described by the complement concept in Boolean algebra.

a	$f(a)$
0	1
1	0

$$f(a) = \bar{a}$$

Any variable has its true (uncomplemented) and false (complemented) forms.

A NOT gate is used to form one from the other. A true form of a variable is sometimes called the assertion form, and the false, the negation form.

NAND. The NAND gate is a combination of an AND gate followed by a NOT gate. Hence, its truth table is

a	b	ab	$f(a, b)$
0	0	0	1
0	1	0	1
1	0	0	1
1	1	1	0

$$f(a, b) = \overline{ab}$$

The key to understanding a NAND gate is to notice that the output is 0 if and only if its inputs are simultaneously 1.

Several other interesting properties of the NAND gate are shown below:

$$f(a, b) = \overline{ab} = \bar{a} + \bar{b} \quad [\text{T12(b)}]$$
$$f(a, a) = \bar{a} + \bar{a} \quad (\text{P2})$$
$$= \bar{a} \quad [\text{P3(a)}]$$
$$f(\bar{a}, \bar{b}) = \overline{\bar{a}\bar{b}} \quad (\text{P2})$$
$$= a + b \quad [\text{T12(b)}]$$

A NAND gate with both of its inputs alike acts like a NOT gate. A NAND gate with complemented inputs acts like an OR gate. Hence NAND gates may be used to implement AND, OR, and NOT gates as shown in Fig. 2.7.

NOR. The NOR gate is derived by combining the functions of an OR operator followed by a NOT operator.

a	b	$a + b$	$f(a, b)$
0	0	0	1
0	1	1	0
1	0	1	0
1	1	1	0

$$f(a, b) = \overline{a + b}$$

The key to remembering the function of a NOR gate is the first row of the truth table; the output of a NOR gate is 1 if and only if both inputs are simultaneously 0.

NOR gates may also be used to generate AND, OR, and NOT operations as shown below:

$$f(a, b) = \overline{a + b} = \bar{a}\bar{b} \quad [\text{T12(a)}]$$
$$f(a, a) = \bar{a} \cdot \bar{a} \quad (\text{P2})$$
$$= \bar{a} \quad [\text{P3(b)}]$$
$$f(\bar{a}, \bar{b}) = \overline{\bar{a} + \bar{b}} \quad (\text{P2})$$
$$= ab \quad [\text{T12(a)}]$$

Figure 2.8 shows the operations in symbolic form.

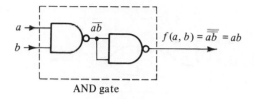

AND gate

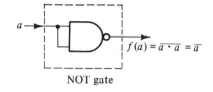

NOT gate

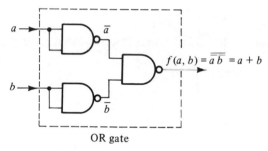

OR gate

Fig. 2.7　Uses of NAND gates.

EXCLUSIVE OR. The EXCLUSIVE-OR operation is defined by the truth table below:

a	b	$f(a, b)$
0	0	0
0	1	1
1	0	1
1	1	0

$$f(a, b) = a \oplus b$$

The output of the EXCLUSIVE-OR gate is 1 if and only if its inputs are not simultaneously equal. In other words, when the inputs are different, the output is 1. The EXCLUSIVE-OR is so named because of its relation to the OR gate. The two differ in the input combination $a = 1$, $b = 1$. The EXCLUSIVE-OR excludes this combination, giving an output 0, whereas the OR gate includes this combination and is therefore synonymously called the INCLUSIVE-OR.

A common relation which is related to the EXCLUSIVE-OR is the COINCIDENCE operation, which is merely the complement of the EXCLUSIVE-OR. By definition

$$f(a, b) = \overline{a \oplus b} = a \odot b$$

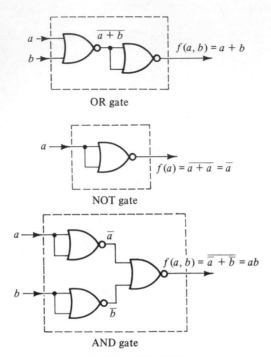

$f(a, b) = a + b$

OR gate

$f(a) = \overline{a + a} = \overline{a}$

NOT gate

$f(a, b) = \overline{\overline{a} + \overline{b}} = ab$

AND gate

Fig. 2.8   Use of the NOR gate.

Another expression for the EXCLUSIVE-OR is

$$a \oplus b = \bar{a}b + a\bar{b}$$
$$= (\bar{a} + \bar{b})(a + b) \quad [\text{T16(a)}] \tag{2-2}$$

Hence,

$$a \odot b = \overline{a \oplus b} = \overline{\bar{a}b + a\bar{b}} \qquad (\text{P2})$$
$$= \overline{\bar{a}b} \cdot \overline{a\bar{b}} \qquad\qquad [\text{T12(a)}]$$
$$= (a + \bar{b})(\bar{a} + b) \qquad [\text{T12(b)}]$$
$$= ab + \bar{a}\bar{b} \qquad\qquad [\text{T16(a)}] \tag{2-3}$$

Several other useful relationships involving the EXCLUSIVE-OR are shown below:

$$a \oplus a = 0$$
$$a \oplus \bar{a} = 1$$
$$a \oplus 0 = a$$
$$a \oplus 1 = \bar{a}$$
$$a \oplus \bar{b} = a \odot b$$
$$a \oplus b = b \oplus a$$
$$a \oplus (b \oplus c) = (a \oplus b) \oplus c$$

The reader may verify that these relations are valid by constructing truth tables for them.

Analysis of Switching Networks

Switching networks may be built by interconnecting the gates we have presented in Table 2.3. These networks are used to perform specific functions inside the digital computing system. Any given switching network may be completely represented by a Boolean expression or function, and, thus, all the power of Boolean algebra may be applied to manipulate the switching function into any form we desire.

An important point to note is that all Boolean expressions may be written in terms of AND, OR, and NOT operations. Hence, any switching network may be constructed using only NAND gates (or NOR gates), as shown in Fig. 2.7 (or Fig. 2.8).

Example.

Consider the typical network shown in Fig. 2.9(a). Each of the internal signals P_i may be expressed as

$$P_1 = \overline{ab}$$
$$P_2 = \overline{\bar{a} + c}$$
$$P_3 = b \oplus \bar{c}$$
$$P_4 = P_1 \cdot P_2 = \overline{ab}(\overline{\bar{a} + c})$$

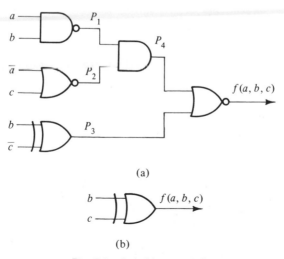

(a)

(b)

Fig. 2.9   Switching networks.

The output is

$$f(a, b, c) = \overline{P_3 + P_4}$$
$$= \overline{(b \oplus \bar{c}) + ab(\bar{a} + c)}$$

To analyze this function we may operate on it using Boolean algebra and equation (2-2):

$$\bar{f}(a, b, c) = (b \oplus \bar{c}) + ab(\bar{a} + c)$$

$$= bc + \bar{b}\bar{c} + ab(\bar{a} + c) \quad \text{[Equation (2-2)]}$$

$$= bc + \bar{b}\bar{c} + (\bar{a} + \bar{b})a\bar{c} \quad \text{(T12)}$$

$$= bc + \bar{b}\bar{c} + a\bar{b}\bar{c} \quad \text{[T11(b)]}$$

$$= bc + \bar{b}\bar{c} \quad \text{[T10(a)]}$$

$$\bar{f}(a, b, c) = b \odot c \quad \text{[Equation (2-3)]}$$

$$f(a, b, c) = b \oplus c$$

This function has been reduced to an EXCLUSIVE-OR gate, which is shown in Fig. 2.9(b). Both switching networks shown in Fig. 2.9 have the same truth table and are therefore equivalent. It is obvious that the one in Fig. 2.9(b) is more desirable since it is less complex.

Example.

The network in Fig. 2.10(a) is defined as

$$f(a, b, c) = \overline{(a \oplus b)(b \oplus c) \cdot \overline{(\bar{a} + \bar{b} + a + c)}}$$

$$= \overline{(a \oplus b)(b \oplus c)} + \bar{a} + \bar{b} + a + c \quad \text{[T12(a)]}$$

$$= (a \oplus b)(b \oplus c) + (\bar{a} + \bar{b}) \cdot (a + c) \quad \text{[T12(b)]}$$

$$= (a\bar{b} + \bar{a}b)(b\bar{c} + \bar{b}c) + (\bar{a} + \bar{b})(a + c) \quad \text{[Equation (2-2)]}$$

$$= a\bar{b}b\bar{c} + a\bar{b}\bar{b}c + \bar{a}bb\bar{c} + \bar{a}b\bar{b}c + (\bar{a} + \bar{b})(a + c) \quad \text{[P6(b)]}$$

$$= a\bar{b}c + \bar{a}b\bar{c} + \bar{a}c + a\bar{b} \quad \text{[P7(b), T8(a), T16(b)]}$$

$$= \bar{b}c + \bar{a}b\bar{c} + \bar{a}c + a\bar{b} \quad \text{[T15(a)]}$$

$$= \bar{b}c + \bar{a}b + \bar{a}c + a\bar{b} \quad \text{[T15(a)]}$$

$$= \bar{b}c + \bar{a}b + a\bar{b} \quad \text{[T13(a)]}$$

$$= \bar{b}c + a \oplus b \quad \text{[Equation (2-2)]}$$

Notice that this is the form of the switching network in Fig. 2.10(b).

The truth table for the function derived in the last example may be found using the technique previously used in Boolean algebra:

a b c	$\bar{b}c$	$a \oplus b$	$f(a, b, c)$
0 0 0	0	0	0
0 0 1	1	0	1
0 1 0	0	1	1
0 1 1	0	1	1
1 0 0	0	1	1
1 0 1	1	1	1
1 1 0	0	0	0
1 1 1	0	0	0

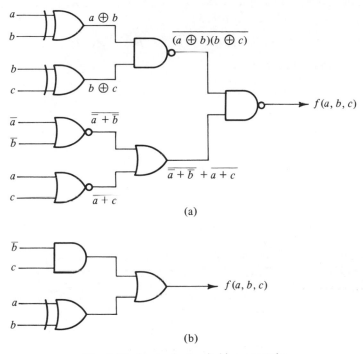

Fig. 2.10   Equivalent switching networks.

The column $\bar{b}c$ is 1 whenever $\bar{b} = 1$ and $c = 1$ or whenever $b = 0$ and $c = 1$. The column $a \oplus b$ is 1 whenever $a \neq b$. These two columns are ORed to create $f(a, b, c)$; therefore, $f(a, b, c)$ is 0 whenever both $\bar{b}c$ and $a \oplus b$ are 0.

In this section we have taken a given switching network, analyzed it by writing down the switching function, simplified it using Boolean algebra, and obtained an equivalent but less complicated network.

Algebraic Forms for Switching Functions

Thus far we have seen several different forms for Boolean functions; for example, see Table 2.2. Now we shall define some specific forms of functions which will be very useful in subsequent chapters.

SP and PS Forms

Switching functions in the *sum of products* (SP) form are constructed by summing (ORing) product (ANDed) terms; the product terms are formed by ANDing complemented and uncomplemented variables. Example product terms are

$$A\bar{B}C$$
$$\bar{B}\bar{D}$$
$$\bar{A}C\bar{D}$$

A sum of products function of four variables, A, B, C, D, which uses these three product terms is shown below:

$$f_1(A, B, C, D) = A\bar{B}C + \bar{B}\bar{D} + \bar{A}C\bar{D}$$

Another example follows:

$$f_2(x_1, x_2, x_3) = x_1\bar{x}_3 + x_2\bar{x}_3 + x_1x_2x_3$$

This function has three variables and three product terms.

Switching functions in *product of sums* (PS) form are constructed by ANDing sum (ORed) terms; the sum terms are formed by ORing complemented and uncomplemented variables as shown below:

$$\bar{A} + B + C$$
$$\bar{B} + C + \bar{D}$$
$$A + \bar{C} + D$$

A product of sums function of four variables, A, B, C, D, which uses these three product terms follows:

$$f_3(A, B, C, D) = (\bar{A} + B + C)(\bar{B} + C + \bar{D})(A + \bar{C} + D)$$

Another example PS function is

$$f_4(W, X, Q) = (Q + \bar{W})(X + \bar{Q})(W + X + Q)(\bar{W} + \bar{X})$$

This is a PS function of three variables, W, X, Q, and four sum terms.

Canonical Forms

Canonical forms for Boolean or switching functions are SP and PS forms with special characteristics.

Minterms. If a product term of a function of n variables contains all n variables one time in complemented or uncomplemented form, the product term is called a *minterm*. If the function is composed completely of minterms, the function is said to be in *canonical SP form;* for example,

$$f_5(A, B, C) = \bar{A}B\bar{C} + AB\bar{C} + \bar{A}BC + ABC \tag{2-4}$$

is a canonical function of three variables with four minterms.

To simplify the minterm notation the variables are coded as follows:

Variables: 1

Complements: 0

Using this code the minterms of $f_5(A, B, C)$ may be written in one of the following equivalent forms:

	Minterm Code	Minterm List
$\bar{A}B\bar{C}$	010	m_2
$AB\bar{C}$	110	m_6
$\bar{A}BC$	011	m_3
ABC	111	m_7

The minterms are written in the form m_i, where i is the decimal integer of the corresponding binary code for the minterm. Thus, $f_5(A, B, C)$ may be compactly written as

$$f_5(A, B, C) = m_2 + m_6 + m_3 + m_7$$
$$= m_2 + m_3 + m_6 + m_7 \qquad (2\text{-}5a)$$

A further simplification results if the function is written in the *minterm list form* as shown below:

$$f_5(A, B, C) = \sum m(2, 3, 6, 7) \qquad (2\text{-}5b)$$

Both equations (2-5a) and (2-5b) are canonical SP forms for $f_5(A, B, C)$. The functions in equations (2-4) and (2-5a) and (2-5b) are also equivalent.

The order of the variables in the functional notation in equations (2-5a) and (2-5b) is very important. This fact can be easily demonstrated by changing the order relation of the variables in the function $f_5(A, B, C)$ to $f_6(B, C, A)$ as shown below:

$$f_6(B, C, A) = \sum m(2, 3, 6, 7)$$
$$= m_2 + m_3 + m_6 + m_7$$
$$\quad\; 010 \quad 011 \quad 110 \quad 111$$
$$= \bar{B}C\bar{A} + \bar{B}CA + BC\bar{A} + BCA$$
$$= \bar{A}\bar{B}C + A\bar{B}C + \bar{A}BC + ABC \qquad (2\text{-}6)$$

Note that (2-6) is *not* identical to (2-4)—even though the minterm lists are the same. Further manipulation of the above equation yields

$$f_6(A, B, C) = f_6(B, C, A)$$
$$= \bar{A}\bar{B}C + \bar{A}BC + A\bar{B}C + ABC$$
$$\quad\; 001 \qquad 011 \qquad 101 \qquad 111 \quad \text{(minterm code)}$$
$$= m_1 + m_3 + m_5 + m_7$$
$$= \sum m(1, 3, 5, 7) \qquad (2\text{-}7)$$

Equations (2-6) and (2-7) are equal; the difference in minterm lists reflects the ordering of the variables in the functional notation.

The truth table for $f_6(A, B, C)$ can be easily derived:

Row No.	Inputs A B C	$m_1,$ $\bar{A}\bar{B}C$	$m_3,$ $\bar{A}BC$	$m_5,$ $A\bar{B}C$	$m_7,$ ABC	Output, $f_6(A, B, C)$
0	0 0 0	0	0	0	0	0
1	0 0 1	1	0	0	0	1
2	0 1 0	0	0	0	0	0
3	0 1 1	0	1	0	0	1
4	1 0 0	0	0	0	0	0
5	1 0 1	0	0	1	0	1
6	1 1 0	0	0	0	0	0
7	1 1 1	0	0	0	1	1

A careful examination of the table indicates that each row is numbered according to the decimal code, and that the only 1's which appear in the table are those in row i which are produced by minterm m_i. Hence, in general we may eliminate all intermediate steps and simply write down the truth table directly from the minterm list as shown below for the function $f_5(A, B, C)$:

Row No.	Inputs A B C	Output, $f_5(A, B, C)$
0	0 0 0	0
1	0 0 1	0
2	0 1 0	1
3	0 1 1	1
4	1 0 0	0
5	1 0 1	0
6	1 1 0	1
7	1 1 1	1

$$f_5(A, B, C) = \sum m(2, 3, 6, 7)$$

In addition the truth table for $\bar{f}_5(A, B, C)$ is

Row No.	Inputs A B C	$f_5(A, B, C)$	$\bar{f}_5(A, B, C)$
0	0 0 0	0	1
1	0 0 1	0	1
2	0 1 0	1	0
3	0 1 1	1	0
4	1 0 0	0	1
5	1 0 1	0	1
6	1 1 0	1	0
7	1 1 1	1	0

$$\bar{f}_5(A, B, C) = \sum m(0, 1, 4, 5)$$

The table indicates that $\bar{f}_5(A, B, C)$ has 1's in rows 0, 1, 4, and 5, and therefore

$$\bar{f}_5(A, B, C) = \sum m(0, 1, 4, 5)$$

and

$$f_5(A, B, C) = \sum m(2, 3, 6, 7)$$

Notice that all the minterms composed of three variables (totaling $2^3 = 8$) are contained in either the minterm list for $f_5(A, B, C)$ or $\bar{f}_5(A, B, C)$. In general the 2^n minterms of n variables will always appear in either the canonical SP form for $f(x_1, x_2, \ldots, x_n)$ or $\bar{f}(x_1, x_2, \ldots, x_n)$.

For example, if

$$f_7(A, B, Q, Z) = \sum m(0, 1, 6, 7)$$

the complement will contain 12 $(2^4 - 4)$ minterms as follows:

$$\bar{f}_7(A, B, Q, Z) = \sum m(2, 3, 4, 5, 8, 9, 10, 11, 12, 13, 14, 15)$$
$$= \sum m(2\text{--}5, 8\text{--}15)$$

One last point is demonstrated by noting, from Boolean algebra, that

$$f(x_1, x_2, \ldots, x_n) + \bar{f}(x_1, x_2, \ldots, x_n) = 1$$

However, since

$$f(x_1, x_2, \ldots, x_n) + \bar{f}(x_1, x_2, \ldots, x_n) = \sum_{i=0}^{2^n-1} m_i$$

then

$$\sum_{i=0}^{2^n-1} m_i = 1 \qquad (2\text{-}8)$$

In other words, the sum (OR) of all the minterms of n variables ($m_0, \ldots, m_{2^n-1}$) is equal to 1. Now let us turn to the canonical PS terms.

Maxterms. If a sum term of a function of n variables contains all n variables one time in complemented or uncomplemented form, the sum term is called a *maxterm*. If a function is composed of a product of sum terms, each of which is a maxterm, the function is said to be in *canonical PS form*. For example,

$$f_8(A, B, C) = (A + B + C)(A + B + \bar{C})(\bar{A} + B + C)(\bar{A} + B + \bar{C})$$

is a canonical function of three variables with four maxterms.

We adopt a special notation for maxterms, as for minterms, with one *major* difference; the coding is interchanged as indicated below:

Variables: 0

Complements: 1

The maxterms of $f_8(A, B, C)$ become

	Maxterm Code	Maxterm List
$A + B + C$	0 0 0	M_0
$A + B + \bar{C}$	0 0 1	M_1
$\bar{A} + B + C$	1 0 0	M_4
$\bar{A} + B + \bar{C}$	1 0 1	M_5

The maxterms are abbreviated as M_i, where i is the decimal integer of the corresponding binary code for the maxterm. Thus,

$$f_8(A, B, C) = M_0 M_1 M_4 M_5$$
$$= \prod M(0, 1, 4, 5) \tag{2-9}$$

The latter form is called *maxterm list form*. These two expressions are canonical PS forms for $f_8(A, B, C)$. Again, as in equations (2-5a), and (2-5b), the ordering of the variables in (2-9) is very important.

The truth table for $f_8(A, B, C)$ is

Row No.	Inputs A B C	$M_0,$ $A+B+C$	$M_1,$ $A+B+\bar{C}$	$M_4,$ $\bar{A}+B+C$	$M_5,$ $\bar{A}+B+\bar{C}$	$f_8(A, B, C)$
0	0 0 0	0	1	1	1	0
1	0 0 1	1	0	1	1	0
2	0 1 0	1	1	1	1	1
3	0 1 1	1	1	1	1	1
4	1 0 0	1	1	0	1	0
5	1 0 1	1	1	1	0	0
6	1 1 0	1	1	1	1	1
7	1 1 1	1	1	1	1	1

Each row in the table is numbered according to the decimal code, as was done before in the minterm case. Note that the only 0's which appear in the table are those in row i which are produced by maxterm M_i. Hence, as in the minterm case, the truth table can be generated by inspection from the maxterm list. Comparing the truth tables for $f_5(A, B, C)$ and $f_8(A, B, C)$ indicates that

$$f_5(A, B, C) = \sum m(2, 3, 6, 7)$$
$$= f_8(A, B, C)$$
$$= \prod M(0, 1, 4, 5) \tag{2-10}$$

Hence the functions $f_5(A, B, C)$ and $f_8(A, B, C)$ are equal and therefore equation (2-10) shows both the canonical SP and canonical PS forms for $f_5(A, B, C)$.

Now let us examine a second example:

$$f_9(A, B, C) = \underset{001}{(A + B + \bar{C})} \underset{011}{(A + \bar{B} + \bar{C})} \underset{101}{(\bar{A} + B + \bar{C})} \underset{111}{(\bar{A} + \bar{B} + \bar{C})}$$
$$= M_1 M_3 M_5 M_7$$
$$= \prod M(1, 3, 5, 7)$$

The maxterms place zeroes in rows 1, 3, 5, and 7 of the truth table for $f_9(A, B, C)$ as shown on the following page:

Row No.	Inputs A B C	Output, $f_9(A, B, C)$	$f_9(A, B, C) = \prod M(1, 3, 5, 7)$
0	0 0 0	1	
1	0 0 1	0	
2	0 1 0	1	
3	0 1 1	0	
4	1 0 0	1	
5	1 0 1	0	
6	1 1 0	1	
7	1 1 1	0	

From the truth table for $f_9(A, B, C)$, one observes that

$$f_9(A, B, C) = \sum m(0, 2, 4, 6)$$

Then

$$\bar{f}_9(A, B, C) = \sum m(1, 3, 5, 7)$$
$$= m_1 + m_3 + m_5 + m_7$$
$$\quad\;\; 001 \quad\; 011 \quad\; 101 \quad\; 111 \qquad \text{(minterm code)}$$
$$= \bar{A}\bar{B}C + \bar{A}BC + A\bar{B}C + ABC$$

Consequently,

$$f_9(A, B, C)$$
$$= \overline{\bar{A}\bar{B}C + \bar{A}BC + A\bar{B}C + ABC}$$
$$= \overline{\bar{A}\bar{B}C} \cdot \overline{\bar{A}BC} \cdot \overline{A\bar{B}C} \cdot \overline{ABC} \qquad\qquad\qquad \text{[T12(a)]}$$
$$= (A + B + \bar{C})(A + \bar{B} + \bar{C})(\bar{A} + B + \bar{C})(\bar{A} + \bar{B} + \bar{C}) \quad \text{[T12(b)]}$$
$$\quad\;\; 001 \qquad\qquad 011 \qquad\qquad 101 \qquad\qquad 111 \qquad \text{(maxterm code)}$$
$$= M_1 M_3 M_5 M_7$$
$$= \prod M(1, 3, 5, 7)$$

Therefore, we have algebraically shown that

$$f_9(A, B, C) = \prod M(1, 3, 5, 7) = \sum m(0, 2, 4, 6)$$

which is clearly evident by inspection of the truth table.

    In manipulating the function $f_9(A, B, C)$ a relationship between minterms and maxterms became apparent:

$$\bar{m}_1 = \quad \overline{\bar{A}\bar{B}C} \quad = A + B + \bar{C} = M_1$$
$$\qquad\qquad 001 \qquad\qquad 001$$
$$\qquad\quad \text{minterm code} \quad\; \text{maxterm code}$$

$$\bar{m}_3 = \quad \overline{\bar{A}BC} \quad = A + \bar{B} + \bar{C} = M_3$$
$$\qquad\qquad 011 \qquad\qquad 011$$
$$\qquad\quad \text{minterm code} \quad\; \text{maxterm code}$$

In the general case,

$$\bar{m}_i = M_i$$
$$\bar{M}_i = \bar{\bar{m}}_i = m_i \qquad (2\text{-}11)$$

and therefore minterms and maxterms are complements.

Before leaving the subject of maxterms, let us examine the canonical PS form for $\tilde{f}_9(A, B, C)$. The truth table for this function is shown below:

Row	Inputs	$f_9(A, B, C)$	Output,
No.	A B C		$\tilde{f}_9(A, B, C)$
0	0 0 0	1	0
1	0 0 1	0	1
2	0 1 0	1	0
3	0 1 1	0	1
4	1 0 0	1	0
5	1 0 1	0	1
6	1 1 0	1	0
7	1 1 1	0	1

$$\tilde{f}_9(A, B, C) = \prod M(0, 2, 4, 6)$$

Zeroes appear in rows 0, 2, 4, and 6; hence,

$$\tilde{f}_9(A, B, C) = \prod M(0, 2, 4, 6)$$

and therefore

$$f_9(A, B, C) = \prod M(1, 3, 5, 7)$$

The function $f_9(A, B, C)$ has three variables and hence eight maxterms, all of which appear in the list for either $f_9(A, B, C)$ or $\tilde{f}_9(A, B, C)$. From Boolean algebra we know that

$$f_9(A, B, C) \cdot \tilde{f}_9(A, B, C) = 0$$

and therefore

$$(M_0 M_2 M_4 M_6)(M_1 M_3 M_5 M_7) = 0$$

$$\prod_{i=0}^{2^3-1} M_i = 0 \qquad (2\text{-}12)$$

In general, for n variables

$$\prod_{i=0}^{2^n-1} M_i = 0$$

Let us summarize the results of this section using $f_5(A, B, C)$ and (2-10):

$$f_5(A, B, C) = \sum m(2, 3, 6, 7) = \prod M(0, 1, 4, 5)$$
$$\tilde{f}_5(A, B, C) = \sum m(0, 1, 4, 5) = \prod M(2, 3, 6, 7)$$

The full meaning of these expressions is now illustrated using a new function $f_{10}(W, X, Y, Z)$. Suppose we are given

$$f_{10}(W, X, Y, Z) = \prod M(0, 4\text{-}8, 10, 12, 15)$$

The function has four variables, W, X, Y, Z, and is specified in canonical PS, or maxterm list, form. From this information we may write down the minterm list for $f_{10}(W, X, Y, Z)$ and the minterm and maxterm lists for $\bar{f}_{10}(W, X, Y, Z)$:

$$f_{10}(W, X, Y, Z) = \prod M(0, 4\text{--}8, 10, 12, 15)$$
$$= \sum m(1, 2, 3, 9, 11, 13, 14)$$
$$\bar{f}_{10}(W, X, Y, Z) = \prod M(1, 2, 3, 9, 11, 13, 14)$$
$$= \sum m(0, 4\text{--}8, 10, 12, 15)$$

Expansion to Canonical Form

Any switching function may be written in canonical form from its truth table; it may also be expanded into its canonical forms using the postulates and theorems of Boolean algebra.

Sum of products expansion. If a switching function is given in SP form, it may be expanded to canonical SP form through repeated use of Theorem 14(a).

Example.

$f_2(x_1, x_2, x_3)$
$= x_1 \bar{x}_3 + x_2 \bar{x}_3 + x_1 x_2 x_3$
$= x_1 x_2 \bar{x}_3 + x_1 \bar{x}_2 \bar{x}_3 + x_2 \bar{x}_3 + x_1 x_2 x_3$ [T14(a)]
$= x_1 x_2 \bar{x}_3 + x_1 \bar{x}_2 \bar{x}_3 + x_1 x_2 \bar{x}_3 + \bar{x}_1 x_2 \bar{x}_3 + x_2 x_2 x_3$ [T14(a)]
$= x_1 x_2 \bar{x}_3 + x_1 \bar{x}_2 \bar{x}_3 + \bar{x}_1 x_2 \bar{x}_3 + x_1 x_2 x_3$ [T8(a)]
      1 1 0   1 0 0   0 1 0   1 1 1   (minterm code)
$= m_6 + m_4 + m_2 + m_7$
$= \sum m(2, 4, 6, 7)$

This same technique can be used to expand any SP function to canonical form.

Product of sums expansion. If a switching function is specified in PS form, then it may be expanded to canonical PS form by repeatedly using Theorem 14(b).

Example.

$f_4(W, X, Q)$
$= (Q + \bar{W})(X + \bar{Q})(W + X + Q)(\bar{W} + \bar{X})$
$= (\bar{W} + X + Q)(\bar{W} + \bar{X} + Q)(X + \bar{Q})(W + X + Q)(\bar{W} + \bar{X})$
                                                 [T14(b)]
$= (\bar{W} + X + Q)(\bar{W} + \bar{X} + Q)(W + X + \bar{Q})$
    $\cdot (\bar{W} + X + \bar{Q})(W + X + Q)(\bar{W} + \bar{X} + Q)(\bar{W} + \bar{X} + \bar{Q})$ [T14(b)]
$= (\bar{W} + X + Q)(\bar{W} + \bar{X} + Q)(W + X + \bar{Q})$
      100   110   001
    $\cdot (\bar{W} + X + \bar{Q})(W + X + Q)(\bar{W} + \bar{X} + \bar{Q})$ [T8(b)]
      101   000   111   (maxterm code)
$= M_4 M_6 M_1 M_5 M_0 M_7$
$= \prod M(0, 1, 4\text{--}7)$

Sometimes one might prefer to work with the SP form when expanding to canonical PS form, so the procedure indicated in the following example is an alternative.

Example.

$$\bar{f}_4(W, X, Q) = (\bar{W} + Q)(X + \bar{Q})(W + X + Q)(\bar{W} + \bar{X})$$

$$= W\bar{Q} + \bar{X}Q + \bar{W}\bar{X}\bar{Q} + WX \qquad \text{(T12)}$$

$$= WX\bar{Q} + W\bar{X}\bar{Q} + W\bar{X}Q + \bar{W}\bar{X}Q$$
$$\qquad + \bar{W}\bar{X}\bar{Q} + WXQ + WX\bar{Q} \qquad \text{[T14(a)]}$$

$$= \underset{1\ 1\ 0}{WX\bar{Q}} + \underset{1\ 0\ 0}{W\bar{X}\bar{Q}} + \underset{1\ 0\ 1}{W\bar{X}Q} + \underset{0\ 0\ 1}{\bar{W}\bar{X}Q}$$

$$\qquad + \underset{0\ 0\ 0}{\bar{W}\bar{X}\bar{Q}} + \underset{1\ 1\ 1}{WXQ} \qquad \begin{array}{l}\text{[T8(a)]}\\ \text{(minterm code)}\end{array}$$

$$= m_6 + m_4 + m_5 + m_1 + m_0 + m_7$$

$$\bar{f}_4(W, X, Q) = \sum m(0, 1, 4\text{–}7)$$

$$f_4(W, X, Q) = \prod M(0, 1, 4\text{–}7)$$

Note that the latter technique offers no real advantage over the previous one.

Synthesis of Switching Networks

Thus far we have introduced several tools for use in analyzing and synthesizing switching networks. These tools include Boolean algebra, switching devices, truth tables, and Venn diagrams. In this section we shall employ some of these tools to design and implement switching networks.

AND-OR and NAND Networks

If a given Boolean function is to be implemented in AND-OR or NAND logic, it must be expressed in sum of products form. For example, the following function

$$f_{11}(p, q, r, s) = p\bar{r} + qrs + \bar{p}s$$

is directly implemented in AND-OR logic in Fig. 2.11(a).

A simple translation using Boolean algebra may be employed to transform a sum of products expression into an appropriate form for direct NAND implementation:

$$f_{11}(p, q, r, s) = \overline{\overline{p\bar{r} + qrs + \bar{p}s}} \qquad \text{(involution)}$$

$$= \overline{\overline{p\bar{r}} \cdot \overline{qrs} \cdot \overline{\bar{p}s}} \qquad \text{[T12(a)]}$$

$$= \overline{x_1 \cdot x_2 \cdot x_3}$$

where

$$x_1 = \overline{p\bar{r}}$$
$$x_2 = \overline{qrs}$$
$$x_3 = \overline{\bar{p}s}$$

The NAND realization for this function is shown in Fig. 2.11(b). The techniques employed above may be used on any sum of products function.

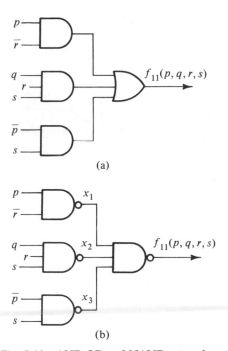

(a)

(b)

Fig. 2.11 AND-OR and NAND networks.

OR-AND and NOR Networks

If a specified Boolean function is to be implemented in OR-AND or NOR logic, it must be expressed in product of sums form. For example, the following function

$$f_{12}(A, B, C, D) = (\bar{A} + B + C)(B + C + D)(\bar{A} + D)$$

is realized directly in OR-AND logic in Fig. 2.12(a).

We may use the same Boolean algebra transformation which we employed previously to express $f_{12}(A, B, C, D)$ in an appropriate form for direct NOR implementation:

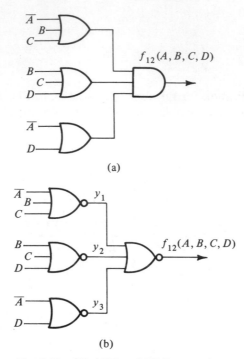

(a)

(b)

Fig. 2.12   OR-AND and NOR networks.

$$f_{12}(A, B, C, D) = \overline{\overline{(\bar{A} + B + C)(B + C + D)(\bar{A} + D)}} \qquad \text{(involution)}$$
$$= \overline{\overline{\bar{A} + B + C} + \overline{B + C + D} + \overline{\bar{A} + D}} \qquad \text{[T12(b)]}$$
$$= \overline{y_1 + y_2 + y_3}$$

where

$$y_1 = \overline{\bar{A} + B + C}$$
$$y_2 = \overline{B + C + D}$$
$$y_3 = \overline{\bar{A} + D}$$

The NOR realization for this function is shown in Fig. 2.12(b). This method may be generalized to implement any product of sums function in NOR logic.

Networks which have a structure like those shown in Figs. 2.11 and 2.12 are referred to as *two-level networks*. Input signals must pass through two levels of gates before reaching the output. The first level is defined as the level containing the gate which produces the output. Gates which receive the circuit inputs are on the second level. When NOT gates are required on input lines, a *three-level network* is produced. A network has n levels when at least one input signal must pass through n gates before reaching the output.

Boolean functions in the SP form or the PS form can be implemented in two-level networks when the inputs are available in both complemented and uncomplemented form. A three-level network is required when only one form of the inputs is available. However, in the latter case, only NOT gates are needed on level 3.

Canonical Form to Two-Level NAND Networks

At this point the reader has all the tools necessary to take a switching function expressed in minterm or maxterm list form and implement it in NAND logic.

The implementation procedure is outlined below:

1. Express the function in minterm list form.
2. Write out the minterms in variable notation.
3. Simplify the function in sum of products form using Boolean algebra.
4. Use Theorem 12(a) and involution to transform the expression into the NAND formulation.
5. Draw the NAND logic diagram.

This procedure will now be illustrated using $f_{13}(X, Y, Z) = \sum m(0, 3, 4, 5, 7)$.

Example.

1. $f_{13}(X, Y, Z) = \sum m(0, 3, 4, 5, 7)$.
2. $f_{13}(X, Y, Z) = m_0 + m_3 + m_4 + m_5 + m_7$
$$\phantom{f_{13}(X, Y, Z) =} 000 \quad 011 \quad 100 \quad 101 \quad 111$$
$$= \bar{X}\bar{Y}\bar{Z} + \bar{X}YZ + X\bar{Y}\bar{Z} + X\bar{Y}Z + XYZ \quad [\text{T14(a)}].$$
3. $f_{13}(X, Y, Z) = \bar{Y}\bar{Z} + YZ + XZ$.
4. $f_{13}(X, Y, Z) = \overline{\overline{\bar{Y}\bar{Z} + YZ + XZ}} \quad (\text{Involution})$
$$= \overline{\overline{\bar{Y}\bar{Z}} \ \overline{YZ} \ \overline{XZ}} \quad [\text{T12(a)}].$$
5. The NAND network is demonstrated in Fig. 2.13(a).

The logic diagram of Fig. 2.13(a) is said to be a *minimum SP realization* of the switching function. This example completely illustrates the design procedure.

Canonical Form to Two-Level NOR Networks

The procedure of the last section may be modified as follows to implement $f_{13}(X, Y, Z)$ in NOR logic:

1. Express the function in maxterm list form.
2. Write out the maxterms in variable notation.
3. Simplify the function in product of sums form using Boolean algebra.

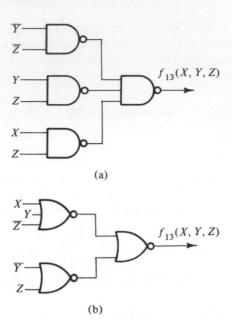

(a)

(b)

Fig. 2.13   Canonical form to NAND and NOR.

4. Use Theorem 12(b) and involution to transform the expression to NOR formulation.
5. Draw the NOR logic diagram.

Example.

$$f_{13}(X, Y, Z) = \sum m(0, 3, 4, 5, 7)$$

1. $f_{13}(X, Y, Z) = \prod M(1, 2, 6)$.
2. $f_{13}(X, Y, Z) = M_1 \cdot M_2 \cdot M_6$
   $$001 \quad 010 \quad 110$$
   $$= (X + Y + \bar{Z})(X + \bar{Y} + Z)(\bar{X} + \bar{Y} + Z).$$

3. $f_{13}(X, Y, Z) = (X + Y + \bar{Z})(\bar{Y} + Z)$ [T14(b)].
4. $f_{13}(X, Y, Z) = \overline{(X + Y + \bar{Z})(\bar{Y} + Z)}$ (Involution)
   $$= \overline{X + Y + \bar{Z}} + \overline{\bar{Y} + Z}$$ [T12(b)].

5. The NOR Network is shown in Fig. 2.13(b) and is said to be a *minimum PS realization* of the switching function. Each of the networks shown in Fig. 2.13 implements the function $f_{13}(X, Y, Z)$.

Timing Diagrams

A *timing diagram* is a graphical representation of input and output signal relationships in a switching network. Often intermediate signals are also illustrated. The timing diagram may include consideration of physical time delays introduced by the switching devices as the signals propagate through the network.

A properly chosen timing diagram can depict all the information contained in the truth table as shown in Fig. 2.14. A 1 is represented by a *high*

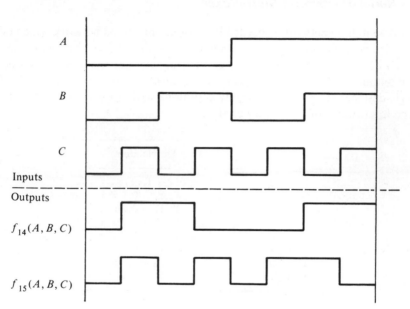

Fig. 2.14 Timing diagram.

Inputs			Outputs	
A	B	C	$f_{14}(A, B, C)$	$f_{15}(A, B, C)$
0	0	0	0	0
0	0	1	1	1
0	1	0	1	0
0	1	1	0	1
1	0	0	0	0
1	0	1	0	1
1	1	0	1	1
1	1	1	1	0

signal; a 0, by a *low* signal. The input and output signals are drawn on the diagram for

$$f_{14}(A, B, C) = \sum m(1, 2, 6, 7)$$
$$f_{15}(A, B, C) = \sum m(1, 3, 5, 6)$$

Timing diagrams are usually drawn for a given logic design problem; once the timing diagram is available, we can write the canonical forms and use the procedures of previous sections to derive NAND and NOR network realizations.

Serial-to-Parallel Multiplexer

A switching network is needed in a communications network which takes a serial bit stream on a single input line and distributes the bits to one of seven output lines as specified by control signals. Let the input signal be X, the outputs be $Y_1, Y_2, \ldots, Y_7$, and the control signals be A, B, and C. The logic designer is free to choose any coding he wishes for the control signals. The following is one arbitrary choice:

A	B	C	Distribution
0	0	0	$Y_i = 0; i = 1, \ldots, 7$
0	0	1	$Y_1 = X; Y_i = 0, i \neq 1$
0	1	0	$Y_2 = X; Y_i = 0, i \neq 2$
0	1	1	$Y_3 = X; Y_i = 0, i \neq 3$
1	0	0	$Y_4 = X; Y_i = 0, i \neq 4$
1	0	1	$Y_5 = X; Y_i = 0, i \neq 5$
1	1	0	$Y_6 = X; Y_i = 0, i \neq 6$
1	1	1	$Y_7 = X; Y_i = 0, i \neq 7$

The logic equations for the output functions are

$$Y_1 = m_1 X = \bar{A}\bar{B}CX$$
$$Y_2 = m_2 X = \bar{A}B\bar{C}X$$
$$\cdot$$
$$\cdot$$
$$\cdot$$
$$Y_7 = m_7 X = ABCX$$

The logic network for the serial-to-parallel multiplexer is shown in Fig. 2.15.

Fan-in and Fan-out

Fan-in may be defined as the number of inputs of a particular logic gate. The electronic limitations usually place a maximum on the number of inputs a manufacturer can furnish for a particular circuit type. To avoid confusion, manufacturers supply a variety of logic modules to meet almost every need of the logic designer. For example, gates might be available in one package type as follows:

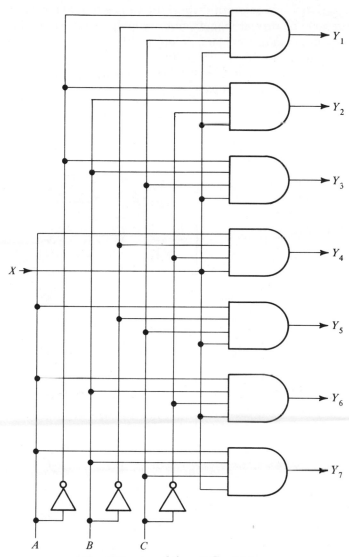

Fig. 2.15 A serial-parallel multiplexer.

Four each two-input NAND's

Three each three-input NOR's

Two each five-input NAND's

Each of these gates have fan-in of 2, 3, and 5, respectively.

Fan-out may be defined as the number of other gates driven by the output of the gate in question. Again, electrical circuit limitations restrict the number of other gates any one gate can drive (8 to 10 is a typical fan-out limit). If more gates must be driven, manufacturers supply *power* gates which drive many more gates than the standard circuit; an alternative is to double invert a signal to obtain more fan-out capability.

Examine the circuit in Fig. 2.16. A table is presented in the figure illustrating fan-in and fan-out for each gate.

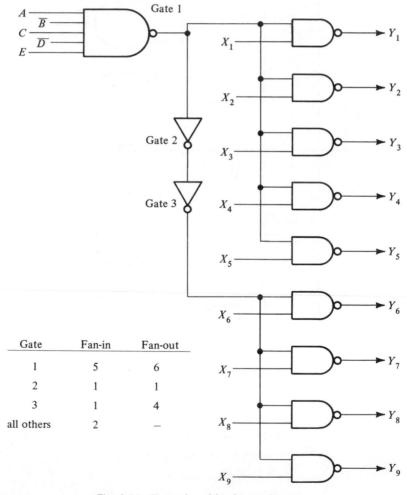

Gate	Fan-in	Fan-out
1	5	6
2	1	1
3	1	4
all others	2	—

Fig. 2.16   Examples of fan-in and fan-out.

Automatic Club Card

As a last example of the synthesis of switching networks, let us design an automatic club card system for a university faculty club. The club members are divided into four classes: instructors, assistant professors, associate professors, and professors. The clubhouse is arranged into four areas: the first area contains the ballroom, dining room, and recreation room; the second, the library and conference room; the third, the casino; and the fourth the bar and lounge. As might be expected, certain areas are restricted for certain classes of members. The restrictions are shown below:

Member Class	Prohibited from
Professors	None
Associate professors	Area 4
Assistant professors	Areas 3 and 4
Instructors	Areas 2, 3, and 4

To enforce the above restrictions, a plastic card is issued to all members with a series of coded holes punched in it. The card must be inserted into a slot beside the doorways into areas 2, 3, and 4. Let us design a logic control unit for these three doors.

First we must choose a code to give each of the member classes. The professors insist that the code be chosen so that an assistant professor cannot drill extra holes in his card and become a professor. Let us adopt the following 4-bit code:

	$C_1\ C_2\ C_3\ C_4$	$A_2\ A_3\ A_4$
Professors	0 0 0 1	1 1 1
Associate professors	0 0 1 1	1 1 0
Assistant professors	0 1 1 1	1 0 0
Instructors	1 1 1 1	0 0 0

Please note that a hole in the card corresponds to a 1; hence, an envious professor may become an assistant professor by drilling two extra holes in his card (provided he gets them in the right places).

From the preceding table the logic equations for the control units are

$$A_2 = \bar{C}_1\bar{C}_2\bar{C}_3C_4 + \bar{C}_1\bar{C}_2C_3C_4 + \bar{C}_1C_2C_3C_4$$
$$= \bar{C}_1\bar{C}_2C_4 + \bar{C}_1C_3C_4$$
$$A_3 = \bar{C}_1\bar{C}_2\bar{C}_3C_4 + \bar{C}_1\bar{C}_2C_3C_4 = \bar{C}_1\bar{C}_2C_4$$
$$A_4 = \bar{C}_1\bar{C}_2\bar{C}_3C_4$$

The club member inserts his card into the slot, and if he is allowed through the door, the signal A_i goes to 1 and the door lock is released. Several electromechanical devices are needed to examine the holes in the cards and to release the door lock; however, the logic design portion of this example is completed.

Summary

This chapter has examined switching networks. Boolean algebra is the foundation upon which the analysis and synthesis of switching circuits rests; therefore much time was spent in developing Boolean algebra as a familiar tool. Boolean algebra was then used to both simplify Boolean functions and to expand them to minterm and maxterm canonical forms. Last, Boolean algebra was used in the synthesis of several example switching networks. At this point the reader should be familiar with the concepts of Venn diagrams, truth tables, minterms, maxterms, timing diagrams, and duality and should be able to apply them to problems in combinational logic network analysis and synthesis. The reader is directed to references [3–6] for additional discussions of these topics.

REFERENCES

1. BOOLE, G., *An Investigation of the Laws of Thought, on Which Are Founded the Mathematical Theories of Logic and Probability*, 1849. Reprinted by Dover Publications, Inc., New York, 1954.

2. CHU, Y., *Digital Computer Design Fundamentals*. New York: McGraw-Hill Book Company, 1962.

3. HILL, F. J., and G. R. PETERSON, *Introduction to Switching Theory and Logical Design*. New York: John Wiley & Sons, Inc., 1968.

4. MALEY, G. A., and J. EARLE, *The Logic Design of Transistor Digital Computers*. Englewood Cliffs, N.J.: Prentice-Hall, Inc., 1963.

5. MCCLUSKEY, E. J., JR., *Introduction to the Theory of Switching Circuits*. New York: McGraw-Hill Book Company, 1965.

6. DIETMEYER, D. L., *Logic Design of Digital Systems*. Boston: Allyn and Bacon, Inc., 1971.

PROBLEMS

2.1. Using Boolean algebra simplify the following expressions:
   (a) $f(w, x, y, z) = x + xyz + \bar{x}yz + wx + \bar{w}x + \bar{x}y$.
   (b) $f(A, B, C, D, E) = (AB + C + D)(\bar{C} + D)(\bar{C} + D + E)$.
   (c) $f(x, y, z) = y\bar{z}(\bar{z} + \bar{z}x) + (\bar{x} + \bar{z})(\bar{x}y + \bar{x}z)$.

2.2. Simplify the following Boolean expressions:
   (a) $f(A, B, C, D)$
   $$= \overline{(A + \bar{C} + D)(\bar{B} + C)(A + \bar{B} + D)(\bar{B} + \bar{C})(\bar{B} + C + \bar{D})}.$$
   (b) $f(A, B, C, D)$
   $$= \overline{AB + \bar{A}\bar{D} + B\bar{D} + \bar{A}B + C\bar{D}A + \bar{A}D + CD + \bar{A}\bar{B}\bar{C}}.$$
   (c) $f(A, B, C, D) = \overline{A\bar{B}C} + AB + \overline{ABC} + A\bar{C} + AB\bar{C}.$
   (d) $f(A, B, C) = \overline{(AB + \bar{A})(AB + C)} + AB\bar{A} + \bar{A}\bar{B}C + (A + B)(\bar{A} + C).$
   (e) $f(A, B, C) = (\bar{A} + \bar{B})(A + \bar{A}B)(\bar{A} + \bar{B} + \bar{A}BC) + (A + B)(\bar{A} + C).$

2.3. Find the minimum equivalent circuit for the one shown in Fig. P2.1.

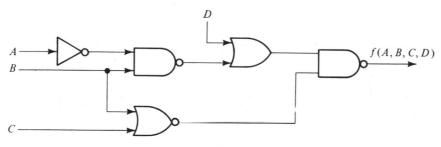

Fig. P2.1

2.4. Given the function $f(x, y, z)$ below, write $f(x, y, z)$ as a sum of minterms and as a product of maxterms:
$$f(x, y, z) = x\bar{y} + x\bar{z}$$

2.5. Find the minterm and maxterm list forms for the function defined by the logic diagram in Fig. P2.2.

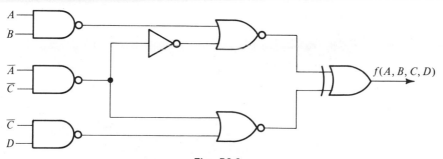

Fig. P2.2

2.6. Find the simplest Boolean expression for the functions given below:
   (a) $f(A, B, C) = \sum m(1, 4, 5).$
   (b) $f(A, B, C, D) = \prod M(0, 2, 4, 5, 8, 11, 15).$
   (c) $f(A, B, C, D) = \sum m(0, 2, 5, 8, 9, 10, 13).$

2.7. Given the timing diagram in Fig. P2.3, find the simplest Boolean expression for $f(A, B, C)$.

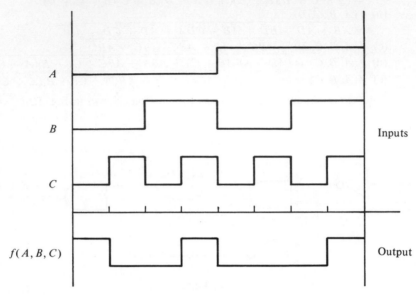

Fig. P2.3

2.8. Given the function

$$f(A, B, C, D) = \sum m(1, 2, 3, 5, 6, 7, 8, 9, 12, 14)$$

find the minimum two-level NOR realization of this function.

2.9. Given the network shown in Fig. P2.4, find the minimum two-level NOR realization.

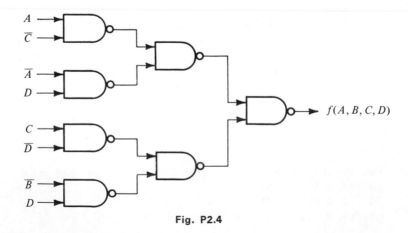

Fig. P2.4

2.10. For the timing diagram shown in Fig. P2.5, find both a minimum NAND and NOR network realization.

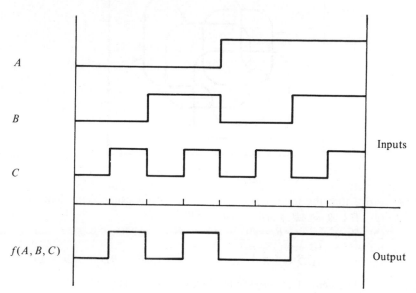

Fig. P2.5

2.11. Use Venn diagrams to determine which of the following Boolean functions are equivalent:

$$f_1(A, B, C) = A\bar{B}\bar{C} + B + \bar{A}\bar{B}C$$
$$f_2(A, B, C) = \bar{A}\bar{B}\bar{C} + B + A\bar{B}C$$
$$f_3(A, B, C) = \bar{A}\bar{C} + AC + B\bar{C} + \bar{A}B$$
$$f_4(A, B, C) = A\bar{C} + AB + B\bar{C} + \bar{A}C$$

2.12. Sketch the following functions on a Venn diagram:
(a) $f(A, B) - AB + \bar{A}\bar{B}$.
(b) $f(A, B, C) = AB + \bar{A}\bar{C}$.
(c) $f(A, B, C, D) = A + \bar{B}CD + \bar{A}BD$.
(d) $f(A, B, C, D) = \bar{A}B + C\bar{D}$.
Hint: Each new variable is represented by a contour which divides each disjoint segment of the Venn diagram into two segments. A four-variable Venn diagram is shown in Fig. P2.6.

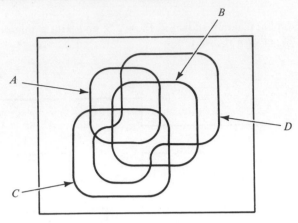

Fig. P2.6

2.13. Prove that the following expressions are valid using Venn diagrams:
   (a) $A + B = A\bar{B} + \bar{A}B + AB = \overline{\bar{A}\bar{B}}$.
   (b) $A\bar{C} + BC + A\bar{B} = \bar{B}\bar{C} + \bar{A}B + AC$.
   (c) $\bar{A}C + AB + \bar{B}\bar{C} = \bar{A}\bar{B} + BC + A\bar{C}$.
   (d) $AD + A\bar{C}\bar{D} + AB + \bar{A}BD + \bar{A}\bar{B}\bar{C} = AB + BD + AD + \bar{B}\bar{C}$.

2.14. Use Theorem 11 to simplify the following expressions:
   (a) $\bar{X} + XAB\bar{C} + \bar{B}C$.
   (b) $\bar{X}\bar{Y} + (X + Y)Z$.
   (c) $Z(\bar{Z} + AB\bar{C}) + \bar{A}\bar{B}$.
   (d) $(\bar{X} + \bar{Y})(XY + Z)$.

2.15. Use Theorem 12 to complement the following expressions:
   (a) $X(Y + \bar{Z}(Q + \bar{R}))$.
   (b) $X + Y(\bar{Z} + Q\bar{R})$.
   (c) $XY + A\bar{C} + IQ$.
   (d) $(A + B\bar{C})(\bar{A} + \bar{D}E)$.

2.16. Apply Boolean algebra Theorem 13 to simplify the following expressions:
   (a) $QR + \bar{X}Q + RX$.
   (b) $(X + Y)Z + \bar{X}\bar{Y}W + ZW$.
   (c) $(\bar{X} + Y)WZ + X\bar{Y}V + VWZ$.
   (d) $(X + Y + Z + \bar{W})(V + X)(\bar{V} + Y + Z + \bar{W})$.

2.17. Use Theorem 19 to transform each of the following functions to the format

$$f(A, B, C, Q) = \bar{Q}f_\alpha(A, B, C) + Qf_\beta(A, B, C)$$
$$= [\bar{Q} + f_\gamma(A, B, C)][Q + f_\delta(A, B, C)]$$

Find $f_\alpha, f_\beta, f_\gamma$, and f_δ when
   (a) $f(A, B, C, Q) = (Q + \bar{A})(\bar{B} + C) + \bar{Q}\bar{C}$.
   (b) $f(A, B, C, Q) = A\bar{B}\bar{C} + Q\bar{A} + \bar{Q}C$.
   (c) $f(A, B, C, Q) = (A + \bar{B} + Q)(\bar{A} + \bar{Q} + C)$.
   (d) $f(A, B, C, Q) = AB\bar{C} + \bar{A}C$.

2.18.   Find truth tables for the following Boolean functions:
     (a) $f(A, B) = A + \bar{B}$.
     (b) $f(A, B, C) = AB + \bar{A}C$.
     (c) $f(a, b, c) = a\bar{b}c + b\bar{c}$.
     (d) $f(a, b, c) = a(b + \bar{c})(\bar{b} + c)$.

2.19.   Find truth tables for the following Boolean functions:
     (a) $f(A, B, C, D) = AB\bar{C}D + ABC\bar{D}$.
     (b) $f(A, B, C, D) = AB + \bar{A}\bar{B} + C\bar{D}$.
     (c) $f(A, B, C, D) = A(\bar{B} + C\bar{D}) + \bar{A}B\bar{C}D$.

2.20.   Find truth tables for the following Boolean functions:
     (a) $f(A, B, C) = A \oplus B + \overline{AC}$.
     (b) $f(A, B, C) = (A \oplus B)C + \bar{A}(B \oplus C)$.
     (c) $f(A, B, C, D) = (\bar{A} \oplus B)(A \oplus \bar{B}) + B \oplus C \oplus D$.

2.21.   Find the output functions for the network of Fig. P2.7. Find the minterm list form for each function.

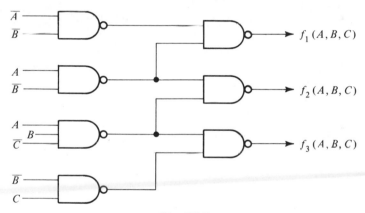

Fig. P2.7

2.22.   Find the minterm and maxterm list forms for the Boolean functions of Problem 2.18. Use any method.

2.23.   Find the canonical SP form for the Boolean functions of Problem 2.19. Use any technique.

2.24.   Find the canonical PS form for the Boolean functions of Problem 2.20. Use any method.

2.25.   Find a minimal two-level NAND realization for each of the following Boolean functions:
     (a) $f(A, B, C) = \sum m(0, 2, 3, 7)$.
     (b) $f(A, B, C, D) = \sum m(0, 2, 8, 10, 14, 15)$.
     (c) $f(A, B, C, D, E) = \sum m(4, 5, 6, 7, 25, 27, 29, 31)$.

2.26. Obtain a minimal two-level NOR realization for the following Boolean functions:
(a) $f(A, B, C) = \sum m(0, 2, 3, 7)$.
(b) $f(A, B, C, D) = \sum m(0, 2, 8, 10, 14, 15)$.
(c) $f(A, B, C, D, E) = \sum m(0–3, 8–24, 26, 28, 30)$.

2.27. Find a logic network realization for the Boolean function

$$f(A, B, C, D) = \sum m(7, 9, 12–15)$$

using NAND gates which have a fan-in of 2 and a fan-out of 5. Use as few gates as you can.

2.28. Implement the Boolean function of Problem 2.27 using NOR gates with a fan-in of 2 and a fan-out of 5.

2.29. A burglar alarm is designed so that it senses four input signal lines. Line A is from the secret control switch, line B is from a pressure sensor under a steel safe in a locked closet, line C is from a battery-powered clock, and line D is connected to a switch on the locked closet door. The following conditions produce a logic 1 voltage on each line:

    A: The control switch is closed.
    B: The safe is in its normal position in the closet.
    C: The clock is between 1000 and 1400 hours.
    D: The closet door is closed.

Design control logic for the burglar alarm which produces a logic 1 (rings a bell) when the safe is moved and the control switch is closed, or when the closet is opened after banking hours, or when the closet is opened with the control switch open. Use two levels of NAND logic for your implementation.

2.30. A long hallway has three doors, one at each end and one in the middle. A switch is located at each door to operate the incandescent lights along the hallway. Label the switches A, B, and C. Design a logic network to control the lights.

3

Minimization
of
Switching
Networks

In our previous work we have found that the simplification of Boolean functions via the Boolean algebra is a difficult task, at best. In other words, in the Boolean algebra there exists no road map which can be followed, and hence one must search for the best approach like a mountain climber relying on intuition and past experience. To perform the minimization of Boolean functions efficiently, one obviously must have at his disposal viable techniques which are standard and systematic and thus provide the road map to the desired answer. In the following pages two such methods will be presented. The first method, called the Karnaugh map, is a graphical technique, and the second approach, referred to as the Quine-McCluskey method, is a tabular technique.

Karnaugh Maps

The Karnaugh map is actually nothing more than an extension of the concepts of truth tables, Venn diagrams, and minterms. To make the extension explicit, let us now transform a Venn diagram into a Karnaugh map. Consider the Venn diagram shown in Fig. 3.1(a). The two variables A and B are represented by designated subdivisions of the universal set. Figure 3.1(b) illustrates that each unique disjoint subdivision of the Venn diagram is

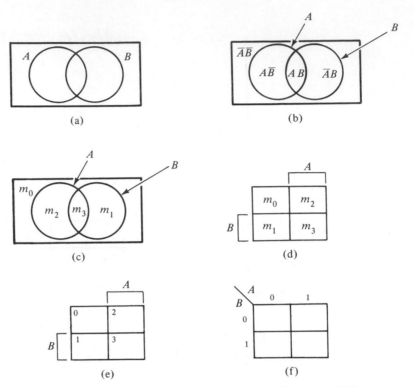

Fig. 3.1   Venn diagram and equivalent K-map for two variables.

formed by the intersections AB, $\bar{A}B$, $A\bar{B}$, and $\bar{A}\bar{B}$. The reader should note that these intersections are just the minterms of two variables. The subdivisions of the Venn diagram are relabeled as minterms m_0, m_1, m_2, and m_3 in Fig. 3.1(c). This form of the Venn diagram has unequal areas for the four minterms. We may adjust the areas and make them all the same, as shown in Fig. 3.1(d). Note that adjacent areas of the Venn diagram are also adjacent in Fig. 3.1(d). However now one-half the diagram represents the variable A and one-half also represents B. Since the minterm notation is identified with each square on the diagram, we may omit the letter m and leave only the subscript, as seen in Fig. 3.1(e). This is one form of the Karnaugh map. A second form for the Karnaugh map is shown in Fig. 3.1(f).

It is important to note that the Karnaugh map is a graphical or pictorial representation of a truth table and hence there exists a one-to-one mapping between the two. The truth table has one row for each minterm while the Karnaugh map has one square per minterm.

To find the Karnaugh map for three variables, follow the development of Fig. 3.2. An important point which requires careful analysis is the step

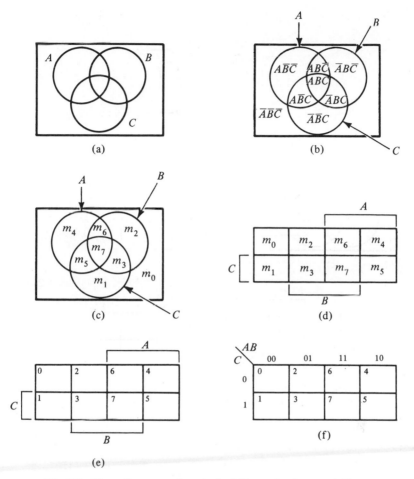

Fig. 3.2 Venn diagram and equivalent K-map for three variables.

between Fig. 3.2(c) and (d). Consider the minterm, m_0. This minterm is adjacent to m_1, m_2, and m_4 in Fig. 3.2(c). However, in Fig. 3.2(d), m_0 is not physically adjacent to m_4. To reconcile this inconsistency, the left and right edges of the map are considered to be the same line. In other words, the left edge can be folded over until·it touches the right edge, making the Karnaugh map for three variables appear as a cylinder. In practice the map is drawn as in Fig. 3.2(e) or (f) and the left and right edges are imagined to be coincident.

The K-maps for two, three, four, five, and six variables are demonstrated in Fig. 3.3(a) and (b). These maps combine all the familiar features that logic designers use in switching circuit synthesis. Either set of maps may be used at the reader's discretion. K-maps of more than six variables are impractical for most problems.

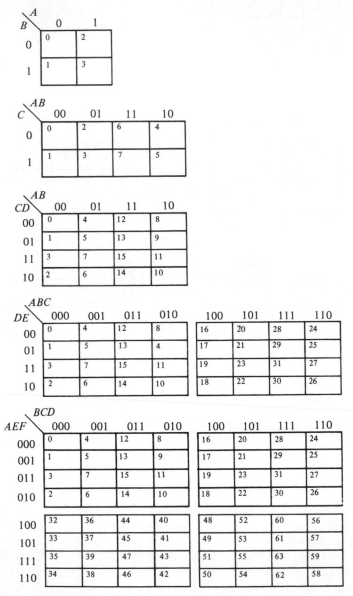

Fig. 3.3(a) *K*-maps for two through six variables.

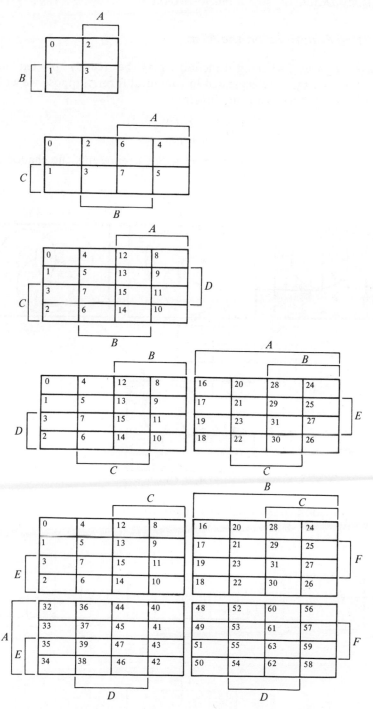

Fig. 3.3(b) Alternate K-maps for two through six variables.

Plotting Functions on the Map

Canonical form. Switching functions may be readily plotted on a Karnaugh map if they are expressed in canonical form. Suppose we wish to find the K-map for the following function:

$$f(A, B, C) = \sum m(0, 3, 5)$$
$$= m_0 + m_3 + m_5$$

Using Venn diagrams, the function $f(A, B, C)$ represents the shaded area shown below:

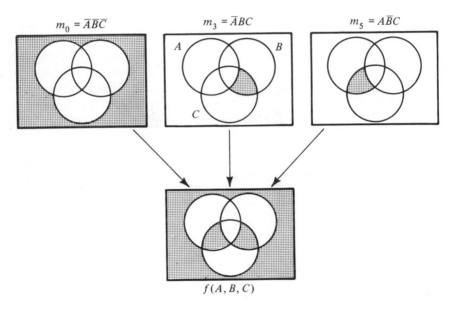

$$f(A, B, C)$$

This same function constructed on K-maps follows:

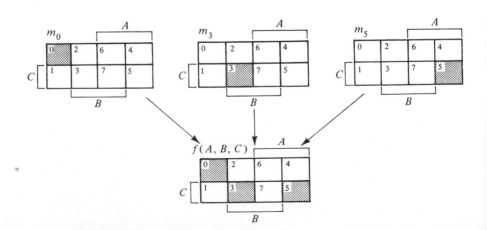

Shaded areas are *not* normally used on K-maps. Instead we employ the familiar 1 and 0 that we used in truth tables, with the shaded areas represented by 1. This change is now made in the last example:

$$f(A, B, C) = \sum m(0, 3, 5)$$

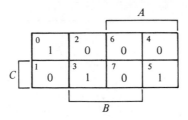

It is important to note that the above is simply the truth table for the function $f(A, B, C) = \sum m(0, 3, 5)$ in another form. One further simplification of notation is usually made: leaving the zeroes off the map. Thus, a blank on the map is understood to be a 0, or that the minterm is "absent" from the function. The final maps for $f(A, B, C)$ are

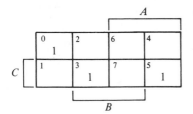 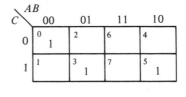

Example.

Let us plot the following function on a K-map:

$$f(a, b, Q, G) = \sum m(0, 3, 5, 7, 10\text{–}15)$$

A most important point should be noted about the ordering of the variables. As was demonstrated in the last chapter, the minterm numbers in the list change if the order of the variables is altered. Therefore, the order of the variables in the function *fixes* the order of the variables on the K-map. The following map is equivalent to the one above:

	Q		
0 1	1	3 1	2
8	9	11 1	10 1
12 1	13 1	15 1	14 1
4	5 1	7 1	6

b (left bracket), a (right bracket), G (bottom bracket)

Sum of products form. To plot a sum of products function onto a K-map, one could expand it to canonical form and use the technique of the last section. This is *not* recommended. A more natural approach is found by again employing the Venn diagram. Let us examine the following function:

$$f(A, B, C) = AB + B\bar{C} + A\bar{B}C$$

Following the procedure demonstrated earlier, the Venn diagrams for each term may be "unioned" in order to construct the function as shown below.

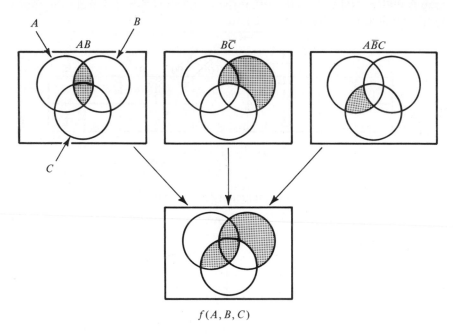

$$f(A, B, C)$$

Performing the same operation via K-maps yields

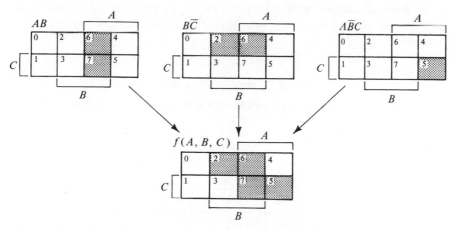

Using the standard K-map notation we obtain the map

From this map we note that the function written in standard minterm form is

$$f(A, B, C) = \sum m(2, 5, 6, 7)$$

Thus, K-maps can be conveniently used to expand an SP function into canonical form.

The following examples will serve to illustrate the immediate previous results. We shall also use the two types of K-maps shown in Fig. 3.3 (as well as a combination of the two) for the benefit of the reader.

Example.

$$f(A, B, C) = AB + B\bar{C}$$

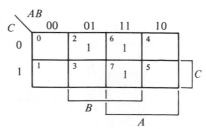

In this example we note that minterm m_6 appears in both AB and $B\bar{C}$. The multiple use of minterms is the rule, rather than the exception, in switching functions.

Example.

$$f(A, B, C, D) = AB\bar{C} + \bar{B}C + CD$$

The representation of this function on the K-map is shown below:

Example.

$$f(A, B, C, D, E) = AB + \bar{C}D + DE + \bar{A}\bar{D}\bar{E}$$

Given the Boolean function in canonical form the following examples illustrate how to place these functions on a K-map.

Example.

$$f(A, B, C) = \sum m(0, 3, 4, 7)$$

Example.

$$f(A, B, C, D) = \sum m(1, 4, 8, 9, 10, 12, 13)$$

CD \ AB	00	01	11	10
00	0	4 — 1	12 — 1	8 — 1
01	1 — 1	5	13 — 1	9 — 1
11	3	7	15	11
10	2	6	14	10 — 1

Example.

$$f(A, B, C, D, E) = \sum m(0, 2, 3, 5, 8, 10, 13, 16, 18, 19, 24, 26, 29)$$

DE \ ABC	000	001	011	010
00	0 — 1	4	12	8 — 1
01	1	5 — 1	13 — 1	9
11	3 — 1	7	15	11
10	2 — 1	6	14	10 — 1

DE \ ABC	100	101	111	110
00	16 — 1	20	28	24 — 1
01	17	21	29 — 1	25
11	19 — 1	23	31	27
10	18 — 1	22	30	26 — 1

Simplification of Boolean Functions

The K-map will now be used to obtain a minimal sum of products (MSP) expression for a Boolean function. By *minimal sum of products* we mean an expression that is equivalent to the original expression but which contains a minimum number of terms in which a minimum number of literals are present.

Simplification of functions on the K-map is expedited by the fact that on the map Boolean terms that are logically adjacent are also physically adjacent. In other words, each block on the map differs from another adjacent block by only a single variable. We illustrate combining terms by drawing a ring around the terms which when combined yield a simpler expression—that is, one with fewer literals.

The following example illustrates both the Boolean algebra and map simplification.

Example.

Given the function

$$f(A, B, C, D) = \sum m(1, 2, 4, 6, 9)$$

The simplification of this function via Boolean algebra is as follows:

$$f(A, B, C, D) = \underbrace{\bar{A}\bar{B}\bar{C}D + \bar{A}\bar{B}C\bar{D} + \bar{A}B\bar{C}\bar{D} + \bar{A}BC\bar{D} + A\bar{B}\bar{C}D}_{\text{step-1}}$$

$$= \bar{B}\bar{C}D + \underbrace{\bar{A}\bar{B}C\bar{D} + \bar{A}B\bar{C}\bar{D} + \bar{A}BC\bar{D}}_{\text{step-2}}$$

$$\underbrace{\qquad\qquad\qquad\qquad\qquad\qquad}_{\text{step-3}}$$

$$= \bar{B}\bar{C}D + \bar{A}C\bar{D} + \bar{A}B\bar{D}$$

The map simplification is shown below:

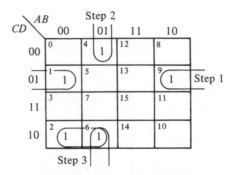

Since opposite edges of the map are actually coincident, the "horse shoes" above are really circles. These circles indicate the manner in which two minterms are combined to yield a simpler Boolean expression. In step 1 minterms 1 and 9, which are adjacent on the map, are combined. Note when comparing the two blocks we see that the variable which changes from 0 to 1 is the variable A, and hence when the two minterms are combined this variable is eliminated as shown in the Boolean algebra approach above. Minterms 4 and 6 on the map are combined in step 2. Comparing the two blocks we see that they differ only in the variable C, and hence this variable is eliminated when blocks 4 and 6 are combined. Combining blocks 2 and 6 eliminates the variable B. Thus, the three steps on the map are equivalent to the corresponding steps indicated in the Boolean algebra above. The reader is reminded, as is demonstrated, that minterms can be used more than once because $A = A + A + A + \cdots$, as shown in Chapter 2.

There are five important points to keep in mind when dealing with K-maps: (1) Each block (minterm) on K-maps of two, three, four, five, etc., variables have two, three, four, five, etc., blocks (minterms), respectively, that are logically adjacent. (2) When combining terms (i.e., blocks) on a K-map we always group blocks in powers of 2, i.e., two blocks, four blocks, eight blocks, etc. Grouping two blocks eliminates one variable, grouping four blocks eliminates two variables, etc. (3) In combining blocks on the map, always begin with those blocks for which there are the fewest number of adjacent blocks; minterms with multiple adjacencies are combined later in the minimization process. (4) Group as many blocks together as is possible; the larger the group, the fewer the number of literals in that product term. (5) Make as few groups as possible cover all the blocks (minterms) of the function; the fewer the groups, the fewer the number of product terms in the minimized function. In other words, a minterm may be used as many times as it is needed in steps 4 and 5; however, it must be used at least once. As soon as all minterms are covered once, *stop*.

Let us recall each of these points as we examine the following examples.

Example.

$$f(A, B, C, D) = \sum m(0, 1, 3, 8, 9, 11, 13, 14)$$

First, we plot the function on the map:

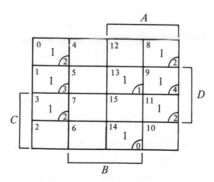

Second, we count the number of adjacencies for each minterm; the number is shown in the lower right-hand corner of the minterm block:

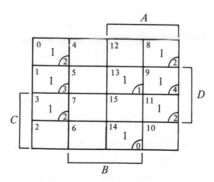

Third, we begin the simplification process by choosing first the minterm m_{14} which has no adjacencies:

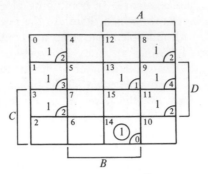

$$f(A, B, C, D) = ABC\bar{D} + \cdots$$

This minterm must be taken as a group by itself; hence, the first term in the minimized function is $ABC\bar{D}$.

Next, we examine minterms with one adjacency; m_{13} is the only one. Consequently, m_{13} has only *one* way of being grouped and that is with m_9 as shown below:

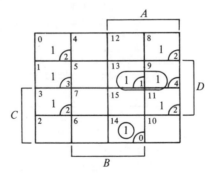

$$(A, B, C, D) = ABC\bar{D} + A\bar{C}D + \cdots$$

Now we have two product terms in the minimized function. Note that the portion of the K-map occupied by the minterms m_9 and m_{13} is completely inside of A, outside of C, and inside of D; hence, it is represented by $A\bar{C}D$. One minterm lies inside of B, and one outside. Therefore B is the variable eliminated.

There are four minterms with two adjacencies: m_0, m_3, m_8, and m_{11}. We pick one of these to group at random, say m_3. Note that m_3 is adjacent to m_1 and m_{11}. Since m_9 is also available (any minterm may be used as many times as it is needed), we may form a large group of four minterms as shown at the top of page 123:

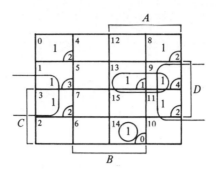

$$f(A, B, C, D) = ABC\bar{D} + A\bar{C}D + \bar{B}D + \cdots$$

By combining these four minterms we have eliminated two variables. The resulting group lies completely outside of B and inside of D; hence, the product term $\bar{B}D$ is added to the minimized function.

The combination of minterms 1, 3, 9, and 11 can also be demonstrated via Boolean algebra. Writing the minterms in variable form we obtain

$$\bar{A}\bar{B}\bar{C}D + \bar{A}\bar{B}CD + A\bar{B}\bar{C}D + A\bar{B}CD$$

Now grouping minterms 1 and 3 together and minterms 9 and 11 together eliminates the variable C from each pair. This combination can be seen on the map and reduces the four terms above to the two terms below:

$$\bar{A}\bar{B}D + A\bar{B}D$$

Now these two terms which represent combined blocks 1 and 3 and combined blocks 9 and 11, respectively, can be grouped to eliminate the variable A, thus reducing the four terms to one term, $\bar{B}D$. Note that four blocks have been combined to eliminate two literals.

Finally, there are still two minterms which have not been accounted for. These two, m_0 and m_8, can be grouped with m_3 and m_9 to form a last group of four minterms. This last group adds the final product term $\bar{B}\bar{C}$ to the function $f(A, B, C, D)$, and hence the final map and the reduced function are given below:

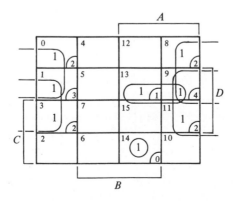

$$f(A, B, C, D) = ABC\bar{D} + A\bar{C}D + \bar{B}D + \bar{B}\bar{C}$$

We defy the reader to find a simpler SP form. Note that minterms m_0, m_3, m_8, m_{13}, and m_{14} were covered once; m_1, twice; and m_9, thrice.

Several other examples are now illustrated in rapid order:

Example.

$$f(A, B, C) = \sum m(1, 2, 3, 6)$$

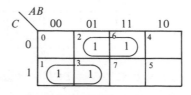

$$f(A, B, C) = \bar{A}C + B\bar{C}$$

Example.

$$f(A, B, C, D) = \sum m(0, 1, 2, 7, 8, 9, 10, 15)$$

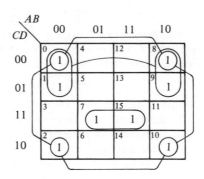

$$f(A, B, C, D) = \bar{B}\bar{D} + \bar{B}\bar{C} + BCD$$

Example.

$$f(A, B, C, D) = \sum m(3, 4, 6, 8, 9, 12, 14)$$

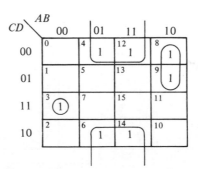

$$f(A, B, C, D) = \bar{A}\bar{B}CD + B\bar{D} + A\bar{B}\bar{C}$$

Example.

$$f(A, B, C, D) = \sum m(5, 7\text{--}15)$$

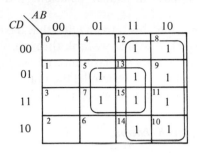

$$f(A, B, C, D) = A + BD$$

Example.

$$f(A, B, C, D, E) = \sum m(0, 2, 4, 7, 10, 12, 13, 18, 23, 26, 28, 29)$$

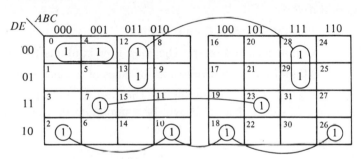

$$f(A, B, C, D, E) = \bar{A}\bar{B}\bar{D}\bar{E} + BC\bar{D} + \bar{B}CDE + \bar{C}D\bar{E}$$

Example.

$$f(A, B, C, D, E) = \sum m(1, 3, 4, 9, 11\text{--}13, 15, 17, 19, 22, 25, 27, 29, 30, 31)$$

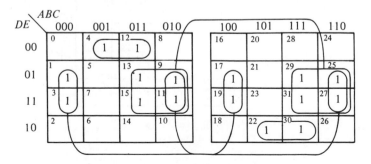

$$f(A, B, C, D, E) = BE + \bar{C}E + \bar{A}C\bar{D}\bar{E} + ACD\bar{E}$$

For five-variable maps, each minterm can have only five possible adjacencies; for example, the adjacencies for m_8 are m_0, m_9, m_{10}, m_{12}, and m_{24}. m_{16} is not adjacent to m_8; that is why we leave a space in the map. Hence, minterms which appear in similar position in the two parts of the map combine.

Another way to state this is to imagine that the two halves of the map are transparent and stacked so that we look through blocks 0–15 and see blocks 16–31. In this configuration similar minterms on each half are logically adjacent and hence combine. For example, the minterm combinations 13 and 29, 7 and 23, 4 and 20, etc., can be grouped to eliminate the variable A.

PS Form Using K-Maps

The simplification procedure of the recent section used K-maps to minimize a function in SP form. Suppose we wish to have a minimum two-level PS form instead. A very simple algorithm which achieves this is stated as follows:

Algorithm 3-1.

STEP 1. Plot the function, f, on a K-map.

STEP 2. Complement the map. The map now contains the function, $\bar{f}$.

STEP 3. Minimize $\bar{f}$ in SP form using the rules of the last section.

STEP 4. Since $f = \bar{\bar{f}}$ by involution, use Theorem 12 of Chapter 2 on the SP function for $\bar{f}$ in step 3. The result will be a minimum PS function for f.

Example.

$$f(A, B, C, D) = \sum m(4, 5, 7, 8, 10\text{–}13, 15)$$

STEP 1.

STEP 2.

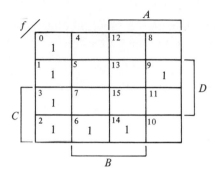

STEP 3.

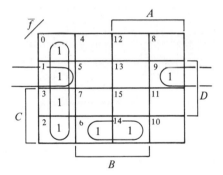

$$\bar{f}(A, B, C, D) = BC\bar{D} + \bar{B}\bar{C}D + \bar{A}\bar{B}$$

STEP 4.

$$\bar{f}(A, B, C, D) = BC\bar{D} + \bar{B}\bar{C}D + \bar{A}\bar{B}$$

$$f(A, B, C, D) = \overline{BC\bar{D} + \bar{B}\bar{C}D + \bar{A}\bar{B}} \qquad\qquad \text{(Involution)}$$

$$\qquad = \overline{BC\bar{D}} \cdot \overline{\bar{B}\bar{C}D} \cdot \overline{\bar{A}\bar{B}} \qquad\qquad\qquad \text{[T12(b)]}$$

$$\qquad = (\bar{B} + \bar{C} + D)(B + C + \bar{D})(A + B) \quad \text{[T12(a)]}$$

After some practice at minimizing switching functions in minimum PS form, one can eliminate some of the steps in Algorithm 3-1. First, we need not complement the K-map. Simply group the 0's instead of the 1's on the original K-map using the rules of the last section. Second, when writing down the minimum function, one can perform step 4 concurrently by complementing each variable as it is recorded. The resulting algorithm follows.

Algorithm 3-2.

STEP 1. Plot the function on a K-map.

STEP 2. Group the zeroes of the function using the rules of the previous section.

STEP 3. Write the minimum PS function directly from the K-map complementing the variables at the same time.

Example.

Minimize the function

$$f(A, B, C, D) = \sum m(4, 5, 7, 8, 10\text{–}13, 15)$$

in PS form.

STEPS 1 and 2.

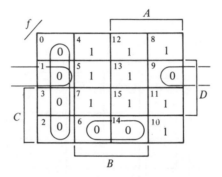

STEP 3.

$$f(A, B, C, D) = (A + B)(B + C + \bar{D})(\bar{B} + \bar{C} + D)$$

The reader should compare this example with the last one and note the simplification.

Although Algorithm 3-2 is faster, the possibility of manual errors is much higher than for Algorithm 3-1. Therefore, Algorithm 3-1 is recommended for the novice logic designer.

Don't Care Conditions

In the design of digital circuits one often encounters cases in which the switching function is not completely specified. In other words, a function may be required to contain certain minterms, omit certain minterms, with the remaining minterms being optional; that is, certain minterms may be included in the logic design if they help simplify the logic circuit. A minterm which is optional is called a *don't care* minterm.

Don't cares arise in two ways. First of all, sometimes certain input combinations are never applied to a switching network; hence, if they never occur, their minterms may be used in any manner we choose. A second way in which don't care conditions arise is the case where all input combinations do occur for a given network but the output is required to be 1 or 0 only for certain combinations. The don't care minterms will be labeled d_i instead of m_i as is shown below.

Canonical form. Suppose that we are given a function $f(A, B, C)$ which is to have minterms m_0, m_1, and m_5 and don't care conditions d_2 and d_6. The minterm list form for this function is

$$f(A, B, C) = \sum m(0, 1, 5) + d(2, 6)$$

The maxterm list form is

$$f(A, B, C) = \prod M(3, 4, 7) \cdot D(2, 6)$$

Here the don't care maxterms D_i are just the don't care minterms since they both may be 1 or 0. Hence,

$$\bar{f}(A, B, C) = \sum m(3, 4, 7) + d(2, 6)$$
$$= \prod M(0, 1, 5) \cdot D(2, 6)$$

Now let us plot this function on the K-map:

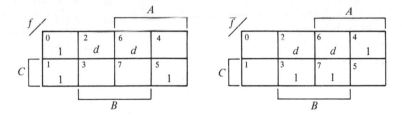

Note that we place a d on the map inside the block for each optional minterm.

Map simplifications. In the use of don't cares there is one additional rule which we adjoin to those previously discussed for minimizing functions via maps. Recall that the don't cares by definition can be either 0 or 1. Hence in minimizing terms in SP form, we choose the don't cares to be 1 *if* in doing so the set of blocks on the map which can be grouped together is larger than would otherwise be possible without including the don't cares. In other words, with regard to don't cares we can take them or leave them depending on whether they do or do not aid in the simplification of a function.

The functions f and $\bar{f}$ shown above can be minimized in the manner shown below:

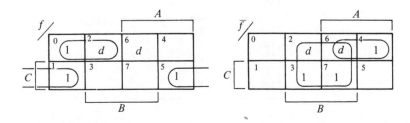

As can be seen from the figure

$$f(A, B, C) = \bar{A}\bar{C} + \bar{B}C$$

and

$$\bar{f}(A, B, C) = B + A\bar{C}$$

Now by complementation of $\bar{f}$

$$\begin{aligned}
\bar{\bar{f}}(A, B, C) &= \overline{B + A\bar{C}} \\
&= \bar{B}(\bar{A} + C) \\
&= \bar{B}\bar{A} + \bar{B}C
\end{aligned}$$

Note that $\bar{\bar{f}}$ is not identical to f. The discrepancy often occurs because of the presence of the don't cares. Note, however, that both f and $\bar{\bar{f}}$ cover the required minterms m_0, m_1 and m_5.

The following examples will serve to illustrate how don't cares occur and how they are used.

Example.

Suppose one needs a logic circuit as shown below with a 4-bit BCD input and single output. The input will be the BCD representation for the decimal digits $0, 1, \ldots, 9$. The circuit is to be used to indicate roundoff conditions; i.e., if the input is 5, 6, 7, 8, or 9, then a 1 should be produced at the output, and if the input is less than 5, a 0 should appear at the output.

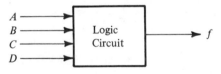

The truth table for this operation is shown below:

ABCD	Minterm	f
0000	0	0
0001	1	0
0010	2	0
0011	3	0
0100	4	0
0101	5	1
0110	6	1
0111	7	1
1000	8	1
1001	9	1
1010	10	d
1011	11	d
1100	12	d
1101	13	d
1110	14	d
1111	15	d

Note that the don't cares appear in the table because these particular inputs do not represent BCD digits and hence cannot possibly occur. Hence the output function f is

$$f(A, B, C, D) = \Sigma\, m(5, 6, 7, 8, 9) + d(10, 11, 12, 13, 14, 15)$$

Plotting this function on the map yields the figure below:

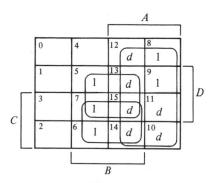

From the map

$$f(A, B, C, D) = A + BD + BC$$
$$= \Sigma\, m(5, 6, 7, 8, 9, 10, 11, 12, 13, 14, 15)$$

Note how much simpler this function is than it would have been without the inclusion of the don't cares. In addition note that in the above simplification all the don't cares were used (i.e., chosen to be 1's). This will *not* always be the case, as shown in the next example.

Example.

Consider the digital system given below:

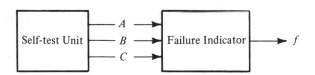

The self-testing unit contains various subsystems. Because of the subsystem configuration, the output employs three lines. If a failure is detected in the unit, it will manifest itself in one of the following outputs $ABC = 000$ or 001. If no failure has occurred, the output will be $ABC = 011$ or 111. The self-testing unit is designed so that no other outputs can possibly occur. Therefore the output function of the failure indicator circuit is

$$f(A, B, C) = \Sigma\, m(0, 1) + d(2, 4, 5, 6)$$

Plotting this function on the map yields

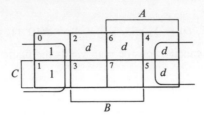

The simplification indicated on the map results in an output function equal to

$$f(A, B, C) = \bar{B}$$
$$= \sum m(0, 1, 4, 5)$$

Note that in this case only selected don't cares were used (chosen to be equal to 1).

Other Applications Using Maps

In this section we shall illustrate other useful applications of the Karnaugh maps.

Expansion of PS functions to canonical form. The expansion of a general PS function to canonical form is a tedious and complicated procedure via the Boolean algebra; however, it can be readily accomplished through use of the map. The procedure is described by the following four steps:

1. Given f in PS form, obtain $\bar{f}$ in SP form.
2. Plot $\bar{f}$ on the map.
3. From the map write down the canonical form for $\bar{f}$ in minterm list form.
4. Obtain the canonical PS form for f from the list of step 3, or involution.

This procedure is demonstrated in the following example.

Example.

Obtain the canonical PS form for the function

$$f(A, B, C) = (\bar{A} + \bar{B})(\bar{B} + C)(\bar{A} + B + \bar{C})$$

STEP 1. $\bar{f}$ in SP form is

$$\bar{f}(A, B, C) = \overline{(\bar{A} + \bar{B})(\bar{B} + C)(\bar{A} + B + \bar{C})}$$
$$= AB + B\bar{C} + A\bar{B}C$$

STEP 2. The map for $\bar{f}$ is

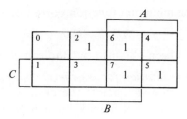

STEP 3. $\bar{f}$ in canonical form is

$$\bar{f}(A, B, C) = \sum m(2, 5, 6, 7)$$
$$= \bar{A}B\bar{C} + A\bar{B}C + AB\bar{C} + ABC$$

STEP 4. f in PS form is then

$$f(A, B, C) = \bar{\bar{f}}(A, B, C) = \prod M(2, 5, 6, 7)$$
$$f(A, B, C) = \bar{\bar{f}}(A, B, C)$$
$$= (A + \bar{B} + C)(\bar{A} + B + \bar{C})(\bar{A} + \bar{B} + C)(\bar{A} + \bar{B} + \bar{C})$$

Demonstrating the equivalence of functions. The K-map can be used to either demonstrate or check the equivalence of two or more functions. The following example indicates how this is done.

Example.

Using the K-map we can check the equivalence of the two functions below:

$$f_1 = AB + \bar{A}CD + \bar{A}BD$$
$$f_2 = ABC + \bar{A}CD + BD + B\bar{C}A$$

The maps for the two functions are shown below, together with the set of groupings which correspond to each term in the function:

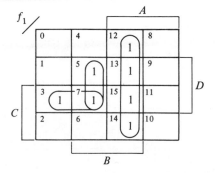

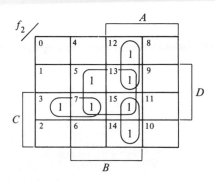

From the map it is immediately obvious that each function contains exactly the same minterms and hence the functions are equivalent. Note also from the map that the minimum function corresponding to either f_1 or f_2 is

$$f = BD + \bar{A}CD + AB$$

which could have also been obtained by Boolean algebra.

Minimum NAND realization for a general function given in mixed form. In the design of modern logic circuits the designer is often called upon to realize a general function, which may have been obtained from a word description of a problem, using only NAND gates. This realization can be easily accomplished using the steps below:

1. Given f in mixed form, use the Boolean algebra to write f in SP form.
2. Plot f on the K-map.
3. Minimize f in SP(NAND) form.
4. Write f in NAND notation.
5. Draw the NAND network.

The example which follows illustrates the steps.

Example.

We want to realize the following function in minimum NAND form:

$$f = D(\bar{A} + AB(C + \bar{B} + \bar{D})) + \bar{A}\bar{B}\bar{C}\bar{D}$$

STEP 1. Reducing the function to SP form,

$$f = D(\bar{A} + AB(C + \bar{B} + \bar{D})) + \bar{A}\bar{B}\bar{C}\bar{D}$$
$$= D(\bar{A} + ABC + AB\bar{D}) + \bar{A}\bar{B}\bar{C}\bar{D}$$
$$= \bar{A}D + ABCD + \bar{A}\bar{B}\bar{C}\bar{D}$$

STEP 2. Placing this function on the map,

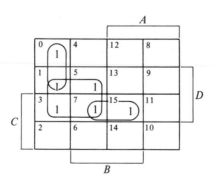

STEP 3. The minimum f in SP(NAND) form is

$$f = \bar{A}D + \bar{A}\bar{B}\bar{C} + BCD$$

STEP 4. Writing f in NAND notation using involution,

$$f = \overline{\bar{A}D + \bar{A}\bar{B}\bar{C} + BCD}$$

$$f = \overline{\overline{\bar{A}D} \cdot \overline{\bar{A}\bar{B}\bar{C}} \cdot \overline{BCD}}$$

STEP 5. Finally the minimum NAND realization is shown below:

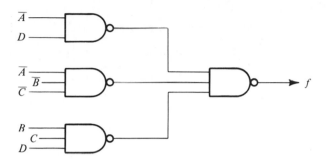

Timing diagrams. As a last example application let us use the Karnaugh map to find a minimum two-level NOR network as specified by a timing diagram.

Example.

Consider the following timing diagram:

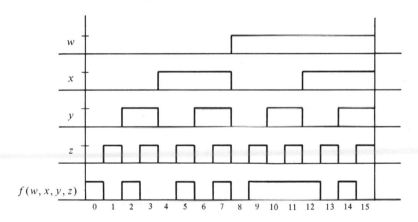

The steps to be employed in solving this problem are

1. From the timing diagram, write the function in minterm list form.
2. Plot the function f on a K-map.
3. Complement the map. The map now displays $\bar{f}$.
4. Minimize $\bar{f}$ to SP form using the K-map simplification procedure.
5. Complement $\bar{f}$ to find $f = \bar{\bar{f}}$ in minimum PS form.
6. Use involution to find f in NOR notation and thus obtain the NOR network.

From the timing digram

STEP 1. $f(w, x, y, z) = \sum m(0, 2, 5, 7, 9\text{--}12, 14)$.

STEP 2. The K-map for f is

		w		
0 1	4	12 1	8	
1	5 1	13	9 1	
3	7 1	15	11 1	z
2 1	6	14 1	10 1	

y x

STEP 3. The K-map for $\bar{f}$ is

		w		
0	4 1	12	8 1	
1 1	5	13 1	9	
3 1	7	15 1	11	z
2	6 1	14	10	

y x

STEP 4. Minimizing $\bar{f}$ on the map we obtain

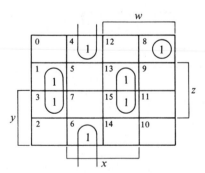

$$\bar{f} = w\bar{x}\bar{y}\bar{z} + wxz + \bar{w}\bar{x}z + \bar{w}x\bar{z}$$

STEP 5.

$$f = \bar{\bar{f}} = \overline{w\bar{x}\bar{y}\bar{z} + wxz + \bar{w}\bar{x}z + \bar{w}x\bar{z}}$$
$$= (\bar{w} + x + y + z)(\bar{w} + \bar{x} + \bar{z})(w + x + \bar{z})(w + \bar{x} + z)$$

Step 6.

$$f = \hat{f} = \overline{(\bar{w} + x + y + z)(\bar{w} + \bar{x} + \bar{z})(w + x + \bar{z})(w + \bar{x} + z)}$$
$$= \overline{\bar{w} + x + y + z} + \overline{\bar{w} + \bar{x} + \bar{z}} + \overline{w + x + \bar{z}} + \overline{w + \bar{x} + z}$$

The logic diagram for this function is

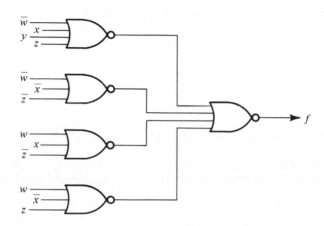

Boolean Algebra and K-Maps

Now that the reader is familiar with both Boolean algebra and Karnaugh maps, we may illustrate the correspondence between the two.

Example.

On three-variable K-maps show that Postulate 6(a) is valid. Let

$$f_1(a, b, c) = a + bc$$
$$f_2(a, b, c) = (a + b)(a + c)$$

But

$$\hat{f}_2(a, b, c) = \bar{a}\bar{b} + \bar{a}\bar{c}$$

The resulting K-maps are

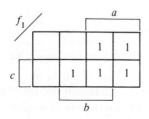   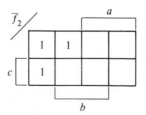

Hence, $f_1 = \hat{\hat{f}}_2 = f_2$.

Example.

Minimize the function $f(a, b, c) = ab + \bar{a}c + bc$. The K-map for f is

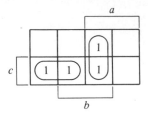

The minimized function is

$$f(a, b, c) = ab + \bar{a}c$$

as predicted by Theorem 13(a) in Boolean algebra.

This completes our discussion of Karnaugh maps. Complete mastery of this subject is essential for one to synthesize practical digital networks.

Hazards in Switching Networks

All physical devices have a measurable response time or delay associated with them. For logic gates, this response time is seen as a lag in an output change caused by an input change. Consider the two-input AND gate with response time Δt shown in Fig. 3.4(a). The response of the gate when the x_1 input changes from 0 to 1 to 0 ($0 \rightarrow 1 \rightarrow 0$) while $x_2 = 1$ is given in the timing diagram shown in Fig. 3.4(b). Note that the output changes occur at a time Δt later than the corresponding input changes.

The response time of most logic devices is very short. However, the response time is seldom the same for any two devices even of the same type. Such relative differences in response time may cause undesirable events to occur in a switching network. These undesirable events are referred to as *hazards*.

To illustrate a hazard, consider the network shown in Fig. 3.5(a). Assume that gates 1, 2, and 3 have response times Δt_1, Δt_2, and Δt_3, respectively. Also, assume that $\Delta t_1 > \Delta t_2 > \Delta t_3$. For convenience, let $\Delta t_1 = 2\Delta t_2$. Figure 3.5 gives the timing diagram of the circuit for a particular input sequence. The change of x_3 at t_1 causes y_2 to change at t_2, which in turn produces a change in z at t_3. This is the expected sequence of events with $t_2 = t_1 + \Delta t_2$ and $t_3 = t_2 + \Delta t_3$. A change of x_2 at t_4 causes no change in output of any gate. However, at t_5 the change of x_1 initiates an interesting sequence of events. First, since $\Delta t_2 < \Delta t_1$, the change in x_1 causes y_2 at t_6 to change from 1 to 0 *prior* to y_1 changing from 0 to 1 at t_8. Hence z changes from 1 to 0 at t_7 and from 0 to 1 at t_9. This change in z is not indicated by the logic description of the network and hence is not the correct behavior of the network.

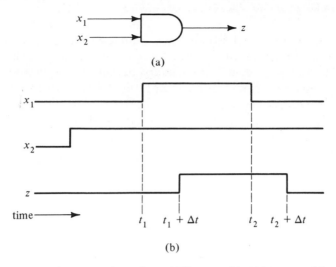

(a)

(b)

Fig. 3.4 Response time of an AND gate: (a) AND gate with response time Δt; (b) a typical response.

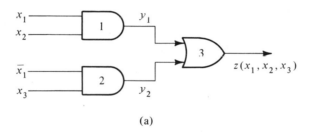

(a)

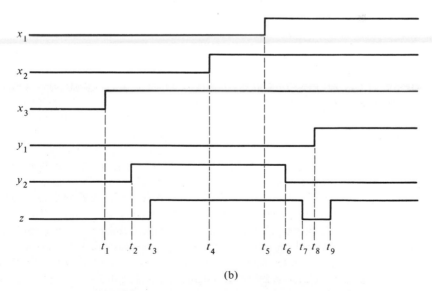

(b)

Fig. 3.5 Illustration of a static hazard: (a) network with static hazard; (b) timing diagram.

Changes like the one illustrated here are referred to as static hazards. In general, a *static hazard* is the condition where a single variable change (x_1 in the example) *may* produce a momentary output change when no output change should occur. Note that no hazard would occur in the above example if the relative delays were such that $\Delta t_1 \leq \Delta t_2$.

The cause of the above hazard condition can be seen by looking at the K-map of the network:

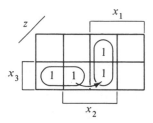

Note that the hazard exists when a changing input (from $x_1 = 0$, $x_2 = 1$, $x_3 = 1$ to $x_1 = x_2 = x_3 = 1$) requires the corresponding minterms to be covered by different product terms. The hazard can be avoided by grouping the minterms as shown below:

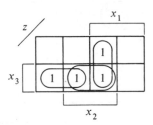

Hence, in general hazards can be removed by covering all pairs of minterms with a common product term. Therefore the removal of hazards requires the addition of redundant gates to a network, resulting in a nonminimum realization. Figure 3.6 shows the hazard-free realization of the above example.

The above discussion was primarily concerned with static hazards known as 1 hazards. The output should remain at logic 1 but temporarily drops to logic 0, producing a transient pulse which is sometimes called a *glitch*. Static 0 hazards are also implied by the definition of static hazard and can occur. However, a network which is free of static 1 hazards is free of static 0 hazards.

A second type of hazard known as a *dynamic hazard* may also exist in a network. This type of hazard is also caused by a special relative response time condition but occurs after an input transition which normally produces an output change. Such hazards cause output responses of $0 \to 1 \to 0 \to 1$ for

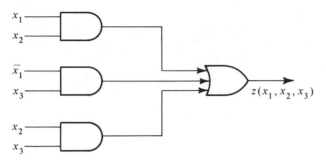

Fig. 3.6 Hazard-free network.

normal $0 \rightarrow 1$ changes or $1 \rightarrow 0 \rightarrow 1 \rightarrow 0$ for normal $1 \rightarrow 0$ changes. Networks which are free of static hazards are also free of dynamic hazards.

Quine-McCluskey Method

The Quine-McCluskey (Q-M) method is a tabular approach to Boolean function minimization. Basically the Q-M method has two advantages over the K-map. First, it is a straightforward, systematic method for producing a minimal function which is less dependent on the designer's ability to recognize patterns than the K-map method. Second, the method is a viable scheme for a large number of variables as opposed to the K-map, which in general is limited to about five or six variables. In general, the Q-M method is a systematic method which performs an exhaustive search and determines all combinations of logically adjacent minterms.

Before we proceed two important terms must be defined: prime implicant and essential prime implicant. These definitions are also applicable to K-maps. A *prime implicant* is a product term which cannot be combined with others to yield a term with fewer literals. An *essential prime implicant* is a prime implicant that covers at least one minterm of the function that is not covered by another prime implicant. In an attempt to make these two terms explicit, consider the example shown below:

Example.

The function $f(A, B, C, D) = \sum m(2, 3, 4, 5, 7, 8, 10, 13, 15)$ is shown on the K-map at the top of page 142.

On the K-map a prime implicant is equivalent to a set of blocks that is not a subset of a set containing a larger number of blocks. The prime implicants for this example, listed according to the minterms covered, are 2–3, 3–7, 4–5, 5–7–13–15, 8–10, and 2–10. Note that some of the minterms are covered more than once. However, the prime implicant 4–5 is an essential prime implicant because it covers minterm 4, which is not covered by any

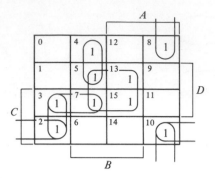

other prime implicant. There are two other essential prime implicants. Can you identify them?

The Quine-McCluskey method is summarized by the steps listed below. The exact meaning of each step will be illustrated by the examples which follow.

STEP 1. List all the minterms of the function to be minimized in their binary representation. Separate them into groups according to the number of 1 bits in their binary representation.

STEP 2. Perform an exhaustive search for adjacent minterms and combine them into minterm lists in a minimizing table. The final result is a list of prime implicants of the switching function.

STEP 3. Construct a prime implicant chart which lists minterms along the horizontal and prime implicants along the vertical with X entries indicating that certain prime implicants cover certain minterms.

STEP 4. Select a minimum number of prime implicants which cover all the minterms of the switching function.

A complete example will now be presented which demonstrates the four steps listed above.

Example.

The Q-M technique will be used to minimize the function
$$f(A, B, C, D) = \sum m(2, 4, 6, 8, 9, 10, 12, 13, 15)$$
The K-map listing for this example is shown on p. 143 and the reader is encouraged to try his hand at obtaining a minimal function via the map method.

To begin the Q-M minimization technique (step 1) the minterms are grouped according to the number of 1's in the binary representation of the minterm number. This grouping of terms is illustrated in the table below the K-map.

Once this table has been formed step 2 of the method specifies that an exhaustive search for all combinations of logically adjacent terms be initiated. The method of performing this functional reduction is summarized here and

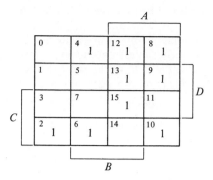

Minterms	$ABCD$	
2	0010	
4	0100	Group 1 (a single 1)
8	1000	
6	0110	
9	1001	Group 2 (two 1's)
10	1010	
12	1100	
13	1101	Group 3 (three 1's)
15	1111	Group 4 (four 1's)

explained in detail below. Consider the minimizing table below containing the three minterm lists. Two terms can be combined if and only if they differ in a single literal. Hence, in list 1 we can combine terms in group 1 only with those in group 2. When all the combinations between these two groups have been made and they have been entered in list 2, a line is drawn under these combinations and we begin combining the terms in group 2 with those in group 3. This simple procedure is repeated from one list to another in order to generate the entire minimizing table.

List 1			List 2			List 3		
Minterm	$ABCD$		Minterms	$ABCD$		Minterms	$ABCD$	
2	0010	✓	2, 6	0–10	PI_2	8, 9, 12, 13	1–0–	PI_1
4	0100	✓	2, 10	–010	PI_3			
8	1000	✓	4, 6	01–0	PI_4			
6	0110	✓	4, 12	–100	PI_5			
9	1001	✓	8, 9	100–	✓			
10	1010	✓	8, 10	10–0	PI_6			
12	1100	✓	8, 12	1–00	✓			
13	1101	✓	9, 13	1–01	✓			
15	1111	✓	12, 13	110–	✓			
			13, 15	11–1	PI_7			

There are a number of items in the table which beg for explanation. Note that the first element in list 2 indicates that minterms 2 and 6 have been combined since they differ in only a single literal. Note that the terms differed in the variable B and hence a dash appears in that position in the combination 2, 6, indicating that variable B was eliminated when the two minterms were combined. This combination can be easily checked by Boolean algebra:

$$\text{Minterm } 2 = \bar{A}\bar{B}C\bar{D}$$

$$\text{Minterm } 6 = \bar{A}BC\bar{D}$$

and

$$\bar{A}\bar{B}C\bar{D} + \bar{A}BC\bar{D} = \bar{A}C\bar{D} \quad \text{or} \quad \bar{A} \quad C\bar{D} \quad \text{or} \quad 0\text{--}10$$

Each minterm in list 1 that is combined with another is checked off, indicating that it appears in a larger set. Although a term may be combined more than once, it is only checked off once.

Once list 2 has been generated from list 1, an exhaustive search is made to combine the terms in list 2 to generate list 3. It is at this point that it becomes evident why it is important to indicate which of the variables has been eliminated. Since, as before, two terms in list 2 can be combined only if they differ in a single literal, only terms which have the same literal missing (i.e., a dash in the same position) can possibly be combined. Note that in list 2 minterm combinations 8, 12 and 9, 13 and also 8, 9 and 12, 13 can be combined to yield the term 8, 9, 12, 13 in list 3. Inspection of list 2 shows that minterm combinations 8, 12 and 9, 13 are both missing the same literal and differ by one other literal. The same is true for the other combination. Hence all four terms are checked off in the table. No other terms in the table can be combined. Hence, all the terms which are not checked off in the entire table are prime implicants and as such are labeled $PI_1 \cdots PI_7$.

The function could now be realized as a sum of all the prime implicants; however, we are looking for a minimal realization, and hence we want to use only the smallest number that are actually required. To determine the smallest number of prime implicants required to realize the function we form a *prime-implicant chart* as shown below; the formation of this chart is step 3 of the Q-M method:

	2	4	6	✓ 8	✓ 9	10	✓ 12	✓ 13	✓ 15
*PI_1				X	Ⓧ		X	X	
PI_2	X		X						
PI_3	X					X			
PI_4		X	X						
PI_5		X					X		
PI_6				X		X			
*PI_7								X	Ⓧ

The double horizontal line through the chart between PI_1 and PI_2 is used to separate prime implicants which contain different numbers of literals.

An examination of the minterm columns indicates that minterms 9 and 15 are each covered by only one prime implicant (shown circled). Therefore prime implicants 1 and 7 must be chosen, and hence they are essential prime implicants (as indicated by the asterisks). Note that in choosing these two prime implicants we have also covered minterms 8, 9, 12, 13, and 15 shown checked in the table.

The problem now remaining is that of selecting as few additional (non-essential) prime implicants as are necessary to cover the minterms 2, 4, 6, and 10. The selection of a minimal cover is the last step of the Q-M method. In general this is accomplished by forming a reduced prime-implicant chart. This reduced chart is shown below; note that the chart contains only the minterms that remain to be covered:

	2	4	6	10
PI_2	X		X	
PI_3	X			X
PI_4		X	X	
PI_5		X		
PI_6				X

Prime implicants PI_5 and PI_6 could obviously have been omitted because they are covered by PI_4 and PI_3, respectively. Hence, ignoring PI_5 and PI_6 for the moment we notice that the minterms 2, 4, 6, and 10 can be most efficiently covered (with the minimum number of prime implicants) by choosing PI_3 and PI_4. Therefore a minimal realization of the original function would be

$$f(A, B, C, D) = PI_1 + PI_3 + PI_4 + PI_7$$
$$= 1\text{-}0\text{-} + \text{-}010 + 01\text{-}0 + 11\text{-}1$$
$$= A\bar{C} + \bar{B}C\bar{D} + \bar{A}B\bar{D} + ABD$$

The corresponding groupings of the minterms on the K-map is shown below:

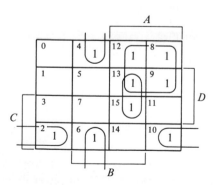

Covering Procedure

The problem of selecting a minimum number of prime implicants to realize a Boolean switching function is sometimes called the *covering problem*.

The following procedure may be employed to systematically choose a minimum number of nonessential prime implicants from the prime-implicant chart.

The first step is to remove all essential prime implicant rows from the chart as well as the minterm columns which they cover. Then the resulting chart is further reduced as described below.

A row (column) i of a PI chart *covers* row (column) j if row (column) i contains an X in each column (row) that row (column) j contains an X. Each row represents a nonessential prime implicant PI_i, while each column represents a minterm m_i of the switching function. For example, consider the PI chart below for the switching function

$$f(A, B, C, D) = \sum m(0, 1, 5\text{--}11, 13\text{--}15)$$

	0	1	5	6	7	8	9	10	11	13	14	15
*PI_1	Ⓧ	X				X	X					
PI_2		X	X				X			X		
PI_3			X		X					X		X
PI_4						X	X	X	X			
PI_5							X		X	X		X
PI_6								X	X		X	X
*PI_7				Ⓧ	X						X	X

For this PI chart PI_1 and PI_7 are essential PI and are marked with asterisks. Now we remove these two rows as well as all columns in which the rows have X entries. The following reduced PI chart is generated:

	5	10	11	13
PI_2	X			X
PI_3	X			X
PI_4		X	X	
PI_5			X	X
PI_6		X	X	

According to the definition of row and column covering stated earlier, row PI_2 covers row PI_3, row PI_4 covers row PI_6, column 11 covers column 10, and column 13 covers column 5.

Rules for PI chart reduction can be stated as follows:

RULE 1. A row that is covered by another row may be eliminated from the chart. When identical rows are present, all but one of the rows may be eliminated. Be cautious in removing PI's of fewer literals.

RULE 2. A column that covers another column may be eliminated. All but one column from a set of identical columns may be eliminated.

If one applies these rules to the previous PI chart, the following reduced PI chart is obtained:

	5	10
**PI$_2$	X	
**PI$_4$		X

Hence, we may choose PI$_2$ and PI$_4$ along with the essential PI$_1$ and PI$_7$ to obtain a minimum cover for the switching function.

A type of PI chart which requires a special approach to accomplish reduction will now be discussed. A *cyclic* PI chart is a chart which contains no essential PI and which cannot be reduced by rules 1 and 2 above. An example of a cyclic chart is shown below for the switching function

$$f(A.\ B,\ C) = \sum m(1, 2, 3, 4, 5, 6)$$

	1	2	3	4	5	6
PI$_1$	X		X			
PI$_2$		X	X			
PI$_3$		X				X
PI$_4$				X		X
PI$_5$				X	X	
PI$_6$	X				X	

The procedure to follow for cyclic chart reduction is to arbitrarily select one PI from the chart. The row corresponding to this PI and the columns corresponding to the minterms covered by the PI are then removed from the chart. If the resulting reduced chart is not cyclic, then rules 1 and 2 may be applied. However, if another cyclic chart is produced, the procedure for a cyclic chart is repeated, and another arbitrary choice is made. For example, arbitrarily choose PI$_1$ in the cyclic chart above. The noncyclic chart below is obtained by removing row PI$_1$ and columns 1 and 3:

	2	4	5	6
PI$_2$	X			
PI$_3$	X			X
PI$_4$		X		X
PI$_5$		X	X	
PI$_6$		X		

Rules 1 and 2 may now be applied to further reduce this chart. Row PI$_3$ covers row PI$_2$; hence row PI$_2$ may be removed. Row PI$_5$ covers row PI$_6$ which can be eliminated. The resulting reduced chart is shown below:

	2	4	5	6
**PI$_3$	X			X
PI$_4$		X		X
**PI$_5$		X	X	

PI$_3$ and PI$_5$ must be chosen to cover the chart.

A minimum cover for the switching function is PI_1, PI_3, and PI_5. Other minimal covers also exist.

The previous discussion is summarized in the covering procedure listed below:

STEP 1. Identify essential PI's if any exist in the original chart. Identify nonessential PI's on reduced charts (from step 4) if any minterm is covered by a single PI.

STEP 2. Remove rows corresponding to the identified essential and nonessential PI's. Remove columns corresponding to minterms covered by the removed rows.

STEP 3. If a cyclic chart results after completing step 2, go to step 5. Otherwise, apply the reduction procedure of rules 1 and 2.

STEP 4. If a cyclic chart results from step 3, then to to step 5. Otherwise, return to step 1.

STEP 5. Apply the cyclic chart procedure. Repeat step 5 until a void chart occurs or until a noncyclic chart is produced. In the latter case, return to setp 1.

The procedure terminates when step 2 or step 5 produces a void chart. A *void* chart contains no rows or columns. On the first application of step 1, prime implicants are found which must be identified to cover minterms for which only one X appears in its column. They are identified by an asterisk and are essential PI. On the second and succeeding applications of step 1 (determined by step 4) nonessential prime implicants are identified by a double asterisk from reduced PI charts.

Example.

The application of the covering procedure will now be demonstrated for

$$f(A, B, C, D) = \sum m(1, 3, 4, 6, 7, 9, 13, 15)$$

From the Q-M method or a K-map the following PI chart is generated:

	1	3	4	6	7	9	13	15
PI_1	X	X						
*PI_2			⊗	X				
PI_3		X			X			
PI_4				X	X			
PI_5					X			X
PI_6							X	X
PI_7						X	X	
PI_8	X					X		

Now we apply the covering procedure.

STEP 1. PI_2 is an essential PI for minterm 4. It is marked with an asterisk.

STEP 2. The row representing PI_2 is removed, along with the columns for minterms 4 and 6. Thus we obtain the following reduced PI chart:

	1	3	7	9	13	15
**PI_1	X	X				
PI_3		X	X			
~~PI_4~~			X			
PI_5			X			X
PI_6					X	X
PI_7				X	X	
PI_8	X			X		

STEP 3. Row PI_3 covers row PI_4. Hence row PI_4 is removed from the chart (shown above as a waved line). No further reduction by rules 1 and 2 is possible.

STEP 4. The reduced chart is cyclic. Go to step 5.

STEP 5. Arbitrarily choose PI_1 as a nonessential PI. It is marked as a double asterisk in the chart above. Remove row PI_1 and columns 1 and 3 from the chart as shown below:

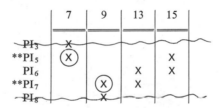

	7	9	13	15
~~PI_3~~	X			
**PI_5	⊗			X
PI_6			X	X
**PI_7		⊗	X	
~~PI_8~~		X		

This reduced chart is noncyclic, so go to step 1.

STEP 1. No PI's are identified.

STEP 2. No action is required.

STEP 3. Row PI_5 covers row PI_3 and row PI_7 covers row PI_8. Rows PI_3 and PI_8 are removed from the chart (a waved line in the chart above).

STEP 4. The chart is not cyclic. Go to step 1.

STEP 1. PI_5 and PJ_7 are identified by double asterisks as nonessential prime implicants.

STEP 2. Remove rows PI_5 and PI_7 and columns 7, 9, 13, and 15. This yields a void table.

This completes our presentation of the covering problem. This technique is also used in Chapters 4 and 12. Examples of the covering problem appear frequently in theory of computer logic design.

Functions with Don't Cares

The minimization of functions involving don't cares proceeds exactly as shown in the example above with one important exception, which will be demonstrated by the example below.

Example.

We want to use the Q-M approach to minimize the function

$$f(A, B, C, D, E) = \sum m(2, 3, 7, 10, 12, 15, 27) + d(5, 18, 19, 21, 23)$$

Following the procedure demonstrated in the example above, *all* the minterms and don't cares are listed in the minimizing table and combined in the manner previously illustrated. The results of this procedure are shown in the following table:

List 1			List 2			List 3		
Minterm	*ABCDE*		Minterm	*ABCDE*		Minterm	*ABCDE*	
2	00010	√	2, 3	0001–	√	2, 3, 18, 19	–001–	PI$_1$
			2, 10	0–010	PI$_4$			
3	00011	√	2, 18	–0010	√	3, 7, 19, 23	–0–11	PI$_2$
5	00101	√				5, 7, 21, 23	–01–1	PI$_3$
10	01010	√	3, 7	00–11	√			
12	01100	PI$_7$	3, 19	–0011	√			
18	10010	√	5, 7	001–1	√			
			5, 21	–0101	√			
7	00111	√	18, 19	1001–	√			
19	10011	√						
21	10101	√	7, 15	0–111	PI$_5$			
			7, 23	–0111	√			
15	01111	√	19, 23	10–11	√			
23	10111	√	19, 27	1–011	PI$_6$			
27	11011	√	21, 23	101–1	√			

A prime-implicant chart for the example must now be obtained. It is at this point that the method differs from that described earlier. Since some of the terms in list 1 are don't cares, there is no need to cover them. Only the specified minterms must be covered, and thus they are the only minterms that appear in the prime implicant chart, as shown on page 151.

It can be seen from the chart that the essential prime implicants are PI$_4$, PI$_5$, PI$_6$, and PI$_7$. Since only minterm 3 is not covered by the essential prime implicants, a reduced prime-implicant chart is not necessary. The minimal realizations for the function are

$$f(A, B, C, D, E) = PI_1 + PI_4 + PI_5 + PI_6 + PI_7$$

or

$$f(A, B, C, D, E) = PI_2 + PI_4 + PI_5 + PI_6 + PI_7$$

	✓ 2	3	✓ 7	✓ 10	✓ 12	✓ 15	✓ 27
PI_1	X	X					
PI_2		X	X				
PI_3			X				
$*PI_4$	X			⊗			
$*PI_5$			X			⊗	
$*PI_6$							⊗
$*PI_7$					⊗		

In terms of the variables

$$f(A, B, C, D, E) = \bar{B}\bar{C}D + \bar{A}\bar{C}D\bar{E} + \bar{A}CDE + A\bar{C}DE + \bar{A}BC\bar{D}\bar{E}$$

or

$$f(A, B, C, D, E) = \bar{B}DE + \bar{A}\bar{C}D\bar{E} + \bar{A}CDE + A\bar{C}DE + \bar{A}BC\bar{D}\bar{E}$$

Systems with Multiple Outputs

In the design of many digital systems it is often necessary to implement more than one output function with some given set of input variables. Using the techniques developed thus far, the problem can be solved by treating each function individually. However, there exists a potential for sharing gates and thus obtaining a simpler and less expensive design.

The extension of the tabular method to the multiple output case is performed essentially as it was in the singular case with the following exceptions:

1. To each minterm we must affix a flag to show in which function it appears.
2. Two minterms can be combined only if they both possess one or more common flags, and the term which results from the combination carries only flags that are common to both minterms.
3. Each term in the minimizing table can be checked off only if all the flags which the term possesses appear in the term resulting from the combination.

Example.

The tabular method will be used to obtain a minimum realization for the functions

$$f_\alpha(A, B, C, D) = \sum m(0, 2, 7, 10) + d(12, 15)$$
$$f_\beta(A, B, C, D) = \sum m(2, 4, 5) + d(6, 7, 8, 10)$$
$$f_\gamma(A, B, C, D) = \sum m(2, 7, 8) + d(0, 5, 13)$$

List 1

Minterm	ABCD	Flags	
0	0000	$\alpha\gamma$	$\checkmark$
2	0010	$\alpha\beta\gamma$	PI_{10}
4	0100	β	$\checkmark$
8	1000	$\beta\gamma$	PI_{11}
5	0101	$\beta\gamma$	$\checkmark$
6	0110	β	$\checkmark$
10	1010	$\alpha\beta$	$\checkmark$
12	1100	α	PI_{12}
7	0111	$\alpha\beta\gamma$	PI_{13}
13	1101	γ	$\checkmark$
15	1111	α	$\checkmark$

List 2

Minterms	ABCD	Flags	
0, 2	00-0	$\alpha\gamma$	PI_2
0, 8	-000	γ	PI_3
2, 6	0-10	β	PI_4
2, 10	-010	$\alpha\beta$	PI_5
4, 5	010-	β	$\checkmark$
4, 6	01-0	β	$\checkmark$
8, 10	10-0	β	PI_6
5, 7	01-1	$\beta\gamma$	PI_7
5, 13	-101	γ	PI_8
6, 7	011-	β	$\checkmark$
7, 15	-111	α	PI_9

List 3

Minterms	ABCD	Flags	
4, 5, 6, 7	01--	β	PI_1

Note that this example will also demonstrate a minimization with don't cares present. The minimizing table is shown on page 152.

Consider the combination 0, 8 in list 2. This term is generated for function $f_\gamma(A, B, C, D)$ from minterms 0 and 8 in list 1. Minterm 8 cannot be checked because its entire label $\beta\gamma$ is not included in the label for minterm 0. In fact, minterm 0 has a check due to the term 0, 2 in list 2.

Although all our minimizing tables thus far have had three lists, in general, the number of lists can be any integer less than or equal to $n + 1$, where n is the number of input variables for the Boolean function, or functions in the multiple output case. The prime-implicant chart for the minimizing table is shown below:

		f_α ✓ 0	✓ 2	7	✓ 10	f_β ✓ 2	✓ 4	✓ 5	f_γ ✓ 2	7	8
*PI$_1$	β						Ⓧ	X			
*PI$_2$	$\alpha\gamma$	Ⓧ	X						X		
PI$_3$	γ										X
PI$_4$	β						X				
*PI$_5$	$\alpha\beta$		X		Ⓧ	X					
PI$_6$	β										
PI$_7$	$\beta\gamma$							X		X	
PI$_8$	γ										
PI$_9$	α			X							
PI$_{10}$	$\alpha\beta\gamma$		X			X			X		
PI$_{11}$	$\beta\gamma$										X
PI$_{12}$	α										
PI$_{13}$	$\alpha\beta\gamma$		X							X	

(handwritten note at left: 2,6 beside PI$_4$)

The chart illustrates that PI$_1$, PI$_2$, and PI$_5$ are essential prime implicants. The reduced prime implicant chart appears below; note that the prime implicants covering only don't cares have been omitted:

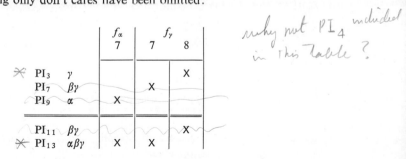

		f_α 7	f_γ 7	8
✳ PI$_3$	γ			X
PI$_7$	$\beta\gamma$		X	
PI$_9$	α	X		
PI$_{11}$	$\beta\gamma$			X
✳ PI$_{13}$	$\alpha\beta\gamma$	X	X	

(handwritten note at right: why not PI$_4$ included in this table?)

It is obvious that the best set of remaining prime implicants is PI$_3$ and PI$_{13}$. We choose PI$_3$ rather than PI$_{11}$ because it has fewer literals. Hence the minimum realizations for the three functions are

$$f_\alpha = PI_2 + PI_5 + PI_{13}$$
$$f_\beta = PI_1 + PI_5$$
$$f_\gamma = PI_2 + PI_3 + PI_{13}$$

or

$$f_\alpha = \bar{A}\bar{B}\bar{D} + \bar{B}C\bar{D} + \bar{A}BCD$$
$$f_\beta = \bar{A}B + \bar{B}C\bar{D}$$
$$f_\gamma = \bar{A}\bar{B}\bar{D} + \bar{B}\bar{C}\bar{D} + \bar{A}BCD$$

It is important to note that PI_2, PI_5, and PI_{13} are generated only once but used to implement two of the functions.

Summary

Graphical and tabular methods for minimization of switching functions have been presented. The ramifications of each technique were discussed in detail. The graphical technique employs the Karnaugh map, which was shown to be nothing more than a convenient representation of the Venn diagram. The Quine-McCluskey method, which is a tabular approach, employs an efficient exhaustive search in the minimization process. The latter minimization technique is also suitable for programming on a digital computer. In addition, a discussion of hazards in combinational logic networks was given.

REFERENCES

1. CHU, Y., *Digital Computer Design Fundamentals*. New York: McGraw-Hill Book Company, 1962.

2. HUFFMAN, D. A., "The Design and Use of Hazard-Free Switching Networks," *J. ACM*, Vol. 4, No. 1, January 1957, pp. 47–62.

3. KARNAUGH, M., "The Map Method for Synthesis of Combinational Logic Circuits," *AIEE Comm. Electronics*, November 1953, pp. 593–599.

4. MCCLUSKEY, E. J., *Introduction to the Theory of Switching Circuits*. New York: McGraw-Hill Book Company, 1965.

5. MCCLUSKEY, E. J., "Minimization of Boolean Functions," *Bell Sys. Tech. J.*, November 1956, pp. 1417–1444.

6. QUINE, W. V., "The Problem of Simplifying Truth Functions," *Am. Math. Monthly*, Vol. 59, 1952, pp. 521–531.

7. VEITCH, E. W., "A Chart Method for Simplifying Truth Functions," *Proc. Computing Machinery Conf.*, May 2–3, 1952, pp. 127–133.

PROBLEMS

3.1. Plot the following functions on the Karnaugh map:
  (a) $f(A, B, C) = \bar{A}\bar{B} + \bar{B}C + \bar{A}C$.
  (b) $f(A, B, C, D) = \bar{B}\bar{C}D + \bar{A}B\bar{C} + AB\bar{D}$.
  (c) $f(A, B, C, D, E) = \bar{B}\bar{C}\bar{E} + \bar{B}CE + C\bar{D}E + \bar{A}BC\bar{D} + AB\bar{C}D\bar{E}$.

3.2. Minimize the following functions via the K-map:
  (a) $f(A, B, C) = \sum m(3, 5, 6, 7)$.
  (b) $f(A, B, C, D) = \sum m(0, 1, 4, 6, 9, 13, 14, 15)$.
  (c) $f(A, B, C, D) = \sum m(0, 1, 2, 8\text{--}15)$.
  (d) $f(A, B, C, D, E) = \sum m(3, 4, 6, 9, 11, 13, 15, 18, 25, 26, 27, 29, 31)$.
  (e) $f(A, B, C, D, E) = \sum m(1, 5, 8, 10, 12\text{--}15, 17, 21, 24, 26, 31)$.

3.3. Minimize the following functions containing don't cares via the K-map:
  (a) $f(A, B, C, D) = \sum m(2, 9, 10, 12, 13) + d(1, 5, 14)$.
  (b) $f(A, B, C, D) = \sum m(1, 3, 6, 7) + d(4, 9, 11)$.
  (c) $f(A, B, C, D, E) = \sum m(3, 11, 12, 19, 23, 29) + d(5, 7, 13, 27, 28)$.

3.4. The circuit in Fig. P3.1 accepts BCD inputs for the decimal digits 0–9. The output is to be 1 only if the input is odd. Design the minimum logic circuit to accomplish this.

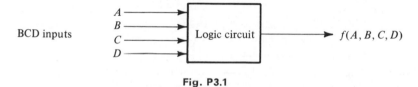

Fig. P3.1

3.5. Use the K-map to expand the PS functions below to canonical form:
  (a) $f(A, B, C) = (A + \bar{B})(\bar{A} + B)(B + \bar{C})$.
  (b) $f(A, B, C, D) = (A + \bar{D})(\bar{A} + C)$.

3.6. Realize the following function with a minimum number of NAND gates:

$$f(A, B, C, D) = (A + B)(A + \bar{C})BD + ABC\bar{D} + A\bar{B}D$$

3.7. Obtain the minimum NAND and NOR realization for the following function:

$$f(A, B, C, D) = \sum m(2, 3, 4, 5, 10, 11, 12, 14)$$

3.8. Minimize the following functions via the Quine-McCluskey method:
  (a) $f(A, B, C, D) = \sum m(0, 2, 4, 5, 7, 9, 11, 12)$.
  (b) $f(A, B, C, D, E) = \sum m(0, 1, 2, 7, 9, 11, 12, 23, 27, 28)$.

3.9. Use the Quine-McCluskey method to minimize the following functions with don't cares:
  (a) $f(A, B, C, D) = \sum m(0, 6, 9, 10, 13) + d(1, 3, 8)$.
  (b) $f(A, B, C, D) = \sum m(1, 4, 7, 10, 13) + d(5, 14, 15)$.

3.10. Minimize the following multiple output functions using the Q-M technique:
(a) $f_a(A, B, C, D) = \sum m(0, 1, 2, 9, 15)$
$f_b(A, B, C, D) = \sum m(0, 2, 8, 12, 15)$.
(b) $f_a(A, B, C, D) = \sum m(3, 7, 9, 14) + d(1, 4, 6, 11)$
$f_b(A, B, C, D) = \sum m(6, 7, 12) + d(3, 14)$.

3.11. Design a switching network which accepts BCD inputs and gives an output of logic 1 only when the input decimal digit is divisible by 3. Use a four-variable K-map to design your circuit.

3.12. Design a switching network which has five input variables and one output variable. Four of the input variables represent BCD digits, while the fifth is a control line. While the control line is at logic 0, the output should be logic 1 only if the BCD digit is greater than or equal to 5. While the control line is high, the output should be logic 1 only if the BCD digit is less than or equal to 5.

3.13. Design a multiple output logic network whose input is BCD data and whose outputs are defined below:
f_1: Detects input digits which are divisible by 4.
f_2: Detects numbers greater than or equal to 3.
f_3: Detects numbers less than 7.

3.14. Use K-maps to expand the following Boolean functions to canonical SP form:
(a) $f(A, B, C) = (\bar{A} + B)(A + B + \bar{C})(\bar{A} + C)$.
(b) $f(A, B, C, D) = A\bar{B} + \bar{A}CD + B\bar{C}\bar{D}$.
(c) $f(A, B, C, D) = (A + \bar{B})(C + \bar{D})(\bar{A} + \bar{C})$.
(d) $f(A, B, C, D, E) = \bar{A}E + BCD$.

3.15. Determine which of the following functions are equivalent:
$$f_1(A, B, C, D) = AC + BD + A\bar{B}\bar{D}$$
$$f_2(A, B, C, D) = A\bar{B}\bar{D} + AB + \bar{A}B\bar{C}$$
$$f_3(A, B, C, D) = BD + A\bar{B}\bar{D} + ACD + ABC$$
$$f_4(A, B, C, D) = AC + A\bar{B}\bar{C}\bar{D} + \bar{A}BD + B\bar{C}D$$
$$f_5(A, B, C, D) = (B + \bar{D})(A + B)(A + \bar{C})$$

3.16. Find both NAND and NOR logic implementations for the following equations; use only two levels of logic:
(a) $f(A, B, C) = (A + \bar{B})(\bar{A} + C) + \bar{B}\bar{A}C$.
(b) $f(A, B, C, D) = (\bar{A}(B + \bar{C}(D + A))) + AC\bar{D}$.

3.17. Design a multiple output combinational network which has two input signals x_0 and x_1, two control signals c_0 and c_1, and two output functions f_0 and f_1. The control signals have the following effect on the outputs:

c_0 c_1	f_0 f_1
0 0	0 0
0 1	x_0 0
1 0	0 x_1
1 1	x_0 x_1

For example, when $c_0 = 0$ and $c_1 = 1$, then $f_0(x_0, x_1, c_0, c_1) = x_0$ and $f_1(x_0, x_1, c_0, c_1) = 0$.

3.18. Use K-maps to find the following functions:
(a) $f_1(A, B, C, D) - f_\alpha(A, B, C, D) \cdot f_\beta(A, B, C, D)$,
(b) $f_2(A, B, C, D) = f_\alpha(A, B, C, D) + f_\beta(A, B, C, D)$,
(c) $f_3(A, B, C, D) = \bar{f}_1(A, B, C, D) \cdot f_2(A, B, C, D)$,
(d) $f_4(A, B, C, D) = f_\alpha(A, B, C, D) \oplus f_\beta(A, B, C, D)$
where

$$f_\alpha(A, B, C, D) = AB + BD + \bar{A}\bar{B}C$$
$$f_\beta(A, B, C, D) = \bar{A}B + B\bar{D}$$

3.19. (a) Use K-maps to generate all the prime implicants for the following multiple output logic network; find a two-level NOR realization:

$$f_\alpha(A, B, C, D) = AB + BD + \bar{A}\bar{B}C$$
$$f_\beta(A, B, C, D) = \bar{A}B + B\bar{D}$$

(b) Repeat part (a) using the multiple output Quine-McCluskey technique. Compare your prime implicant charts.

3.20. Use a K-map to find the following forms of the given Boolean function:
(a) The canonical SP form.
(b) The canonical PS form.
(c) A NAND gate realization.
(d) A NOR gate realization.

$$f(A, B, C, D, E) = B\bar{D}E + A\bar{B}D + \bar{A}C\bar{D}E + A\bar{C}E$$

4

Computer-Aided
Design
of
Switching
Networks

In recent years computers with their great computational power have assumed an important role in the design of scientific systems. The computer has relieved the system designer of many routine calculations and allowed him more time for creativity and innovation in design technology. The digital computer has made the design of large, complex systems routine in cases which were impossible to complete by hand.

The implementation of large switching networks is an example of one design problem which can be impractical to solve by hand. In the preceding chapter we have presented several techniques for minimizing combinational logic networks. However, these techniques are not well suited for the manual solution of problems involving six or more Boolean variables because the probability of human error in the minimization procedure in such cases is rather high. To effectively minimize logic networks containing a large number of Boolean variables, a minimization algorithm is developed in this chapter for use with a digital computer.

Introduction

Computer-aided design (CAD) of logic networks may be subdivided into two categories: first, synthesis of single-output networks; and second, synthesis of multiple-output networks. In this chapter we shall address only the first subdivision. This chapter develops a general-purpose design automation algorithm which minimizes a Boolean function in two-level sum of products (SP) form. The effectiveness of this CAD algorithm will be demonstrated by example.

There are many automated logic implementation systems in use today which can be employed once a minimum function has been obtained. For example, General Electric Co. has developed a system which produces data for a numerically controlled wiring machine from a logic block diagram. The wiring machine then completes the synthesis process.

Now it is possible to see how one computer may be used to design and construct a more advanced one. The first computer is given a numerically controlled wiring machine as a peripheral device, and then the first computer is programmed to minimize and implement another machine. International Business Machines Corp. has successfully used this technique in producing their System/360 and 370 models. With this brief motivation, let us now examine the CAD algorithm of this chapter.

The Cellular Structure [1-2]

The notation which will be employed to represent the cellular structure is the same as that used in the Quine-McCluskey method in Chapter 3. That is, a variable in complemented form is represented by 0, a variable in uncomplemented form (true form) by 1, and the absence of a variable by –. Then a Boolean product term may be written as

$$\mathbf{c} = (c_n c_{n-1} \cdots c_1)$$

where each c_i $(i = 1, n)$ is called a *component* of $\mathbf{c}$ and is a member of the set $\{0, 1, -\}$. The product term $\mathbf{c}$ is said to be a *cell* of the cellular structure to be defined later.

Example.

Given the Boolean function

$$C(A, B, C, D) = AB\bar{C}D + A\bar{B}D + \bar{A}\bar{D} + \bar{B}C$$

the corresponding cellular notation is

$$f(A, B, C, D) = \mathbf{c}_1 + \mathbf{c}_2 + \mathbf{c}_3 + \mathbf{c}_4$$
$$= (1101) + (10\text{--}1) + (0\text{--}\,\text{--}0) + (\text{--}01\text{--})$$

This is identical to the Q-M notation.

The n-Cube

The set $C = \{0, 1, -\}$ is a partially ordered set in which the order relation $\geq$ is defined as shown in Fig. 4.1. That is,

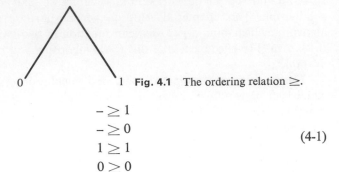

Fig. 4.1   The ordering relation $\geq$.

$$
\begin{aligned}
- &\geq 1 \\
- &\geq 0 \\
1 &\geq 1 \\
0 &\geq 0
\end{aligned}
\tag{4-1}
$$

The relation $\geq$ may be extended to cells as follows. If $\mathbf{x} = (x_n x_{n-1} \cdots x_1)$ and $\mathbf{y} = (y_n y_{n-1} \cdots y_1)$ are cells and $x_i \geq y_i$ for $i = 1, n$, then we say that $\mathbf{x} \supseteq \mathbf{y}$, or $\mathbf{x}$ contains $\mathbf{y}$.

The partially ordered set

$$
C^n = \{(c_n c_{n-1} \cdots c_1) \,|\, c_i \in C\} = \{\mathbf{c} \,|\, c_i \in C\}
\tag{4-2}
$$

with the order relation $\supseteq$ is called the *cellular n-cube* $(C^n, \supseteq)$.

Example.

Suppose $\mathbf{x} = (11{-}1)$ and $y = (1101)$ are members of the cellular 4-cube $(C^4, \supseteq)$; then $\mathbf{x} \supseteq \mathbf{y}$ since $1 \geq 1$, $1 \geq 1$, $- \geq 0$, and $1 \geq 1$. Please note that the relation $\geq$ is *not* the mathematical "greater than or equal to" relation.

Order. The *order* of a cell $\mathbf{c}$ in $(C^n, \supseteq)$ is equal to the number of components c_i which are equal to $-$. Thus, a 1-cell has one component equal to $-$, etc. A 0-cell is called a *vertex* of the cellular n-cube $(C^n, \supseteq)$ and is represented by a special symbol $\mathbf{v}$. There are 2^n vertices in the n-cube $(C^n, \supseteq)$. The reader should now realize that a vertex is simply a minterm.

Example.

The cellular n-cube of dimension 3 is shown in Fig. 4.2(a). Note that there are 2^3 0-cells or vertices, i.e., (000), (001), . . . , (111). Each edge of the 3-cube corresponds to a 1-cell; cell (01$-$) is illustrated in the figure. Each 2-cell, such as (1$--$), corresponds geometrically to a plane in the cellular structure. A K-map of three variables is shown in Fig. 4.2(b). Note that each vertex of the cube corresponds to a minterm block on the K-map. Adjacent minterms 2 and 3 combine to form cell (01$-$). Similarly, minterms 4, 5, 6, and 7 combine to form the cell (1$--$).

Minimum and maximum vertices. Two vertices which are extremely useful in representing a cell $\mathbf{c}$ of $(C^n, \supseteq)$ are the *minimum vertex*, min($\mathbf{c}$), and *maximum vertex*, max($\mathbf{c}$). Min($\mathbf{c}$) is determined by replacing each $-$ component of the cell $\mathbf{c}$ with a 0. Max($\mathbf{c}$) is found by replacing each $-$ with a 1.

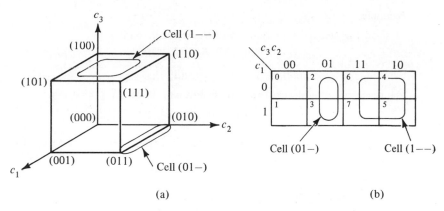

Fig. 4.2   A cellular n-cube: (a) cellular 3-cube; (b) Karnaugh map.

Example.

Given the cell $c_2 = (10$–$1)$ from an earlier example, the maximum and minimum vertices are

$$\max(c_2) = (1011)$$
$$\min(c_2) = (1001)$$

The maximum and minimum vertices completely describe a particular cell c of the n-cube $(C^n, \supseteq)$.

The Decimal Transform

In dealing with cells and vertices of the cellular structure for Boolean functions, one soon is burdened by manipulating so many 1's and 0's. Therefore we adopt a convention utilizing a *decimal transform* to improve our notation.

Consider the vertex $\mathbf{v} = (v_n v_{n-1} \cdots v_1)$ of the n-cube $(C^n, \supseteq)$. This vertex (minterm) has a decimal representation defined by the expression

$$\delta(\mathbf{v}) = \sum_{i=1}^{n} v_i \cdot 2^{i-1} \tag{4-3}$$

where v_i is equal to 0 or 1. In Chapter 2 we used $\delta(\mathbf{v})$ as the minterm subscript.

Example.

Given the vertex $\mathbf{v} = (1001)$ its decimal representation is

$$\delta(\mathbf{v}) = 1 \times 2^3 + 0 \times 2^2 + 0 \times 2^1 + 1 \times 2^0 = (9)_{10}$$

and hence this vertex corresponds to minterm m_9.

Similarly, each cell c in an n-cube $(C^n, \supseteq)$ has a decimal representation defined as

$$D(\mathbf{c}) = (\delta(\min(\mathbf{c})), \delta(\max(\mathbf{c}))) \tag{4-4}$$

Example.

Find the decimal representation for the cell $\mathbf{c} = (10\text{--}1)$.

$$\max(\mathbf{c}) = (1011) \qquad \delta(\max(\mathbf{c})) = 11$$
$$\min(\mathbf{c}) = (1001) \qquad \delta(\min(\mathbf{c})) = 9$$

The corresponding decimal representation is

$$D(\mathbf{c}) = (9, 11)$$

Notation. In the remainder of this chapter a capital letter will be used to denote the decimal transform of a vertex labeled with the corresponding lowercase letter. In other words, if $\mathbf{v}$ is a vertex, then

$$V = \delta(\mathbf{v}) \tag{4-5}$$

is the corresponding decimal transform defined in equation (4-3).

In addition we also employ the notation

$$D(\mathbf{c}) = (I, J) \tag{4-6}$$

where

$$I = \delta(\min(\mathbf{c}))$$
$$J = \delta(\max(\mathbf{c}))$$

This will eliminate most occurrences of the symbol $\delta(\ )$, making the equations more readable.

Example.

Find the vertices of the cell $\mathbf{c} = (0\text{--}1\text{--}01)$ and find its decimal transform.

This 2-cell has 2^2 vertices, two of which are $\min(\mathbf{c})$ and $\max(\mathbf{c})$. The other two can be obtained by replacing — by the remaining combinations of 1 and 0. That is,

$$\mathbf{v}_1 = \min(\mathbf{c}) = (001001) \longrightarrow V_1 = 9 = I$$
$$\mathbf{v}_2 = \phantom{\min(\mathbf{c})} = (001101) \longrightarrow V_2 = 13$$
$$\mathbf{v}_3 = \phantom{\min(\mathbf{c})} = (011001) \longrightarrow V_3 = 25$$
$$\mathbf{v}_4 = \max(\mathbf{c}) = (011101) \longrightarrow V_4 = 29 = J$$

Hence the decimal transform is

$$D(\mathbf{c}) = (I, J) = (9, 29)$$

Note that $9 < 13 < 25 < 29$ and hence it is seen that

$$I \leq V_i \leq J \tag{4-7}$$

for every vertex $\mathbf{v}_i$ of cell $\mathbf{c}$ in the n-cube $(C^n, \supseteq)$.

This completes our presentation of the cellular structure itself. Now let us examine some containment properties of the cellular n-cube which are useful in minimizing Boolean switching functions.

Containment Properties [1-2]

Some of the properties of the decimal representation for cells of the n-cube are useful in defining relations which exist between cells and vertices. Those properties which are used in the algorithm to arrive at a minimum, nonredundant, cover (realization) for a Boolean function are now discussed.

AND. The logic AND for Boolean variables has been defined in Chapter 2. When this operation is performed on two vertices, the individual components of the vertices are ANDed to yield another vertex, so that

$$\mathbf{v}_i \cdot \mathbf{v}_j = \mathbf{v}_k \tag{4-8a}$$

The manner in which the operation is performed is illustrated by the following example.

Example.

Given two vertices of a 5-cube

$$\mathbf{v}_1 = (10011)$$

and

$$\mathbf{v}_2 = (10101)$$

then the AND operation yields

$$\begin{aligned}
\mathbf{v}_1 \cdot \mathbf{v}_2 &= (10011) \cdot (10101) \\
&= (1 \cdot 1, 0 \cdot 0, 0 \cdot 1, 1 \cdot 1) \\
&= (10001)
\end{aligned}$$

which is, of course, another vertex. Note that the resultant vertex indicates immediately the positions in which both $\mathbf{v}_1$ and $\mathbf{v}_2$ contain a 1 component.

Sometimes the notation

$$V_i \cdot V_j = V_k \tag{4-8b}$$

will be used instead of (4-8a) for simplicity to indicate the AND operation on two vertices. However, the decimal transforms V_i and V_j must be converted to binary components and then the AND operation can be performed.

Containment. If two vertices $\mathbf{v}_1$ and $\mathbf{v}_2$ of the n-cube satisfy the relation

$$\mathbf{v}_1 \cdot \mathbf{v}_2 = \mathbf{v}_1$$

then we say that $\mathbf{v}_1$ is related to $\mathbf{v}_2$ by the relation

$$\mathbf{v}_2 \longrightarrow \mathbf{v}_1 \tag{4-9a}$$

meaning that $\mathbf{v}_1$ is *contained* in $\mathbf{v}_2$. In other words, $\mathbf{v}_2$ has a 1 component in every position in which $\mathbf{v}_1$ has a 1 component. In decimal transform notation this means if

$$V_1 \cdot V_2 = V_1$$

then

$$V_2 \longrightarrow V_1 \qquad (4\text{-}9b)$$

The AND operation is used to show containment and is the basis of the CAD minimization algorithm which follows. One can show that containment defined by (4-2) is not equivalent to (4-9). Containment for cells ($\supseteq$) and for vertices ($\longrightarrow$) are different relations.

Now we list several theorems, stated without proof, which form a basis for the design algorithm.

Theorem 1.

For every cell $\mathbf{c}$ of an n-cube $(C^n, \supseteq)$, $\max(\mathbf{c}) \longrightarrow \min(\mathbf{c})$, or $I \cdot J = I$, where $D(\mathbf{c}) = (I, J)$.

This theorem provides a simple method for determining if a pair of minterms (vertices) of a Boolean function can be combined to form a cell. If I and J are two minterms of an nth-order Boolean function and if $I \cdot J = I$, then $J \longrightarrow I$, and hence from Theorem 1, (I, J) is the decimal transform of a cell of $(C^n, \supseteq)$ with minimum vertex I and maximum vertex J. We shall call (I, J) a cell of $(C^n, \supseteq)$ for convenience.

Example.

Given two minterms 10 and 14 of a fourth-order Boolean function, determine if (10, 14) is a cell of $(C^4, \supseteq)$. If so, find the cell.

$$I = 10, \quad i = (1010)$$
$$J = 14, \quad j = (1110)$$
$$I \cdot J, \quad \mathbf{i} \cdot \mathbf{j} = (1010) \cdot (1110)$$
$$= (1010) = \mathbf{i}$$
$$I \cdot J = I, \quad J \longrightarrow I$$

Hence (10, 14) is a cell of $(C^4, \supseteq)$. Since the minimum vertex is (1010) and the maximum vertex is (1110), the cell (I, J) is represented by (1–10), where the – is placed in the component positions corresponding to those in which the maximum and minimum vertices differ.

Theorem 2.

Vertex $\mathbf{v}$ is contained in cell $\mathbf{c}$, expressed as

$$\mathbf{c} \supseteq \mathbf{v}$$
$$(I, J) \supseteq V$$

if and only if

$$\max(\mathbf{c}) \longrightarrow \mathbf{v} \longrightarrow \min(\mathbf{c})$$

or

$$I \cdot V = I, \quad V \cdot J = V$$

This theorem is used to determine if a vertex (minterm) of the n-cube is contained in a cell (I, J). A cell represents a group of minterms. Hence, we say that a cell which contains a vertex *covers* that vertex.

Example.

Determine if minterm m_{11} is covered by the cell $(10, 15)$. The vertices in decimal and binary form are

$$I = 10, \quad \mathbf{i} = (1010)$$
$$V = 11, \quad \mathbf{v} = (1011)$$
$$J = 15, \quad \mathbf{i} = (1111)$$

Since

$$I \cdot V = 10 \cdot 11 = 10 = I$$
$$V \cdot J = 11 \cdot 15 = 11 = V$$

the vertex V is contained in cell (I, J):

$$(10, 15) \supseteq 11$$

Theorem 2 finds frequent use when one is trying to find essential prime implicants from a prime-implicant chart. The prime implicants are represented by cells and Theorem 2 allows us to test for minterm coverage using the logical AND operation which a digital computer performs very rapidly.

Theorem 3.

If

$$\min(\mathbf{c}_2) \longrightarrow \min(\mathbf{c}_1)$$
$$\max(\mathbf{c}_1) \longrightarrow \max(\mathbf{c}_2)$$

then

$$\mathbf{c}_1 \supseteq \mathbf{c}_2$$

In decimal notation, if

$$I_1 \cdot I_2 = I_1$$

and

$$J_2 \cdot J_1 = J_2$$

then

$$(I_1, J_1) \supseteq (I_2, J_2)$$

This theorem gives the criterion for containment of one cell in another cell. Again, based on the logical AND operation, the digital computer can rapidly test to see if one product term of a Boolean function contains another. This theorem is used to perform the equivalent task, for the CAD algorithm, of generating the minimizing table and the list of prime implicants of the Quine-McCluskey method.

Example.

Show that $(10, 15) \supseteq (14, 15)$. In decimal and binary notation

$$(I_1, J_1) = (10, 15), \quad c_1 = (1\text{-}1\text{-})$$
$$(I_2, J_2) = (14, 15), \quad c_2 = (111\text{-})$$

Since

$$I_1 \cdot I_2 = (10) \cdot (14) = (1010) \cdot (1110) = (1010) = I_1$$
$$J_2 \cdot J_1 = (15) \cdot (15) = (1111) \cdot (1111) = (1111) = J_2$$

by Theorem 3,

$$(10, 15) \supseteq (14, 15)$$

An analysis of the two cells c_1 and c_2 in the last example shows that they differ in only one component position: cell c_1 has a – in this position and c_2 has a 1. Since $- \geq 1$, $c_1 \supseteq c_2$ by equation (4-2).

Theorem 4.

If v_1 and v_2 are vertices of an n-cube and $v_2 \longrightarrow v_1$, then

$$\delta(v_1) \leq \delta(v_2)$$

or

$$V_1 \leq V_2$$

where $\leq$ is the mathematical "less than or equal to" relation.

This theorem says that in order for vertex v_2 to contain vertex v_1 the decimal transform of the former must be greater that that of the latter. We extend this theorem for use with cells.

Theorem 5.

If c_1 and c_2 are cells of an n-cube and $c_1 \supseteq c_2$, then

$$\delta(\min(c_1)) \leq \delta(\min(c_2))$$
$$\delta(\max(c_2)) \leq \delta(\max(c_1))$$

or in decimal notation, if $(I_1, J_1) \supseteq (I_2, J_2)$ then

$$I_1 \leq I_2 \leq J_2 \leq J_1$$

This theorem uses the comparison features of the digital computer to test for containment. Earlier we pointed out that Theorem 3 is used to find the prime implicants of a Boolean function. Theorem 5 may be used as a "screening" test for a pair of cells before Theorem 3 is applied. Used together they form the basis of a fast computerized algorithm for generating prime implicants.

Example.

For the cells

$$c_1 = (10, 15)$$
$$c_2 = (14, 15)$$

we know that $(10, 15) \supseteq (14, 15)$ from the previous example. Since

$$10 \le 14 \le 15 \le 15$$

Theorem 5 is also satisfied.

In summary, the relations of Theorems 3, 4, and 5 are used to test the following conditions:

1. A vertex V is covered by cell (I, J) if and only if

$$I \le V \le J$$
$$I \cdot V = I \tag{4-10}$$

and

$$V \cdot J = V$$

2. A cell (I_2, J_2) is covered by another cell (I_1, J_1) if and only if

$$I_1 \le I_2 \le J_2 \le J_1$$
$$I_1 \cdot I_2 = I_1 \tag{4-11}$$

and

$$J_2 \cdot J_1 = J_2$$

Equations (4-10) and (4-11) will be employed in the generation of prime implicants, as is demonstrated in the example below.

Example.

Consider the Boolean function

$$f(w, x, y, z) = \sum m(1, 3, 5, 7)$$

The vertices of the 4-cube for this function are $V_1 = 1$, $V_2 = 3$, $V_3 = 5$, and $V_4 = 7$. We may use Theorem 1 to generate other cells of the function by testing each pair of vertices as follows:

$$1 \cdot 7 = (0001) \cdot (0111) = (0001) = 1$$
$$\therefore (1, 7) \text{ is the cell } (0 - - 1)$$
$$1 \cdot 5 = (0001) \cdot (0101) = (0001) = 1$$
$$\therefore (1, 5) \text{ is the cell } (0 - 0 \ 1)$$
$$1 \cdot 3 = (0001) \cdot (0011) = (0001) = 1$$
$$\therefore (1, 3) \text{ is the cell } (0 \ 0 - 1)$$
$$3 \cdot 7 = (0011) \cdot (0111) = (0011) = 3$$
$$\therefore (3, 7) \text{ is the cell } (0 - 1 \ 1)$$
$$3 \cdot 5 = (0011) \cdot (0101) = (0001) = 1$$
$$\therefore (3, 5) \text{ is } not \text{ a cell}$$
$$5 \cdot 7 = (0101) \cdot (0111) = (0101) = 5$$
$$\therefore (5, 7) \text{ is the cell } (0 \ 1 - 1)$$

Once the cells have been generated we may use equation (4-11) to test for containment as follows: To check (1, 7) and (1, 5),

$$1 \leq 1 \leq 5 \leq 7$$
$$1 \cdot 1 = 1$$
$$5 \cdot 7 = 5$$

Hence, $(1, 7) \supseteq (1, 5)$. Similarly, one may show that $(1, 7)$ also contains $(1, 3)$, $(3, 7)$ and $(5, 7)$. Because cell $(1, 7)$ contains all the minterms of the function, it covers the complete function and is the only prime implicant. Therefore,

$$f(w, x, y, z) = (1, 7) = (0- -1)$$
$$= \bar{w}z$$

The reader should keep in mind that the procedure used in the example above is equivalent to that performed by Boolean algebra, Karnaugh maps, and the Quine-McCluskey procedure. The function above can be simplified by inspection on a K-map to yield $f(w, x, y, z) = \bar{w}z$. Also note that by organizing the test for cells (Theorem 1) in the order shown above (i.e., comparing the lowest numbered minterm with the largest, etc.), the largest cells of the Boolean function are generated first. This procedure guarantees the entries of the largest prime implicants into the prime-implicant chart employed in the algorithm. This approach is equivalent to grouping the largest possible number of blocks on the K-map.

The reader should now be able to use the properties of the cellular n-cube $(C^n, \supseteq)$ in minimizing Boolean functions.

The Minimization Algorithm [3-5]

The containment properties of the cellular n-cube are now used to develop an algorithm to select prime implicants, essential and nonessential. The algorithm is suitable for implementation on a general-purpose digital computer in a procedure-oriented language such as FORTRAN IV. A flow chart which describes the general method of minimization is shown in Fig. 4.3. The step-by-step procedure is outlined below:

STEP 1. Specify the order of the Boolean function and its minterms and don't cares. Then combine the minterms and don't cares and arrange these terms in increasing order. (Note that a term refers to both minterms and don't cares.)

STEP 2. Choose the pair (II, JJ), where II is the term of lowest magnitude and JJ is the term of highest magnitude.

STEP 3. Check the pair (II, JJ) to see if it forms a cell, i.e., $II \cdot JJ = II$.

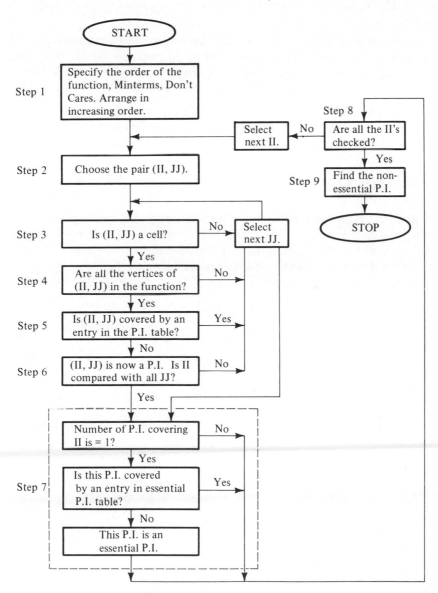

Fig. 4.3   The minimization algorithm.

If this pair does form a cell, go to step 4. If this pair does not form a cell, select the next highest term in the function as *JJ* and repeat this step.

STEP 4. Generate all the vertices (terms) of the cell (*II, JJ*). If all the vertices are included in the function as minterms or don't cares, then go to step 5. If not, choose the next highest term in the function as *JJ* and go to step 3.

STEP 5. Check cell (*II, JJ*) to see if it is contained in an entry in the prime-implicant table. (*Note*: on the first pass through the algorithm the prime-implicant table will be empty.) If not, go to step 6. If contained, select the next highest term in the function as *JJ* and go to step 3.

STEP 6. Cell (*II, JJ*) is now a prime implicant and is entered in that table. If *II* has been compared with all other terms in the function greater than *II*, proceed to step 7. Otherwise, select the next highest term with function as *JJ* and go to step 3.

At this point the prime-implicant table contains all the prime implicants that cover term *II*.

STEP 7. Check the number of prime implicants that cover *II*; if there is only one, then this prime implicant may be an essential prime implicant. Hence, test the prime implicant to see if it is already contained (or covered) in the essential prime-implicant table. If contained, go to the next step. If not, enter this prime implicant in the essential prime implicant table.

STEP 8. Repeat steps 2–7 with *II* equal to each term in the function.

We have now found all the prime implicants of the function and have selected all the essential prime implicants.

STEP 9. Find all minterms that are not covered by essential prime implicants. Select the best set of prime implicants which cover all these uncovered minterms. These prime implicants are nonessential prime implicants.

The essential prime implicants together with the nonessential prime implicants represent the function in minimum form. The process of choosing the nonessential prime implicants has been discussed in Chapter 3. Step 9 essentially follows the procedure used in the Quine-McCluskey method. The procedure has been modified to make it computationally efficient [6].

Let us now apply the algorithm manually to a simple example Boolean function.

Example.

Minimize the function

$$f(A, B, C, D) = \sum m(0, 2, 4) + d(10)$$

Function order: 4

Minterm list: 0, 2, 4

Don't care list: 10

STEP 1. 0, 2, 4, 10.

STEP 2. (*II, JJ*) = (0, 10).

STEP 3. $0 \cdot 10 = (0000) \cdot (1010) = (0000) = 0$

$(0, 10) = \text{cell} (-0-0)$

STEP 4. Vertices of $(0, 10)$ are $0, 2, 8, 10$. Vertex 8 is not a minterm. Next $JJ = 4 \longrightarrow (II, JJ) = (0, 4)$.

STEP 3. $0 \cdot 4 = (0000) \cdot (0100) = (0000) = 0$

$(0, 4) = \text{cell} (0-00)$

STEP 4. Vertices of $(0, 4)$ are 0 and 4. Vertices 0 and 4 are minterms.

STEP 5. $(0, 4)$ is not contained in the PI table.

STEP 6. $PI_1 = (0-00)$. Next $JJ = 2 \longrightarrow (II, JJ) = (0, 2)$.

STEP 3. $0 \cdot 2 = (0000) \cdot (0010) = (0000) = 0$

$(0, 2) = \text{cell} (00-0)$

STEP 4. Vertices of $(0, 2)$ are 0 and 2. Vertices 0 and 2 are minterms.

STEP 5. Does PI_1 contain $(0, 2)$? By equation (4-11)

$$0 \leq 0 \leq 2 \leq 4$$

$$0 \cdot 0 = (0000) \cdot (0000) = (0000) = 0$$

$$2 \cdot 4 = (0010) \cdot (0100) = (0000) = 0$$

Fails. Hence, $(0, 2)$ not contained in the PI table.

STEP 6. $PI_2 = (00-0)$.

STEP 7. Minterm 0 is covered by PI_1 and PI_2. Therefore, there is no essential PI.

STEP 8. Next $II = 2 \longrightarrow (II, JJ) = (2, 10)$.

STEP 3. $2 \cdot 10 = (0010) \cdot (1010) = (0010) = 2$

$(2, 10) = \text{cell} (-010)$

STEP 4. Vertices of $(2, 10)$ are 2 and 10. Vertices are minterms (or don't cares).

STEP 5. Does PI_1 or PI_2 contain (-010)? No.

STEP 6. $PI_3 = (-010)$. Next $JJ = 4 \longrightarrow (II, JJ) = (2, 4)$.

STEP 3. $2 \cdot 4 = (0010) \cdot (0100) = (0000) = 0$

Not a cell. Next JJ is complete; go to step 7.

STEP 7. Minterm 2 is covered by PI_2 and PI_3. No essential PI thus far.

STEP 8. Next $II = 4 \longrightarrow (II, JJ) = (4, 10)$.

STEP 3. $4 \cdot 10 = (0100) \cdot (1010) = (0000) = 0$

$(4, 10)$ is not a cell. Next JJ is complete; go to step 7.

STEP 7. Minterm 4 is covered by PI_1 only. $PI_1 = (0-00)$ is *essential*.

STEP 8. Next II is complete.

STEP 9. PI_1 covers 0 and 4. Minterm 2 is covered by PI_2 or PI_3. Choose PI_2.

The solution is

$$f(A, B, C, D) = PI_1 + PI_2$$
$$= (0{-}00) + (00{-}0)$$
$$= \bar{A}\bar{C}\bar{D} + \bar{A}\bar{B}\bar{D}$$

The algorithm of Fig. 4.3 has been implemented in FORTRAN IV in reference [7]; complete flow charts and listings are found there.

The computer solution to the last example is shown below:

THE BOOLEAN FUNCTION IS OF ORDER 4

MINTERMS
0   2   4

DON'T CARES
10

PRIME IMPLICANTS
(0, 4)   0–00
(0, 2)   00–0
(2, 10)   –010

THE ESSENTIAL P.I. ARE   0–00

NONESSENTIAL P.I. ARE   00–0

Although the manual manipulation of the algorithm seems cumbersome, the procedure is quite natural for the digital computer. The logical AND and $\leq$ comparisons greatly increase the speed of solution over the conventional Quine-McCluskey approach.

Example Results

The following examples are computer solutions to typical combinational logic minimization problems.

Example.

Minimize the following fourth-order function:

$$f(A, B, C, D) = \sum m(0, 2, 4, 5, 6, 9, 10) + d(7, 11, 12, 13, 14, 15)$$

For comparison both the Karnaugh map and computer simplifications of this function will be shown. The K-map for $f(A, B, C, D)$ is shown in Fig. 4.4. Note from the K-map that

m_0 is covered only by PI_1; hence PI_1 is essential.
m_5 is covered only by PI_3; hence PI_3 is essential.
m_9 is covered only by PI_4; hence PI_4 is essential.

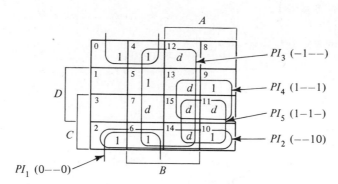

Fig. 4.4   K-map of the function.

Only minterm number 10, i.e., m_{10}, remains to be covered. It can be covered by PI_2 or PI_5. If PI_2 is chosen as the nonessential prime implicant, the results are identical to those obtained by the computer algorithm shown below:

THE BOOLEAN FUNCTION IS OF ORDER 4

MINTERMS

0   2   4   5   6   9   10

DON'T CARES

7   11   12   13   14   15

PRIME IMPLICANTS

(0, 6)	0 – – 0
(2, 14)	– – 1 0
(4, 15)	– 1 – –
(9, 15)	1 – – 1
(10, 15)	1 – 1 –

THE ESSENTIAL P.I. ARE   0 – – 0

– 1 – –

1 – – 1

NONESSENTIAL P.I. ARE   – – 1 0

Hence the minimized function is

$$f(A, B, C, D) = PI_1 + PI_3 + PI_4 + PI_2$$
$$= (0- -0) + (-1- -) + (1- -1) + (- -10)$$
$$= \bar{A}\bar{D} + B + AD + C\bar{D}$$

Two other examples which indicate the use of the computer algorithm in function minimization are presented below.

Example.

THE BOOLEAN FUNCTION IS OF ORDER 6

MINTERMS

3   7   12   14   15   19   27   28   29   31   35   39   44   45   46   48   49
50   52   53   55   56   57   59   60   62   63

DON'T CARES
0   11   13   23   30   32   43   47   51   54   61

PRIME IMPLICANTS

(0, 32)	– 0 0 0 0 0
(3, 63)	– – – – 1 1
(12, 63)	– – 1 1 – –
(32, 48)	1 – 0 0 0 0
(48, 61)	1 1 – – 0 –
(48, 55)	1 1 0 – – –
(49, 63)	1 1 – – – 1
(52, 63)	1 1 – 1 – –

THE ESSENTIAL P.I. ARE

– – – – 1 1
– – 1 1 – –
1 1 0 – – –
1 1 – – 0 –

NONESSENTIAL P.I. ARE

NONE

Example.

THE BOOLEAN FUNCTION IS OF ORDER 8

MINTERMS
17   20   21   23   25   32   34   35   38   39   48   49   53   54   64   65   66
70   71   72   73   84   85   86   87   98   99   100   101   102   114   115
116   117   118   119   132   133   134   135   136   137   151   152   153

DON'T CARES
0   10   11   12   13   14   15   26   27   28   29   30   31   42   43   44   45
46   47   58   59   60   61   62   63   74   75   76   77   78   79   90   91
92   93   94   95   106   107   108   109   110   111   122   123   124   125
126   127   138   139   140   141   142   143   154   155   156   157   158
159   160   161   162   163   164   165   166   167   168   169   170   171
172   173   174   175   176   177   178   179   180   181   182   183   184
185   186   187   188   189   190   191   192   193   194   195   196   197
198   199   200   201   202   203   204   205   206   207   208   209   210
211   212   213   214   215   216   217   218   219   220   221   222   223
224   225   226   227   228   229   230   231   232   233   234   235   236
237   238   239   240   241   242   243   244   245   246   247   248   249
250   251   252   253   254   255

PRIME IMPLICANTS

(0, 64)	0 – 0 0 0 0 0 0
(0, 32)	0 0 – 0 0 0 0 0
(10, 255)	– – – – 1 – 1 –
(12, 255)	– – – – 1 1 – –
(17, 53)	0 0 – 1 0 – 0 1
(17, 29)	0 0 0 1 – – 0 1
(20, 93)	0 – 0 1 – 1 0 –

(21, 125)	0 – – 1 – 1 0 1
(21, 95)	0 – 0 1 – 1 – 1
(23, 223)	– – 0 1 – 1 1 1
(25, 159)	– 0 0 1 1 – – 1
(32, 176)	– 0 1 – 0 0 0 0
(32, 162)	– 0 1 0 0 0 – 0
(34, 238)	– – 1 0 – – 1 0
(34, 235)	– – 1 0 – 0 1 –
(34, 175)	– 0 1 0 – – 1 –
(38, 254)	– – 1 – – 1 1 0
(48, 177)	– 0 1 1 0 0 0 –
(49, 181)	– 0 1 1 0 – 0 1
(53, 253)	– – 1 1 – 1 0 1
(64, 202)	– 1 0 0 – 0 – 0
(64, 201)	– 1 0 0 – 0 0 –
(66, 238)	– 1 – 0 – – 1 0
(70, 254)	– 1 – – – 1 1 0
(70, 223)	– 1 0 – – 1 1 –
(72, 207)	– 1 0 0 1 – – –
(84, 255)	– 1 – 1 – 1 – –
(98, 254)	– 1 1 – – – 1 0
(98, 251)	– 1 1 – – 0 1 –
(100, 254)	– 1 1 – – 1 – 0
(100, 253)	– 1 1 – – 1 0 –
(114, 255)	– 1 1 1 – – 1 –
(132, 239)	1 – – 0 – 1 – –
(135, 255)	1 – – – – 1 1 1
(136, 255)	1 – – – 1 – –
(160, 255)	1 – 1 – – – – –
(192, 255)	1 1 – – – – – –

THE ESSENTIAL P.I. ARE

```
0 – 0 1 – 1 0 –
– 0 1 0 – – 1 –
– – 1 – – 1 1 0
– 1 0 0 – 0 0 –
– 1 0 – – 1 1 –
– 1 1 – – 1 0 –
1 – – 0 – 1 – –
1 – – – 1 – – –
```

NONESSENTIAL P.I. ARE

```
0 0 – 1 0 – 0 1
– – 0 1 – 1 1 1
– 0 0 1 1 – – 1
– 0 1 – 0 0 0 0
– 1 – 0 – – 1 0
– 1 1 – – 0 1 –
– 1 – 1 – 1 – –
```

Summary

The algorithm described in this chapter is basically a Quine-McCluskey type of procedure. However, the containment properties of the cellular n-cube representation greatly minimize the number of comparisons. The ordering of minterms and don't cares (lowest first, highest last) helps in finding the largest prime implicant first, thus avoiding the possibility of entering a term into the PI table which may be found later to be covered by a new cell.

The computer implementation of the algorithm [7], which requires $46K$ bytes of core memory on an IBM 360/50, is fast and flexible. In general results indicate that on an IBM System 360/50 a fourth-order function can be minimized in approximately 1 second and an eighth-order function can be minimized in approximately 40 seconds.

The input data may be in integer, binary, or a mixed format, and the implementation will minimize not only the uncomplemented function but the complemented one as well.

A complete FORTRAN IV source listing of the algorithm is found in [7].

REFERENCES

1. PRATHER, R. E., *Introduction to Switching Theory: A Mathematical Approach.* Boston: Allyn and Bacon, Inc., 1967.

2. CARROLL, C. C., and G. E. JORDAN, "A Fast Algorithm for Boolean Function Minimization," Project THEMIS Tech. Report, *Report No. AU-T-3*, Auburn University, Auburn, Alabama, December 1968.

3. SHIVA, S. G., and H. T. NAGLE, JR., "A Fast Algorithm for Complete Minimization of Boolean Functions," Project THEMIS Tech. Report, *Report No. AU-T-24*, Auburn University, Auburn, Alabama, June 1972.

4. MOTT, H., and C. C. CARROLL, "Numerical Procedures for Boolean Function Minimization," *IEEETEC*, Vol. EC-13, No. 4, p. 470, August 1964.

5. CARROLL, C. C., and W. A. HORNFECK, "An Algorithm for Fast Boolean Function Minimization Using Properties of Cellular N-Cube," Project THEMIS Tech. Report, *Report No. AU-T-16*, Auburn University, Auburn, Alabama, August 1970.

6. BUBENIK, V., "Weighting Method for Determination of the Irredundant Set of Prime Implicants," *IEEETEC*, Vol. C-21, No. 12, December 1972, pp. 1449–1451.

7. SHIVA, S. G., and H. T. NAGLE, JR., "Computer Aided Design of Digital Networks," Parts 1, 2, and 3, *Electronic Design*, Vol. 22, 1974 (submitted for publication).

PROBLEMS

4.1. Minimize the following functions in two-level sum of product form:
   (a) $f(A, B, C) = \sum m(1, 2, 3, 6)$.
   (b) $f(A, B, C, D) = \sum m(0, 1, 2, 6, 8, 9, 11, 15) + d(5, 10)$.
   (c) $f(A, B, C, D) = \sum m(0, 2, 3, 5, 7, 8, 12, 15) + d(4, 10, 13)$.
   (d) $f(A, B, C, D) = \sum m(0, 1, 2, 6, 7, 11, 12, 14) + d(4, 13, 15)$.
   (e) $f(A, B, C, D) = \sum m(0, 2, 7, 8, 9, 10, 12, 13) + d(3)$.

4.2. Find a minimum two-level NAND implementation for the following functions:
   (a) $f(A, B, C, D, E) = \sum m(0, 2, 3, 12, 14, 15, 17, 20, 21, 22, 23, 24, 25, 26,$
       $27, 29) + d(13, 18, 30)$.
   (b) $f(A, B, C, D, E) = \sum m(0, 1, 2, 3, 7, 8, 12, 14, 17, 18, 20, 21)$
       $+ d(23, 24, 25, 29, 30, 31)$.
   (c) $f(A, B, C, D, E) = \sum m(0, 1, 2, 3, 5, 7, 8, 10, 16, 18, 21, 23, 24, 25, 26,$
       $29, 30, 31)$.
   (d) $f(A, B, C, D, E) = \sum m(0, 2, 3, 7, 9, 15, 18)$.

4.3. Find a minimum two-level NOR implementation for the following functions:
   (a) $f(A, B, C, D, E) = \sum m(1, 4, 7, 14, 17, 20, 21, 22, 23)$
       $+ d(0, 3, 6, 19, 30)$.
   (b) $f(A, B, C, D, E) = \sum m(3, 11, 12, 19, 23, 29) + d(5, 7, 13, 27, 28)$.
   (c) $f(A, B, C, D, E, F) = \sum m(1, 2, 4, 7, 9, 12, 13, 14, 25, 27, 30, 35, 37, 40,$
       $41, 42, 55, 64) + d(10, 18, 19, 22, 29, 32, 44, 45,$
       $46, 47, 51, 52, 53, 58, 59, 60, 61, 62)$.
   (d) $f(A, B, C, D, E, F) = \sum m(3, 9, 13, 21, 29, 32, 35, 38, 43, 46, 51, 54,$
       $59, 60, 62) + d(1, 5, 7, 19, 25, 31, 48, 56, 63)$.

4.4. Find minimum two-level NAND and NOR realizations for the following switching functions:
   (a) $f(A, B, C, D, E, F) = \sum m(0, 2, 10, 11, 21, 24, 30, 34, 41, 47, 48, 52,$
       $57, 58, 61, 62) + d(1, 8, 18, 28, 38, 43, 51, 56, 63)$.
   (b) $f(A, B, C, D, E, F, G) = \sum m(2, 6, 7, 12, 13, 63, 75, 89, 101, 102, 106,$
       $111, 116, 118, 119, 121, 123, 124, 125, 126)$.
   (c) $f(A, B, C, D, E, F, G) = \sum m(0, 1, 3, 4, 5, 6, 7, 8, 10, 16, 20–38, 58, 62,$
       $90–99, 142, 150–159, 198, 200, 225–229, 240,$
       $241, 242)$.

4.5. Minimize the following functions in two-level sum of products form:
   (a) $f(A, B, C, D, E, F, G, H) = \sum m(0, 1, 2, 3, 9, 10, 12, 15, 19, 21, 25, 38,$
       $39, 47, 48, 52, 60, 71, 75, 130, 131, 149, 170,$
       $171, 210, 255) + d(5, 55, 56, 83, 89, 90, 114,$
       $121, 122, 124, 135, 180, 185, 197, 199, 200)$.
   (b) $f(A, B, C, D, E, F, G, H) = \sum m(0–5, 7, 13, 14, 15, 19, 31, 45, 48, 55,$
       $60, 61, 63, 64, 75, 80, 81, 99, 100, 101, 121,$
       $127, 128, 131, 166, 188–197, 200, 224–228,$
       $231, 245, 254, 255) + d(8, 9, 50–53, 65, 66,$
       $67, 94, 95, 244, 246–253)$.

(c) $f(A, B, C, D, E, F, G, H) = \sum m(0, 2, 4, 8, 9, 10, 23, 53, 68, 96) +$
$d(1, 3, 5, 11, 24, 55, 65, 73, 97, 98)$.

(d) $f(A, B, C, D, E, F, G, H) = \sum m(0, 1, 15, 23, 73, 79, 81, 90, 91, 92, 93,$
$104, 107, 111, 150, 152, 157, 163, 181, 190,$
$195\text{–}198, 211, 220, 230, 231, 244, 255)$
$+ d(4, 6, 7, 10, 25, 29, 40, 42, 50, 55, 70,$
$74, 77, 106, 112, 119, 132, 145, 183, 225)$.

4.6. Expand the following switching functions to minterm list form:

(a) $f(A, B, C, D, E, F) = \bar{A}BE + \bar{B}C\bar{D}F + A\bar{E}\bar{F}$.

(b) $f(A, B, C, D, E, F) = A\bar{B}\bar{E} + B\bar{C}D\bar{F} + \bar{A}EF$.

(c) $f(A, B, C, D, E, F, G, H) = AB + \bar{C}\bar{D} + EF + \bar{G}\bar{H}$.

(d) $f(A, B, C, D, E, F, G, H) = (A + B)(\bar{C} + \bar{D})(E + F)(\bar{G} + \bar{H})$.

4.7. Minimize the following functions in two-level sum of product form:

(a) $f(A, B, C, D, E) = A\bar{B}CD + B\bar{D}E + AC\bar{D}E + \bar{B}C\bar{E} + A\bar{E}$.

(b) $f(A, B, C, D, E, F)$
$= (\bar{A} + \bar{C} + E + F)(B + C + \bar{F})(\bar{B} + D + F)(\bar{A} + B + D + \bar{E} + F)$
$(A + C + \bar{F})$.

5

Special
Topics
in
Combinational
Logic

In Chapters 2, 3, and 4 we have discussed the fundamentals of combinational logic circuit analysis and synthesis. Here we extend the concepts presented earlier and introduce the reader to functional decomposition, NAND/NOR synthesis, multivalued logic, application of read only memories (ROM's), and threshold logic. The special topics are presented independently and may be examined in any sequence.

Functional Decomposition

Introduction

Functional decomposition is basically a process by which a complex switching function is separated or decomposed into a set of smaller functions. In other words, it is a technique for realizing a switching function of n variables by a number of functions with less than n variables. The realization of a complex switching function by a set of smaller functions is very advantageous in devices such as integrated circuits where the use of smaller standard modules can produce an economical design that is easy to troubleshoot.

In the material which follows we shall introduce the basic concepts and ideas of decomposition primarily through examples. The reader interested in the many facets and ramifications of this subject is referred to the works of Ashenhurst [1] and Curtis [2].

Simple Disjunctive Decomposition

Let $f(X) = f(x_1, x_2, \ldots, x_n)$ be a switching function of n-variables. A *simple disjunctive decomposition* of f exists if and only if there exist disjoint subsets, $Y = (y_1, y_2, \ldots, y_i)$ and $Z = (z_1, z_2, \ldots, z_j)$, of X whose union is X and switching functions F_1 and F_2 such that

$$f(X) = F_2(F_1(Y), Z) \tag{5-1}$$

Figure 5.1 illustrates equation (5-1) in diagram form. The variables in Y are called *bound variables*, whereas the variables in Z are referred to as *free variables*.

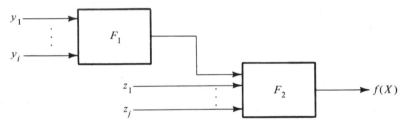

Fig. 5.1   The form of a simple disjunctive decomposition.

To form a simple disjunctive decomposition, we must find a separation of X into Y and Z and also define the functions F_1 and F_2 such that equation (5-1) is satisfied. A simple disjunctive decomposition does not exist for all switching functions.

To aid us in determining if a function can be disjunctively decomposed (and if so what the resultant decomposition is) we employ what is called a partition map or decomposition chart. On this map the free variables are listed down the side and the bound variables are listed across the top. Two typical partition maps for a function of four variables are shown in Fig. 5.2. The partition map is like a K-map with a different ordering for the cell locations. Note however that the cell numbers placed in the partition map are based on the original variable ordering sequence (x_1, x_2, x_3, x_4). The following example will illustrate the use of partition maps for determining a decomposition.

Example.

We want to disjunctively decompose the following function:

$$f(x_1, x_2, x_3, x_4) = \sum m(0, 1, 3, 4, 5, 8, 12, 13)$$

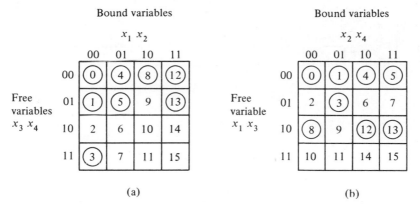

Fig. 5.2 Two typical four-variable partition maps.

Two of the partition maps for this function are shown in Fig. 5.2. A circle around a cell number indicates a minterm of the function.

It will now be shown that the function can be decomposed as follows:

$$f(x_1, x_2, x_3, x_4) = F_2(F_1(x_2, x_4), x_1, x_3)$$

From equation (5-1) it follows that for a given combination of values of the free variables, the function f must be equal to either 0, 1, F_1, or $\bar{F}_1$. This condition cannot be established for the map in Fig. 5.2(a). However, the map in Fig. 5.2(b) readily yields the desired condition if $F_1(\bar{F}_1)$ is defined according to the second row or to the third row.

Defining F_1 by the second row yields

$$F_1(x_2, x_4) = \bar{x}_2 x_4$$

Hence, the function $f(x_1, x_2, x_3, x_4)$ can be written as follows:

$$
\begin{aligned}
f(x_1, x_2, x_3, x_4) &= (1)\,\bar{x}_1\bar{x}_3 + F_1(x_2, x_4)\bar{x}_1 x_3 + \bar{F}_1(x_2, x_4)x_1\bar{x}_3 + (0)\,x_1 x_3 \\
&= \bar{x}_1\bar{x}_3 + (\bar{x}_2 x_4)\bar{x}_1 x_3 + (\overline{\bar{x}_2 x_4})x_1\bar{x}_3 \\
&= F_2(F_1(x_2, x_4), x_1, x_3)
\end{aligned}
$$

Figure 5.3 shows a realization of f based on the above decomposition.

The procedure outlined in the previous example is used in general to accomplish the decomposition; i.e., examine partition maps for rows that correspond only to 0, 1, F_1, or $\bar{F}_1$. Our search for the proper row conditions can be expedited by looking at what is called *column multiplicity*. This term is defined as the number of distinct column patterns in the partition map. It can be shown that a simple disjunctive decomposition exists if and only if the column multiplicity is less than or equal to two. Examination of Fig. 5.2(b) indicates that only two different column patterns are present in the partition map and hence the function plotted can be disjunctively decomposed (as we have just seen).

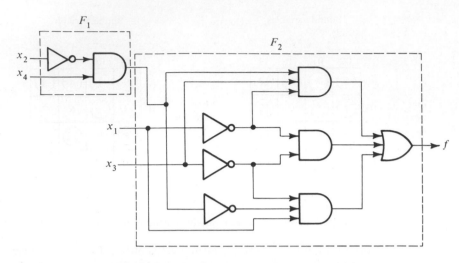

Fig. 5.3   Realization of $f(x_1, x_2, x_3, x_4) = \Sigma\, m(0, 1, 3, 4, 5, 8, 12, 13)$.

The following example will not only serve to illustrate the complete decomposition procedure but will also serve to demonstrate some of the other salient features of the analysis.

Example.

We will now try to find a simple disjunctive decomposition for the function

$$f(x_1, x_2, x_3, x_4) = \sum m(0, 1, 2, 7, 10, 11, 12, 13)$$

All the partition maps for this function for which the number of bound variables is greater than or equal to two are shown in Fig. 5.4. Note that if the number of bound variables is less than two the decomposition would be trivial. Note also that for completeness three maps in addition to those shown in Fig. 5.4 are required. However, if in the analysis we also view the last three maps sideways (i.e., rotate them 90° thus interchanging the free and bound variables), then all possible combinations of two and three bound variables are exhibited by the maps.

A close examination of the partition maps indicates that only the map in Fig. 5.4(b) has a column multiplicity of two or less. Therefore this map can be used to obtain a simple disjunctive decomposition of the form

$$f(x_1, x_2, x_3, x_4) = F_2(F_1(x_1, x_3, x_4), x_2)$$

Choosing the first row of the partition map as $F_1(x_1, x_3, x_4)$ then

$$f(x_1, x_2, x_3, x_4) = \bar{x}_2 F_1(x_1, x_3, x_4) + x_2 \bar{F}_1(x_1, x_3, x_4)$$

where

$$F_1(x_1, x_3, x_4) = \bar{x}_1\bar{x}_3 + x_3\bar{x}_4 + x_1 x_3.$$

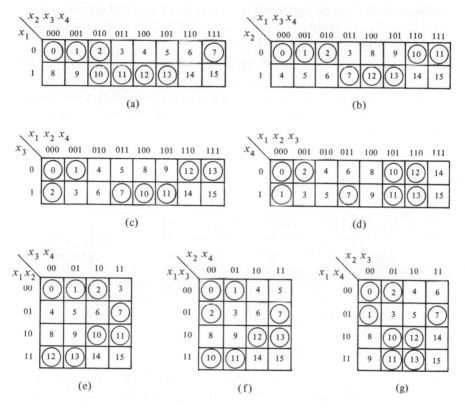

Fig. 5.4 Partition maps for $f(x_1, x_2, x_3, x_4) = \Sigma \, m \, (0, 1, 2, 7, 10, 11, 12, 13)$.

Using either Boolean algebra or the K-map we can easily show that the above function is equivalent to the original one.

Functions with don't cares can also be decomposed. We simply designate the don't cares on the partition map by a line through the appropriate numbers and then selectively circle the don't cares that will yield a column multiplicity of two or less.

Simple Nondisjunctive Decomposition

Switching functions that cannot be decomposed in the simple disjunctive form can sometimes be written in a form known as a simple nondisjunctive decomposition. We will consider only the definition of this form here and refer the interested reader to the references for further discussion of the subject.

Let $f(X) = f(x_1, x_2, \ldots, x_n)$ be a switching function of n-variables. A *simple nondisjunctive decomposition* of f exists if and only if there exist subsets $Y_1 = (y_1, \ldots, y_i)$ and $Y_2 = (y_{i-k}, \ldots, y_n)$, $i > k \geq 1$, of X whose union is X and switching functions F_1 and F_2 such that

$$f(X) = F_2(F_1(Y_1), Y_2) \tag{5-2}$$

Figure 5.5 shows equation (5-2) in diagram form.

The observant reader will note that the simple nondisjunctive decomposition is a generalization of the simple disjunctive decomposition where the subsets of X are not required to be disjoint.

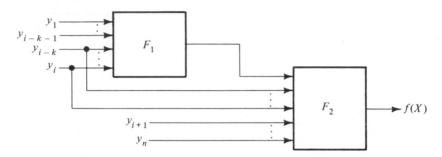

Fig. 5.5   The form of a simple nondisjunctive decomposition.

Complex Decompositions

A complex decomposition is merely many simple decompositions on a single function. In other words, once a simple decomposition has been realized, the decomposed function should be remapped. If this remapped function can be decomposed again, then a complex decomposition has been achieved. This procedure should be repeated until no further decompositions can be realized.

There are several forms of complex decompositions. A *multiple* decomposition occurs when all previous decompositions are in the set of free variables. If all previous decompositions are in the set of bound variables, then an *iterative* decomposition results. Both multiple and iterative decompositions can be either disjunctive or nondisjunctive. Although we will not treat the subject of complex decompositions here, the reader can find a discussion of this subject in the references cited earlier.

Hardware Reduction Through Decomposition

In addition to the advantages listed earlier for decomposition we add the fact that in many cases decomposition results in a reduction in the amount of hardware required to realize a Boolean function. This reduction in general becomes significant when the order of the function is large.

The performance index for hardware reduction includes the number of gates and the number of inputs to gates. The following example provides an indication of the reduction in hardware that can be achieved through decomposition. For a function of higher order the difference would be even more striking.

Example.

Consider the following Boolean function:

$$f(x_1, x_2, x_3, x_4, x_5) = \sum m(0, 2, 5, 7, 12, 14, 17, 19, 20, 22, 29, 31)$$

A viable partition map for this example is shown in Fig. 5.6. The simple disjunctive decomposition is described by the equations

$$F_1(x_1, x_5) = \bar{x}_1 x_5 + x_1 \bar{x}_5$$

$$F_2(F_1, x_2, x_3, x_4) = \bar{x}_2 \bar{x}_3 \bar{F}_1 + \bar{x}_2 x_3 F_1 + x_2 x_3 \bar{F}_1$$

This realization requires 3 two-input NANDS, 4 three-input NANDS, 5 inverters, and 23 inputs to gates. Minimizing this function in the standard form via the K-map leads to the following hardware requirements: 6 four-input NANDS, 1 six-input NAND, 4 inverters, and 34 inputs to gates.

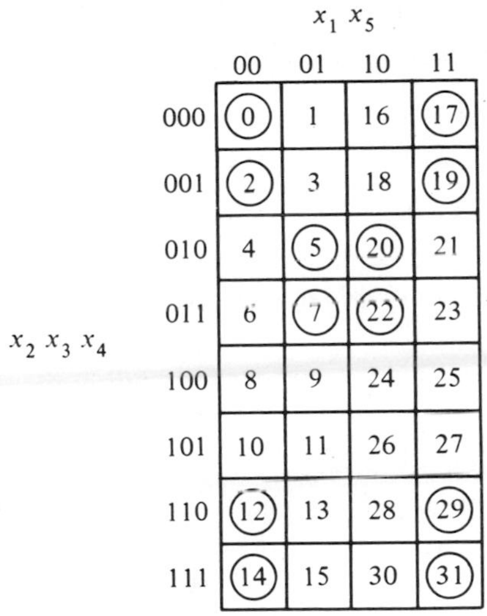

$$x_1\, x_5$$

$x_2\, x_3\, x_4$	00	01	10	11
000	⓪	1	16	⑰
001	②	3	18	⑲
010	4	⑤	⑳	21
011	6	⑦	㉒	23
100	8	9	24	25
101	10	11	26	27
110	⑫	13	28	㉙
111	⑭	15	30	㉛

Fig. 5.6 Partition map for the function $f(x_1, x_2, x_3, x_4, x_5) = \sum m(0, 2, 5, 7, 12, 14, 17, 19, 20, 22, 29, 31)$.

NAND and NOR Synthesis

Introduction

In this section we shall discuss NAND and NOR synthesis and present three techniques by which a Boolean function can be realized in either NAND or NOR form. The three techniques which will be employed are the double complement technique, the transform method, and the map factoring approach.

Although NAND and NOR synthesis techniques can be somewhat complex, especially for multilevel logic functions, they are important for a number of reasons. In general, NAND and NOR logic is more economical. NAND and NOR are each logically complete, and hence any Boolean function can be realized with only NAND and NOR gates. This property is especially important in the manufacture of integrated circuits (IC's) employing large scale integration (LSI). These IC chips may contain thousands of NAND or NOR gates which are later interconnected to realize particular Boolean functions.

NAND and NOR logic is more flexible to implement. For example, NAND and NOR gates contain built-in amplification compared to AND and OR gates, which can be passive devices. In addition, any Boolean expression can be realized with three-level NAND or NOR logic with uncomplemented input variables. The three-level design minimizes the amount of delay through the circuit, and the use of only uncomplemented inputs minimizes the number of input signal lines.

With these basic facts in mind we now attack the synthesis process for both the NAND and NOR logic. Our objective will be to implement the Boolean expressions with a minimum amount of hardware.

NAND Synthesis

Double complement method. The simplest method of realizing a Boolean function with NAND gates is the double complement technique. This technique applies involution and then De Morgan's theorem to a Boolean function in sum of products (SP) form. The resulting expression can be directly realized with only NAND gates. Since this method was presented in Chapter 2, it will not be elaborated here. The usefulness of this technique lies in its simplicity; however, the resulting circuit is not guaranteed to be in a minimal form.

Transform method. An extension of the previous technique the transform method is more versatile and in general provides a better opportunity to achieve a minimal circuit.

In subsequent material we shall be referring to the number of gating levels in a circuit. Figure 5.7(a) illustrates the manner in which we label gate levels.

As a prelude to the transform method, consider the following example.

Example.

We want to realize the following function using both AND/OR and NAND logic:

$$f(A, B, C, D, E, F) = (\bar{A} + \bar{B})C + (\bar{D} + \bar{E})F$$

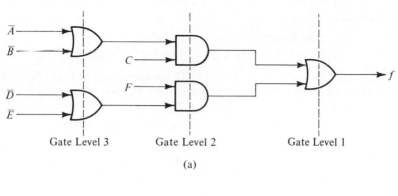

Gate Level 3   Gate Level 2   Gate Level 1

(a)

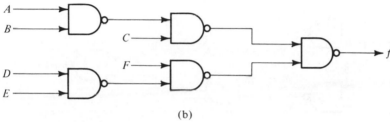

(b)

Fig. 5.7 Equivalent forms for $f(A, B, C, D, E) = (\bar{A} + \bar{B})C + (\bar{D} + \bar{E})F$: (a) OR-AND-OR network form; (b) NAND network form.

The function can be directly realized in AND/OR logic as shown in Fig. 5.7(a). Using the double complement method the above function can be transformed to NAND form and the resulting circuit is shown in Fig. 5.7(b).

An examination of Fig. 5.7 indicates that the OR-AND-OR form transforms directly to NAND form by replacing all gates with NAND gates and complementing the input variables to odd levels of gating.

In view of the above discussion the rules for the transform method for NAND synthesis are

RULE 1. Factor the Boolean expression into an SP form so that OR gates lie on the odd levels of gating and AND gates lie on the even levels. Attempt to achieve a form in which the uncomplemented variables enter even levels of gating and the complemented variables enter odd levels of gating.

RULE 2. Transform the AND/OR circuit to NAND form by replacing all gates with NAND gates and complementing the input variables on all odd gate levels.

The example which follows illustrates not only the use of the rules but also one of the algebraic tricks which can be employed to either juggle the Boolean function into a viable form or to reduce the amount of hardware required to implement the function.

Example.

Consider the following Boolean expression:

$$f(A, B, C, D) = (\bar{A} + \bar{B})C + (\bar{A} + \bar{C})B$$

This function can be realized in NAND form as shown in Fig. 5.8(a). However, if we expand the function through the addition of redundant literals, we obtain

$$f(A, B, C, D) = (\bar{A} + \bar{B} + \bar{C})C + (\bar{A} + \bar{B} + \bar{C})B$$

The realization of this function in NAND form is shown in Fig. 5.8(b). Hence, through the addition of redundant terms we have achieved another NAND realization with one less gate.

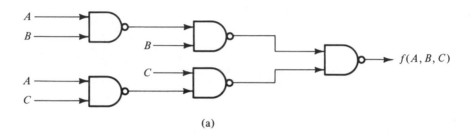

(a)

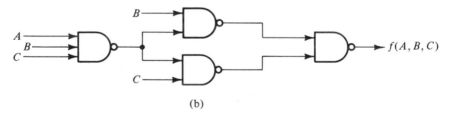

(b)

Fig. 5.8 Equivalent NAND forms.

Other viable tricks involve performing a partial multiplication on the function or an application of the associate law of Boolean algebra. Each of these techniques helps to manipulate the original function into a form such that the application of the transform yields a circuit which is simpler than the original one.

Although the application of these tricks may appear to be simple guesswork, the individual who is very experienced in Boolean algebra manipulation will encounter little difficulty in spotting the application of these techniques in NAND synthesis.

Map factoring. Map factoring is a graphical technique employing the K-map which provides a convenient means of deriving a NAND or NOR realization of a Boolean function. Although the method is straightforward, only through experience can one consistently derive minimum realizations.

The important ideas which form the basis of the map factoring technique for NAND synthesis will now be introduced.

The literals entering an even gate level appear at the output as 1's of the function, as shown in Fig. 5.9(a). Literals entering an odd gate level appear at the output as 0's of the function, as shown in Fig. 5.9(b).

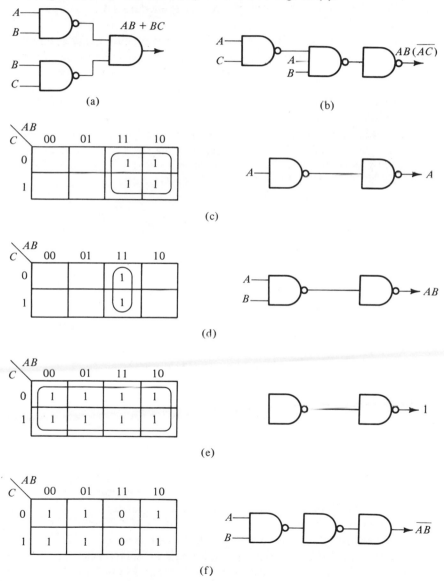

Fig. 5.9 Basic properties of map factoring.

We shall be concerned with what we call loops on the map, and we note that for a function of at least one variable a gate with a single literal input loops half of the map as illustrated in Fig. 5.9(c). In a similar manner for a function of at least two variables, a gate with an input of two literals will loop one-fourth of the map, as shown in Fig. 5.9(d). A less obvious but very important fact is that a gate with no input literals will loop the entire map. As an aid to understanding this point the reader is encouraged to compare Fig. 5.9(e) and (f).

Another basic principle in map factoring is that we can *inhibit* one region on the map from another region by an appropriate interconnection of gates. This fact is illustrated by the following example.

Example.

Consider the gate structure and corresponding maps shown in Fig. 5.10. Note that the loop represented by the input literal to gate 2 (i.e., *A*) is inhibited at the input to gate 2 by the loop representing the input literals to gate 1 (i.e., *AC*), as shown in Fig. 5.10(b), resulting in the loop shown in Fig. 5.10(c).

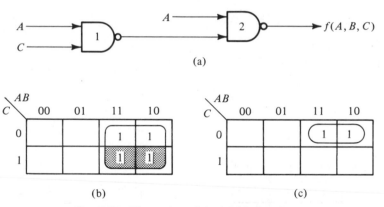

Fig. 5.10   Illustration of the inhibit function.

As can be seen in the previous example the word *loop* is used as a synonym for the phrase "area represented by the inputs." Hence, in general we say that the area represented by the input literals to gate 2 is inhibited at the input to gate 2 by the intersection of the areas representing the inputs to gate 1 and the inputs to gate 2, provided the output of gate 1 is connected as an input to gate 2. The previous example is a direct illustration of this point.

One other important term must be defined before we begin NAND synthesis. A *permissible loop* on the map is a loop that can be formed by employing only uncomplemented literals with or without inhibitions. The set of permissible loops for a two-variable function are shown in Fig. 5.11.

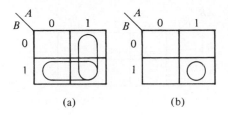

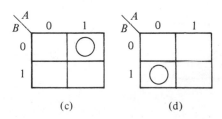

Fig. 5.11 Permissible loops for a 2-variable function: (a) A and B; (b) AB; (c) A inhibited by B, A inhibited by AB; (d) B inhibited by A, B inhibited by AB.

We now have the background to proceed with NAND synthesis by map factoring.

Example.

We want to synthesize the following function with NAND logic:

$$f(A, B, C) = \sum m(1, 4, 6)$$

A plot of this function on the map is shown in Fig. 5.12(a). Minterms 4 and 6 are generated via the technique shown in Fig. 5.12(b). Minterm 1 is obtained by the procedure shown in Fig. 5.12(c). Hence, the complete NAND realization is shown in Fig. 5.12(d). Note that the direct realization of this function with uncomplemented inputs requires six gates. The reader should compare this final step with that of the analysis example presented earlier which illustrates that the output function is actually the input to the gates on level 2.

NOR Synthesis

Double complement method. As in NAND synthesis, the double complement method can be applied in NOR synthesis also. In Chapter 2, it was shown that the double complement applied to a Boolean function in product of sums (PS) form leads directly to a NOR realization. Although this method is applicable to simple two-level logic expressions, special techniques are required for more complex functions.

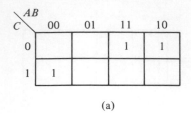

(a)

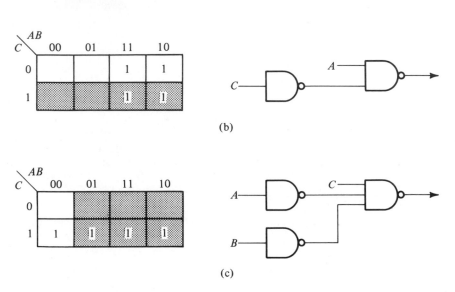

(b)

(c)

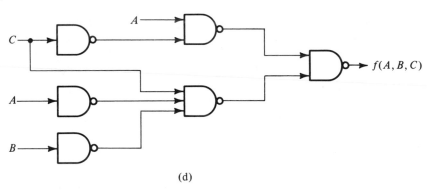

(d)

Fig. 5.12   NAND synthesis of the function $f(A, B, C) = \Sigma\, m(1,\ 4, 6)$.

Transform method. The transform method for NOR synthesis is closely related to that described earlier for NAND synthesis. The rules for NOR synthesis are

RULE 1. Factor the Boolean expression into a PS form with AND gates on odd levels and OR gates on even levels. Attempt to achieve a form in which the uncomplemented variables enter even levels of gating and the complemented variables enter odd levels of gating.

RULE 2. Transform the AND/OR circuit to NOR form by replacing all gates with NOR gates and complementing the input variables on all odd gate levels.

The following example illustrates the use of one of the algebraic tricks applicable to NOR synthesis.

Example.

Suppose we are given the following function to be realized in NOR form:

$$f(A, B, C, D) = (AB + \bar{C}\bar{D})$$

Although this function is not in a standard NOR form, we can employ the distributive law to achieve the proper format, i.e.,

$$f(A, B, C, D) = (AB + \bar{C})(AB + \bar{D})$$

This form will place complemented variables on even levels of gating; hence, instead we apply the distributive law such that

$$f(A, B, C, D) = (\bar{C}\bar{D} + A)(\bar{C}\bar{D} + B)$$

The resulting network is shown in Fig. 5.13.

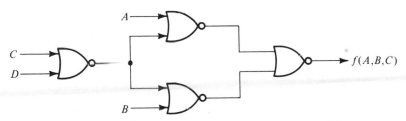

Fig. 5.13 NOR network for $f(A, B, C, D) = AB + \bar{C}\bar{D}$.

Map factoring. A NOR realization with map factoring basically follows the same procedure presented earlier for NAND synthesis with the exception that we associate zeroes with uncomplemented literals and we loop all regions of the map where the function is equal to zero. The following example will illustrate the method.

Example.

The NOR realization for the function

$$f(A, B, C) = \prod M(1, 2, 5, 7)$$

is derived in Fig. 5.14.

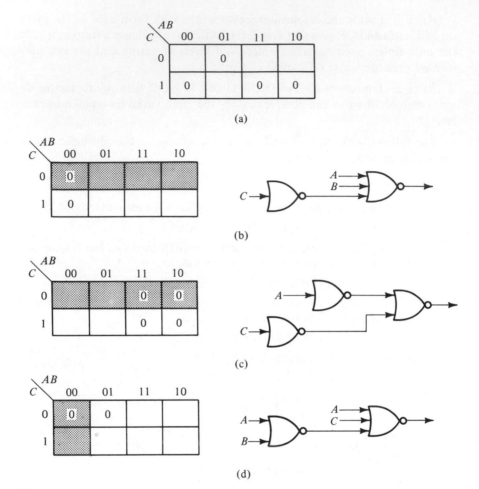

(a)

(b)

(c)

(d)

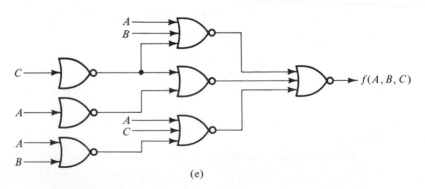

(e)

Fig. 5.14 NOR realization for $f(A, B, C) = \Pi\, M(1, 2, 5, 7)$.

In addition to the approach just presented, a NOR realization can also be derived via a NAND realization. A NAND gate realization for the dual of a function $f(X)$ is first obtained and then the NAND gates are replaced with NOR gates; the resulting circuit realizes the function $f(X)$.

This concludes our presentation of NAND and NOR synthesis. The interested reader is referred to references [3] and [4] for further information. A particularly attractive method for finding minimal three-level NAND realizations is presented in [5].

Multivalued Logic

In all our past discussions all switching functions and logic gates have been based on the binary number system. Each signal line carries only two items of information. However, if one generalizes the concept of a switching function to allow each signal line to have N values, then an N-valued logic system is established. An N-valued logic system is also said to be a *multivalued logic* system for $N \geq 2$.

The Algebra

Many different algebras for multivalued logic functions have been proposed [6–10], the most notable being the original one by Post [6]. The algebra presented herein is an extension of the Postian algebra [11]; it is defined by the operators

$$\text{AND:} \quad A \cdot B = \min(A, B)$$

$$\text{OR:} \quad A + B = \max(A, B)$$

$$\text{CYCLE:} \quad A^{\overset{\rightarrow B}{}} = A \text{ plus } B \,(\text{mod } N)$$

$$\text{COMPLEMENT:} \quad \bar{A} = P \text{ minus } A \text{ where } P = N \text{ minus } 1$$

In these definitions, N is the base of the algebra. Each of the operators is defined for the general case where $N = $ any integer ≥ 2. The AND, OR, and CYCLE operators are identical to those defined by Post [6] and in themselves constitute the Postian system of multivalued algebra. The algebra presented herein is therefore the Postian algebra modified by the addition of the COMPLEMENT operator.

As the Postian algebra is known to be sufficient to represent all N-valued functions and is included in this algebra, this algebra must also be sufficient to represent all functions of N values.

The algebra thus defined obeys several basic relations as previously presented by Post [6] and Smith [7] and other relations dependent on the COMPLEMENT operator. The theorems presented below are valid for any base $N \geq 2$. The identity elements are represented by 0 and P where $P = N - 1$.

Theorem 1. Identity elements

(a) $x + 0 = x$.

(b) $x \cdot P = x$.

Theorem 2. Identity elements

(a) $x \cdot 0 = 0$.

(b) $x + P = P$.

Theorem 3. Idempotence

(a) $x \cdot x = x$.

(b) $x + x = x$.

Theorem 4.

(a) $x + \bar{x} \neq P, N > 2, x \neq 0, P$.

(b) $x \cdot \bar{x} \neq 0, N > 2, x \neq 0, P$.

Theorem 5.

(a) $\overset{\to 0}{x} + \overset{\to 1}{x} + \cdots + \overset{\to P}{x} = P$.

(b) $\overset{\to 0}{x} \cdot \overset{\to 1}{x} \cdot \cdots \cdot \overset{\to P}{x} = 0$.

Theorem 6. Involution (COMPLEMENT)

$$\bar{\bar{x}} = x$$

Proof.

$$\bar{x} = P - x$$
$$\bar{\bar{x}} = P - \bar{x}$$
$$= P - (P - x)$$
$$= P - P + x$$
$$= x$$

Theorem 7. Involution (CYCLE)

$$\overset{\to N}{x} = x$$

Theorem 8. Absorption

(a) $x + (x \cdot y) = x$.

(b) $x \cdot (x + y) = x$.

Theorem 9. Commutative

(a) $x + y = y + x$.

(b) $x \cdot y = y \cdot x$.

Theorem 10. Associative

(a) $x + (y + z) = (x + y) + z$.

(b) $x \cdot (y \cdot z) = (x \cdot y) \cdot z$.

Theorem 11. Distributive

(a) $x + (y \cdot z) = (x + y) \cdot (x + z)$.
(b) $x \cdot (y + z) = x \cdot y + x \cdot z$.

Theorem 12. De Morgan's law

(a) $\bar{x} + \bar{y} = \overline{x \cdot y}$.
(b) $\bar{x} \cdot \bar{y} = \overline{x + y}$.

Proof.

(a) $\bar{x} + \bar{y} = \max[\bar{x}, \bar{y}]$
$= \max[P - x, P - y]$
$= P - \min[x, y]$
$= P - x \cdot y$
$= \overline{x \cdot y}$

(b) $\bar{x} \cdot \bar{y} = \min[\bar{x}, \bar{y}]$
$= \min[P - x, P - y]$
$= P - \max[x, y]$
$= \overline{x + y}$.

Theorem 13.

$$\overline{\overset{\to a}{x}} = \bar{x}^{\overset{\to (N-a)}{}}, \quad 0 \le a \le P$$

Proof.

$$\overline{\overset{\to a}{x}} = P - \overset{\to a}{x}$$
$$= P - (x + a), \qquad \mod N$$
$$= P - x - a, \qquad \mod N$$
$$= P - x + N - a, \qquad \mod N$$
$$= (P - x) + (N - a), \quad \mod N$$
$$= \bar{x} + (N - a), \qquad \mod N$$
$$= \bar{x}^{\,(N-a)}$$

For the special case of $N = 2$, both the CYCLE operation $\overset{\to P}{x}$ and the multivalued COMPLEMENT operation $\bar{x}$ are equivalent to the COMPLEMENT operation of binary Boolean algebra. Of those properties attributed in the binary Boolean algebra to the COMPLEMENT operator, when generalized to multivalued algebra, some are properties of the CYCLE operator and some are properties of the multivalued COMPLEMENT operator. For $N > 2$, however, neither CYCLE nor COMPLEMENT is able to assume all the properties of the binary COMPLEMENT operator. For example, as shown in Theorem 4, a multivalued variable combined with its complement under either the AND or OR operator does not result in an identity element. As shown in Theorem 5, the CYCLE operator does obey this basic concept. On the other hand, as shown in Theorem 12 as presented by Su and Sarris [12], the multivalued COMPLEMENT operator satisfies De Morgan's laws.

Representation of Functions

Functions of one or more N-valued variables may be represented in a truth table or map form just as in the binary case; see Fig. 5.15. Functions may also be represented algebraically in both canonical and reduced form as either a product of sums or as a sum of products.

A	B	$F(A,B)$
0	0	1
0	1	2
0	2	0
1	0	1
1	1	1
1	2	1
2	0	0
2	1	0
2	2	1

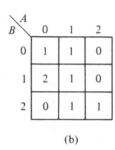

(a)   (b)

Fig. 5.15   A function of two 3-valued variables: (a) truth table; (b) map.

A canonical sum term of K variables ($K \geq 1$) is defined as a term whose truth table contains one nonzero value, and a canonical product term is defined as a term whose truth table contains only one value not equal to the identity element P. Any function may therefore be represented as a logical sum of canonical sum terms or as a logical product of canonical product terms. Furthermore, a canonical sum term of K variables may be represented as a logical product of K canonical sum terms of a single variable and a canonical product term as a logical sum of K canonical product terms of a single variable. Thus the canonical forms are

$$f(x_1, \ldots, x_K) = \sum_F \prod_{i=1}^{K} x_i^*$$

$$f(x_1, \ldots, x_K) = \prod_F \sum_{i=1}^{K} x_i^{**}$$

where x^* and x_i^{**} represent, respectively, a canonical sum term and a canonical product term of x_i. Thus the canonical sum terms and the canonical product terms are similar to the binary minterms and maxterms. However, for $N \geq 3$ the canonical terms of a single variable themselves involve a logical sum or product which may also be operated on by the CYCLE operator. For this reason, functions may not be algebraically minimized from the canonical form in this algebra at its present state of development.

Minimization is possible, however, using a map-oriented process patterned after that presented by Smith [7]. The following definitions apply to this process:

1. *Literal.* A literal is one appearance of a variable.
2. *Permutation.* A literal or group of literals is said to be permuted if it is operated on by either the CYCLE or COMPLEMENT operator or both.
3. *Term.* A term is a literal or any group of literals combined under the AND or OR operators. Any logical product or sum of terms or any permutation of a term is also a term.
4. *Implicant.* In the sum of products form, a term implies (is an implicant of) a function if its value in every position of the truth table is less than or equal to the corresponding value of the function. In the product of sums form, the value of the implicant must be greater than or equal to the value of the function in every position of the truth table.
5. *Cost.* Any estimate of the cost of a function must be both simple to apply and a reasonably accurate estimate of the expense of implementing the function. The cost estimate used herein will be the total number of AND and OR operators required regardless of permutations plus the number of permutations of a literal.
6. *Cover.* A term is said to cover some portion of a function if it implies the function, and its value in some position of the truth table is equal to that of the function.
7. *Prime implicant.* An implicant of a function is said to be a prime implicant of that function if it covers some portion S of the function and there exists no other term of lower cost which also covers S.

Since the term *prime implicant* is defined for both the sum of products and product of sums forms, any function may be represented as either a sum of prime implicants or a product of prime implicants. A prime implicant of K variables may also be represented as a sum or a product of K or fewer terms of one variable or some permutation thereof. These terms of one variable may not be canonical terms. To evaluate the cost of the prime implicants, it is necessary to know the cost of each function of a single variable. These functions are listed along with their minimum algebraic form and cost in Fig. 5.16 for $N = 2$ and $N = 3$, respectively. The canonical sum and product terms are indicated in these tables by one and two asterisks, respectively. The column labeled minimum form gives the structure of the function within some permutation of the CYCLE operator. The column labeled CYCLE gives the permutation.

The minimization process then consists of finding all prime implicants of a function and selecting the lowest cost subset of these which covers the function. The first step in the determination of the minimal subset of prime

x	Logic Value		Canonical Form	Minimum Form	Cost
	0	1			
f_0	0	0		0	0
f_1	0	1	*, **	x	0
f_2	1	0	*, **	$\bar{x}$	1
f_3	1	1		1	0

(a)

x	0	1	2	Canonical Form	Minimum Form	Cycle	Cost
f_0	0	0	0		0		0
f_1	0	0	1	*	$1 + x$	2	1
f_2	0	0	2	*	$1 \cdot \bar{x}$	2	2
f_3	0	1	0	*	$1 + \vec{x}^1$	2	2
f_4	0	1	1		$1 \cdot x$		1
f_5	0	1	2		x		0
f_6	0	2	0	*	$1 \cdot \vec{x}^2$	2	2
f_7	0	2	1		$\bar{x}$	1	1
f_8	0	2	2	**	$1 + \bar{x}$	1	2
f_9	1	0	0	*	$1 + \bar{x}$	2	2
f_{10}	1	0	1		$1 \cdot \vec{x}^2$		2
f_{11}	1	0	2		$\bar{x}$	2	1
f_{12}	1	1	0		$1 \cdot \bar{x}$		2
f_{13}	1	1	1		1		0
f_{14}	1	1	2		$1 + x$		1
f_{15}	1	2	0		x	1	1
f_{16}	1	2	1		$1 + \vec{x}^1$		2
f_{17}	1	2	2	**	$1 \cdot x$	1	1
f_{18}	2	0	0	*	$1 \cdot x$	2	1
f_{19}	2	0	1		x	2	1
f_{20}	2	0	2	**	$1 + \vec{x}^1$	1	2
f_{21}	2	1	0		$\bar{x}$		1
f_{22}	2	1	1		$1 + \bar{x}$		2
f_{23}	2	1	2	**	$1 \cdot \vec{x}^2$	1	2
f_{24}	2	2	0	**	$1 + x$	1	1
f_{25}	2	2	1	**	$1 \cdot \bar{x}$	1	2
f_{26}	2	2	2		2		0

(b)

Fig. 5.16 Functions of a single variable: (a) functions of one 2-valued variable; (b) functions of one 3-valued variable.

implicants is to select all essential prime implicants. If some portion of the function is covered by only one prime implicant, that prime implicant is said to be essential. The method of Chapter 3 may be used to assist in the selection of the lowest cost subset of prime implicants to cover the remainder of the function.

The method is demonstrated below for the sum of products and product of sums forms for the function of Fig. 5.15.

Example.

Find a sum of products form for the function

$$A:\quad 000 \quad 111 \quad 222$$
$$B:\quad 012 \quad 012 \quad 012$$

					Cost
$f(A, B)$:	120	111	002		
PI$_1$:	120	110	000	$f_{21}(A) \cdot f_{15}(B) = \bar{A} \cdot \overset{\rightarrow 1}{B}$	3
PI$_2$:	000	001	001	$f_5(A) \cdot f_1(B) = A \cdot \overset{\longrightarrow 2}{(1 + B)}$	2
PI$_3$:	000	111	000	$f_3(A) = (1 + \overset{\rightarrow 1}{A})^2$	2
PI$_4$:	000	001	002	$f_5(A) \cdot f_2(B) = A \cdot \overset{\longrightarrow 2}{(1 \cdot \bar{B})}$	3
	↑x	xxx	↑		

Prime implicants 1 and 4 are essential and cover the function. Therefore,

$$f(A, B) = \bar{A} \cdot \overset{\rightarrow 1}{B} + A \cdot \overset{\longrightarrow 2}{(1 \cdot \bar{B})}$$

Example.

Find a product of sums form for the function

					Cost
$f(A, B)$:	120	111	002		
PI$_1$:	120	121	222	$f_5(A) + f_{15}(B) = A + \overset{\rightarrow 1}{B}$	2
PI$_2$:	222	112	002	$f_{21}(A) + f_2(B) = \bar{A} + \overset{\longrightarrow 2}{1 \cdot \bar{B}}$	4
PI$_3$:	222	112	012	$f_{21}(A) + f_5(B) = \bar{A} + B$	2
PI$_4$:	222	112	102	$f_{21}(A) + f_{11}(B) = \bar{A} + \overset{^,2}{\underset{\rightarrow 1}{B}}$	3
PI$_5$:	222	111	222	$f_{23}(A) = 1 \cdot \overset{\rightarrow 2}{A}$	2
PI$_6$:	122	122	122	$f_{17}(B) = 1 \cdot \overset{\rightarrow 1}{B}$	1
PI$_7$:	122	122	022	$f_{12}(A) + f_8(B) = 1 \cdot \bar{A} + \overset{\longrightarrow 1}{(1 + \bar{B})}$	5
	x↑	x x			

The single 0 value for $f(A, B)$ must be covered by PI$_1$. The remaining terms may be selected using the covering procedure of Chapter 3; observe that PI$_2$ covers all remaining nontrivial values. The resulting equation is

$$f(A, B) = (A + \overset{\rightarrow 1}{B}) \cdot [\bar{A} + \overset{\longrightarrow 2}{(1 \cdot \bar{B})}]$$

This completes our introduction to multivalued logic. The reader should investigate the listed references for further theory and applications of multi-valued logic.

Read Only Memory Logic

Introduction

The ROM is by definition a read only memory device. In fact, we shall see in the following material that a ROM device simply generates a specific set of output signals for a given combination of input signals. The input-output relationship is a permanent one which is established by the physical structure of the device. Since the output for any input is independent of the past history of the device, the ROM is a random access memory which acts like a combinational logic network.

In the sections which follow we shall present the basic structure of the ROM and some of its many applications.

The Basic ROM

The ROM is basically a two-port network. In its simplest form, as shown in Fig. 5.17, it consists of an $N \times M$ matrix of elements which interconnect the decoded data input lines to the data output lines. The specific memory requirements determine the matrix dimensions, and in general M can be less than, equal to, or greater than N. The size of the ROM is equal to the number of words ($N = 2^n$) multiplied by the length of the words (M); n is the number

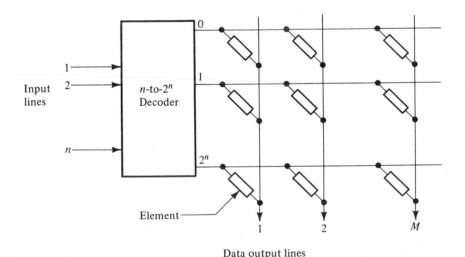

Data output lines

Fig. 5.17   Basic ROM structure.

of coded input lines. (See decoders in Chapter 11.) Typical sizes are 256 bits and 4,096 bits, although much larger units are in use.

The type of memory depends on the type of element, and the choice of the type of element depends on many factors such as cost, speed, reliability, flexibility, and the like. The coupling element, which interconnects the input and output lines, will store either a 1 or a 0 and thus it provides the memory. These coupling elements range from simple passive devices to magnetic, optical, and semiconductor devices.

In a standard ROM the elements are not modified. However, if the ROM is changed so that the elements may be repetitively modified, the resulting device is called a read mostly memory (RMM). In general there is a wide differential between the read time and the write time in a RMM—read time is many orders of magnitude faster than the write time.

ROM's have been in existence for many years. However, only with the advent of LSI, which has produced some radical changes not only in the implementation of memories but also in memory design philosophy, could we begin to realize the full potential of the ROM. LSI provides the mechanism for realizing large ROM's with reasonable size and power constraints.

Applications

There are many uses of ROM's and some of these uses will be discussed in the following material via a number of simple examples.

One of the most basic and useful applications of ROM's is code conversion. To accomplish code conversion using an ROM, all that is required is a truth table which relates the output code word to each possible input code word. The ROM is then programmed directly from the truth table. Off-the-shelf ROM's exist which convert among the following codes: Baudot teletypewriter code, ASCII, EBCDIC, BCD, and the like.

To illustrate the code conversion procedure a simple, although not economically practical, example will be given.

Example.

We wish to use an ROM to convert from binary to Gray code. The truth table for the code conversion is shown in Fig. 5.18(a). The ROM is programmed from the truth table and a block diagram of the ROM indicating the conversion from binary 0111 to Gray code 0100 is shown in Fig. 5.18(b).

Another form of code converter is the look-up table. Tables of such things as trigonometric functions, logarithms, and exponentials can be easily implemented with ROM's. In addition, numerical calculations which can be tabularized such as addition, subtraction, and multiplication, can also be readily implemented with a ROM.

Decimal Number	Binary $B_3 B_2 B_1 B_0$	Gray Code $G_3 G_2 G_1 G_0$
0	0000	0000
1	0001	0001
2	0010	0011
3	0011	0010
4	0100	0110
5	0101	0111
6	0110	0101
7	0111	0100
8	1000	1100
9	1001	1101
10	1010	1111
11	1011	1110
12	1100	1010
13	1101	1011
14	1110	1001
15	1111	1000

(a)

(b)

Fig. 5.18 Binary to Gray code converter: (a) truth table; (b) ROM block diagram.

Example.

The block diagram shown in Fig. 5.19 is a system of ROM'S used to implement an 8-bit by 8-bit high-speed binary multiplier [13]. The ROM's are used as multiplication look-up tables. The partial products generated by the ROM's are then added to yield the final product.

In addition to the many types of code conversion applications, ROM's are also useful in logic design [14].

Example.

Consider the logic function

$$f(A, B, C) = ABC + A\bar{B}\bar{C} + \bar{A}\bar{B}C + \bar{A}BC$$

This function is shown on the K-map in Fig. 5.20(a). The implementation of this function with an ROM would require an 8×1 memory because

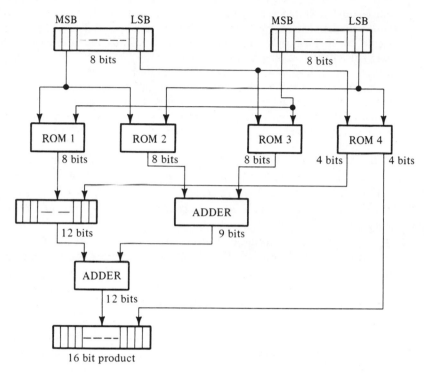

Fig. 5.19 Implementation of a high-speed binary multiplier with ROM's.

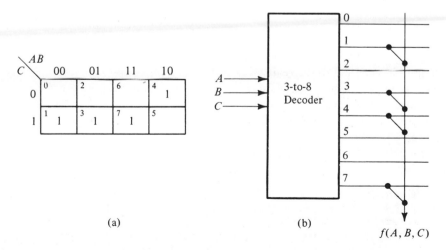

Fig. 5.20 ROM logic realization: (a) K-map; (b) ROM logic.

there are eight possible combinations of three variables in the sum. The minterms would be stored as 1's and the remaining three variable combinations would be stored as 0's. In Fig. 5.20(a) the address of $A\bar{B}\bar{C}$ would be 100 on the map and the corresponding output would be a 1. This same address would be the memory's input for this minterm. Thus, every square on the map has a corresponding bit in the storage array with a coupling element to store a 1 in the locations representing each minterm. The ROM array for this function is shown in Fig. 5.20(b) in a configuration similar to that of Fig. 5.17 for $M = 1$. If any minterm of the function is addressed, the output will be a 1. If any of the other remaining combinations are addressed, then the output will be 0 since there are no coupling elements for these combinations.

Another very useful application of ROM's is in microprogramming. In microprogramming a stored program in memory is used to replace a hardwired control unit. The use of microprogramming will in general reduce the amount of control logic, provide easy use of special instructions, and reduce debugging and fault location time [15].

ROM's are used in communication systems. For example, multiplexers and demultiplexers can be obtained using ROM sequencers. ROM's can also be employed to generate a Hamming single error correcting code by using the information bits as an input address to the ROM, which in turn generates the proper parity bits.

Finally, ROM's can be interconnected in series, parallel, or series-parallel configurations. The usefulness of the ROM is improved significantly through interconnection. Using this technique many functions can be performed with reduced bit requirements and with little, if any, increase in peripheral circuitry.

Threshold Logic

This section will be devoted to a discussion of a logic device known as a threshold gate and to the realization of Boolean functions with such gates. A threshold gate is more powerful from the logical point of view than the more standard gates such as AND, OR, NOT, NAND, and NOR gates. Hence, the number of gates required to realize a given Boolean function is generally fewer when threshold gates are used instead of the standard gates. Disadvantages of the use of threshold gates will be considered later.

Basic Definitions

A *threshold gate* (T-gate) is a logic device with binary-valued inputs $x_1, \ldots, x_n$ and a binary-valued output y. Associated with each input x_i is a real number a_i known as the *weight* or *coefficient* of the input. A real number

T called the threshold is associated with the gate. The output value of a T-gate is given as a function of the input values as follows:

$$y = 1 \quad \text{if and only if} \quad \sum_{i=1}^{n} a_i x_i \geq T$$

$$y = 0 \quad \text{if and only if} \quad \sum_{i=1}^{n} a_i x_i < T \tag{5-3}$$

where the sum and product operations are arithmetic. A T-gate is represented pictorially as shown in Fig. 5.21(a).

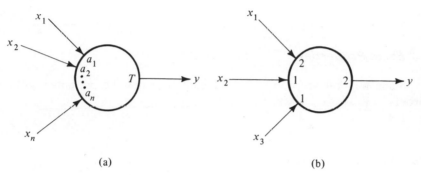

(a)   (b)

Fig. 5.21   The threshold gate: (a) symbol of a general threshold gate; (b) T-gate that realizes $y = x_1 + x_2 x_3$.

The output of a T-gate will be represented in two distinct forms. Clearly, a T-gate realizes a Boolean function. Hence, the output of a T-gate can be represented by a Boolean function as follows:

$$y = f(x_1, \ldots, x_n)$$

An alternative representation is given below:

$$y = \langle A(x_1, \ldots, x_n) \rangle_T \tag{5-4}$$

where $A(x_1, \ldots, x_n) = \sum_{i=1}^{n} a_i x_i$ and is called the *separating function* of the T-gate. Equation (5-4) is called the separating function representation of the gate.

Example.

Consider the T-gate shown in Fig. 5.21(b):

$$y = \langle 2x_1 + x_2 + x_3 \rangle_2$$

The Boolean function realized by the gate can be determined by constructing a truth table as shown in Table 5.1. From the truth table it follows that the following Boolean function is realized by the T-gate:

$$y = x_1 + x_2 x_3$$

TABLE 5.1

$x_1x_2x_3$	Separating Function, $2x_1 + x_2 + x_3$	Relation to $T = 2$	y
000	0	$<$	0
001	1	$<$	0
010	1	$<$	0
011	2	$=$	1
100	2	$=$	1
101	3	$>$	1
110	3	$>$	1
111	4	$>$	1

Basic Properties

Some well-known properties of T-gates will now be presented without proof.

Let

$$y = \left\langle \sum_{i=1}^{n} a_i x_i \right\rangle_T$$

be the output of a T-gate.

1. If $a_1 = a_2 = \cdots = a_n = T$, then y is the Boolean function $x_1 + x_2 + \cdots + x_n$.
2. If $a_1 = a_2 = \cdots = a_n$ and $T = na_1$, then y is the Boolean function $x_1 x_2 \cdots x_n$.
3. If k is a real number, then

$$y = \left\langle k + \sum_{i=1}^{n} a_i x_i \right\rangle_{k+T}.$$

4. If k is a positive real number, then

$$y = \left\langle k \sum_{i=1}^{n} a_i x_i \right\rangle_{kT}.$$

5. $\bar{y} = \left\langle -\sum_{i=1}^{n} a_i x_i \right\rangle_{-T}.$

6. $y^d = \left\langle \sum_{i=1}^{n} a_i x_i \right\rangle_{\sigma - T}$, where y^d is the dual function of y and $\sigma = \sum_{i=1}^{n} a_i$.

Example.

A T-gate realization of the three-variable OR and the three-variable AND is given below:

$$x_1 + x_2 + x_3 = \langle x_1 + x_2 + x_3 \rangle_1$$
$$x_1 x_2 x_3 = \langle x_1 + x_2 + x_3 \rangle_3$$

Property 3 is useful for changing the signs of coefficients. The following example illustrates this procedure.

Example.

A Boolean function has the T-gate realization

$$y = \langle -2x_1 - x_2 + x_3 \rangle_{-1}$$

Determine an equivalent realization that requires only positive weights. Observe that $x_i = 1 - \bar{x}_i$. Then

$$
\begin{aligned}
y &= \langle -2(1 - \bar{x}_1) - (1 - \bar{x}_2) + x_3 \rangle_{-1} \\
&= \langle -2 + 2\bar{x}_1 - 1 + \bar{x}_2 + x_3 \rangle_{-1} \\
&= \langle -3 + 2\bar{x}_1 + \bar{x}_2 + x_3 \rangle_{-1} \\
&= \langle 3 - 3 + 2\bar{x}_1 + \bar{x}_2 + x_3 \rangle_{3-1} \\
&= \langle 2\bar{x}_1 + \bar{x}_2 + x_3 \rangle_2
\end{aligned}
$$

Realization of Boolean Functions

Many Boolean functions can be realized by a single T-gate. These functions are called *linearly separable* (ℓ.s.) functions or *threshold* functions. However, most Boolean functions cannot be realized with a single T-gate. Such functions are known as *nonlinearly separable* (non-ℓ.s.) functions and can be realized by a network of T-gates.

Consider now the problem of determining a T-gate realization of ℓ.s. functions. A realization of a given function is obtained by choosing values for the separating function coefficients and for the threshold. This can be accomplished by finding a solution to a set of simultaneous linear inequalities. The following example illustrates this procedure.

Example.

Determine a T-gate realization of the Boolean function

$$f(x_1, x_2, x_3) = x_1 \bar{x}_2 + x_3$$

Table 5.2 presents the truth table of f along with the set of inequalities to be solved. The inequalities are obtained as follows. For each combination of

TABLE 5.2

$x_1 x_2 x_3$	f	Inequalities
000	0	$0 < T$
001	1	$a_3 \geq T$
010	0	$a_2 < T$
011	1	$a_2 + a_3 \geq T$
100	1	$a_1 \geq T$
101	1	$a_1 + a_3 \geq T$
110	0	$a_1 + a_2 < T$
111	1	$a_1 + a_2 + a_3 \geq T$

x_1, x_2, and x_3, include a_i, $i = 1, 2, 3$, in the sum if and only if $x_i = 1$. A linear sum is set $\geq T$ if the corresponding input combination is a minterm of f and is set $< T$ if the corresponding input combination is not a minterm of f.

There are several approaches that can be used to solve a set of simultaneous linear inequalities. Among these are trial and error, algebraic elimination, and linear programming. The following is a solution to the given set:

$$a_1 = 1$$
$$a_2 = -1$$
$$a_3 = 2$$
$$T = 1$$

Figure 5.22(a) shows this realization.

The reader should observe that in general there is no unique solution to a set of inequalities. Another valid solution to this problem is

$$a_1 = 1$$
$$a_2 = -\tfrac{3}{4}$$
$$a_3 = -1\tfrac{1}{2}$$
$$T = \tfrac{1}{2}$$

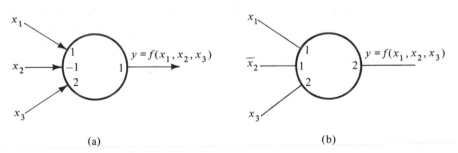

(a)   (b)

Fig. 5.22 Realization of $f(x_1, x_2, x_3) = x_1 \bar{x}_2 + x_3$: (a) T-gate realization; (b) realization with positive weights.

If complemented input variables are available, a realization requiring only positive coefficients is desirable from the point of view of physical realizability. As illustrated earlier, property 3 can be used to convert a given realization to a realization requiring only positive weights. Figure 5.22(b) gives a positive weight realization for the function considered in the previous example.

Many T-gate realization procedures have been developed that indirectly solve the set of inequalities. These procedures are complex and beyond the scope of this text. However, in general, the indirect procedures are superior to the direct method from a computational point of view.

As mentioned earlier, most Boolean functions are not realizable with a single T-gate. A necessary but not sufficient condition for a function to be ℓ.s. will now be discussed. Let $f(x_1, \ldots, x_n)$ be a Boolean function. Then f is a *unate* function if and only if no variable appears both uncomplemented and complemented when f is written in a minimum sum of products form.

Example.

The following are both unate functions:

$$f_1(x_1, x_2, x_3) = x_1 + x_2 x_3$$
$$f_2(x_1, x_2, x_3) = \bar{x}_1 \bar{x}_2 + \bar{x}_3$$

On the other hand, the following functions are not unate:

$$f_3(x_1, x_2) = x_1 x_2 + \bar{x}_1 \bar{x}_2$$
$$f_4(x_1, x_2, x_3) = x_1 \bar{x}_2 + x_2 x_3$$

All linearly separable functions are unate. Therefore all nonunate functions are nonlinearly separable. But, unate functions are not necessarily linearly separable.

Example.

Functions f_1 and f_2 in the previous example are unate and ℓ.s. Functions f_3 and f_4 are not unate and therefore are not ℓ.s. The following function is unate but not ℓ.s.:

$$f_5(x_1, x_2, x_3, x_4) = x_1 x_2 + x_3 x_4$$

Procedures are available for determining T-gate realizations of non-ℓ.s. functions. However, such procedures are beyond the scope of this text. The following example illustrates a T-gate network realization.

Example.

The non-ℓ.s. function $x_1 \bar{x}_2 + \bar{x}_1 x_2$ has the realization given below:

$$f(x_1, x_2) = \langle -x_1 + x_2 + 2\langle x_1 - x_2 \rangle_1 \rangle_1$$

Figure 5.23 shows the realization symbolically.

Savings in the number of gates can be obtained when using T-gates to realize Boolean functions. This advantage is offset, however, by a number of factors. Two of these factors are the complexity of realization procedures and the complexity of the circuits required to build a reliable T-gate. Hence, T-logic is used in realizations only when the need to save gates is the prime consideration.

The reader interested in learning more about threshold logic should consult references such as [16], [17], and [18].

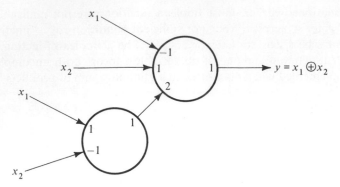

Fig. 5.23   A T-gate network.

Summary

This chapter has introduced a wide range of special topics in combinational logic circuit implementation. In particular, functional decomposition, NAND/NOR synthesis, multivalued logic, ROM logic, and threshold logic were mentioned. The coverage is by no means complete and is intended to create interest in the reader in the various subject areas. The reader is referred to the listed references for more detailed presentations.

REFERENCES

1. ASHENHURST, R. L., "The Decompositions of Switching Functions," *Proc. Symp. Theory of Switching*, 1957.

2. CURTIS, H. A., *Design of Switching Circuits*. New York: Van Nostrand Reinhold Company, 1962.

3. MALEY, G. A., and J. EARLE, *The Logical Design of Transistor Digital Computers*. Englewood Cliffs, N.J.: Prentice Hall, Inc., 1963.

4. BRADLEY, D. B., "A Survey of Boolean Function Realization Using NAND and NOR Logic", M.S. Thesis, Auburn University, Auburn, Ala., 1970.

5. GIMPEL, J. F., "The Minimization of TANT Networks," *IEEETEC*, Vol. EC-16, February 1967, pp. 18–38.

6. POST, E. L., "Introduction to a General Theory of Elemental Propositions," *Am. J. Math.*, Vol. 43, 1921, pp. 163–185.

7. SMITH, W. R., III, "Some Algebraic Properties and Minimization Techniques for Multivalued Lattice Logics," *Conference Record of the 1972 Symposium on the Theory and Applications of Multiple-valued Logic Design*, Buffalo, N.Y., May 25–26, 1972, pp. 163–174.

8. J. B. ROSSER, and A. R. TURQUETTE, *Many Valued Logics*. Amsterdam: North-Holland Publishing Company, 1952.

9. MUEHLDORF, E. I., "Multivalued Switching Algebras and Their Application in Digital Systems," *Proc. National Electronics Conf.*, Vol. XV, 1959, pp. 467–480.

10. VRANESIC, Z. G., E. S. LEE, and K. C. SMITH, "A Many-Valued Algebra for Switching Systems," *IEEE Trans. Computers*, Vol. C-19, No. 10, October 1970, pp. 964–971.

11. IRVING, T. A., and H. T. NAGLE, "An Approach to Multivalued Sequential Logic," *Conference Record of the 1973 Symposium on the Theory and Applications of Multiple-valued Logic Design*, Toronto, Canada, May 24–25, 1973, pp. 89–105.

12. SU, S. Y. H., and A. A. SARRIS, "The Relationship Between Multivalued Switching Algebra and Boolean Algebra Under Different Definitions of Complement," *IEEE Trans. Computers*, Vol. C-21, No. 5, May 1972, pp. 479–485.

13. JOHNSON, N., "Improved Binary Multiplication System," *Electronics*, January 11, 1973, pp. 6–7.

14. SIMMONS, J. D., JR., "The Read-only Memory and its Applications in Logic Design," M.S. Thesis, Auburn University, Auburn, Ala., March 1971.

15. JORDAN, W. F., "Memory Arrays Come on Strong," *Electronics*, Vol. 41, No. 21, December 1968, pp. 54–56.

16. LEWIS, P. M., II and C. L. COATES, *Threshold Logic*. New York: John Wiley & Sons, Inc., 1967.

17. DERTOUZAS, MICHAEL L., *Threshold Logic: A Synthesis Approach*. Cambridge, Mass.: The M.I.T. Press, 1965.

18. SHENG, C. L., *Threshold Logic*. New York: Academic Press, Inc., 1969.

PROBLEMS

5.1. Derive a simple disjunctive decomposition for the function
$$f(x_1, x_2, x_3, x_4) = \sum m(0, 2, 4, 6, 8, 11, 13, 15)$$

5.2. Repeat Problem 5.1 for the function
$$f(x_1, x_2, x_3, x_4) = \sum m(1, 2, 3, 4, 7, 10, 11, 12, 13)$$

5.3. Obtain a simple nondisjunctive decomposition for the function
$$f(x_1, x_2, x_3, x_4) = \sum m(0, 3, 7, 8, 11)$$

5.4. Repeat Problem 5.3 for the function
$$f(x_1, x_2, x_3, x_4) = \sum m(0, 2, 5, 9, 10, 13, 14)$$

5.5. Obtain a simple disjunctive decomposition for the following function with don't cares:

$$f(x_1, x_2, x_3, x_4) = \sum m(0, 5, 6, 9, 10, 15) + d(3, 8)$$

5.6. Use partial multiplication to obtain a NAND realization for the function

$$f(A, B, C, D) = (A + B)(\bar{C} + \bar{D})$$

5.7. Obtain a NAND realization for the function

$$f(A, B, C) = \sum m(1, 2, 3, 5, 6)$$

5.8. Use map factoring to obtain a NAND realization for

$$f(A, B, C) = \sum m(2, 4, 6)$$

5.9. Obtain a NAND realization for the following function using map factoring:

$$f(A, B, C) = \sum m(0, 2, 4)$$

5.10. Obtain a NOR network for the following function via the transform method:

$$f(A, B, C) = \bar{A}B + AB\bar{C} + \bar{A}C$$

5.11. Use map factoring to obtain a NOR realization for

$$f(A, B, C) = \prod M(1, 2, 3)$$

5.12. Plot the maps for the following functions of two three-valued variables:
(a) $f(A, B) = (\bar{A} + \overset{\rightarrow 1}{B}) \cdot \overset{\rightarrow 2}{A}$.
(b) $f(A, B) = (A \cdot \overset{\rightarrow 2}{B}) + \overline{2 \cdot B}$.

5.13. Plot the maps for the following functions of two four-valued variables:
(a) $f(A, B) = (\bar{A} + \overset{\rightarrow 1}{B}) \cdot \overset{\rightarrow 3}{A}$.
(b) $f(A, B) = (A \cdot \overset{\rightarrow 3}{B}) + \overline{1 \cdot B}$.

5.14. Find an algebraic expression for the multivalued function of Fig. P5.1.

A	B	$f(A, B)$
0	0	0
0	1	0
0	2	1
1	0	1
1	1	2
1	2	2
2	0	0
2	1	2
2	2	1

Fig. P5.1

5.15. Determine a T-gate realization of each of the following ℓ.s. functions:
(a) $f_a(x_1, x_2, x_3) = x_1 x_2 + \bar{x}_3$.
(b) $f_b(x_1, x_2, x_3) = x_1 x_2 + x_1 x_3$.
(c) $f_c(x_1, x_2, x_3) = x_1 x_2 + x_1 x_3 + x_2 x_3$.
(d) $f_d(x_1, x_2, x_3, x_4) = x_1 + x_2 + x_3 + x_4$.

5.16. Which of the following functions are not ℓ.s.?
   (a) $g_a(x_1, x_2, x_3) = x_1\bar{x}_2 + x_1\bar{x}_3$.
   (b) $g_b(x_1, x_2) = x_1x_2 + \bar{x}_1\bar{x}_2$.
   (c) $g_c(x_1, x_2, x_3, x_4) = x_1\bar{x}_2 + x_3\bar{x}_4$.

5.17. Determine a realization of the non-ℓ.s. function below using a network of two T-gates:

$$f(x_1, x_2, x_3) = x_1x_2 + \bar{x}_2x_3$$

Hint: One T-gate can realize the function $g(x_1, x_2, x_3) = x_1x_2 + x_1x_3$.

6

Introduction to Sequential Devices

The basic concept of a sequential device is an important one which is fundamental in the design of digital systems. The sequential concept is not, however, restricted to digital systems. For example, consider the operation of an elevator in a four-story building. The elevator acts as a sequential device because its actions are determined by input signals from its control panels (both on board and on each floor) and its present position at floor 1, 2, 3, or 4. Also the elevator must in some way "remember" its present position in order to determine its next floor transition. Therefore we define the *present state* of the elevator as a description of its current floor position including a history of its past floor transitions. The *next state* (and hence the next floor position) of the elevator is determined by its present state and its *input*, which consists of the condition of the control buttons on the control panels located in the elevator and stationed on each floor. Once the next state is determined a *state transition* is ordered by sending a command to the pulley motor, which drives the elevator to a new floor. The concepts of present state, next state, input, and state transition are fundamental in the study of sequential logic circuits.

Another simple example of a sequential device and one that finds wide application in digital systems is a counter. This device can be employed to perform such functions as counting the number of cars entering a parking lot or keeping track of certain functions being performed within a large computer system.

Recall that in combinational logic networks, the output is a function of only the current input. In sharp contrast to this, the output of sequential devices depends not only on the current input but previous inputs as well, as seen above in the elevator example. This history of the input is made available through the use of storage devices, i.e., memory. It is the use of this memory which adds a new dimension to logic design by providing the capability to solve numerous problems which cannot be handled by combinational logic alone.

Models for Sequential Circuits

Block Diagram Representation

In our study of combinational logic networks we found that we could represent these circuits as shown in Fig. 6.1(a). The mathematical relationship which describes this network is

$$z_i = f_i(x_1, x_2, \ldots, x_n), \quad i = 1, \ldots, m \tag{6-1}$$

This equation simply states that the output is a function of only the present input. All the signals in the above equation are assumed to be either of the two values 0 or 1.

The model for the sequential circuit is shown in Fig. 6.1(b). The n-tuples $(x_1, \ldots, x_n)$ will be referred to as the *input*, the m-tuples $(z_1, \ldots, z_m)$ will be called the *output*, and the r-tuples $(y_1, \ldots, y_r)$ and $(Y_1, \ldots, Y_r)$ represent the *present state* and *next state*, respectively. The relationships which exist among these variables may be expressed mathematically as

$$z_i = g_i(x_1, \ldots, x_n, y_1, \ldots, y_r), \quad i = 1, \ldots, m \tag{6-2}$$

$$Y_i = h_i(x_1, \ldots, x_n, y_1, \ldots, y_r), \quad i = 1, \ldots, r \tag{6-3}$$

Equations (6-2) and (6-3) may be written in vector notation as

$$z = g(x, y) \tag{6-4}$$

$$Y = h(x, y) \tag{6-5}$$

where

$$z = \begin{bmatrix} z_1 \\ z_2 \\ \cdot \\ \cdot \\ \cdot \\ z_m \end{bmatrix}, \quad x = \begin{bmatrix} x_1 \\ x_2 \\ \cdot \\ \cdot \\ \cdot \\ x_n \end{bmatrix}, \quad y = \begin{bmatrix} y_1 \\ y_2 \\ \cdot \\ \cdot \\ \cdot \\ y_r \end{bmatrix}, \quad Y = \begin{bmatrix} Y_1 \\ Y_2 \\ \cdot \\ \cdot \\ \cdot \\ Y_r \end{bmatrix} \tag{6-6}$$

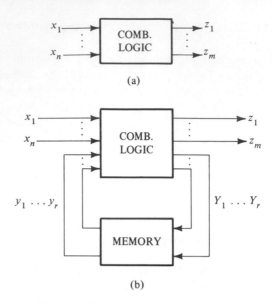

Fig. 6.1 The sequential circuit model.

All the vectors in equation (6-6) are time-dependent; we shall adopt the convention that vector $\mathbf{y}$ has the value $\mathbf{y}(t_k)$ at time t_k. Occasionally we shall examine a signal $\mathbf{y}(t)$ at evenly spaced points in time. If $t_k = k\,\Delta t$ (k an integer), then

$$\mathbf{y}(t_k) = \mathbf{y}(k\,\Delta t) \triangleq \mathbf{y}^k$$

where Δt is some fixed increment of time.

The memory devices in the block diagram of Fig. 6.1 may be of several types: semiconductor flip-flops, magnetic devices, delay lines, mechanical relays, rotation switches, and many others. Many of these memory devices will be examined later.

The input signals x_i and output signals z_j for Fig. 6.1 may also assume a variety of forms. Several of these forms will be explored later.

State Tables and Diagrams

The logic equations (6-2) and (6-3) and vector equations (6-4) and (6-5) completely define the behavior of the sequential circuit modeled in Fig. 6.1 for a given memory device. However, the description, although complete, does not present a very lucid picture of the relationships which exist among the pertinent variables. The functional relationship which exists among the input, output, present state, and next state is very vividly illustrated by either the state table or the state diagram. The *state diagram* is a graphical representation of a sequential circuit in which the states of the circuit are represented by circles and the state transitions (the path from the present state **y** to the next state **Y**) are shown by arrows. Each arrow is labeled with the input **x** and the resulting circuit output **z**, as shown in Fig. 6.2(a).

Figure 6.2(b) illustrates the *state table* representation. All circuit input vectors **x** are listed across the top, while all state vectors **y** are listed down the left side. Entries in the table are the next state **Y** and the output **z**. The table is read as follows: For an input **x** with the sequential circuit in state **y**, the circuit will proceed to the next state **Y** with an output **z**.

In practice, the state diagrams and tables are usually labeled using symbols rather than vectors. For example, consider a sequential circuit with

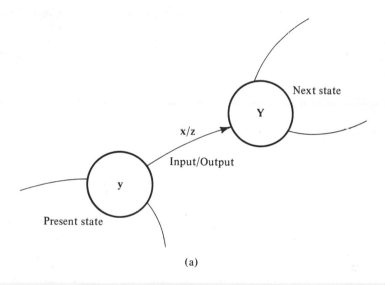

(a)

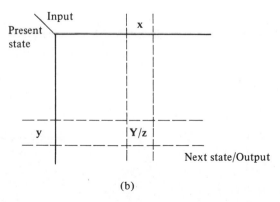

(b)

Fig. 6.2 State tables and diagrams: (a) state diagram; (b) state table.

two present-state variables y_1 and y_2. Then

$$\mathbf{y} = \begin{bmatrix} y_1 \\ y_2 \end{bmatrix}$$

Therefore, the vector $\mathbf{y}$ can have any of four possible values:

$$\mathbf{y} = \begin{bmatrix} 0 \\ 0 \end{bmatrix} \equiv A, \qquad \mathbf{y} = \begin{bmatrix} 1 \\ 0 \end{bmatrix} \equiv C,$$

$$\mathbf{y} = \begin{bmatrix} 0 \\ 1 \end{bmatrix} \equiv B, \qquad \mathbf{y} = \begin{bmatrix} 1 \\ 1 \end{bmatrix} \equiv D,$$

Thus, the sequential circuit has only four possible states, which may be labeled A, B, C, and D. In general, if r represents the number of memory devices in a circuit with N_s states, these two quantities are related by the expression

$$2^{r-1} < N_s \leq 2^r \tag{6-7}$$

This expression will be used in later chapters.

Example.

Consider a sequential circuit having one input variable x, two state variables y_1 and y_2, and one output variable z:

$$\begin{aligned} \text{Inputs:} \quad & x = 0 \\ & x = 1 \end{aligned}$$

$$\begin{aligned} \text{States:} \quad & [y_1 y_2] = [00] \equiv A \\ & [y_1 y_2] = [01] \equiv B \\ & [y_1 y_2] = [10] \equiv C \\ & [y_1 y_2] = [11] \equiv D \end{aligned}$$

$$\begin{aligned} \text{Outputs:} \quad & z = 0 \\ & z = 1 \end{aligned}$$

The state diagram for this sequential circuit is defined by Fig. 6.3. Let us assume that the circuit is initially in state A; if an input of $x = 0$ is now applied, the next state is D and the output is $z = 0$. This information may be

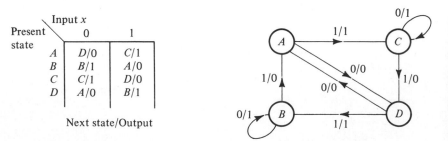

Present state	Input x	
	0	1
A	$D/0$	$C/1$
B	$B/1$	$A/0$
C	$C/1$	$D/0$
D	$A/0$	$B/1$

Next state/Output

Fig. 6.3 Example sequential circuit.

read from either the state diagram or the state table. Now consider the application of the following input sequence to the circuit:

$$x = 0110101100$$

The circuit will behave as follows when the initial state is A:

Present state:	A	D	B	A	D	B	B	A	C	C
Input:	0	1	1	0	1	0	1	1	0	0
Next state:	D	B	A	D	B	B	A	C	C	C
Output:	0	1	0	0	1	1	0	1	1	1
Time:	0	1	2	3	4	5	6	7	8	9

Hence, this input sequence applied to the machine in state A causes the output sequence

$$z = 0100110111$$

and leaves the circuit in final state C.

Mealy Model

A Mealy model for a sequential circuit is shown in Fig. 6.4. The Mealy model is called a transition-assigned circuit because the circuit output is associated with the state transitions. All the state diagrams and tables presented thus far in this chapter have been of the Mealy model configuration.

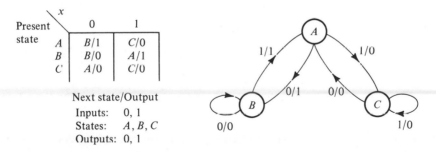

Present state	0	1
A	$B/1$	$C/0$
B	$B/0$	$A/1$
C	$A/0$	$C/0$

Next state/Output
Inputs: 0, 1
States: A, B, C
Outputs: 0, 1

Fig. 6.4 The Mealy model.

Moore Model

A second arrangement for a state diagram is shown in Fig. 6.5. This type is called the Moore model for a sequential circuit and it is distinguished from the Mealy model by identifying the outputs with the present state of the device. The output is then included inside the circles representing the states of the circuit.

The state table is also in a new format. The output may be removed from the next state entries in the state table since each next state will always have

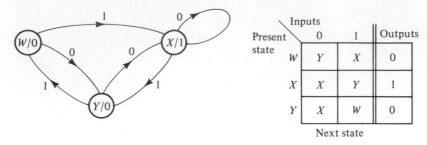

Moore Model State Table

	Inputs		
Present state	0	1	Outputs
W	Y	X	0
X	X	Y	1
Y	X	W	0

Next state

Fig. 6.5   Moore model for a sequential circuit.

the same output entry; a new column of outputs is shown. It is important to remember that these outputs belong to the present state and not the next one.

The output functional relationship given in equations (6-2) and (6-4) can be modified, respectively, as follows for Moore-type circuits:

$$z_i = g_i(y_1, \ldots, y_r), \quad i = 1, \ldots, m$$

$$\mathbf{z} = \mathbf{g}(\mathbf{y})$$

This follows since the outputs are determined by the present state only.

Consider the following input sequence to the Moore example with the starting state W:

$$\text{Input:} \quad 0 \ \ 0 \ \ 0 \ \ 1 \ \ 1 \ \ 1$$
$$\text{Present state:} \quad W \ Y \ X \ X \ Y \ W$$
$$\text{Next state:} \quad Y \ X \ X \ Y \ W \ X$$
$$\text{Output:} \quad 0 \ \ 0 \ \ 1 \ \ 1 \ \ 0 \ \ 0$$

The output is always identified by the present state from either the state diagram or state table.

Analysis of Sequential Circuits

General

In the previous section we examined several models for sequential circuits. The analysis of circuits will now be covered. *Analysis* is the process of determining the output response of a given circuit to a given input sequence. Before proceeding with the analysis of sequential circuits it is appropriate to define some new terms.

The operation of some sequential circuits modeled in Fig. 6.1(b) is controlled by a synchronizing pulse signal called a *clock*. The clock is usually applied to the "memory" portion of the diagram. A circuit which is controlled by a clock is termed a *synchronous sequential circuit*. One devoid of a clock signal is called an *asynchronous sequential circuit*. All sequential circuits may be placed in one of these categories.

An Introductory Example

Let us now consider the problem of analyzing a sequential circuit defined by a logic diagram similar to Fig. 6.1(b). For such a sequential circuit we need to determine the state table or state diagram which defines its operation. As an example, consider the sequential circuit shown in Fig. 6.6. This sequential circuit is built of AND, OR, and NOT gates and a memory device called a D flip-flop (delay flip-flop). For illustrative purposes the circuit is drawn in the form of the model presented in Fig. 6.1(b). It is assumed that the circuit operates in a synchronous manner under the control of an external clock; this means that the memory changes state only during a clock pulse.

The D flip-flop. The D flip-flop is a memory device with two input signals C and D, as shown in Fig. 6.6. The behavior of the D flip-flop is demonstrated in Fig. 6.7. Data are input to the flip-flop on the D terminal; however, the data enter the flip-flop only when the clock pulse C goes to 1. In other words, the clock pulse C is normally 0, and on a 0 → 1 (zero to one) transition of the

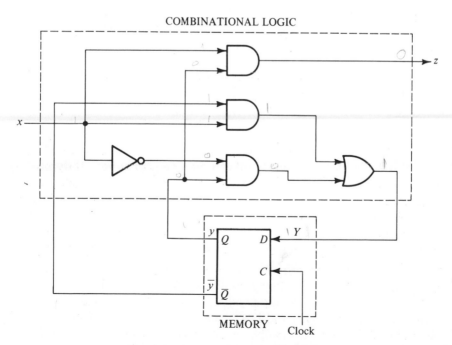

COMBINATIONAL LOGIC

Fig. 6.6 An example sequential circuit.

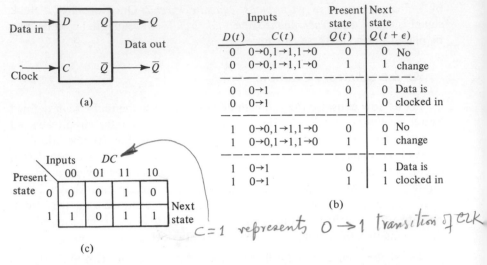

Inputs		Present state	Next state	
$D(t)$	$C(t)$	$Q(t)$	$Q(t + \epsilon)$	
0	0→0,1→1,1→0	0	0	No
0	0→0,1→1,1→0	1	1	change
0	0→1	0	0	Data is
0	0→1	1	0	clocked in
1	0→0,1→1,1→0	0	0	No
1	0→0,1→1,1→0	1	1	change
1	0→1	0	1	Data is
1	0→1	1	1	clocked in

(a)

(b)

$C = 1$ represents $0 \to 1$ transition of clk

(c)

Fig. 6.7 The D flip-flop: (a) logic symbol; (b) truth table; (c) state table.

clock, the data input D is transferred to the output terminals. The data arrive at the output terminals Q and $\bar{Q}$ after a transient time delay period ϵ through the device itself. A flip-flop which acts on a $0 \longrightarrow 1$ transition is said to be *edge-triggered*. We shall discuss this important concept in more detail later in the chapter.

The characteristics of the device are summarized by the truth table and state table of Fig. 6.7. Another convenient description of the D flip-flop is the next state equation given below:

$$Q^{k+1} = D^k C^k + Q^k \bar{C}^k \tag{6-8}$$

In equation (6-8), a logic value 1 for C^k, by definition, represents a $0 \longrightarrow 1$ transition; a logic value 0 on the other hand represents no transition ($1 \longrightarrow 1$, $0 \longrightarrow 0$) or a $1 \longrightarrow 0$ transition. In other words, the D flip-flop is triggered by the $0 \longrightarrow 1$ edge of the clock pulse. Perhaps a more vivid understanding can be obtained if we examine a timing diagram for the device as shown in Fig. 6.8. Note that the output signal Q is just the input data D time-delayed Δt seconds; Δt is the period of the clock and ϵ is the clock pulse width, which is chosen to be equal to the flip-flop transient time delay for convenience in drawing timing diagrams.

Timing diagram. Let us now examine the behavior of the circuit in Fig. 6.6. The operation of the D flip-flop has just been described and the characteristics of the AND, OR, and NOT gates were demonstrated in Chapter 2. A timing diagram for the example sequential circuit can be constructed for a given input sequence and a fixed starting state.

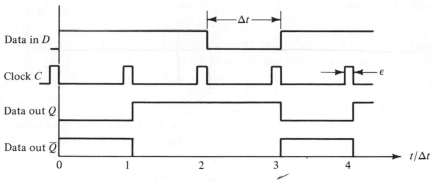

Fig. 6.8 Timing diagram for the D flip-flop.

This sequential circuit has only one flip-flop and hence only two states, 0 and 1. The input, output, and state conditions for this network are summarized below:

$$\text{Inputs:} \quad x = 0$$
$$x = 1$$
$$\text{States:} \quad y = 0$$
$$y = 1$$
$$\text{Outputs:} \quad z = 0$$
$$z = 1$$

The logic equations for the example are given here:

$$z = xy$$
$$Y = x\bar{y} + \bar{x}y = x \oplus y \tag{6-9}$$

Using equations (6-9) one can build the timing diagram shown in Fig. 6.9. The

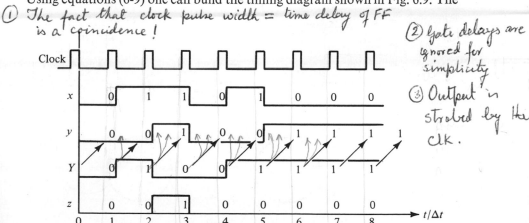

Fig. 6.9 Timing diagram for Fig. 6.6.

input sequence is

$$x = 01101000$$

and the starting state is $y = 0$. During the interval $t = 0$ to $t = 1$, the input is $x = 0$ and the present state is $y = 0$. Hence,

$$z = xy = 0 \cdot 0 = 0$$

$$Y = x \oplus y = 0 \oplus 0 = 0$$

Therefore the clock pulse at $t = 1$ clocks the next state $Y = 0$ into the D flip-flop. During the period $t = 1$ to $t = 2$, the present state is $y = 0$ and the input is $x = 1$:

$$z = xy = 1 \cdot 0 = 0$$

$$Y = 1 \oplus 0 = 1$$

As the clock pulse at $t = 2$ occurs the state of the sequential device will change to 1, etc. In a similar manner the remainder of the timing diagram is determined.

From the timing diagram we observe that the output sequence is

$$z = 00100000$$

State diagram and state table. The operation of the sequential circuit of Fig. 6.6 may be completely defined by a state table which lists all possible operating conditions. Let us adopt the notation

$$y(k\,\Delta t) = y^k$$

where k is an integer and Δt is the period between clock pulses. The blank state table is shown in Fig. 6.10(a). To fill in the upper left-hand corner, we

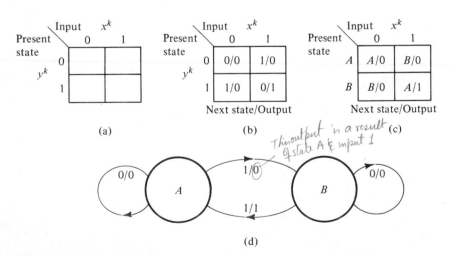

Fig. 6.10   State table and diagram for Fig. 6.6.

① At the clk pulse the o/p is observed and will be a combinatorial result of the I/p and the present state

② Then the present state changes to next state.

must assume a present state $y^k = 0$ and the input $x^k = 0$. Following these signals through the circuit of Fig. 6.6 one finds that the next state is $Y^k = y^{k+1} = 0$ and that the output is $z^k = 0$. Hence, the entry in the upper left block is $y^{k+1}/z^k = 0/0$.

The initial conditions for the upper right block are $y^k = 0$ and $x^k = 1$. Applying these signals in Fig. 6.6 yields $z^k = 0$ and $Y^k = y^{k+1} = 1$. The entry in this block is $y^{k+1}/z^k = 1/0$. The two lower block entries are determined in a similar manner. The results of the analysis are shown in Fig. 6.10(b).

As shown in an earlier example, we sometimes replace the present state vectors **y** of equations (6-4) and (6-5) by symbols to simplify notation; for example, in Fig. 6.10(b), one may represent the states as follows:

$$\mathbf{y} = [y] = [0] \equiv A$$
$$\mathbf{y} = [y] = [1] \equiv B$$

The state diagram and table drawn from the information contained in Fig. 6.10(b) are demonstrated in Fig. 6.10(c) and (d).

Karnaugh maps. It is both interesting and informative to derive the state table shown in Fig. 6.10(b) via the circuit equations and K-maps. In Fig. 6.6 we have noted that

$$z = xy$$
$$Y = x \oplus y$$

Evaluated at time $t = k\,\Delta t$

$$z^k = x^k \cdot y^k$$
$$Y^k = x^k \oplus y^k = y^{k+1}$$

K-maps for the above equations are shown in Fig. 6.11(a) and (b). The state table is constructed by merely combining the two K-maps as shown in Fig. 6.11(c). This table is identical to the one in Fig. 6.10(b).

This completes the analysis of our first example sequential circuit. Later in this chapter many others will be analyzed using the techniques presented here.

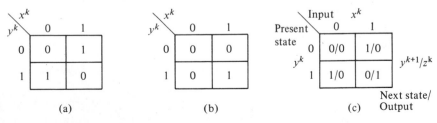

Fig. 6.11   K-maps and the state table for Fig. 6.6: (a) map for $Y^k = y^{k+1}$; (b) map for z; (c) state table.

Memory Devices

As indicated earlier an integral part of the sequential machine is the memory unit. Our discussion will be concerned primarily with the external characteristics of the memory devices and not the detailed internal functions. In other words, our analysis will be confined to the use of these elements in the design of digital systems.

Delay Lines

The simplest memory device is a delay element shown in Fig. 6.12(a). Its storage capability is derived from the fact that it takes a finite amount of time for the signal to propagate through it. Mathematically the delay element's

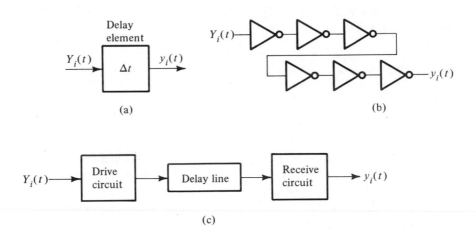

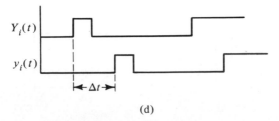

Fig. 6.12   Delay lines: (a) logic symbol; (b) cascaded NOT gates; (c) delay line circuitry; (d) timing diagram.

characteristics are described by the equation

$$y_i(t + \Delta t) = Y_i(t)$$

Hence, the output of the device at time $t + \Delta t$ is equal to the signal inserted into the device at time t.

If we let $t = k \Delta t$, where k is an integer and Δt is the time delay of the device, then

$$y_i[(k + 1) \Delta t] = Y_i(k \Delta t)$$

or

$$y_i^{k+1} = Y_i^k$$

The delay element shown in Fig. 6.12(a) is physically realized by acoustic delay lines, transmission lines, inductor/capacitor networks, cascaded semiconductor gates, and many others. We shall lump all these time-delay devices into one category and label them *delay lines*.

Figure 6.12(b) and (c) illustrates typical delay-line elements. The first one shows six cascaded NOT gates; if each gate has a transient delay time ϵ, then the total delay for the group is $\Delta t = 6\epsilon$. The second example shows a generalized configuration for transmission lines, acoustic devices, and lumped inductor/capacitor circuits used as delay lines. The drive and receive circuits serve to match impedances, reduce reflections, accomplish wave shaping, etc. A timing diagram is presented in Fig. 6.12(d) that illustrates typical waveforms for delay lines.

Flip-Flops

A series of bistable semiconductor electronic devices is available for use as the memory elements in the sequential circuit model of Fig. 6.1(b). The D flip-flop has already been briefly illustrated in Fig. 6.7. In this section we shall examine the D flip-flop again and present several others. Perhaps the three most popular devices are the trigger, set-reset, and JK flip-flops.

Set-reset flip-flop. The SR or set-reset flip-flop is described in Fig. 6.13. It possesses two states, $Q = 1$ and $Q = 0$, and two input signals, a set (S) line and a reset (R) line. An input on the set line of $S = 1$ forces the output $Q = 1$, or in other words the input $S = 1$ sets the flip-flop. A 1 input on the reset line forces the output $Q = 0$, or in other words the input $R = 1$ resets the flip-flop. The input condition $S = R = 0$ causes no change in the flip-flops's state. The input condition $S = R = 1$ is prohibited. If the S and R input terminals are both equal to 1, the behavior of the SR flip-flop is unspecified. The next state equation of an SR flip-flop is given below:

$$Q^{k+1} = S^k + \bar{R}^k Q^k \tag{6-10}$$

An SR flip-flop can be easily constructed from cross-coupled NAND or

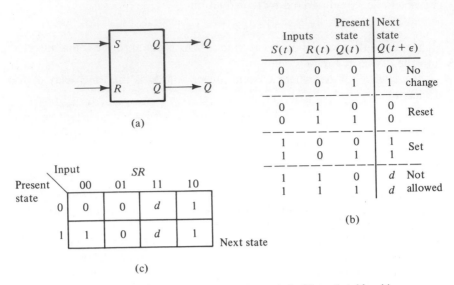

	Inputs		Present state	Next state
	$S(t)$	$R(t)$	$Q(t)$	$Q(t+\epsilon)$
	0	0	0	0 No
	0	0	1	1 change
	0	1	0	0
	0	1	1	0 Reset
	1	0	0	1 Set
	1	0	1	1
	1	1	0	d Not
	1	1	1	d allowed

(a)

(b)

Present state \ Input	SR 00	01	11	10
0	0	0	d	1
1	1	0	d	1

Next state

(c)

Fig. 6.13 Set-reset flip-flop: (a) logic symbol; (b) truth table; (c) state table.

NOR gates, as shown in Fig. 6.14. Let us examine the cross-coupled NOR's. Assume that the output $Q = 0$ and that $S = R = 0$. The upper NOR gate will have as inputs $Q = S = 0$; hence, its output is equal to $\overline{0+0} = 1$ and is labeled $\bar{Q}$. The lower NOR gate then has as its inputs $\bar{Q} = 1$ and $R = 0$; hence, its output is equal to $\overline{0+1} = 0$, the value with which we began.

Suppose that R suddenly goes to 1. The lower gate then has inputs $\bar{Q} = R = 1$ and output $Q = \overline{\bar{Q} + R} = \overline{1+1} = 0$ and remains unchanged in the reset condition; however, if instead S suddenly goes to 1, things begin to happen. First, the output of the upper gate $\bar{Q} = \overline{Q + S} = \overline{0+1} = 0$ and $\bar{Q}$ changes to zero. As $\bar{Q}$ goes to 0, the inputs of the lower gate are affected as follows: $\bar{Q} = 0$, $R = 0$, and thus the output Q ($Q = \overline{\bar{Q} + R} = \overline{0+0} = 1$)

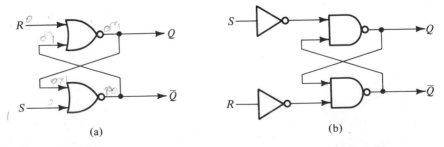

(a)   (b)

Fig. 6.14 Cross-coupled NAND and NOR gates: (a) NOR SR flip-flop; (b) NAND SR flip-flop.

changes to 1, the set condition. Thus, the cross-coupled logic circuits of Fig. 6.14 may be used as SR flip-flops. The reader is encouraged to determine what happens to the cross-coupled NAND circuit when $S = R = 1$, the forbidden condition.

Before leaving the SR flip-flop, let us examine the example timing diagram shown in Fig. 6.15. The important point to note from the diagram is that multiple set or reset pulses act as a single set or reset pulse; the first one causes a state change and all others are ignored. This property of the SR flip-flop renders it very useful in eliminating noise in digital networks; for example, cross-coupled NAND's and NOR's are commonly used to ignore switch bounce in mechanical switches. As the switch is thrown the contacts bounce vigorously for some time, giving a string of narrow pulses. In many cases only a single pulse is desired. The SR flip-flop provides a simple solution to the dilemma.

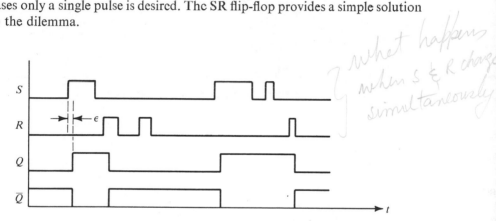

what happens when s & R change simultaneously

Fig. 6.15   Timing diagram for a SR flip-flop.

D flip-flop. The general description of the D (delay) flip-flop was presented in Figs. 6.7 and 6.8. The basic property of the device is that the input data are transferred to the output and held there on a $0 \rightarrow 1$ transition of the clock signal—an edge-triggered flip-flop. To implement such a circuit we may modify the cross-coupled NAND configuration of the SR flip-flop as shown in Fig. 6.16. It is important to remember that the clock input can be normally 1 or normally 0; however, in either case data are always clocked to the output Q on a $0 \rightarrow 1$ transition of the clock input C. The reader is invited to prove this for himself using the properties of NAND gates and Fig. 6.16.

The D flip-flop realization which we just presented is very simple compared to electronic packages for other flip-flop circuit types. Hence, we shall show the logic symbol only for the other flip-flops we shall cover and refer the interested reader to the manufacturer's specification sheets for more detail.

T flip-flop. The T (trigger) flip-flop is a memory device with only one input signal T, as shown in Fig. 6.17. The tables in Fig. 6.17(b) and (c) illustrate that

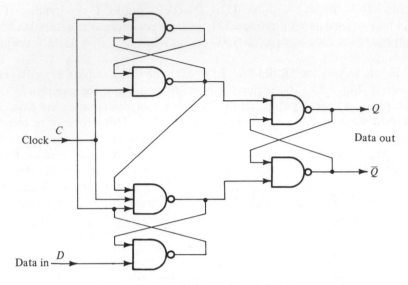

Fig. 6.16 A realization of the D flip-flop.

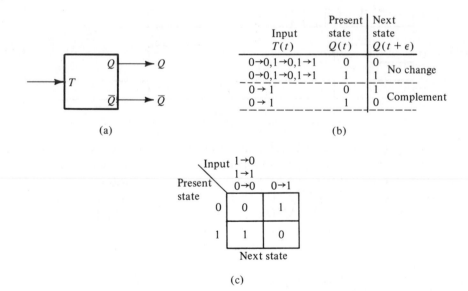

	Input $T(t)$	Present state $Q(t)$	Next state $Q(t + \epsilon)$	
	$0{\to}0, 1{\to}0, 1{\to}1$	0	0	No change
	$0{\to}0, 1{\to}0, 1{\to}1$	1	1	
	$0 \to 1$	0	1	Complement
	$0 \to 1$	1	0	

(a) $\qquad\qquad\qquad$ (b)

Present state \ Input	$1{\to}0$ $1{\to}1$ $0{\to}0$	$0{\to}1$
0	0	1
1	1	0

Next state

(c)

Fig. 6.17 The T flip-flop; (a) logic symbol; (b) truth table; (c) the T flip-flop.

the T flip-flop is a sequential device itself. The flip-flop's states are $Q = 1$ and $Q = 0$. A T flip-flop is also described by the following next-state equation:

$$Q^{k+1} = T^k \bar{Q}^k + \bar{T}^k Q^k \qquad (6\text{-}11)$$

Both the true (Q) and complemented ($\bar{Q}$) output variables are available for use in the combinational logic portion of a sequential circuit.

The key to the flip-flop is that when the input signal T changes from 0 to 1 (abbreviated $0 \longrightarrow 1$), the output Q is complemented, or the flip-flop changes state; hence, the T flip-flop is another edge-triggered device. The transient time delay required for the state change is defined as ϵ in the table and is typically very small compared to the clock pulse interval Δt. This time delay period ϵ is also made equal to the pulse width of the clock signal in order to simplify the timing diagrams for all flip-flop types, except the master/slave type discussed later.

Clocked T flip-flop. The operation of the T flip-flop under clock pulse control is illustrated in Fig. 6.18(a). The control signal T_c allows the clock pulses to be selectively applied to the input terminal T. Each clock pulse that arrives at T causes the flip-flop to change state. A detailed timing diagram is offered in Fig. 6.18(b). The next-state equation for a clocked T flip-flop can be obtained from equation (6-11) by letting $T = T_cC$, where C is the clock signal. Hence, the next-state equation below is obtained:

$$Q^{k+1} = T_c^k C^k \bar{Q}^k + \overline{T_c^k C^k} Q^k \qquad (6\text{-}12)$$

In equation (6.12) the clock variable C^k is interpreted in the same manner as for equation (6-8).

JK flip-flop. The JK flip-flop is in essence a combination of the set-reset and trigger flip-flops. In other words, the JK device acts like the set-reset flip-flop

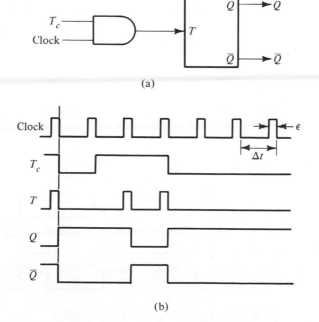

(a)

(b)

Fig. 6.18 The clocked T flip-flop: (a) logic symbol; (b) timing diagram.

except under the condition $J = 1$ and $K = 1$ and in this case it acts like a trigger and changes state. This operation is described in the tables of Fig. 6.19. The operation is also given by the following next-state equation:

$$Q^{k+1} = J^k \bar{Q}^k + \bar{K}^k Q^k \qquad (6\text{-}13)$$

To portray the operating characteristics of the JK flip-flop, the timing diagram of Fig. 6.20 is now analyzed. The two input signals J and K were

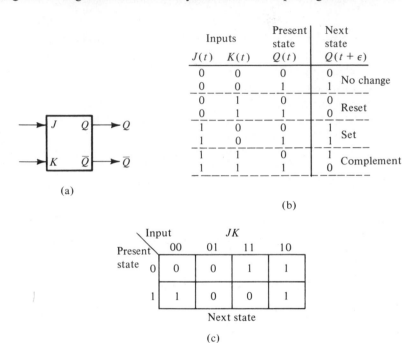

Inputs		Present state	Next state	
$J(t)$	$K(t)$	$Q(t)$	$Q(t+\epsilon)$	
0	0	0	0	No change
0	0	1	1	
0	1	0	0	Reset
0	1	1	0	
1	0	0	1	Set
1	0	1	1	
1	1	0	1	Complement
1	1	1	0	

(a)

(b)

Present state \ Input JK	00	01	11	10
0	0	0	1	1
1	1	0	0	1

Next state

(c)

Fig. 6.19 The JK flip-flop: (a) logic symbol; (b) truth table; (c) state table.

what happens on 01 → 00 direct ?

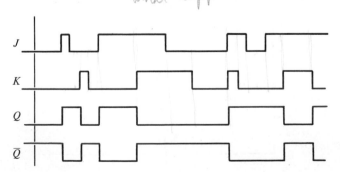

Fig. 6.20 Timing diagram for a JK flip-flop.

arbitrarily chosen to provide a full range of conditions on the flip-flop. The state of the device is initially zero ($Q = 0$) and the first $0 \rightarrow 1$ transition of the output Q is caused by the set action of the J input. A summary of all the state transitions is offered below:

Q Transition	Reason	Inputs J and K
1. $0 \rightarrow 1$	Set	10
2. $1 \rightarrow 0$	Reset	01
3. $0 \rightarrow 1$	Set	10
4. $1 \rightarrow 0$	Complement	11
5. $0 \rightarrow 1$	Complement	11
6. $1 \rightarrow 0$	Complement	11
7. $0 \rightarrow 1$	Set	10

The transitions occur in an unsynchronized or asynchronous manner. Note that transition 4 was activated by the $0 \rightarrow 1$ transition of the K input. The $J = K = 1$ condition makes the flip-flop behave as an edge-triggered device, just like the T flip-flop.

Clocked JK flip-flop. The clocked JK flip-flop presented here has many desirable features which make it a very versatile memory element. See Fig. 6.21. The logic symbol indicates that this flip-flop has five input signals C, J, K, S, and R. The first three are used for synchronous, clocked operation of the device [see Fig. 6.21(b)]; in this mode the set S and reset R inputs are held at zero. Note that the table shows that the clock signal must be normally zero and experience $0 \rightarrow 1 \rightarrow 0$ transitions to initiate a state change in the device. The two transitions are needed because this flip-flop actually has internally two flip-flops in a master/slave configuration. The first transition, $0 \rightarrow 1$, causes the master flip-flop to operate, while the second, $1 \rightarrow 0$, transfers data from the master to the slave. The outputs Q and $\bar{Q}$ come from the slave flip-flop. Figure 6.21(d) demonstrates an example master/slave configuration for the clocked JK flip-flop using a JK and a D flip-flop. The next-state equation for a clocked JK flip-flop is given below:

$$Q^{k+1} = S^k + \bar{R}^k \bar{K}^k Q^k + \bar{R}^k \bar{C}^k Q^k + \bar{R}^k J^k C^k \bar{Q}^k \qquad (6\text{-}14)$$

For this equation to be valid, a value of 1 for C means that C undergoes a $0 \rightarrow 1 \rightarrow 0$ transition, as shown in Fig. 6.21(b). A timing diagram for typical signals into the clocked JK flip-flop is illustrated in Fig. 6.21(e). The reader is encouraged to trace these signals through the master/slave configuration to verify the tables shown in Fig. 6.21(b) and (c). A summary of the conditions which cause the $0 \rightarrow 1$ and $1 \rightarrow 0$ transitions for Q in the timing diagram are outlined follow:

Q Transition	Input Condition
1. $0 \longrightarrow 1$	Static set ($S = 1$)
2. $1 \longrightarrow 0$	Static reset ($R = 1$)
3. $0 \longrightarrow 1$	Static set ($S = 1$)
4. $1 \longrightarrow 0$	Clocked reset ($K = 1$)
5. $0 \longrightarrow 1$	Clocked set ($J = 1$)
6. $1 \longrightarrow 0$	Clocked complement ($J = K = 1$)
7. $0 \longrightarrow 1$	Static set ($S = 1$)

Note that the static set S and reset R override the clocked flip-flop inputs. Since the master/slave configuration is not sensitive to internal time delays,

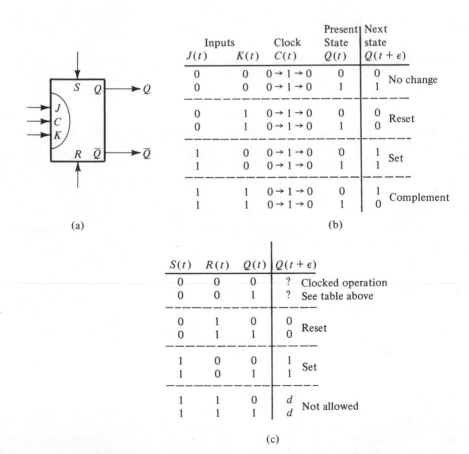

(a)

Inputs		Clock	Present State	Next state	
$J(t)$	$K(t)$	$C(t)$	$Q(t)$	$Q(t + \epsilon)$	
0	0	$0 \to 1 \to 0$	0	0	No change
0	0	$0 \to 1 \to 0$	1	1	
0	1	$0 \to 1 \to 0$	0	0	Reset
0	1	$0 \to 1 \to 0$	1	0	
1	0	$0 \to 1 \to 0$	0	1	Set
1	0	$0 \to 1 \to 0$	1	1	
1	1	$0 \to 1 \to 0$	0	1	Complement
1	1	$0 \to 1 \to 0$	1	0	

(b)

$S(t)$	$R(t)$	$Q(t)$	$Q(t + \epsilon)$	
0	0	0	?	Clocked operation
0	0	1	?	See table above
0	1	0	0	Reset
0	1	1	0	
1	0	0	1	Set
1	0	1	1	
1	1	0	d	Not allowed
1	1	1	d	

(c)

Fig. 6.21 The clocked JK flip-flop: (a) logic symbol (b) truth table for clocked operation ($S = R = 0$); (c) truth table for static operation;

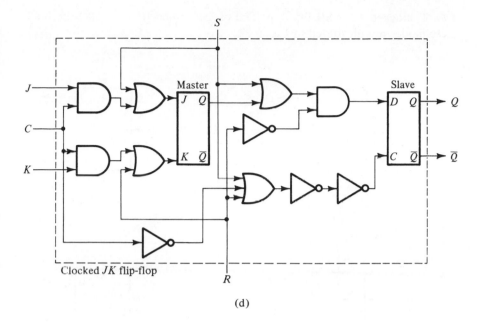

(d)

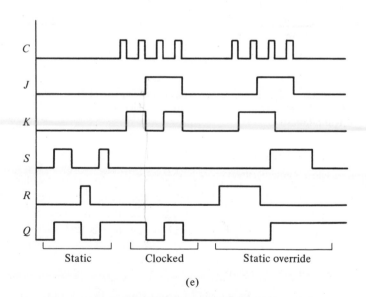

(e)

Fig. 6.21—*Cont.* (d) master/slave configuration; (e) timing diagram.

all timing diagrams envolving them will have zero transient delay. This convention is adopted for convenience in drawing timing diagrams.

The clocked JK flip-flop is a general-purpose device which can operate as a D, T, clocked T, or SR flip-flop. The proper connections to operate in all these modes are illustrated in Fig. 6.22.

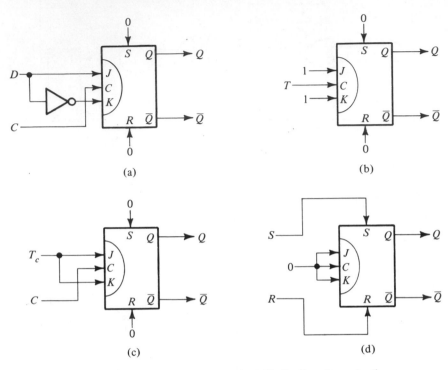

Fig. 6.22   Versatility of the clocked JK flip-flop based on equation (6-14): (a) D flip-flop; (b) T flip-flop; (c) clocked T flip-flop; (d) SR flip-flop.

Other Memory Devices

Many other kinds of storage devices may be used for memory elements in Fig. 6.1(b), several of which are magnetic cores, capacitors, magnetic films, superconductive cryotron elements, and electromechanical relays. The explanation of these devices is beyond the scope of this text.

Types of Sequential Circuits

Sequential circuits may be classified according to their input, output, and memory characteristics. The memory elements studied to this point fall into two categories:

1. Clocked.
2. Unclocked.

The characteristics of both types have been presented in great detail. The input signals to sequential circuits need further consideration. A variety of input signals x_i for the sequential circuit of Fig. 6.1(b) is presented in Fig. 6.23. The signals are shown in four categories:

1. Synchronous pulses.
2. Synchronous levels.
3. Asynchronous pulses.
4. Asynchronous levels.

A synchronous signal is defined as one which is *in step* with a regular, external clock pulse. Outputs may be classified as levels or as pulses.

An input sequence is defined for synchronous levels and pulses as the value of the input signal during the duration ϵ of the clock pulse. Input sequences for asynchronous pulses are defined as a 1 for a pulse and a 0 during intervals when no pulses are present. See Fig. 6.23 for example input sequences. Later in the chapter we shall discuss an example which serves to explain the technique for interpreting asynchronous-level inputs.

The various combinations of input and memory categories may be combined to yield the following four major types of sequential circuits:

Type 1. *Pulsed synchronous:* those sequential circuits which have pulse input signals and clocked memory elements. *I/p Pulses are synchronous too!*

Type 2. *Level synchronous:* those sequential circuits with level input signals and clocked memory units.

Type 3. *Pulsed asynchronous:* those sequential circuits possessing pulsed input signals and unclocked memory devices.

Type 4. *Level asynchronous:* those circuits having level inputs and unclocked memory elements.

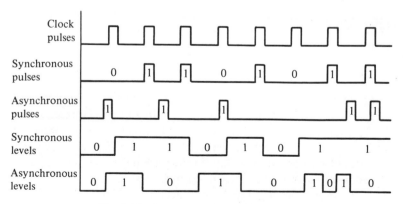

Fig. 6.23 Sequential circuit input signals.

Clock pulses and input pulses should be narrow compared to propagation delay in FFs

The pulses that are not synchronized should not overlap even partially with the clock pulses ie all asynchronous pulses are assumed to be occuring somewhere between the clock pulses otherwise they will cause problems?

240 INTRODUCTION TO SEQUENTIAL DEVICES   Ch. 6

Outputs may be in the form of pulses or levels for types 1, 2, or 3. Only level outputs can be provided in type 4 circuits. Each of the four types of sequential circuits will now be illustrated by an example.

Pulsed Synchronous Circuits (Type 1)

Consider now the problem of analyzing a clocked sequential circuit with synchronous or asynchronous input pulses. In either case, however, only the input pulses which are synchronized with the external clock pulse can affect the next state of the device. Hence, we shall examine the input signals *only during the clock pulse period*. Suppose we analyze the circuit of Fig. 6.24; in the analysis we may use timing diagrams, state tables, K-maps, and state diagrams. This example employs one clocked T flip-flop as described in Fig. 6.18. The clock input is ANDed with the feedback signal T_c to ensure synchronous operation. To completely analyze this circuit we shall develop a timing diagram, state table, and state diagram in a manner similar to our first example in this chapter.

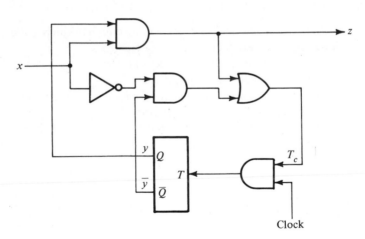

Fig. 6.24 A pulsed synchronous sequential circuit.

Timing diagram. Let us now explore the behavior of the circuit in Fig. 6.24. The operation of the T flip-flop has already been presented in this chapter and the characteristics of AND, OR, and NOT gates were demonstrated in Chapter 2. A specific timing diagram for the example sequential circuit is valid for only one given input sequence and a fixed starting state.

This sequential circuit has only one flip-flop and, hence, only two states, 0 and 1. The input, output, and state conditions for this network are summarized as follows:

* However, the output will be affected by all pulses and should therefore be strobed. Actually the CLK provides timing info for the entire ckt — which includes the input pulses too!

$$\text{Inputs:} \quad x = 0 \quad \text{(no pulse)}$$
$$x = 1 \quad \text{(pulse)}$$
$$\text{States:} \quad y = 0 \quad \text{(no level)}$$
$$y = 1 \quad \text{(level)}$$
$$\text{Outputs:} \quad z = 0 \quad \text{(no pulse)}$$
$$z = 1 \quad \text{(pulse)}$$

The logic equations for the example are given here:

$$z = xy$$
$$T_c = xy + \bar{x}\bar{y} = x \odot y$$

Using these equations, one can construct the timing diagram shown in Fig. 6.25. The clocked T flip-flop characteristics described in Fig. 6.18 are also employed in the timing diagram's construction. The input sequence is

$$x = 01101000$$

and the starting state is 0. During the time $t/\Delta t = 0$ to $t/\Delta t = 1$, the input is $x = 0$ and the present state is $y = 0$. Hence, if we examine the logic equations during the clock pulse at the end of the period,

$$z = xy = 0 \cdot 0 = 0$$
$$T_c = x \odot y = 0 \odot 0 = 1$$

The variable T_c is the control for the T flip-flop. On the $0 \rightarrow 1$ transition of the clock pulse, the signal T_c will allow the clock pulse to trigger the flip-flop

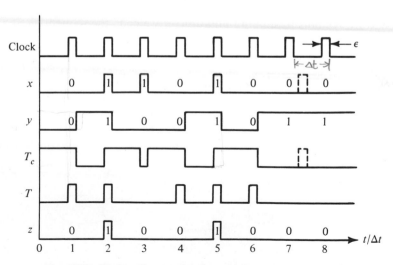

Fig. 6.25   Timing diagram for the pulsed synchronous circuit.

to the 1 state as shown for y in the interval $t/\Delta t = 1$ to $t/\Delta t = 2$. In a similar manner, the entire timing diagram is determined. Notice that all the input pulses are synchronized with the clock. Suppose an asynchronous input pulse occurs after time $t/\Delta t = 7$ (see the dotted pulse in Fig. 6.25); although this asynchronous input pulse causes a change in T_c, the AND gate inhibits its activity and the T input to the flip-flop is unchanged. Hence, only input pulses coincident with clock pulses are considered.

State diagram and state table. The operation of the sequential circuit of Fig. 6.24 is completely defined by its state table, which tabulates all possible operating conditions. The blank state table is shown in Fig. 6.26(a). To fill in the upper left-hand corner of the state table we assume that the present state is zero, i.e., $y^k = 0$ and the input $x^k = 0$; signals are examined only during the period ϵ while the clock pulse is high (1). Following these signals through the circuit of Fig. 6.24 one finds that $z^k = 0$ and $T_c^k = 1$, and hence during the clock pulse the T input to the flip-flop will experience a $0 \longrightarrow 1$ transition. The latter signal will change the flip-flop's state, and hence the entry in the block under examination is $y^{k+1}/z^k = 1/0$. In other words, when the sequential circuit is in state $y^k = 0$ and the input is $x^k = 0$, the circuit changes state so that $y^{k+1} = 1$ and the output produced is $z^k = 0$.

The initial conditions for the upper right-hand block are $y^k = 0$ and $x^k = 1$. These conditions yield $z^k = 0$ and $T_c^k = 0$, and therefore the flip-flop does not change state and hence the block entry is $y^{k+1}/z^k = 0/0$. The two lower-block entries are derived in a similar manner and shown in Fig. 6.26(b). The state table may also be taken from a judiciously chosen timing diagram. The reader is encouraged to try this procedure.

As shown in an earlier example, sometimes the Boolean variable codes are replaced by symbols to simplify notation; if we code the sequential circuit's

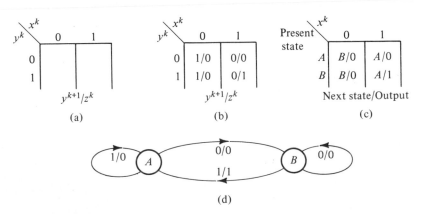

(a)   (b)   (c)

(d)

Fig. 6.26   State table and diagram for Fig. 6.24.

states as

$$0 \equiv A$$
$$1 \equiv B$$

the state table in Fig. 6.26(c) and the state diagram of Fig. 6.26(d) are obtained. At this point we may use the state diagram to determine the response of the circuit to an input sequence:

$$x: \quad 0\ 1\ 1\ 0\ 1\ 0\ 0\ 0$$
$$y: \quad A\ B\ A\ A\ B\ A\ B\ B\ B$$
$$z: \quad 0\ 1\ 0\ 0\ 1\ 0\ 0\ 0$$

The starting state is A ($y = 0$) and the final state is B ($y = 1$). Note that this behavior is identical to the timing diagram of Fig. 6.25, which was to be expected.

Karnaugh maps. K-maps may also be used to determine the state table for pulsed synchronous sequential circuits. The logic equations are

$$z^k = x^k \cdot y^k$$
$$T_c^k = x^k \odot y^k$$

where y^k is the present state and T_c^k determines the next state. K-maps for the above equations are shown in Fig. 6.27(a). The map for T_c defines the signal to the T input of the flip-flop when a clock pulse is present for various conditions of x and y. $T_c = 1$ causes the flip-flop to change state when a clock pulse occurs; for $T_c = 0$, there is no change in state.

Using the map for T_c in Fig. 6.27(a) we must now find the map for the

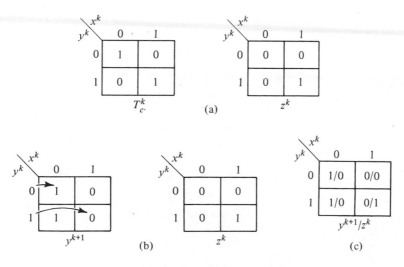

Fig. 6.27 K-maps via the state table.

next state y^{k+1}. This map is derived in Fig. 6.27(b). The K-map variables are the input x^k and the present state y^k. The next-state entry is made by examining the corresponding entries in the map for T_c. The arrows indicate the state changes caused by $T_c = 1$ minterms.

Finally, combining the next-state and output K-maps in Fig. 6.27(b) yields the state table in Fig. 6.27(c), which is identical to the one shown in Fig. 6.26(b). This completes the example.

Level Synchronous Circuits (Type 2)

This type of sequential circuit includes all circuits with clocked memory elements and level input signals whether the levels are synchronized with the clock or not.

The example circuit to be analyzed is that shown in Fig. 6.28. The circuit contains two clocked JK flip-flops and hence has four states. An analysis similar to that presented above for type 1 circuits yields the state table and timing diagram of Fig. 6.29. The input sequence and starting state are

$$x = 0011110$$

$$y_1^0 y_2^0 = 10$$

The equations which describe the circuit's operation are

$$J_1 = xy_2, \qquad J_2 = x, \qquad K_1 = \bar{x},$$

$$K_2 = \bar{x} + \bar{y}_1, \qquad z = xy_1y_2$$

The K-maps for these equations are given in Fig. 6.30. The K-maps for J and

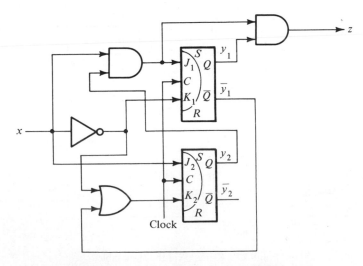

Fig. 6.28   A level synchronous sequential circuit.

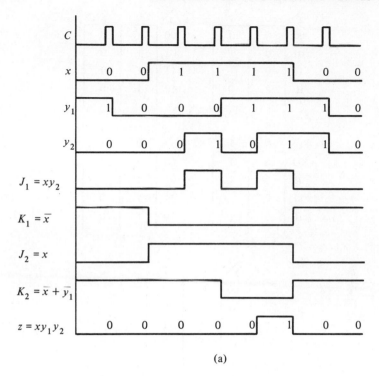

(a)

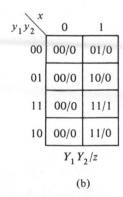

(b)

Fig. 6.29 (a) Timing diagram and (b) state table for circuit of Fig. 6.28.

K are combined into a single table shown in Fig. 6.31(a). Using the J and K signals to determine the state changes yields the table of Fig. 6.31(b). Finally, combining the latter table with the table for the output z we obtain the state table shown in Fig. 6.31(c).

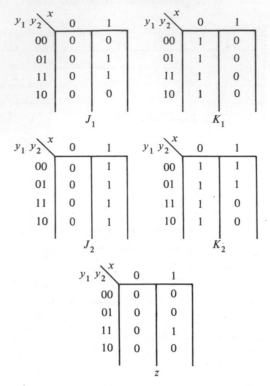

Fig. 6.30 K-maps for logic equations which describe circuit in Fig. 6.28.

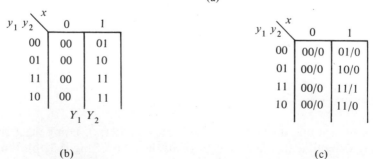

$y_1 y_2$ \ x	0		1	
00	01	01	00	11
01	01	01	10	11
11	01	01	10	10
10	01	01	00	10
	$J_1 K_1$	$J_2 K_2$	$J_1 K_1$	$J_2 K_2$

(a)

$y_1 y_2$ \ x	0	1
00	00	01
01	00	10
11	00	11
10	00	11
	$Y_1 Y_2$	

(b)

$y_1 y_2$ \ x	0	1
00	00/0	01/0
01	00/0	10/0
11	00/0	11/1
10	00/0	11/0

(c)

Fig. 6.31 Combining the K-maps into the state table.

246

Pulsed Asynchronous Circuits (Type 3)

Asynchronous circuits require special attention since there is no clock signal to provide common timing information to the circuit elements. Hence, asynchronous circuits respond immediately to any change of input rather than responding to the input present during the clock pulse. The absence of a clock signal also means that memory element transitions must be initiated by some other means. Therefore, precautions must be taken to avoid timing problems. With this in mind, the following assumptions are often made when considering pulsed asynchronous circuits.

1. Pulses will not occur simultaneously on two or more input lines.
2. Memory element transitions are initiated only by input pulses.
3. Input variables are used only in the uncomplemented or the complemented forms but not both.

The first assumption means that a circuit with n input lines has $n + 1$ input conditions rather than 2^n, as in the case for synchronous circuits. Assumption 2 implies that a state transition can occur only if an input pulse occurs. Hence, the circuit responds only when an input pulse arrives. The third assumption guarantees that all devices trigger on the same edge of each pulse. Keep these assumptions in mind while studying the examples which follow.

Example.

A pulsed asynchronous circuit is shown in Fig. 6.32. The circuit has the following states and inputs:

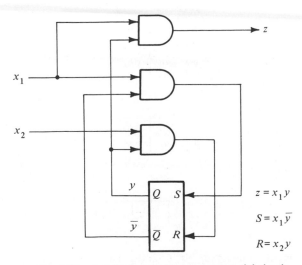

$$z = x_1 y$$
$$S = x_1 \bar{y}$$
$$R = x_2 y$$

Fig. 6.32 A pulsed asynchronous sequential circuit.

$$\text{States:} \quad [y] = 0 \equiv A$$
$$[y] = 1 \equiv B$$
$$\text{Inputs:} \quad [x_1 x_2] = 00 \equiv I_0$$
$$[x_1 x_2] = 10 \equiv I_1$$
$$[x_1 x_2] = 01 \equiv I_2$$

The analysis of this circuit can proceed in much the same fashion as the analysis of a synchronous circuit. The major differences are due to the absence of a clock signal and to the assumptions given above.

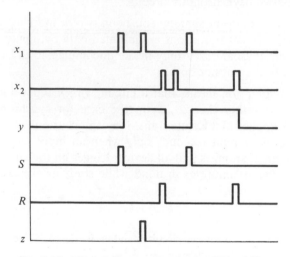

Fig. 6.33 Timing diagram for circuit of Fig. 6.32.

(a)

y^k \ $x_1^k x_2^k$	00	01	10	
0	0/0	0/0	1/0	y^{k+1}/z^k
1	1/0	0/0	1/1	

(b)   Present state

	I_0	I_2	I_1	
A	A/0	A/0	B/0	Next state/Output
B	B/0	A/0	B/1	

(c)   Present state

	x_1	x_2	
A	B/0	A/0	Next state/Output
B	B/1	A/0	

Fig. 6.34 State tables for Fig. 6.32: (a) state table; (b) symbolic state table; (c) simplified state table.

Figure 6.33 shows a timing diagram of the circuit for a typical input sequence. Note that all state transitions correspond to the occurrence of an input pulse.

The state table shown in Fig. 6.34(a) can be constructed from the timing diagram in Fig. 6.33. A symbolic state table is shown in Fig. 6.34(b). A simplified state table is given in Fig. 6.34(c). This table is obtained from the symbolic table by eliminating the I_0 column, by interchanging the I_2 and I_1 columns, and by replacing the symbols I_1 with x_1 and I_2 with x_2. The simplified state table completely describes the circuit behavior.

A K-map development of the state table is given in Fig. 6.35. Since the input condition $x_1x_2 = 11$ is assumed never to occur, the corresponding K-map cells are left unspecified. The final step is accomplished by dropping the 00 and 11 columns from the table and relabeling the 10 column as x_1 and the 01 column as x_2.

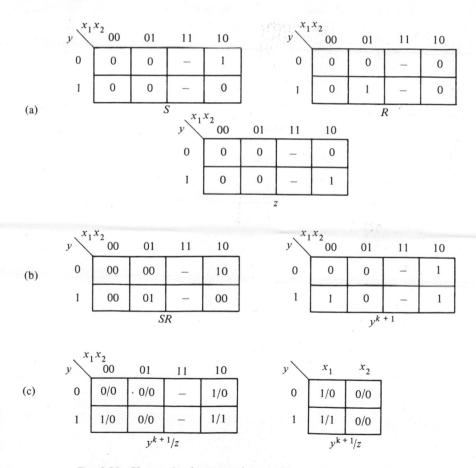

Fig. 6.35 K-map development of state tables: (a) K-maps for the circuit; (b) combined SR map and y^{k+1} map; (c) state tables.

Pulsed asynchronous circuits utilizing memory elements which are not edge-triggered can be analyzed as shown in the above example. The analysis of a circuit which employs edge-triggered flip-flops will be considered next.

Example.

Consider the sequential circuit of Fig. 6.36. The analysis of this example will be completed using a timing diagram. The circuit is described by the logic equations

$$D_1 = \bar{y}_1, \qquad D_2 = \bar{y}_1, \qquad z = xy_1y_2,$$
$$C_1 = xy_2, \qquad C_2 = x$$

The timing diagram for the circuit has been constructed in Fig. 6.37. The input x is asynchronous pulses and the starting state is $y_1 = y_2 = 0$. Notice that only three of the states of the circuit are shown on the diagram.

If the starting state had been $y_1 = 1$ and $y_2 = 0$, the sequential circuit can never change state because

$$D_1 = 0, \qquad D_2 = 0,$$
$$C_1 = 0, \qquad C_2 = x$$

The state variable y_2 will always stay at 0 and inhibit any state change in flip-flop output y_2.

A state table and diagram may be compiled for this circuit if we define the following:

$$
\begin{array}{rll}
\text{Inputs:} & I_0 \equiv \text{no pulse on } x \\
& I_1 \equiv \text{pulse on } x
\end{array}
$$

$$
\begin{array}{rcl c c}
\text{States:} & & & y_1 & y_2 \\
& A & \equiv & 0 & 0 \\
& B & \equiv & 0 & 1 \\
& C & \equiv & 1 & 0 \\
& D & \equiv & 1 & 1
\end{array}
$$

$$
\begin{array}{rl}
\text{Outputs:} & z = 0 \\
& z = 1
\end{array}
$$

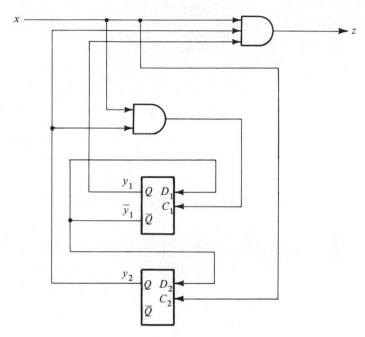

Fig. 6.36   A pulsed sequential circuit with unclocked memory.

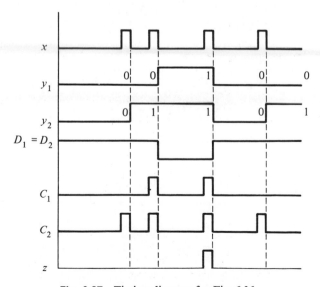

Fig. 6.37   Timing diagram for Fig. 6.36.

The resulting state table and diagram are illustrated in Fig. 6.38. They are derived from the timing diagram in Fig. 6.37. The state diagram has two separate parts. Hence, if state C is the starting state, the sequential circuit is "hung" in a single state. However, if states A, B, or D are the starting states, the circuit behaves as a typical sequential machine.

K-maps can be used for construction of the state table corresponding to the circuit of Fig. 6.36 by using equation (6-8) and by making the following observation. The D flip-flop clock inputs will see a 0 to 1 transition only if an input pulse occurs. Hence, at most one such transition can occur for each input pulse.

The following equations are obtained by using (6-8) and the logic equations corresponding to Fig. 6.36:

$$Y_1 = D_1 C_1 + y_1 \bar{C}_1$$
$$= \bar{y}_1 x y_2 + y_1 (\bar{x} + \bar{y}_2)$$
$$= x \bar{y}_1 y_2 + \bar{x} y_1 + y_1 \bar{y}_2$$
$$Y_2 = D_2 C_2 + y_2 \bar{C}_2$$
$$= \bar{y}_1 x + y_2 \bar{x}$$

The K-map development of the state table is shown in Fig. 6.39.

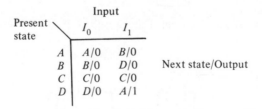

	Input	
Present state	I_0	I_1
A	$A/0$	$B/0$
B	$B/0$	$D/0$
C	$C/0$	$C/0$
D	$D/0$	$A/1$

Next state/Output

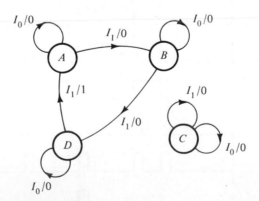

Fig. 6.38 State table and diagram for Fig. 6.36.

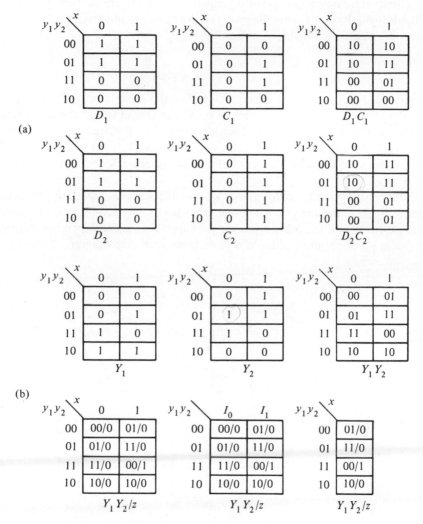

(a)

(b)

Fig. 6.39　K-map state table development: (a) flip-flop input maps; (b) next state maps.

Level Asynchronous Circuits (Type 4)

The last category of sequential circuits contains all those with unclocked memory elements and level inputs, whether synchronized by a clock signal or not. Consider the example circuit defined by Fig. 6.40. The circuit is composed of AND, OR, and NOT gates with one delay line memory element.

The level asynchronous types of sequential circuits are perhaps the most difficult to analyze. A timing diagram for the circuit is shown in Fig. 6.40(b). The logic equations for the circuit are

$$Y = \overline{xy} = \bar{x} + \bar{y}$$
$$z = xy + \bar{x}\bar{y} = x \odot y$$

Observing the equation for Y we notice that the complement of the input signal x serves as a control variable to mask out transitions in the delay line feedback loop. If $x = 0$ ($\bar{x} = 1$), then the next state Y is independent of the present state y. When $x = 1$ ($\bar{x} = 0$), the next state Y is the complement of the present state y, and the sequential circuit cycles back and forth between the 0 and 1 state.

This type of circuit is unique from all the others in that there are no pulses present to aid in the analysis. The other types have input pulses or clock pulses present. In each of the other types we examined the sequential circuit during the pulse duration and produced a state table and state diagram. However,

(a)

(b)

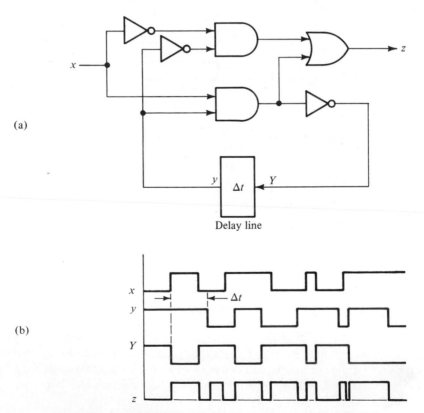

Fig. 6.40   A level asynchronous sequential circuit: (a) logic diagram; (b) timing diagram.

the level asynchronous circuits are more difficult to describe. We shall postpone our discussion of this type until a later chapter, at which time we shall introduce a special notation for handling this unusual case.

Summary

In Chapter 6 we have introduced models for sequential circuits including logic diagrams, state tables and diagrams, and the Mealy and Moore formulations. Examples of all types of synchronous and asynchronous sequential circuits have been analyzed. Also, many practical memory elements have been described. The reader should now be able to take the logic diagram for any given sequential network, provided it is not extremely complicated, apply the analysis techniques of this chapter, and derive a state table or timing diagram description of the circuit. In the next chapter we shall reverse this procedure and find logic diagrams for a specified state table or diagram.

REFERENCES

1. GILL, A., *Introduction to the Theory of Finite-State Machines.* New York: McGraw-Hill Book Company, 1962.

2. HUFFMAN, D. A., "The Synthesis of Sequential Switching Circuits," *J. Franklin Inst.*, Vol. 257, Nos. 3 and 4, March and April 1954, pp. 161–190, 275–303.

3. McCLUSKEY, E. J., JR., *Introduction to the Theory of Switching Circuits.* New York: McGraw-Hill Book Company, 1965.

4. MEALY, G. H., "A Method for Synthesizing Sequential Circuits," *Bell System Tech. J.*, Vol. 34, September 1955, pp. 1045–1079.

5. MILLER, R. E., *Switching Theory*, Vol. II: *Sequential Circuits and Machines*, New York: John Wiley & Sons, Inc., 1965.

6. MOORE, E. F., "Gedanken—Experiments on Sequential Machines," *Automata Studies, Annals of Mathematical Studies*, No. 34. Princeton, N.J.: Princeton University Press, 1956, pp. 129–153.

PROBLEMS

6.1. Construct a state diagram from the following state table:

	x 0	1
A	$D/1$	$B/0$
B	$D/1$	$C/0$
C	$D/1$	$A/0$
D	$B/1$	$C/0$

What is the logic equation for the output variable z?

6.2. Given the state table below, find the output and state sequences for the input sequence

$$x = 010101$$

if the circuit starts in state A:

	x	
	0	1
A	$D/0$	$B/0$
B	$C/0$	$B/0$
C	$B/0$	$C/0$
D	$B/0$	$C/1$

6.3. For the following sequential circuit, determine the output sequence for the input sequence

$$x = 0010110101$$

if the starting state is A. Draw a state diagram for the circuit.

	x	
	0	1
A	$B/0$	$C/1$
B	$C/1$	$B/0$
C	$A/0$	$A/1$

6.4. For the synchronous sequential circuit of Fig. P6.1, find
   (a) The state table using K-maps and $A \equiv 0$, $B \equiv 1$.
   (b) The state diagram if the circuit input is in pulse form.
   (c) The timing diagram for an input sequence $x = 00100110$ and the starting state $y^0 = 1$.

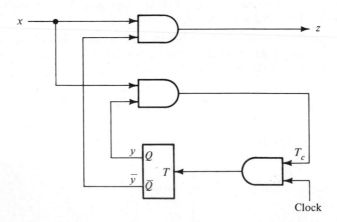

Fig. P6.1

6.5. Given the synchronous sequential circuit of Fig. P6.2 with level inputs,
       (a) Draw a timing diagram for $x = 000101011$ and $y^0 = 0$.
       (b) Find the state diagram.
       (c) Find the state table.

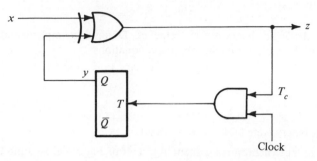

Fig. P6.2

6.6. For the sequential circuit in Fig. P6.3, find
       (a) The state table ($A \equiv 0$, $B \equiv 1$).
       (b) The state diagram.
       (c) A timing diagram if the starting state is $y^0 = 0$ and $x = 001011000$.
       This circuit is level synchronous (type 2).

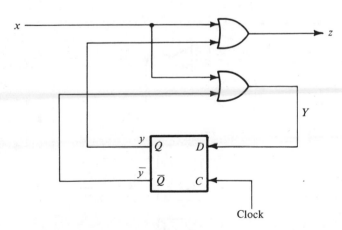

Fig. P6.3

6.7. Draw the logic diagram for a synchronous sequential circuit using clocked
       T flip-flops and the switching functions

$$z = T_{c1} = x\bar{y}_2$$
$$T_{c2} = x \oplus y_1$$

Find a state diagram of the circuit using the assignment

$$\begin{array}{c c c}
 & y_1 & y_2 \\
\hline
A: & 0 & 0 \\
B: & 0 & 1 \\
C: & 1 & 1 \\
D: & 1 & 0 \\
\end{array}$$

6.8. Draw the logic diagram for a clocked D flip-flop implementation of a sequential circuit employing the logic equations

$$Y_1 = \bar{x} \oplus y_1 = x \odot y_1$$

$$Y_2 = x + y_1 + y_2$$

$$z = x y_1 \bar{y}_2$$

Find a binary state table for this circuit.

6.9. Analyze the synchronous sequential circuit of Fig. P6.4. Assume the inputs are binary levels and that the following state assignment is used:

$$\begin{array}{c c c}
 & y_1 & y_2 \\
\hline
A: & 0 & 0 \\
B: & 0 & 1 \\
C: & 1 & 0 \\
D: & 1 & 1 \\
\end{array}$$

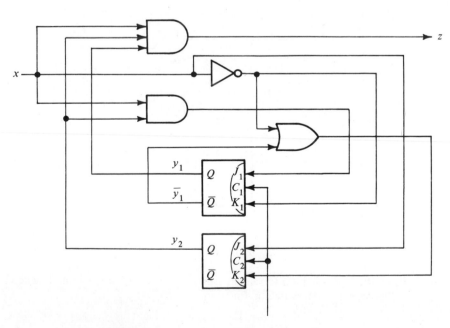

Fig. P6.4

Use K-maps to find
(a) The state table.
(b) The state diagram.

6.10. Consider the asynchronous sequential circuit presented in Fig. P6.5. If the circuit input is synchronous pulses, determine
(a) The state table if $A \equiv 0$, $B \equiv 1$.
(b) The state diagram.
(c) The timing diagram for $x = 010011010$ and $y^0 = 0$.
Hint: You may use K-maps.

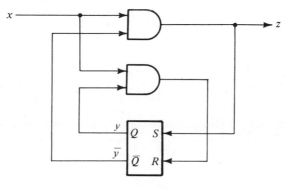

Fig. P6.5

6.11. Analyze the asynchronous sequential circuit of Fig. P6.6. This circuit has synchronous pulses as its input x. Construct
(a) A timing diagram for the input sequence $x = 01101000$ and $y^0 = 0$.
(b) A state table.
(c) A state diagram.

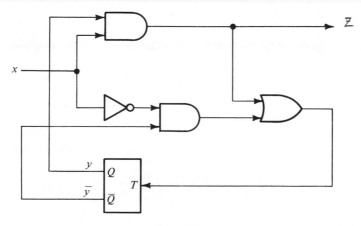

Fig. P6.6

In your solution you may define the pulse widths of the input x to be equal to the time delay of the T flip-flop. Discuss what effect the following condition will have on the operation of this sequential circuit: Allow the input pulse width to be somewhat longer than the flip-flop time delay. Show your conclusions on the timing diagram for (a).

6.12. Analyze the asynchronous sequential circuit of Fig. P6.7 if the circuit input is synchronous pulses. Find

(a) The timing diagram if $x = 01010010100$ and $y_1^0 y_2^0 = 11$.

(b) The state table.

(c) The state diagram.

Hint: K-maps yield incorrect results because assumption 3 for type 3 circuits is violated.

why doesn't this happen in 6.11?

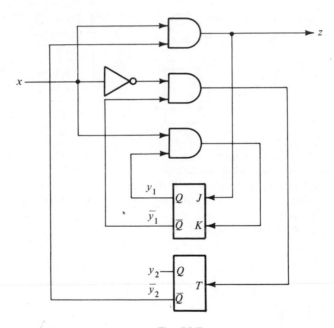

Fig. P6.7

6.13. If the sequential circuit of Fig. P6.8 yields an output sequence

$$z = 1\ 1\ 0\ 1\ 1\ 1\ 1\ 1$$

when one applies the input sequence

$$x = 0\ 1\ 1\ 0\ 1\ 0\ 1\ 0$$

what is the starting state?

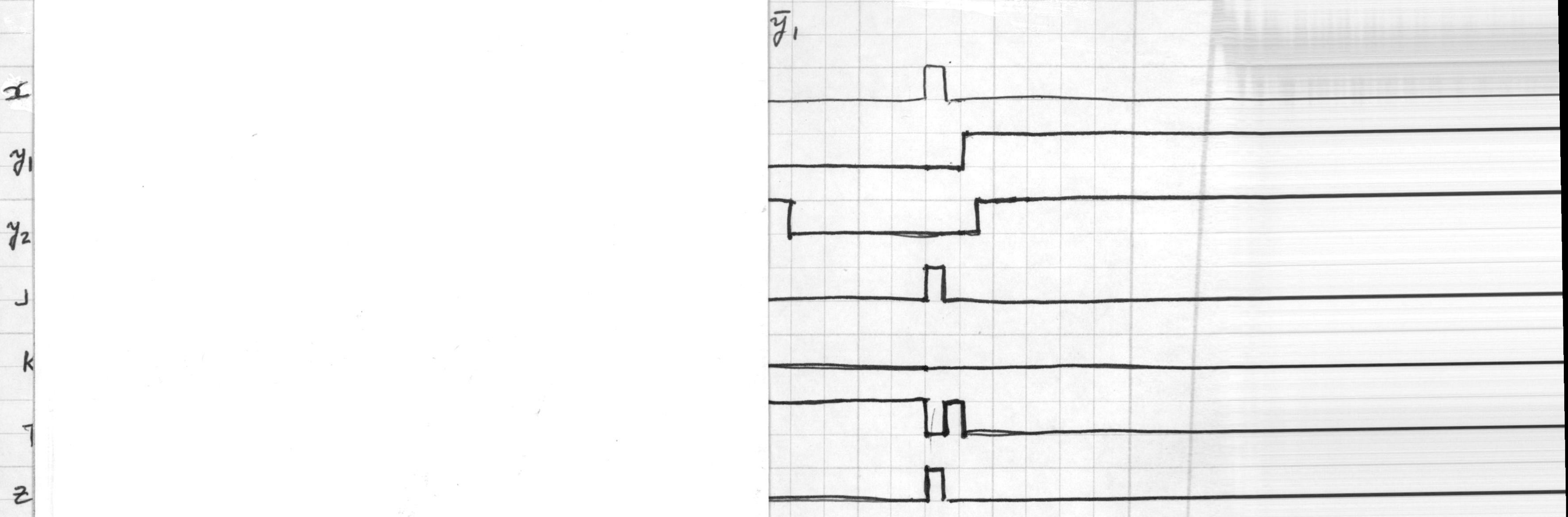

$\overline{y}_1$

x

y_1

y_2

$\lrcorner$

k

$\top$

z

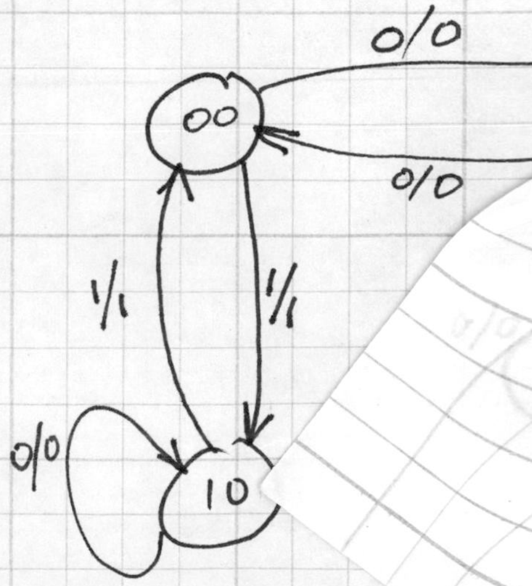

0/0

0/0

1/1   1/1

0/0

00

10

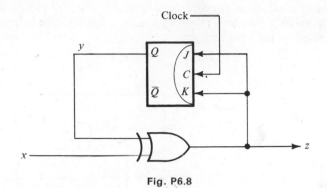

Fig. P6.8

6.14. Find the state table for the sequential circuit in Fig. P6.9.

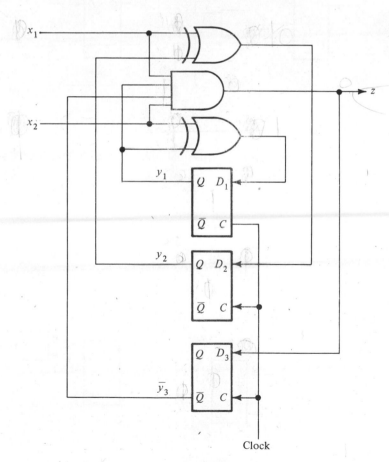

Fig. P6.9

6.15. Consider a sequential circuit consisting of two cascaded circuits illustrated in Fig. P6.10. If the starting state is $y_1 = y_2 = 0$, what is the output sequence generated by the input sequence

$$x = 0\ 1\ 1\ 0\ 1\ 1\ 1\ 0\ 1\ 0$$

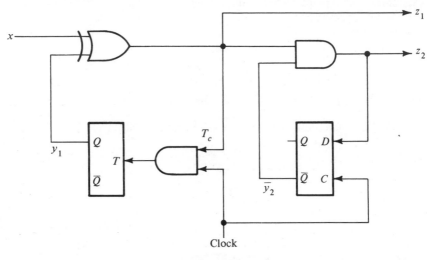

Fig. P6.10

6.16. Find the state diagram for the sequential circuit of Fig. P6.11 using the state assignment

	y_1	y_2
A:	0	0
B:	0	1
C:	1	0
D:	1	1

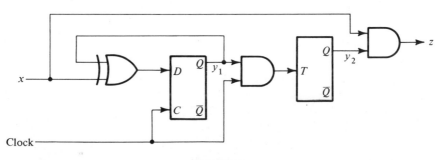

Fig. P6.11

6.17. Construct state diagrams for
    (a) The D flip-flop.
    (b) The SR flip-flop.
    (c) The T flip-flop.
    (d) The JK flip-flop.

6.18. Derive the flip-flop state equations shown in
    (a) Equation (6-8) for D flip-flops.
    (b) Equation (6-10) for SR flip-flops.
    (c) Equation (6-11) for T flip-flops.
    (d) Equation (6-13) for JK flip-flops.

6.19. Derive the state equation of equation (6-14) for clocked JK flip-flops.

6.20. Connect a D flip-flop in such a manner that it will perform like a T flip-flop.

7

Synthesis
of
Synchronous
Sequential
Circuits

In Chapter 6, the analysis of sequential circuits was introduced using several examples. In each case a logic diagram was given and the resulting analysis produced a state table or diagram. In this chapter the reverse procedure, the synthesis process, will be addressed [1–6]. For a given state table or diagram, well-defined tools will be used to generate an equivalent logic diagram for the sequential circuit in question. All sequential circuits in this chapter have clocked memory elements and are thus *synchronous* sequential circuits. These circuits have been classified as type 1 and type 2 circuits in Chapter 6.

In our previous work, each time we analyzed a sequential circuit, we found that the resulting state table was usually completely determined, or specified. However, occasionally a circuit is connected in such a manner that the state table cannot be completely defined (for example, a circuit which causes a 1 input to both the S and R terminals of an SR flip-flop).

The synthesis of synchronous sequential circuits begins with the specification of the desired state table (or diagram). Circuits for which every next state/output pair is completely defined are termed *completely specified circuits*. Those for which several next states or outputs are arbitrary are termed *incompletely specified circuits*. An example of each type of circuit is shown in Fig. 7.1.

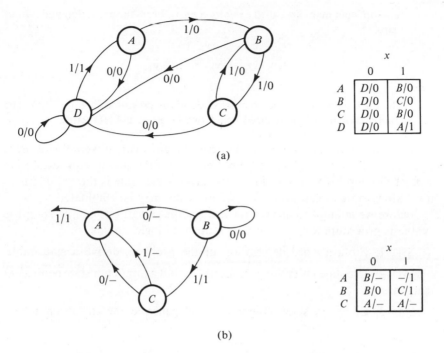

(a)

(b)

Fig. 7.1 Types of sequential circuits: (a) completely specified circuit; (b) incompletely specified circuit.

The term *sequential machine* is often used to refer to the mathematical model of a sequential circuit. However, in the following pages, the terms sequential machine and sequential circuit will be used synonymously.

The Synthesis Procedure

The procedure for designing synchronous sequential circuits will be introduced by a simple example.

Example.

Suppose one needs to find a clocked D flip-flop realization for the sequential circuit defined in Fig. 7.2(a). First we must adopt some coding scheme for the symbolic states. This process is called *state assignment*. We arbitrarily choose the code in Fig. 7.2(b). If one replaces the symbolic states with their code equivalent, he obtains a binary state table, or in other words the *transition table* shown in Fig. 7.2(c). The transition table contains all the necessary information for generating the Boolean functions for the combinational logic portion of the circuit. Then we separate the transition table into an output K-map and D flip-flop input K-maps as shown in Fig. 7.2(d) and (e). The flip-flop input maps are called *excitation maps*. From the excitation and output maps,

$$D_1 = y_1\bar{y}_2 + xy_2$$

$$D_2 = \bar{x}y_1 + x\bar{y}_1 = x \oplus y_1$$

$$z = x\bar{y}_1y_2 + \bar{x}y_1\bar{y}_2$$

The logic diagram for the completed design is presented in Fig. 7.2(f). The combinational logic is realized using two levels of NAND gates.

In the foregoing example several questions remain unanswered. How does one choose the state assignment? What happens if the design requires another type of flip-flop? How do we know the given state table is the "best" one to use? Many state tables have extra states which may be eliminated.

Before we attempt to answer these questions, let us outline the complete synthesis procedure for synchronous sequential logic circuits:

STEP 1. From a word description of the problem, derive a state table.

STEP 2. Use state reduction techniques to find a minimum state equivalent machine.

STEP 3. Choose a state assignment and generate the transition tables.

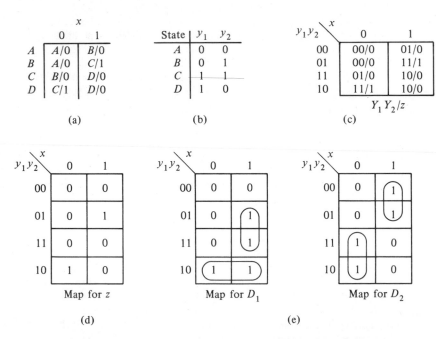

(a)

(b)

(c)

(d)

(e)

Fig. 7.2 An introductory example: (a) state table; (b) state assignment; (c) transition table; (d) output map; (e) excitation maps.

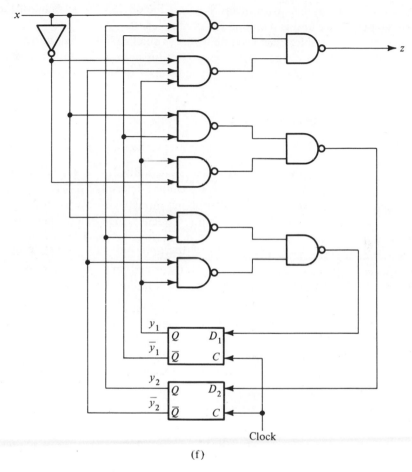

(f)

Fig. 7.2—*Cont.* (f) logic diagram.

STEP 4. Determine the memory device or flip-flop to be used and find the excitation maps.

STEP 5. From the excitation maps, produce the Boolean logic equations. Also, form output maps and determine the output logic equations.

STEP 6. Draw the logic diagram of the sequential circuit using the Boolean logic equations and the chosen memory devices.

The first step requires intuition on the part of the logic designer and must be learned through trial and error experience. Steps 2, 3, and 4 are presented in much detail in this chapter. We shall see that the successful designer employs standard algorithms and rules of thumb in completing these steps. The skills required in step 5 are found in Chapter 3 and hence it is assumed that the reader is familiar with them. Step 6 is the obvious conclusion of the synthesis procedure and is included for completeness.

Now that the problem has been defined, we shall examine techniques for state reduction, state assignment, and excitation map generation for both completely and incompletely specified synchronous sequential circuits.

Completely Specified Circuits

Equivalent States

In a general sense we say that two states are equivalent if we cannot distinguish between them. In other words, we cannot determine in which of two equivalent states a machine starts by applying inputs and observing the outputs. If this condition exists for every input sequence, then one of these states is redundant and can be removed without altering the machine's behavior.

Redundant states normally arise in an early design phase when a word description of the machine's function is transformed into a state diagram or state table. The removal of redundant states is important for a number of reasons:

1. *Cost:* The number of memory elements is directly related to the number of states.
2. *Complexity:* The more states the machine contains, the more complex the machine and its associate circuitry become.
3. *Aids failure analysis:* Diagnostic routines are often predicated upon the assumption that no redundant states exist.

Let us introduce the idea of equivalence through a simple example. Consider the machine shown in Fig. 7.3(a) and (b). Suppose that the machine's initial state is unknown. If an input $x = 0$ is applied to the machine and the output is $z = 1$, all that is known concerning the circuit's initial state is that it was either A or B or C. If the output had been $z = 0$, then the initial state would have been either D or E. In other words, for a single input $x = 0$, all that can be concluded concerning the machine's initial state is that it is either A or B or C if $z = 1$ and either D or E if $z = 0$. Note that a similar conclusion is obtained for the input $x = 1$. Therefore, we conclude that states A, B, and C are equivalent and that states D and E are equivalent for an input sequence of length 1, i.e., 1-equivalent. The machine's behavior for input sequences of lengths 2 and 3 is shown in Fig. 7.3(c) and (d). Note that states B and C and that states D and E are 2-equivalent. States B and C are also 3-equivalent, and in fact it can be shown that these two states are K-equivalent for all K.

With these facts as basic background we now define precisely what is meant by equivalent states.

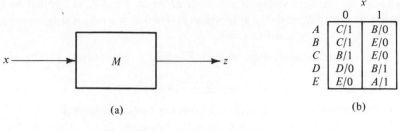

(a)   (b)

| | Input sequences | | | |
Initial state	00	01	10	11
A	11	10	01	00
B	11	10	00	01
C	11	10	00	01
D	00	01	11	10
E	00	01	11	10

Output sequences

(c)

| | Input sequences | | | | | | | |
Initial state	000	001	010	011	100	101	110	111
A	111	110	100	101	011	010	000	001
B	111	110	100	101	000	001	011	010
C	111	110	100	101	000	001	011	010
D	000	001	011	010	111	110	100	101
E	000	001	011	010	111	110	101	100

Output sequences

(d)

Fig. 7.3 Redundant states: (a) machine M; (b) state table; (c) sequences of length two; (d) sequences of length three.

Definition.

The states $S_1, S_2, \ldots, S_j$ of a sequential circuit are said to be equivalent if and only if for every possible input sequence, the same output sequence will be produced by the circuit regardless of whether $S_1, S_2, \ldots, S_j$ is the initial state.

This definition can be stated in another manner for pairs of states. Let

S_k and S_l be the next states of machine M when input I_p is applied to the machine in states S_i and S_j, respectively. Then S_i and S_j are *equivalent* if and only if, for every possible input I_p,

1. The output produced by state S_i is equal to the output produced by state S_j, and
2. The next states S_k and S_l are equivalent.

The second definition can be deduced from the first as follows. If S_i produces a different output for any input I_p than S_j produces for I_p, then S_i and S_j cannot be equivalent. Hence, the first condition is necessary. If S_k and S_l are not equivalent then there is an input sequence $I_1 I_2 \ldots I_m$ that produces a different output sequence for S_k as a starting state than for S_l as a starting state. Therefore $I_p I_1 I_2 \ldots I_k$ will produce a different output sequence for S_i as a starting state than for S_j as a starting state. Hence, S_i and S_j cannot be equivalent unless the second condition is satisfied. Finally, the conditions are clearly sufficient for S_i and S_j to be equivalent; and therefore the two definitions are synonymous. These two conditions form the basis for all state reduction techniques.

Basically, there are three techniques for determining equivalent states:

1. Inspection.
2. Partitioning.
3. The implication table.

Inspection. The simplest and most obvious technique is that of recognizing equivalent states by inspection. In this approach one need only recognize multiple, identical rows in the state table and then remove the redundant states.

Example.

The sequential circuit defined by the state table shown in Fig. 7.4(a) can be reduced by inspection by noting that states B and D perform exactly the same function. Hence, state D can be removed from the table by simply replacing state D in the remainder of the table by its equivalent state B. This procedure results in the state table shown in Fig. 7.4(b).

	x	
	0	1
A	$B/0$	$C/1$
B	$C/0$	$A/1$
C	$D/1$	$B/0$
D	$C/0$	$A/1$

(a)

	x	
	0	1
A	$B/0$	$C/1$
B	$C/0$	$A/1$
C	$B/1$	$B/0$

(b)

Fig. 7.4   State equivalence by inspection: (a) original machine; (b) reduced equivalent machine.

Partitioning. The partitioning approach involves the successive determination of partitions P_K, $K = 1, 2, 3, \ldots, l$, in which each P_K is composed of a number of *blocks*, each of which consists of a group of one or more states. The states contained within a given block of P_K are K-equivalent. In other words given a sequential machine with states $S_1, S_2, \ldots, S_5$, if $P_K = (S_1 S_3)(S_2 S_4)$ (S_5), then P_K contains three blocks and S_1 and S_3 are K-equivalent, as are S_2 and S_4. S_5 is not K-equivalent to any other state in the sequential machine. For clarity, the sequential circuit described by Fig. 7.3(b) will be used as an example in describing the partitioning procedure:

STEP 1. The first partition P_1 is formed by placing two or more states in the same block of P_1 if and only if their *output* is identical for each possible input. For the example of Fig. 7.3(b), $P_1 = (ABC)(DE)$, and hence the states within each block are 1-equivalent. This step guarantees that each block in P_1 satisfies condition 1 for equivalent states.

STEP 2. Successive partitions P_K, $K = 2, 3, 4, \ldots, l$, are derived by placing two or more states in the same block of P_K if and only if for each input value, their next states all lie in a *single* block of P_{K-1}. This iterative procedure is suggested by condition 2 for equivalent states.

In performing this procedure for our example it is necessary to check the groups of states in each block of P_1. In the first block, the next states for A, B, and C with $x = 0$ all lie in the same block of P_1. However, for $x = 1$, the next state of A lies in a different block of P_1 than the next states of B and C. Therefore the block (ABC) contained in P_1 is split into the blocks $(A)(BC)$ in P_2. See Fig. 7.5. The next states of states D and E lie in the same block of

P_0	A	B	C	D	E
$x = 0$	1	1	1	0	0
$x = 1$	0	0	0	1	1
P_1	A	B	C	D	E
$x = 0$	C	C	B	D	E
$x = 1$	B	E	E	B	A
P_2	A	B	C	D	E
$x = 0$	C	C	B	D	E
$x = 1$	B	E	E	B	A
P_3	A	B	C	D	E
$x = 0$	C	C	B	D	E
$x = 1$	B	E	E	B	A
$P_4 = P_3$	A	B	C	D	E

States B and C are equivalent.

Fig. 7.5   State equivalence by partitioning.

P_1 for both $x = 0$ and $x = 1$, and hence D and E will remain in the same block of P_2. Thus,

$$P_2 = (A)(BC)(DE)$$

and the states within each block are 2-equivalent. Hence, P_2 should correspond exactly to Fig. 7.3(c).

Partition P_3 is obtained by examining each block of P_2. The next states of B and C lie in the same block of P_2 for each input, and hence the block (BC) remains intact in P_3. However, the next states for D and E with $x = 1$ lie in different blocks of P_2, and hence these two states must appear in different blocks of P_3. Therefore $P_3 = (A)(BC)(D)(E)$. This agrees with Fig. 7.3(d), and hence only states B and C are 3-equivalent.

This procedure of obtaining successive partitions is repeated until the condition stated in step 3 is obtained.

STEP 3. When $P_{K+1} = P_K$, i.e., once the partition repeats, then the states in each block of P_K that are K-equivalent are $(K + 1)$-equivalent $(K + 2)$-equivalent, etc., and P_K is said to be an *equivalence* partition. In our example a quick check indicates that $P_4 = P_3$ and therefore states B and C are K-equivalent for any K, i.e., equivalent. Condition 2 for equivalent states in now satisfied by P_K.

Example.

The partitions for the state table shown in Fig. 7.6(a) are

$$P_1 = (AD)(BE)(CF)(GH)$$
$$P_2 = (AD)(BE)(CF)(G)(H)$$
$$P_3 = P_2$$

The reduced state table using the symbolic states below is shown in Fig. 7.6(b):

$$A' = (AD), \qquad C' = (CF), \qquad E' = (H),$$
$$B' = (BE), \qquad D' = (G)$$

	x	
	0	1
A	$E/0$	$D/0$
B	$A/1$	$F/0$
C	$C/0$	$A/1$
D	$B/0$	$A/0$
E	$D/1$	$C/0$
F	$C/0$	$D/1$
G	$H/1$	$G/1$
H	$C/1$	$B/1$

(a)

	x	
	0	1
A'	$B'/0$	$A'/0$
B'	$A'/1$	$C'/0$
C'	$C'/0$	$A'/1$
D'	$E'/1$	$D'/1$
E'	$C'/1$	$B'/1$

(b)

Fig. 7.6 Partitioning example: (a) original machine; (b) reduced equivalent machine.

Example.

The state table is shown in Fig. 7.7(a). The partitions are listed below:

$$P_1 = (ACG)(BDEH)(F)$$

$$P_2 = (A)(CG)(BH)(DE)(F), \quad \text{from column } x = 0$$

$$= (A)(C)(G)(BH)(DE)(F), \quad \text{from column } x = 1$$

$$P_3 = P_2$$

Using the following symbolic states yields the reduced state table shown in Fig. 7.7(b):

$$A' = (A), \quad C' = (C), \quad E' = (BH),$$

$$B' = (F), \quad D' = (G), \quad F' = (DE)$$

	x 0	1
A	A/0	B/0
B	H/1	C/0
C	E/0	B/0
D	C/1	D/0
E	C/1	E/0
F	F/1	G/1
G	B/0	F/0
H	H/1	C/0

(a)

	x 0	1
A'	A'/0	E'/0
B'	B'/1	D'/1
C'	F'/0	E'/0
D'	E'/0	B'/0
E'	E'/1	C'/0
F'	C'/1	F'/0

(b)

Fig. 7.7 Partitioning example: (a) original machine; (b) reduced equivalent machine.

Example.

This example illustrates that the techniques described above are applicable for sequential machines with multiple inputs. The state table for a sequential circuit with two input lines is shown in Fig. 7.8(a). The partitions are

$$P_1 = (ADFG)(BCEH)$$

$$P_2 = (AFG)(D)(BCEH)$$

$$P_3 = (AF)(G)(D)(BCH)(E)$$

$$P_4 = P_3$$

The reduced state table is shown in Fig. 7.8(b), where the following state substitution has been used:

$$A' = (AF), \quad C' = (D), \quad E' = (G)$$

$$B' = (BCH), \quad D' = (E),$$

Equivalence relations. Let x and y be elements of a set S. Suppose x and y are related by a property r which is denoted $x \, r \, y$. A *relation R* on the set S

	\(x_1x_2\)			
	00	01	10	11
A	*D*/0	*D*/0	*F*/0	*A*/0
B	*C*/1	*D*/0	*E*/1	*F*/0
C	*C*/1	*D*/0	*E*/1	*A*/0
D	*D*/0	*B*/0	*A*/0	*F*/0
E	*C*/1	*F*/0	*E*/1	*A*/0
F	*D*/0	*D*/0	*A*/0	*F*/0
G	*G*/0	*G*/0	*A*/0	*A*/0
H	*B*/1	*D*/0	*E*/1	*A*/0

(a)

	\(x_1x_2\)			
	00	01	10	11
A′	*C′*/0	*C′*/0	*A′*/0	*A′*/0
B′	*B′*/1	*C′*/0	*D′*/1	*A′*/0
C′	*C′*/0	*B′*/0	*A′*/0	*A′*/0
D′	*B′*/1	*A′*/0	*D′*/1	*A′*/0
E′	*E′*/0	*E′*/0	*A′*/0	*A′*/0

(b)

Fig. 7.8   Multiple input example: (a) original machine; (b) reduced equivalent machine.

is the set of all ordered pairs (s_i, s_j) such that s_i and s_j are elements of S and such that $s_i \, r \, s_j$. R is *reflexive* if and only if $s_i \, r \, s_i$ for all s_i in S. R is *symmetric* if and only if $s_i \, r \, s_j$ implies that $s_j \, r \, s_i$. R is *transitive* if and only if $s_i \, r \, s_j$ and $s_j \, r \, s_k$ imply that $s_i \, r \, s_k$. An *equivalence relation* on S is a relation on S which is symmetric, reflexive, and transitive. The elements of S can be partitioned into disjoint subsets called *equivalence classes* by an equivalence relation.

It can be shown that state equivalence defines an equivalence relation on the set of states of a completely specified sequential machine. Hence, the equivalence classes are used to define the states of the reduced state table.

A relation on S is said to be a *compatibility relation* if and only if the relation is reflexive and symmetric. Compatibility relations define subsets of S referred to as *compatibility classes*. These subsets are not, in general, disjoint. The subject of compatibility classes will be important when the reduction of incompletely specified state tables is discussed later in the chapter.

Implication table. The implication table, like partitioning, is used to determine state equivalence. This technique is more general in that it can be applied to incompletely specified sequential machines; however, it can also be more time consuming than the partitioning approach.

Consider once again the example shown in Fig. 7.3(b). This example will be used to explain the procedure.

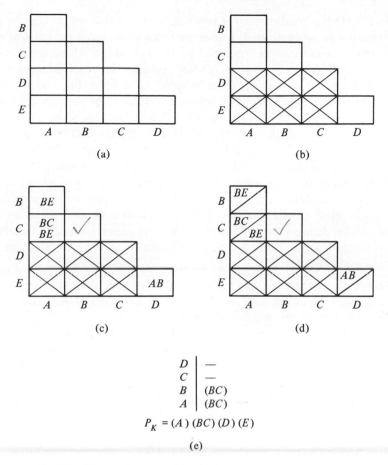

Fig. 7.9 The implication table: (a) implication table; (b) output partitioning; (c) implied pairs; (d) completed table; (e) equivalence partition.

STEP 1. Form the table shown in Fig. 7.9(a), which is derived by listing vertically all states in the state table except the first and listing horizontally all states in the state table except the last. The resulting table displays all possible combinations of two states, and hence each cell in the table corresponding to the intersection of a row and column represents two states being tested for equivalence.

STEP 2. Since only states with identical outputs can possibly be equivalent (condition 1 for equivalent states), an X is placed in the cells corresponding to those pairs of states whose outputs are not equal for every input. This has been done in Fig. 7.9(b) for the example.

STEP 3. Using condition 2 for equivalent states, the vacant cells in Fig. 7.9(b) must now be completed. Into these blocks are placed the pairs of next states whose equivalence is "implied" by the two states whose intersection defines the cell. As an illustration of this, consider the cell defined by states A and B. From the state table it can be seen that in order for A and B to be equivalent states, B and E must be equivalent. Hence, the pair BE is listed in the cell defined by A and B, as shown in Fig. 7.9(c). Note the if the states of the implied pair, B and E, are not equivalent, then there exists an input string beginning with $x = 0$ which will produce different outputs depending on whether the initial state is A or B, meaning A and B are not equivalent.

If the implied pairs for any cell contain only the states which define the cell or if the next states of the two states defining the cell are the same state for a given input, then a check mark ($\checkmark$) is placed in the cell indicating that the two states defining the cell are equivalent by *inspection* and independent of any implied pairs. This condition is illustrated in Fig. 7.9(c) by the cell defined by states B and C.

STEP 4. Once the table has been completely filled, successive passes are made through the entire table to determine if any cells should be crossed off other than those crossed out in step 2.

A cell in the table is crossed out if it contains at least one implied pair which defines a cell in the table that has previously been crossed out. This operation has been performed for the example, and the resulting table is shown in Fig. 7.9(d). For example, the cell defined by A and B was crossed out because it contained the pair BE which defines a cell which was already crossed out. This procedure is repeated until no additional cells can be crossed off.

STEP 5. Finally the table shown in Fig. 7.9(e) is obtained by listing as a column the states which define the horizontal row of the implication table. Then the implication table is examined column by column from right to left to see if any cells are not crossed out. The states which define any cell that has not been crossed out are equivalent and are listed as an equivalent pair in the table in Fig. 7.9(e). Pairs are combined using transitivity:

$$(S_i, S_j)(S_j, S_k) \longrightarrow (S_i, S_j, S_k) \tag{7-1}$$

In the example, all the cells in columns D and C are crossed out and hence dashes are placed in rows D and C in the table of Fig. 7.9(e). In column B of the implication table the cell defined by states B and C is not crossed out and hence the pair (BC) is placed in row B of the table. Row A contains everything in row B plus any other equivalent pairs found in column A of the implication table. The equivalence partition then consists of all the equivalent states found in the last row of the table, i.e., (BC) together with the remaining states of the circuit which are not equivalent to any other state. Note that this equivalence partition is identical to that obtained earlier by partitioning.

Example.

The implication table can be employed to determine the equivalence partition for the sequential circuit shown in Fig. 7.6(a). The analysis for this example is shown in Fig. 7.10.

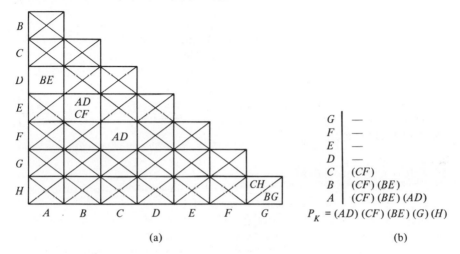

(a)   (b)

Fig. 7.10 Implication table example: (a) implication table; (b) equivalence partition.

Example.

The equivalence partition for the sequential circuit described by the state table of Fig. 7.8(a) is determined in Fig. 7.11. This example, although straight-

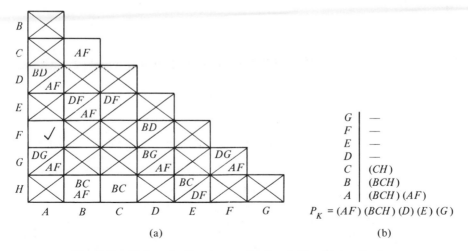

(a)   (b)

Fig. 7.11 State reduction by implication table: (a) implication table; (b) equivalence partition.

forward, does contain one salient feature. In row B of Fig. 7.11(b) is listed the set of equivalent states (BCH). The reason for this is equation (7-1). If B is equivalent to C and H is equivalent to C, then by the transitive property H is equivalent to B. Note that the fact that H is equivalent to B is also illustrated in the implication table by the fact that the cell defined by the two states is not crossed off.

The two examples above, which illustrate the use of the implication table, can be compared with the previously used partitioning method. In general the implication table approach is more routine, but it is also more tedious than the partitioning approach.

In this section we have examined three techniques for minimizing the number of states of synchronous sequential circuits. Any one may be used in the synthesis process.

Flip-Flop Input Tables

In the introductory synthesis example of Fig. 7.2, the edge-triggered D flip-flop was employed for circuit realization. In particular, the characteristics of the D flip-flop were used to generate the excitation maps from the transition table. The transition table defines the necessary state transitions for each memory flip-flop. A *flip-flop input table* may be used to determine the required inputs for each type of flip-flop memory element. Consider the input tables of Fig. 7.12. The D flip-flop is convenient to employ because its next state is

State Transitions		Required Inputs
$Q(t)$	$Q(t+\epsilon)$	$D(t)$
0	0	0
0	1	1
1	0	0
1	1	1

(a)

State Transitions		Required Inputs	
$Q(t)$	$Q(t+\epsilon)$	$S(t)$	$R(t)$
0	0	0	d
0	1	1	0
1	0	0	1
1	1	d	0

(b)

State Transitions		Required Inputs
$Q(t)$	$Q(t+\epsilon)$	$T_c(t)$
0	0	0
0	1	1
1	0	1
1	1	0

(c)

State Transitions		Required Inputs	
$Q(t)$	$Q(t+\epsilon)$	$J(t)$	$K(t)$
0	0	0	d
0	1	1	d
1	0	d	1
1	1	d	0

(d)

Fig. 7.12   Flip-flop input tables: (a) D flip-flop; (b) clocked SR flip-flop; (c) clocked T flip-flop; (d) clocked JK flip-flop.

its present input; hence, the excitation maps are taken directly from the transition table. Any other flip-flop requires the application of its input table of Fig. 7.12 in the production of the excitation K-maps. The flip-flop input tables are derived from the flip-flop descriptions of Chapter 6.

Example.

Let us implement the machine of Fig. 7.2 using clocked JK flip-flops. Assume the same state assignment. The transition table remains unchanged and is reproduced in Fig. 7.13(a) for convenience.

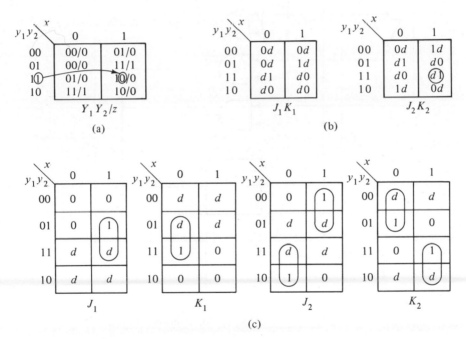

Fig. 7.13 Generating the excitation map: (a) transition table; (b) excitation tables; (c) excitation maps.

The flip-flop input table of Fig. 7.12(d) is used to obtain the excitation tables of Fig. 7.13(b). One state transition is emphasized both in the transition table and in the corresponding entry of the excitation table; i.e., the transition of y_2 shown in Fig. 7.13(a) from 1 to 0 requires $J_2 = d$ and $K_2 = 1$, as illustrated in Fig. 7.13(b). Next the excitation tables are transformed into excitation K-maps and the required Boolean logic equations are minimized as follows:

$$J_1 = xy_2, \qquad K_1 = \bar{x}y_2,$$
$$J_2 = x \oplus y_1, \qquad K_2 = x \odot y_1 = \bar{J}_2$$

The logic diagram is shown in Fig. 7.14. The output logic is unchanged from Fig. 7.2(f).

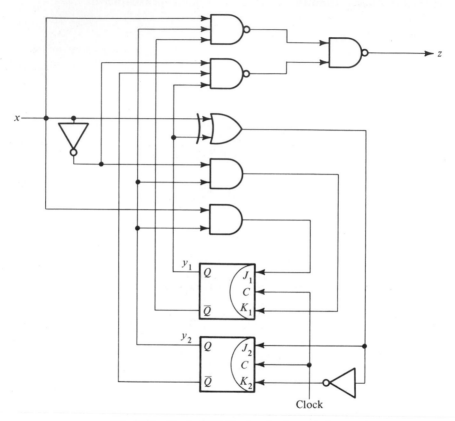

Fig. 7.14   Clocked JK flip-flop implementation.

The last example illustrated a general procedure for finding excitation maps which is valid for all synchronous flip-flop types. A special technique which matches the state equation for the clocked JK flip-flop to a particular application is presented in the section entitled special-sequence counters of Chapter 11. The interested reader may adopt it for clocked JK flip-flops here if he wishes.

Design Examples

The synthesis procedure for synchronous sequential circuits has been presented earlier in this chapter as a six-step process. The reader should now be able to complete all the steps except step 3, state assignment. Let us postpone the development of the theory of this topic and, instead, dwell on some practical applications of the other five steps for the moment. This change of pace has two purposes: first, to allow the reader to practice his skills of state reduction and excitation map generation, and, second, to provide a basis from which to present the state assignment problem.

The design procedure will be demonstrated by several examples. In each example it is assumed that the circuit is under the control of a periodic clock pulse and that transitions in the circuits occur only as initiated by this clock.

Example.

The word description of the problem can be stated as follows: Design a synchronous sequential circuit with one input and one output that recognizes the input sequence 01. In other words, the circuit should produce an output sequence $z = 01$ whenever the input sequence $x = 01$ occurs. For example, if the input sequence is

$$x = 010100000111101$$

then the output sequence will be

$$z = 010100000100001$$

The first step in the design procedure is the construction of a state diagram which represents the input-output behavior described above. The diagram is constructed as shown in Fig. 7.15. First, it is assumed that the machine is in some starting state A and that the first input is a 1. Since a 1 is not the first element in the input string to be recognized, the machine remains in state A and yields an output $z = 0$, as shown in Fig. 7.15(a). However, if the machine is in the initial state A and the input is a 0, then because this input is the first input symbol in the string to be recognized, the machine moves to a new state B and produces an output of 0, as shown in Fig. 7.15(b). Now suppose that the machine is in state B and that the input symbol is a 0. Because this is not the second symbol in the sequence 01, the machine merely remains in state B and yields an output $z = 0$. Finally, if the machine is in state B and the next input symbol is a 1, then the machine moves to state A and produces

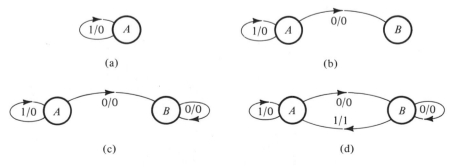

Fig. 7.15   A sequence 01 detector.

an output $z = 1$. Note that this final diagram shown in Fig. 7.15(d) satisfies the input-output sequence given above and thus recognizes the input sequence $x = 01$. The state table which corresponds to the final state diagram is shown in Fig. 7.16(a). A quick check reveals it to be minimum.

The next step in the synthesis procedure is to determine the number of flip-flops required and the state assignment. The relationship between the number of states (N_S) and the number of flip-flops (N_{FF}) is given by the expression

$$2^{N_{FF}-1} < N_S \leq 2^{N_{FF}}$$

For example, a 4-state machine would require two flip-flops, a 10-state machine would require four flip-flops, etc. For the machine described by the state table shown in Fig. 7.16(a), only a single flip-flop is needed. The state assignment is arbitrarily chosen as $A = 0$ and $B = 1$; it could, however, just as easily have been selected in the opposite manner (i.e., $A = 1$, $B = 0$). We shall defer a more detailed discussion of state assignment until later.

Once the state assignment has been chosen, the state table in Fig. 7.16(a) can be redrawn as the transition table of Fig. 7.16(b). Here y^k denotes the present state of the circuit which is the current output of the flip-flop. The symbol y^{k+1} denotes the next state of the machine, i.e., the output of the flip-flop after a transition has occurred. The K-map for the output z is drawn separately merely for simplicity. Suppose that we want to realize the circuit with clocked set-reset flip-flops. The problem then becomes one of determining the proper signals on the set and reset input lines to effect the transitions shown in Fig. 7.16(b). Using the clocked SR flip-flop input table of Fig. 7.12(b), one may derive the excitation maps shown in Fig. 7.16(c). For example, consider the transition in the upper left-hand corner of the transition table

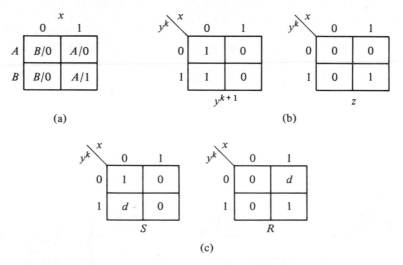

Fig. 7.16 Synthesis of a sequence 01 detector: (a) state table; (b) transition table and output map; (c) excitation maps.

shown in Fig. 7.16(b), i.e., $y^k = 0$, $x = 0$, and $y^{k+1} = 1$. To effect a state change from $y^k = 0$ to $y^{k+1} = 1$, the signals which must appear on the set and reset lines are $S = 1$ and $R = 0$. Hence, these signals appear in the corresponding positions in the excitation maps of Fig. 7.16(c). Next consider the state transition in the upper right-hand corner of the transition table, i.e., $y^k = 0$, $x = 1$, and $y^{k+1} = 0$. Since no change in state must occur, the signal on the set line must be $S = 0$, while the signal on the reset line does not matter; i.e., R is a don't care. The reader should recall that an SR flip-flop will not change to the set state with $S = 0$ and $R = 0$ or $S = 0$ and $R = 1$. The remaining blocks in the excitation maps are determined in a similar manner.

The excitation maps can now be used to derive the Boolean logic circuit equations:

$$S = \bar{x}$$
$$R = x$$
$$z = xy^k$$

The actual circuit obtained from these logic equations is shown in Fig. 7.17(a). The reader may now check the circuit to see if it does indeed recognize the input sequence 01. A timing diagram with x a level input signal is drawn in Fig. 7.17(b).

For completeness the example will also be realized with clocked T and JK flip-flops. If a clocked T flip-flop is used to implement the sequence detector, the excitation map for the flip-flop is shown in Fig. 7.18(a). This table is derived using the transition table in Fig. 7.16(b). Recall that $T_c = 1$ if a state transition is to take place and $T_c = 0$ otherwise. See the input table for a clocked T flip-flop in Fig. 7.12(c). From the excitation map in Fig. 7.18(a), the logic equation for T_c is given by the expression

$$T_c = \bar{x}\bar{y} + xy = x \odot y$$

The output equation is identical to that obtained earlier. The implementation of the logic equation with a clocked T flip-flop is shown in Fig. 7.18(b).

Figure 7.18(c) shows the excitation maps for a realization using clocked JK flip-flops. The corresponding logic equations are given below:

$$J = \bar{x}, \qquad K = x$$

Note that the logic equations for J and K are identical to those for S and R in the set-reset realization and hence the clocked JK flip-flop realization is identical to that shown in Fig. 7.17(a) with the dotted portion replaced by a clocked JK flip-flop.

Example.

In this example the problem is to design a synchronous sequential circuit with one input line and one output line that recognizes the input string $x = 1111$. The circuit is also required to recognize overlapping sequences such that if the input string is

$$x = 1101111111010$$

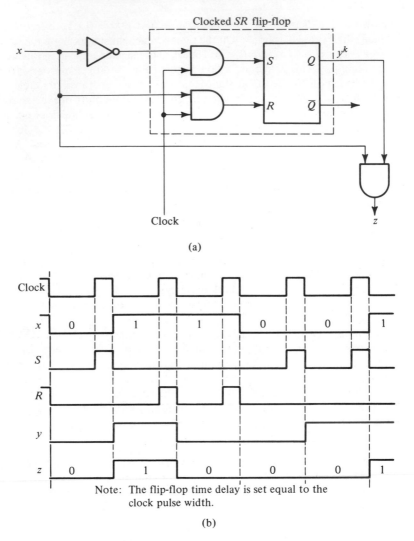

(a)

(b)

Note: The flip-flop time delay is set equal to the clock pulse width.

Fig. 7.17 Circuit implementation: (a) logic diagram; (b) timing diagram ($y^0 = 0$).

then the output string should be

$$z = 0000001111000$$

The reduced state table and corresponding state diagram for the sequential circuit that will recognize the input string $x = 1111$ is shown in Fig. 7.19. Note that assuming that state A is the initial state, the machine changes state every time an input $x = 1$ occurs with the exception of the fourth and succeeding 1's. Every time an $x = 0$ occurs the machine resets by returning to state A. The loop with $x = 1$ at state D satisfies the overlapping input sequence

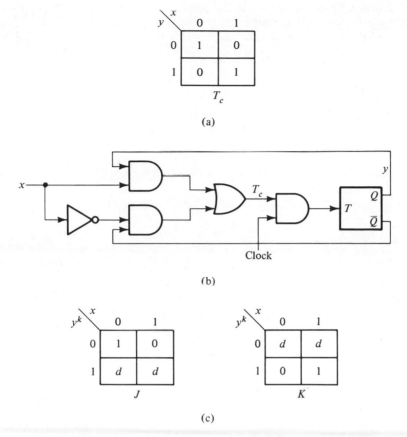

Fig. 7.18 Clocked T and JK flip-flop realizations: (a) clocked T
flip-flop excitation map; (b) clocked T flip-flop implementation;
(c) clocked JK excitation maps.

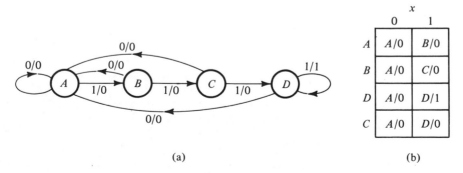

Fig. 7.19 Another sequence detector.

criterion by producing a 1 at the output when the fourth, fifth, sixth, etc., logic 1 occurs at the input.

The state assignment for the example is arbitrarily chosen as follows:

$$A = 00$$
$$B = 01$$
$$C = 10$$
$$D = 11$$

The resulting transition table is shown in Fig. 7.20(a). The output map is shown in Fig. 7.20(b).

The excitation maps for a clocked SR flip-flop realization of the circuit are shown in Fig. 7.21. The logic equations obtained from Fig. 7.21 and Fig. 7.20(b) are

$$S_1 = y_2 x, \qquad S_2 = \bar{y}_2 x, \qquad z = x y_1 y_2,$$
$$R_1 = \bar{x}, \qquad R_2 = \bar{x} + \bar{y}_1 y_2$$

The excitation maps for a clocked T flip-flop realization of the circuit are given in Fig. 7.22(a), and the corresponding logic circuit equations are

$$T_{c1} = y_1 \bar{x} + \bar{y}_1 y_2 x, \qquad z = x y_1 y_2$$
$$T_{c2} = y_2 \bar{x} + \bar{y}_2 x + \bar{y}_1 y_2$$

Excitation maps for a clocked JK flip-flop realization are given in Fig. 7.22(b). The logic equations obtained from these K-maps are given below, and the hardware used to realize the equations is shown in Fig. 7.23:

$$J_1 = y_2 x, \qquad J_2 = x, \qquad z = x y_1 y_2,$$
$$K_1 = \bar{x}, \qquad K_2 = \bar{y}_1 + \bar{x}$$

Example.

Here we want to design a clocked sequential circuit that recognizes the input sequence consisting of exactly two zeroes followed by a 10. In other

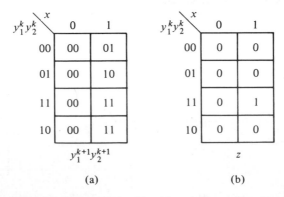

(a)

(b)

Fig. 7.20 The binary state table: (a) transition table; (b) output map.

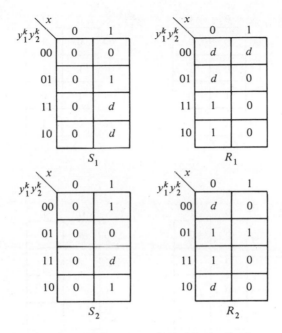

Fig. 7.21 K-maps for a clocked SR realization.

words if the input sequence is

$$x = 001001000010010$$

then the output sequence will be

$$z = 000100100000001$$

The state diagram and corresponding state table are shown in Fig. 7.24. Note that state E is used as a holding state when more than two zeroes occur in sequence. The machine holds in state E awaiting a 1 at the input so that the machine can reset to recognize the proper sequence. Recognition of overlapping sequences is accomplished in the loop from state B to state D. Realization of this circuit in hardware will require three flip-flops. To complete the solution one need only follow the procedure as shown in the previous examples.

Rather than continue with sequence detectors, let us examine another kind of sequential circuit, the up/down counter.

Example.

Design an up/down counter with four states (0, 1, 2, 3) using clocked JK flip-flops. A control signal x is used as follows: When $x = 0$ the machine counts forward (up); when $x = 1$, backward (down). A state diagram depicting this counter is illustrated in Fig. 7.25(a). From this diagram the state table

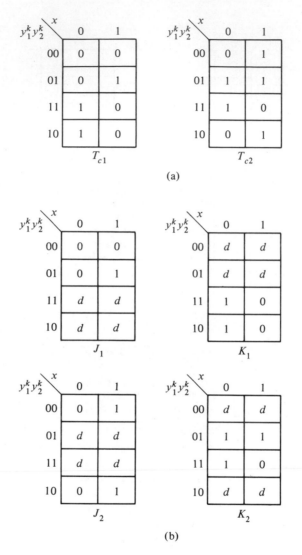

Fig. 7.22 Clocked T and JK realizations: (a) clocked T excitation maps; (b) clocked JK excitation maps.

shown in Fig. 7.25(b) is derived. Notice that the output of the counter is just its present state. If we choose a state assignment

$$0 \longrightarrow 00$$
$$1 \longrightarrow 01$$
$$2 \longrightarrow 10$$
$$3 \longrightarrow 11$$

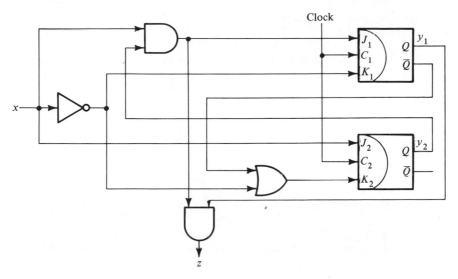

Fig. 7.23 Clocked JK logic diagram.

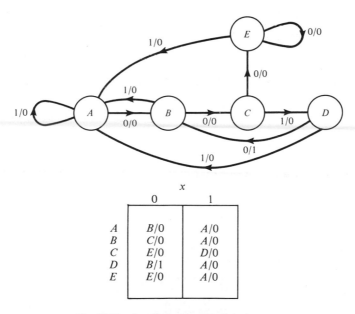

	x	
	0	1
A	B/0	A/0
B	C/0	A/0
C	E/0	D/0
D	B/1	A/0
E	E/0	A/0

Fig. 7.24 Another sequence detector.

which is standard for counters, the transition table may be produced as illustrated in Fig. 7.25(c). Using the input table for the clocked JK flip-flop (see Fig. 7.12), the excitation maps for the two flip-flops y_1 and y_2 are obtained in Fig. 7.25(d). Using these K-maps, the following relations are found:

$$J_1 = K_1 = x\bar{y}_2 + \bar{x}y_2 = x \oplus y_2$$

$$J_2 = K_2 = 1$$

Hence, the logic diagram for the four-state up/down counter is drawn in Fig. 7.26. If the signal x is controlled by a toggle switch and the clock period is very slow (say 1 second), the action of this device may be observed by

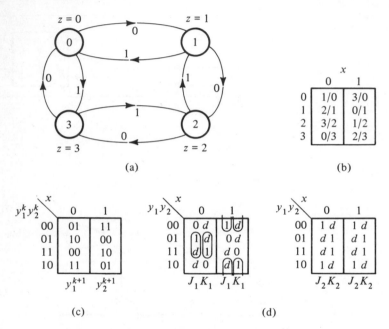

(a)

	x	
	0	1
0	1/0	3/0
1	2/1	0/1
2	3/2	1/2
3	0/3	2/3

(b)

$y_1^k y_2^k$	x 0	1
00	01	11
01	10	00
11	00	10
10	11	01
	y_1^{k+1}	y_2^{k+1}

(c)

$y_1 y_2$	x 0	1
00	0 d	1 d
01	1 d	0 d
11	d 1	d 0
10	d 0	d 1
	$J_1 K_1$	$J_1 K_1$

$y_1 y_2$	x 0	1
00	1 d	1 d
01	d 1	d 1
11	d 1	d 1
10	1 d	1 d
	$J_2 K_2$	$J_2 K_2$

(d)

Fig. 7.25 Up/down counter synthesis: (a) state diagram; (b) state table; (c) transition table; (d) excitation maps.

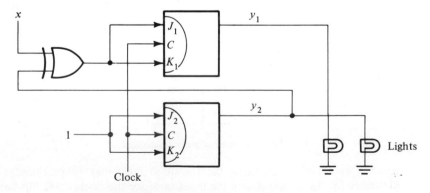

Fig. 7.26 Implementation of an up/down counter.

attaching lights to the flip-flop outputs. In reality; the lights might be light-emitting diodes.

Now let us tackle a more formidable counter design.

Example.

The problem is to use clocked JK flip-flops to design a circuit which counts in the BCD code. The output showing the value of the count is to be in the form of four lights. For example, if the count is 3, then the lights would read OFF, OFF, ON, ON.

Because of its simplicity, the state table can be constructed immediately. Ignoring the output for the moment, the state table for this example is shown Fig. 7.27(a).

To satisfy the output readout, the states will be assigned so that they are a direct indication of the count; i.e., each is assigned its BCD representation, and hence the output can be obtained by merely monitoring the output of the flip-flops and using these signals to turn the lights on and off. Therefore, the state assignment is

$$0 \longrightarrow 0000 \qquad 5 \longrightarrow 0101$$
$$1 \longrightarrow 0001 \qquad 6 \longrightarrow 0110$$
$$2 \longrightarrow 0010 \qquad 7 \longrightarrow 0111$$
$$3 \longrightarrow 0011 \qquad 8 \longrightarrow 1000$$
$$4 \longrightarrow 0100 \qquad 9 \longrightarrow 1001$$

x	0	1
0	0	1
1	1	2
2	2	3
3	3	4
4	4	5
5	5	6
6	6	7
7	7	8
8	8	9
9	9	0

(a)

$y_3^k y_2^k y_1^k y_0^k$ \ x	0	1
0000	0000	0001
0001	0001	0010
0010	0010	0011
0011	0011	0100
0100	0100	0101
0101	0101	0110
0110	0110	0111
0111	0111	1000
1000	1000	1001
1001	1001	0000
1010	*dddd*	*dddd*
1011	*dddd*	*dddd*
1100	*dddd*	*dddd*
1101	*dddd*	*dddd*
1110	*dddd*	*dddd*
1111	*dddd*	*dddd*

$$y_3^{k+1} y_2^{k+1} y_1^{k+1} y_0^{k+1}$$

(b)

Fig. 7.27 State table for the BCD counter: (a) state table; (b) transition table.

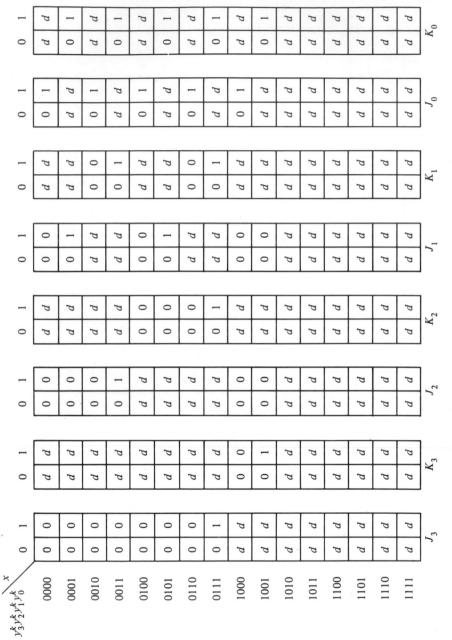

Fig. 7.28 Excitation tables for the BCD counter.

The transition table for this assignment is given in Fig. 7.27(b). Next we derive the excitation maps for the four flip-flops using Fig. 7.12. The resulting tables are presented in Fig. 7.28. The d's in the tables represent don't cares. These tables may be reorganized into ordinary K-map form as shown for input J_2 in Fig. 7.29. All the resulting Boolean logic equations are listed below:

$$J_3 = y_2 y_1 y_0 x, \qquad K_3 = y_0 x$$
$$J_2 = y_1 y_0 x, \qquad K_2 = y_1 y_0 x$$
$$J_1 = \bar{y}_3 y_0 x, \qquad K_1 = y_0 x$$
$$J_0 = x, \qquad K_0 = x$$

Note from the logic equations that the input x acts as a gating signal to disable or enable all flip-flop inputs simultaneously.

The actual implementation of the circuit using clocked JK flip-flops is shown in Fig. 7.30. When the first one is received at the input x and a clock pulse occurs, the rightmost light will illuminate. When the second one appears at the input, the rightmost light turns off, and the light second from the right will illuminate, etc. If a zero appears at the input x, no further change in the illumination pattern will take place.

$y_1^k y_0^k$ \ $y_3^k y_2^k$	\ $x = 0$ 00	01	11	10	$x = 1$ 00	01	11	10
00	0	d	d	0	0	d	d	0
01	0	d	d	0	0	d	d	0
11	0	d	d	d	1	d	d	d
10	0	d	d	d	0	d	d	d

Fig. 7.29　K-map for J_2.

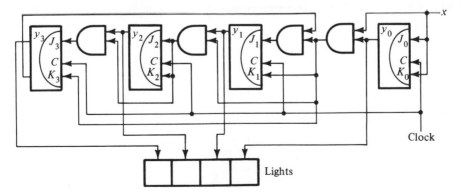

Fig. 7.30　Realization of the BCD counter.

State Assignment

Up to this point we have always merely assumed some state assignment with no discussion of any alternatives. However, it is important for the reader to realize that two different assignments may yield vast differences in hardware. From a purely practical standpoint many engineers might argue that what is needed is a solution; however, if the system being designed is a basic module which will be manufactured in great quantities, a potential cost saving exists if the module can be built with fewer elements.

The following example will illustrate the need for some guidelines in choosing a good state assignment.

Example.

Consider the sequential circuit described by the minimum state table of Fig. 7.31. If the following state assignment is used

	y_1 y_2 y_3			y_1 y_2 y_3
A:	0 0 0		E:	1 0 1
B:	0 0 1		F:	1 1 0
C:	0 1 1		G:	1 1 1
D:	0 1 0			

then the logic equations which implement the circuit are

$$J_1 = \bar{y}_2 x + y_3 x \qquad J_3 = \bar{y}_2$$

$$K_1 = \bar{y}_3 + x \qquad K_3 = y_2$$

$$J_2 = y_3 \qquad z = \bar{y}_3 y_2 \bar{y}_1 \bar{x} + \bar{y}_3 y_1 x$$

$$K_2 = \bar{y}_3$$

Present state	x	
	0	1
A	$B/0$	$E/0$
B	$C/0$	$G/0$
C	$D/0$	$F/0$
D	$A/1$	$A/0$
E	$G/0$	$C/0$
F	$A/0$	$A/1$
G	$F/0$	$D/0$

Next state/Output

Fig. 7.31 A seven-state machine.

Consider also the following assignment:

	y_1 y_2 y_3		y_1 y_2 y_3
A:	0 0 0	E:	1 0 0
B:	0 0 1	F:	1 0 1
C:	0 1 0	G:	1 1 0
D:	0 1 1		

Under this second assignment the logic equations which implement the circuit are

$$J_1 = x\bar{y}_3 + x\bar{y}_2 \qquad J_3 = y_2 + \bar{x}\bar{y}_1$$

$$K_1 = x + y_3 \qquad K_3 = 1$$

$$J_2 = y_1\bar{y}_3 + \bar{y}_1 y_3 \qquad z = xy_1 y_3 + \bar{x}y_2 y_3$$

$$K_2 = y_3 + \bar{x}y_1 + x\bar{y}_1$$

A quick gate count check shows that the first assignment requires three OR gates, four AND gates, and one NOT gate; the second assignment requires six OR gates, nine AND gates, and one NOT gate. Hence, the second assignment requires *twice* as many gates as the first assignment.

The number of possible state assignments for a problem of any significance is quite large. For example, the number of possible state assignments for a 5-state machine is over 100 and the number of possible assignments for a 10-state machine exceeds 10 million. It is unfortunate that no simple and efficient technique for choosing a state assignment exists [7–11]. In place of an optimal solution we shall offer in the following pages a few guidelines to aid the reader in choosing a reasonably good state assignment.

With this motivation, let us now examine several useful techniques for choosing a state assignment. As part of the synthesis procedure, a minimum state table was obtained in order to reduce the required number of memory elements needed to implement the synchronous sequential circuit. Once a minimum number of memory elements has been found, the proper choice of state assignment can drastically reduce the required amount of logic to implement the Boolean switching functions. Previously we have seen that the total number of memory elements N_{FF} is related to the number of states N_S in the circuit by

$$2^{N_{FF}-1} < N_S \leq 2^{N_{FF}}$$

Therefore, there will be

$$N_{SA} = \frac{2^{N_{FF}}!}{(2^{N_{FF}} - N_S)!}$$

ways of assigning the $2^{N_{FF}}$ combinations of binary state assignments to the N_S states. This expression is evaluated for several cases in Fig. 7.32. It should be demonstrated that not all these assignments are unique with respect to the

N_S	N_{FF}	N_{SA}	N_{UA}
1	0	–	–
2	1	2	1
3	2	24	3
4	2	24	3
5	3	6,720	140
6	3	20,160	420
7	3	40,320	840
8	3	40,320	840
9	4	4.15×10^9	10,810,800
10	4	2.91×10^{10}	75,675,600

Fig. 7.32 Number of state assignments.

Boolean logic equations; for example, for a given state assignment we may complement a given bit position to get a new state assignment but the resulting Boolean equations may be derived from the previous ones by complementing the corresponding variable. The new logic equations are no better than the old ones since both true and complemented variables are available from most flip-flop devices.

Suppose we swap two columns in a given state assignment; this results in the swapping of two variables in the Boolean logic equations and the cost of the logic is still essentially unchanged. Therefore, for sequential circuits with only two states, there is really only one choice. For three and four states the 24 possible assignments reduce to just 3 unique ones; see Fig. 7.33. Therefore, it is possible to synthesize the sequential circuit using all three assignments and to choose the best one. The number of possible unique state assignments N_{UA} for a sequential circuit with N_S states is given by

$$N_{UA} = \frac{(2^{N_{FF}} - 1)!}{(2^{N_{FF}} - N_S)! N_{FF}!}$$

Several cases for this expression are shown in Fig. 7.32. For more than four states, complete enumeration is impractical, so techniques for choosing a good assignment are necessary.

State assignment guidelines. Our approach to developing a set of state assignment guidelines is to find several rules which will yield a state assignment

States	Assignments		
	1	2	3
A	00	00	00
B	01	11	10
C	11	01	01
D	10	10	11

Fig. 7.33 Unique state assignments.

which reduces the complexity of the next-state equations for the implementation of a reduced state table. The state assignment problem for this case is to select a state coding which forces large groupings of the logic 1's on the binary transition table, or transition K-map. The larger the groups of logic 1's, the less complex the combinational circuitry becomes. Notice that next-state logic minimization suggests the use of D flip-flops.

To gain insight into finding a good assignment, let us examine an example four-state machine synthesized using all three of its unique state assignments. Consider the state table of Fig. 7.34. First let us realize this reduced circuit using assignment 1 and D flip-flops. Substituting assignment 1 into Fig 7.34 yields the transition table of Fig. 7.35(a), which may be rearranged into K-maps for z, D_2, and D_1, as displayed in Fig. 7.35(b), (c), and (d). Hence, the logic equations for this assignment are

Assignment 1.

$$D_2 = \bar{y}_1\bar{y}_2 + \bar{x}\bar{y}_2 + xy_1y_2$$

$$D_1 = \bar{x}\bar{y}_2 + \bar{x}y_1 + x\bar{y}_1y_2$$

$$z = \bar{y}_1y_2$$

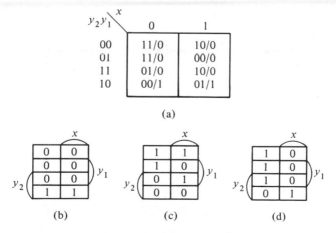

	x	
	0	1
A	$C/0$	$D/0$
B	$C/0$	$A/0$
C	$B/0$	$D/0$
D	$A/1$	$B/1$

Fig. 7.34　A four-state machine.

y_2y_1	x 0	1
00	11/0	10/0
01	11/0	00/0
11	01/0	10/0
10	00/1	01/1

(a)

(b)　　　　(c)　　　　(d)

Fig. 7.35　D flip-flop realization for assignment 1: (a) transition table; (b) K-map for z; (c) K-map for D_2; (d) K-map for D_1.

Figures 7.36 and 7.37 illustrate the same procedures for assignments 2 and 3. The resulting Boolean switching functions are listed below:

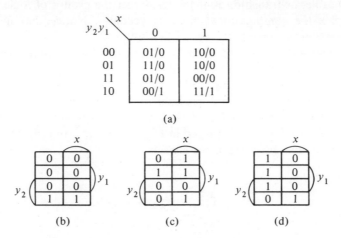

(a)

(b)   (c)   (d)

Fig. 7.36 D flip-flop realization for assignment 2: (a) transition table; (b) K-map for z; (c) K-map for D_2; (d) K-map for D_1.

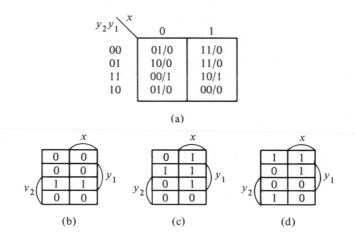

(a)

(b)   (c)   (d)

Fig. 7.37 D flip-flop realization for assignment 3: (a) transition table; (b) K-map for z; (c) K-map for D_2; (d) K-map for D_1.

Assignment 2.

$$D_2 = x\bar{y}_1 + y_1\bar{y}_2$$
$$D_1 = \bar{x}\bar{y}_2 + \bar{x}y_1 + x\bar{y}_1y_2$$
$$z = \bar{y}_1y_2$$

Assignment 3.

$$D_2 = y_1\bar{y}_2 + x\bar{y}_2 + xy_1$$
$$D_1 = x\bar{y}_2 + \bar{x}\bar{y}_1$$
$$z = y_1 y_2$$

Now let us examine the results. If we specify a two-level sum of products logic implementation and count the number of inputs to gates, assignment 1 requires 20; assignment 2, 18; and assignment 3, 15. Assignment 3 gives the best results, but why? Obviously, assignment 3 gives a better grouping of 1's and 0's on the K-maps for D_1, D_2, and z. There are two ways to rearrange the 1's on the K-map: first, vertically by making the 1's combine under the same input, and, second, horizontally by making the 1's combine among the next-state entries for a given present state. These goals are accomplished by adopting the following general state assignment rules:

RULE 1. States which have the same next states for a given input should be given logically adjacent assignments.

RULE 2. States which are the next states of a single present state, under logically adjacent inputs, should be given logically adjacent assignments.

Both of these rules may be applied by inspection of the reduced state table.

Let us apply these rules to the example of Fig. 7.34. Rule 1 says that states A and B should be adjacent because they both go to state C under input 0, or A adj B. Also, A adj C is indicated. Rule 2 yields A adj B, A adj C, B adj D, and C adj D. We may compare the adjacencies of states for the three assignments by plotting the states on two-variable K-maps as shown in Fig. 7.38. It is clear from the K-maps that assignment 3 fulfills all these adjacencies and hence produces the better results for this example.

In general, one is not able to satisfy all the adjacencies suggested by rule 1 and rule 2. He does, however, satisfy as many as possible. Resolve any conflicts in favor of rule 1 because it takes precedence.

Implication graph. Another tool which aids the logic designer in selecting good state assignments is the implication graph. The *implication graph* for a

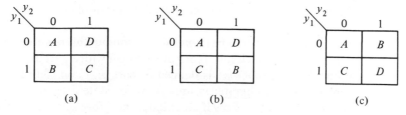

Fig. 7.38   State adjacencies for four-state assignments: (a) assignment 1; (b) assignment 2; (c) assignment 3.

sequential circuit is a flow graph whose nodes represent pairs of states. The nodes are connected by arcs which represent state transitions between *pairs* of states as specified by the state table of the sequential circuit.

Example.

Consider the sequential circuit of Fig. 7.39(a). The implication graph for this circuit is shown in Fig. 7.39(b).

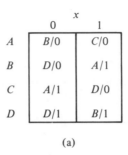

	0	1
A	B/0	C/0
B	D/0	A/1
C	A/1	D/0
D	D/1	B/1

(a)

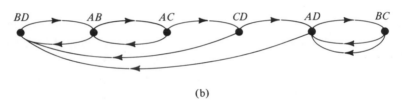

(b)

Fig. 7.39   A four-state machine: (a) state table; (b) implication graph.

An implication graph greatly resembles the implication table presented earlier and contains much of the same information; however, here it is displayed in a graphical form. The implication graph is constructed by first choosing a pair of states, say *BD* in the example, and finding its implied next-state pair, under each input; the implied pairs are entered as new nodes on the graph. No entry is made on the graph if the pair of states has the same next state. For example, states *B* and *D* both go to state *D* under an input of 0. Now the procedure is repeated for each new implied pair until no new implied pairs can be generated.

An implication graph is said to be *complete* if it contains all possible pairs of states for a given sequential circuit. Normally we deal with a partially complete implication graph. A *subgraph* is defined as part of a complete graph.

One particular type of subgraph is important for state assignment, the *closed* subgraph. A subgraph is *closed* if all outgoing arcs for each node within the subgraph terminate on nodes completely contained within the subgraph and if every state of the sequential circuit is represented by at least one node.

Example.

A closed subgraph for the sequential circuit of Fig. 7.40(a) is demonstrated in Fig. 7.40(b). Notice that arcs may *enter* a closed subgraph from the exterior, but none may originate within the closed subgraph and exit.

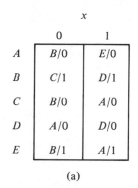

	x	
	0	1
A	*B*/0	*E*/0
B	*C*/1	*D*/1
C	*B*/0	*A*/0
D	*A*/0	*D*/0
E	*B*/1	*A*/1

(a)

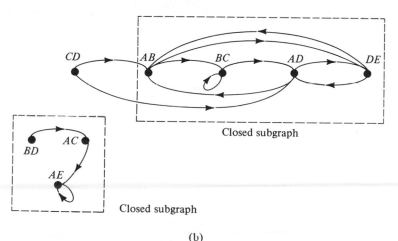

Closed subgraph

Closed subgraph

(b)

Fig. 7.40   Closed subgraphs: (a) state table; (b) implication subgraph.

The implication graph may be used in state assignment selection in the following manner. After one has applied rules 1 and 2 to a reduced state table, he has several suggested adjacencies. He may choose some of these to be implemented in a state assignment. Once he has made two states logically adjacent it is possible to rearrange the state table so that the two states are physically adjacent. Considering these two adjacent states as present states of the sequential circuit, it is desirable to make their next-state pairs adjacent in order to provide larger groupings of 1's on the transition table. The example below illustrates this point.

Example.

Consider the example of Fig. 7.39. The application of rules 1 and 2 to the state table yields

RULE 1. *B* adj *D*.

RULE 2. *B* adj *C*, *D* adj *A*, *A* adj *D*, *D* adj *B*.

The adjacency *B* adj *D* is the most important one. If we make state *B* adjacent to state *D*, it is desirable to make *A* adj *B* as indicated by the implication graph. This adjacency was not suggested by either rule 1 or rule 2. In fact the implication graph also suggests *A* adj *C* and *C* adj *D*. This assignment corresponds to unique assignment 3 of Fig. 7.38(c). The transition table for this assignment is produced in Fig. 7.41. The resulting Boolean switching functions are

$$D_2 = \bar{x}y_2 + \bar{x}\bar{y}_1 + xy_1$$
$$D_1 = \bar{x}y_2 + x\bar{y}_2$$
$$z = xy_2 + \bar{x}y_1$$

These switching functions are optimal for this sequential circuit. The key to success in making the proper state assignment was the advent of *A* adj *B* by

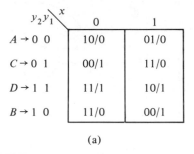

(a)

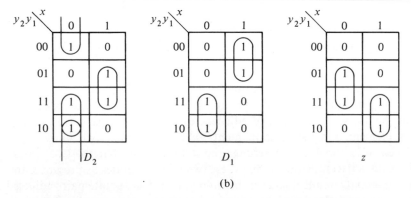

(b)

Fig. 7.41   Example state assignment: (a) transition table; (b) K-maps.

the implication graph. If we had ignored the graph entirely and made our assignment based entirely on rules 1 and 2, we would have arrived at assignment 2 and the realization would have been

$$D_2 = xy_1\bar{y}_2 + \bar{x}\bar{y}_1 + \bar{x}y_2 + \bar{y}_1 y_2$$
$$D_1 = \bar{y}_1\bar{y}_2 + x\bar{y}_1$$
$$z = xy_2 + \bar{y}_1 y_2 + \bar{x}y_1\bar{y}_2$$

which is not optimal.

The last example illustrates the concept of establishing a *chain* of adjacency pairs. The chain is established by assigning adjacent pairs of states in accordance with the transition arcs of the implication graph. The ideal chains are those established by a closed subgraph. If a closed subgraph cannot be established, try to include a contiguous subgraph which contains a large number of transition arcs.

We shall now incorporate the implication graph into our state assignment guidelines by the following rule.

RULE 3. Use the adjacencies suggested by rules 1 and 2 to construct a partially complete implication graph for the reduced state table. Then try to establish a chain of adjacency pairs on a closed or contiguous subgraph.

In applying rules 1, 2, and 3 let us emphasize that rules 1 and 3 are more important than rule 2.

The last state assignment guideline to be discussed is concerned with the mechanics of making the actual code choices. Generally, one tries to minimize the total number of logic 1's on the K-maps and to maximize the number of don't cares. The following rule helps accomplish this goal:

RULE 4. Search the next state portion of the reduced state table for the "most transferred to" state. Assign it the all logic 0 code by placing it on an assignment K-map in the block for minterm 0. Begin assigning other states according to the suggested adjacencies of rules 1, 2, and 3, saving the minterm blocks with the largest numbers of logic 1's in their binary code for last. Satisfy as many of the suggested adjacencies as possible.

This completes the presentation of the state assignment guidelines. The procedure is now illustrated by a complete example.

Example.

Find a D flip-flop realization for the sequential circuit of Fig. 7.42(a).

RULE 1. *A* adj *C*, *B* adj *D*, *A* adj *D*.

RULE 2. *A* adj *D*, *B* adj *E*, *A* adj *E*, *A* adj *B*, *C* adj *D*.

RULE 3. From rules 1 and 2 and the closed subgraph of Fig. 7.42(b), *A* adj *D*, *A* adj *E*, *B* adj *C*, *B* adj *D*, *D* adj *E*.

RULE 4. See Fig. 7.42(c).

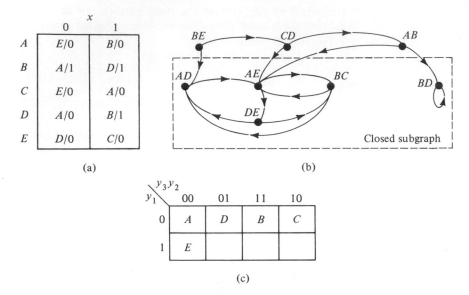

Fig. 7.42 State assignment procedure: (a) state table; (b) closed subgraph; (c) state assignment.

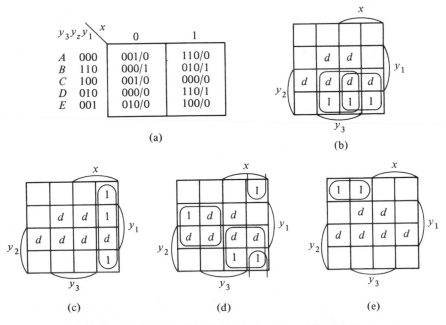

Fig. 7.43 D flip-flop realization: (a) transition table; (b) K-map for z; (c) K-map for D_3; (d) K-map for D_2; (e) K-map for D_1.

From this state assignment the following switching functions are generated as shown in Fig. 7.43:

$$D_3 = x\bar{y}_3$$
$$D_2 = x\bar{y}_3\bar{y}_1 + xy_2 + \bar{x}y_1$$
$$D_1 = \bar{x}\bar{y}_2\bar{y}_1$$
$$z = xy_2 + y_3y_2$$

Output logic. A word about the output equations is in order. In our state assignment procedure we have completely ignored any consideration of minimizing the output logic. If the number of Boolean next-state equations is much larger than the number of output equations, then apply the rules as stated to the next states and accept the results of the output equations. However, if the output equations are a significant part of the implementation logic, rules 1 and 2 are equally applicable for output logic minimization. In this text, however, we restrict ourselves to next-state analysis.

Partitioning. Recall that a *partition*, say P_i, on the set of states for a sequential machine is a collection of disjoint subsets, called *blocks B_{ij}*, which contain all the states of the machine. The process of making a state assignment for the sequential machine is equivalent to forcing a series of partitions with two blocks, called *two-block partitions*, on the set of states, one partition for each memory flip-flop.

Example.

Find the two-block partitions forced on the sequential machine of Fig. 7.42(a) by the assignment of Fig. 7.42(c). The assigned code is listed below:

$$y_3 \; y_2 \; y_1$$

	y_3	y_2	y_1
A:	0	0	0
B:	1	1	0
C:	1	0	0
D:	0	1	0
E:	0	0	1

Each bit column of the assignment separates the states into two blocks, or subsets, those associated with logic 0 and those associated with logic 1:

		B_{31}	B_{32}
$y_3 \longrightarrow P_3$:		(ADE)	(BC)

		B_{21}	B_{22}
$y_2 \longrightarrow P_2$:		(ACE)	(BD)

		B_{11}	B_{12}
$y_1 \longrightarrow P_1$:		$(ABCD)$	(E)

A partition on the set of states of a sequential machine is *closed* if and only if, for any block in the partition, all specified next states under each input fall into a single block of the partition.

Example.

Consider partition P_3 for the sequential machine of Fig. 7.42(a). If one examines the next-state behavior of the blocks of the partition, he observes

Input

Present Block	0	1	
B_{31}	B_{31}	B_{32}	Next
B_{32}	B_{31}	B_{31}	Block

Hence partition P_3 is closed.

The presence of closed partitions on the states of a sequential machine can greatly reduce the dependence of the next-state equations Y_i $(i = 1, r)$ on the present-state variables y_i $(i = 1, r)$. If the closed partition has two blocks, one of the present-state variables y_j can be used to code the blocks; this variable is called a *block bit*. The presence of the closed partition results in the reduced dependency for equation (6-3) in one variable

$$Y_j = h_j(x_1, x_2, \ldots, x_n, y_j)$$

as exemplified by the state assignment of Fig. 7.42(c):

$$Y_3 = x\bar{y}_3$$

Closed partitions may be generated by using an implication graph. One begins by assuming that two states S_i and S_j are in the same partition block. By the definition of a closed partition, the implied next-state pairs of S_iS_j must also lie together in some block of the closed partition. The implied pairs are then combined into disjoint blocks using the properties of equivalence relations.

Example.

Find a closed partition for the state table of Fig. 7.44(a). If states AB are chosen as a starting point, the partial implication subgraph of Fig. 7.44(b) is generated. The implied pairs are

$$(AB), (BC), (AC) \longrightarrow (ABC)$$
$$(DE), (EF), (DF) \longrightarrow (DEF)$$

Hence,

$$P_1 = (ABC)(DEF)$$

is a closed partition for the sequential machine.

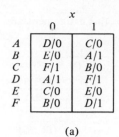

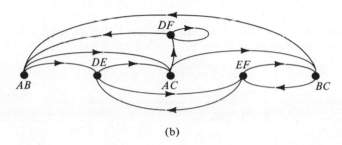

(b)

Fig. 7.44   Closed partitions: (a) state table; (b) partial implication graph.

The closed partition describes a property which exists in certain machines. If the closed partition has two blocks and the state assignment codes these blocks with a block bit, reduced next-state logic equations are obtained. Rule 3 of the state assignment procedure helps the logic designer find state assignments which correspond to closed partitions without requiring him to generate the partitions themselves.

Partition pairs. A second type of reduced dependency, called *cross dependency*, is exhibited by some sequential machines. These machines rely on pairs of partitions which are not necessarily closed. State transitions of sequential machines with cross dependency are described by block transitions between pairs of partitions, as is illustrated by the example below.

Example.

The sequential machine of Fig. 7.31 exhibits cross dependency under the minimal assignment

$$y_1 \; y_2 \; y_3$$

$$
\begin{array}{llll}
A: & 0 & 0 & 0 \\
B: & 0 & 0 & 1 \\
C: & 0 & 1 & 1 \\
D: & 0 & 1 & 0 \\
E: & 1 & 0 & 1 \\
F: & 1 & 1 & 0 \\
G: & 1 & 1 & 1 \\
\end{array}
$$

The two-block partitions for this assignment are

	B_{11}	B_{12}
P_1:	$(ABCD)$	(EFG)

	B_{21}	B_{22}
P_2:	(ABE)	$(CDFG)$

	B_{31}	B_{32}
P_3:	(ADF)	$(BCEG)$

Close examination of the block behavior reveals the block transition table and diagram of Fig. 7.45.

The partitions P_2 and P_3 are not closed, but as a pair, they exhibit reduced dependency as shown by the D flip-flop implementation below:

$$D_1 = x\bar{y}_1 y_3 + \bar{x}y_1 y_3 + x\bar{y}_1\bar{y}_2$$

$$\left.\begin{array}{l} D_2 = y_3 \\ D_3 = \bar{y}_2 \end{array}\right\} \quad \text{Cross dependency}$$

$$z = xy_1\bar{y}_3 + \bar{x}\bar{y}_1 y_2\bar{y}_3$$

The generation of partition pairs is beyond the scope of this text; the interested reader is referred to the listed references at the end of the chapter. Rule 3 of the state assignment procedure presented earlier helps the logic designer find cross-dependent assignments when they exist. Although the state assignment guidelines are not optimal, they can produce good state assignments even for machines with reduced dependency.

It is important for the reader to note that cross dependency which is based on a pair of partitions is a generalization of reduced dependency which is based on a single closed partition. Reduced dependency can be considered to be a special case of cross dependency in which the pair of partitions is formed by using one closed partition twice.

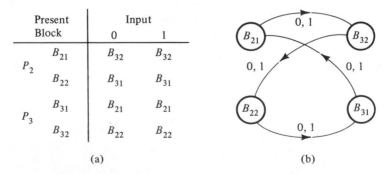

Present Block		Input 0	Input 1
P_2	B_{21}	B_{32}	B_{32}
	B_{22}	B_{31}	B_{31}
P_3	B_{31}	B_{21}	B_{21}
	B_{32}	B_{22}	B_{22}

(a)   (b)

Fig. 7.45   Cross dependency: (a) block transition table; (b) block transition diagram.

Optimal state assignments. Numerous authors have proposed procedures for obtaining "good" or "near-optimal" state assignments, and several claim that their procedure yields "optimal" assignments under some stated criteria of optimality. Several common optimality criteria are listed below:

1. Minimal gate and/or inputs-to-gates circuit.
2. Minimal cost circuit.
3. Circuit with reduced dependency.
4. Criteria 1–3 for a specified flip-flop type.

Several of the better methods for producing near-optimal assignments for D flip-flops are those developed by Dolotta and McCluskey [12], Weiner and Smith [13], and Torng [14]. These methods search for reduced dependency in the specified reduced state table for a sequential machine.

To this point we have examined only the case for D flip-flops. What happens if one wants to use another type? In general, a *good* state assignment for D flip-flops will also be a *good* assignment for other flip-flop types. However, Curtis [15] has shown that an assignment which is optimal, or near-optimal, for one flip-flop type may be far from optimal for another. Curtis has extended the methods of Dolotta and McCluskey and Weiner and Smith to provide near-optimal state assignments for specific flip-flop types, or combinations of flip-flops of different types within one sequential machine realization.

To produce optimal assignments, the computational complexity of the proposed state assignment algorithms require the use of a general-purpose digital computer. Story et al. [16] and Haring [17] have developed such optimal algorithms. Story et al. find an optimal state assignment for clocked JK flip-flops.

For most applications an optimal or near-optimal solution for the state assignment problem is not required; a good assignment is adequate for most cases. However, in cases where an optimal assignment is essential, the logic designer is referred to the open literature for state assignment algorithms which guarantee optimality.

This completes our presentation of the state assignment problem. We have tried to formulate some general guidelines to aid the designer in choosing a state assignment for a given sequential machine. Our guidelines do not guarantee a minimum logic realization. They do, however, generally give much better results than a completely arbitrary choice, as was made earlier in the text.

Incompletely Specified Circuits

A sequential circuit is said to be incompletely specified if its state table contains don't cares. These don't cares arise normally in some circuits due to the fact that only a certain set of inputs can ever be applied. Hence, states and outputs that may occur because of forbidden inputs are never attained and hence we may assign them as a don't care. The following example will illustrate this idea.

Example.

This example describes the design of a detonator circuit as shown in Fig. 7.46(a). When the device is active and $x = 0$, the device rests in an idle state A. The detonation sequence is initiated by setting $x = 1$. The device will count up to 4 and issue a pulse ($z = 1$) to detonate an explosive. The circuitry prior to the detonator circuit is designed so that once the first $x = 1$ occurs the device cannot be reset; i.e., no $x = 0$ input will occur once $x = 1$ is received.

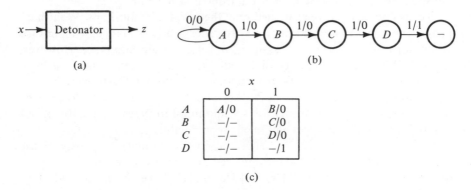

(a)

(b)

	x	
	0	1
A	$A/0$	$B/0$
B	$-/-$	$C/0$
C	$-/-$	$D/0$
D	$-/-$	$-/1$

(c)

Fig. 7.46   Detonator circuit: (a) block diagram; (b) partial state diagram; (c) complete state table.

The partial state diagram and complete state table for the detonator are shown in Fig. 7.46(b) and (c), respectively. Here again note that once the detonator sequence is begun it will continue without interruption until the detonate pulse is generated. The final state is a don't care because the explosive has ignited. In the following analysis the detonator circuit will be realized using clocked T flip-flops. If we choose the state assignment $(y_2 y_1)$ as

$$A = 00 \qquad C = 10$$
$$B = 01 \qquad D = 11$$

all the necessary tables for the circuit realization are shown in Fig. 7.47. The following equations follow directly from the tables:

$$T_{c1} = x$$
$$T_{c2} = y_1$$
$$z = y_1 y_2$$

The actual circuit for the detonator is shown in Fig. 7.48. Since our analysis is valid only during the clock pulse, we use the clock pulse to gate the output.

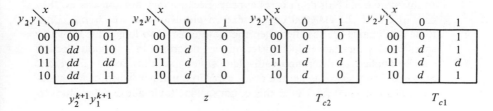

Fig. 7.47   Detonator excitation maps.

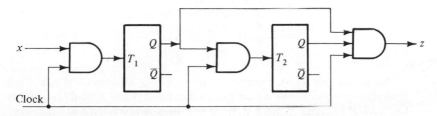

Fig. 7.48   Detonator implementation.

It is important for the reader to realize that incompletely specified circuits have an advantage over completely specified circuits from a hardware realization standpoint. The advantage stems from the presence of don't cares in the state table. In other words, quite often these don't cares can be grouped with the 1's in the excitation maps to produce a simpler circuit than would have been possible if all terms were completely specified. Figure 7.47 illustrates this case.

State Reduction

The minimization of state tables containing don't cares requires special consideration. The following example will quickly illustrate this point.

Example.

Consider the problem of minimizing the following incompletely specified circuit:

	x	
	0	1
A	$B/-$	$E/0$
B	$B/1$	$E/-$
C	$F/0$	$C/0$
D	$B/1$	$A/1$
E	$D/0$	$C/-$
F	$D/-$	$C/1$

In this state table four don't cares appear. Because they are don't cares, they can, of course, be assigned or specified in any way that we choose. Once these don't cares are specified then the state table is no longer incompletely specified and the state reduction techniques described in a previous section can be applied to determine equivalent states and thus reduce the table. Suppose then that we assign the don't cares in a manner which makes states *AB* and *EF* equivalent. Under this condition the table above will reduce to

	x	
	0	1
A'	$A'/1$	$D'/0$
B'	$D'/0$	$B'/0$
C'	$A'/1$	$A'/1$
D'	$C'/0$	$B'/1$

Note that this was a rather obvious simplification since one could see immediately from the original state table that states *A* and *B* would be equivalent as well as states *E* and *F* if the don't cares were assigned in the proper manner. However, if the don't cares in the original table are specified as 0's for present states *A* and *E* and specified as 1's for states *B* and *F*, then states *ACE* and *BDF* are equivalent. Hence, the state table reduces to

	x	
	0	1
A'	$B'/0$	$A'/0$
B'	$B'/1$	$A'/1$

Note that the latter simplification was not the obvious one and yet it yielded the simplest table.

The following ideas provide the basis for state table reduction in incompletely specified circuits.

Applicable input sequences. An input sequence is said to be *applicable* to state S_i of an incompletely specified machine if and only if the following condition is satisfied: When the machine is in S_i and the input sequence is applied, all next states are specified except for possibly the last element of the sequence. For example, the input sequences 0111 and 1111 are applicable to state *A* of the machine defined in Fig. 7.46. But the sequence 11111 is not applicable to state *A*.

Compatible states. Two states S_i and S_j of an incompletely specified machine are said to be *compatible* $(S_i S_j)$ if and only if for each input sequence applicable to S_i and S_j the same output sequence will be produced when the outputs are specified, whether S_i or S_j is the starting state. States A and C in the state reduction example are compatible. Note that the following output sequences produced by input sequence 1111 for starting states A and C are the same when specified:

$$
\begin{array}{cccccc}
\text{Input:} & 1 & 1 & 1 & 1 \\
\text{State:} & A & E & C & C & C \\
\text{Output:} & 0 & - & 0 & 0 \\
\text{State:} & C & C & C & C & C \\
\text{Output:} & 0 & 0 & 0 & 0 \\
\end{array}
$$

State compatibility can be shown to define a compatibility relation on the states of an incompletely specified machine. Hence, a set of compatible states is called a *compatibility class*. A *maximal compatible* is a compatibility class which will not remain a compatibility class if any state not in the class is added. In the previous example (AC), (AE), (CE), and (ACE) are compatibility classes. Of these four compatibility classes only (ACE) is a maximal compatible.

States S_i and S_j of an incompletely specified machine are compatible if and only if the following two conditions are satisfied:

1. The outputs produced by S_i and S_j must be the same, when both are specified, for each possible input I_P.
2. The next states of S_i and S_j must be compatible, when both are specified, for each possible input I_P.

Incompatible states. Two states of an incompletely specified machine which fail to satisfy the two conditions stated above are said to be *incompatible*. A set of incompatible states form an *incompatibility class*. A *maximal incompatible* is an incompatibility class to which no other incompatible state may be added without destroying the class.

Example.

Determine the compatibility-classes and maximal compatibles for the state table of Fig. 7.49(a). The implication table is employed first to determine all pairs of compatible states as shown in Fig. 7.49(b). This table is formed in the same manner as it was in the completely specified case. Note that the presence of don't care output terms allows state B to be paired with state A in one instance and state C in another.

The reduction of the implication table is also performed as it was in the completely specified case. The determination of the compatibility classes is shown in Fig. 7.49(c). Note that this procedure is reminiscent of that used to determine equivalent states in the completely specified case. In the row defined by state G, the pair (GH) is a compatibility class. The bottom row in Fig. 7.49(c) is the set of maximal compatibles.

Examination of the list of maximal compatibles illustrates the fundamental difference between compatibility in incompletely specified circuits and

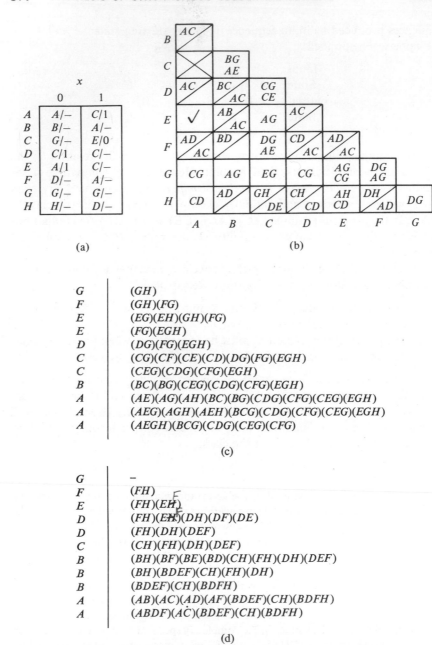

Fig. 7.49 Generating maximal compatibles and incompatibles: (a) state table; (b) implication table; (c) compatibility classes; (d) incompatibility classes.

equivalence in completely specified circuits. In a completely specified circuit if we found that state A was equivalent to state B and that state B was equivalent to state C, we were guaranteed without even checking that states A and C were equivalent because state equivalence is an equivalence relation. However, since the transitive property does not hold in general for incompletely specified circuits, there is no such guarantee. Consider the maximal compatible (BCG) in Fig. 7.49(c). To be able to group all three states together we must have the compatible pairs (BC), (CG), and (BG); i.e., (BC) and (CG) do not automatically imply (BG). A moment's reflection will show that this problem arises due to don't cares in the state table.

Example.

Determine the incompatibility classes and maximal incompatibles for the sequential machine of Fig. 7.49(a). The implication table of Fig. 7.49(b) is employed to generate the incompatibility classes by extracting from it pairs of states which are *not* compatible, as shown in Fig. 7.49(d). The set of maximal incompatibles is the list at the bottom of the table.

The process of generating the maximal compatibles and incompatibles as demonstrated in Fig. 7.49(c) and (d) can be somewhat tedious, and hence we now introduce a graphical technique which aids in this process.

Merger diagrams. The process of finding the maximal compatible sets of states from the compatible pairs derived from the implication table is aided measurably by a graphical technique called the *merger diagram*. First the states of the original machine can be conveniently represented as dots equally spaced around a circle; then a line is used to connect each related (compatible or incompatible) pair of states. This completes the construction of the merger diagram.

The maximal sets of states can be derived from the merger diagram by visually noting those sets in which every state is connected to every other state by a line segment. Thus the maximal sets form regular graphical patterns, as shown in Fig. 7.50. The rules for extracting maximal sets from a merger diagram are

RULE 1. Make each maximal set as large as possible.

RULE 2. Each state of the maximal set must be interconnected with every other state in the set by a line segment.

RULE 3. Each related (compatible or incompatible) pair of states must appear in at least one maximal set.

The application of these rules is now demonstrated by an example.

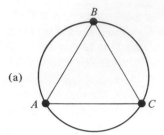

(a)

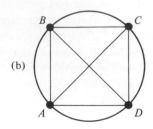

(b)

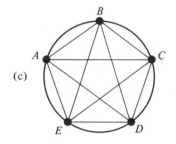

(c)

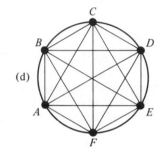

(d)

Fig. 7.50 The merger diagram: (a) three states; (b) four states; (c) five states; (d) six states.

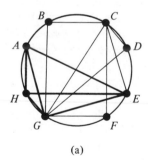

(a)

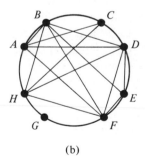

(b)

Fig. 7.51 Example merger diagrams: (a) merger diagram for the maximal compatibles of Fig. 7.49; (b) merger diagram for the maximal incompatibles of Fig. 7.49.

Example.

The merger diagrams of Fig. 7.51 are constructed from the implication table of Fig. 7.49(b). Consider the merger diagram for the maximal compatibles in Fig. 7.51(a). The graphical pattern for the maximal compatible $(AEGH)$ has been emphasized. Note that any attempt to add another compatible state to this graphical grouping ends in failure. All remaining line segments (compatible pairs) may be covered using four triangles (BCG), (CDG), (CEG), and (*CFG*). Hence, we have found the set of maximal compatibles. The set of maximal incompatibles is extracted from Fig. 7.51(b) in a like manner.

The reader is now familiar with the concept of incompletely specified sequential circuits, compatible states, incompatible states, and merger diagrams. With these tools he is now prepared to address the problem of state minimization for incompletely specified sequential circuits.

Minimization procedure. The minimization of an incompletely specified state table for a sequential machine can be an involved process. In general one must select a set of compatibility classes which meets the following three conditions:

1. *Completeness:* The union of all the sets in the chosen set of compatibility classes must contain all the states in the original machine.
2. *Consistency:* The chosen set of compatibility classes must be closed; that is, the implied next states of each compatibility class in the chosen set must be contained by some compatibility class within the set.
3. *Minimality:* The smallest number of compatibility classes which meet the above criterion should be chosen.

Once a set of compatibility classes has been found which meets these conditions, each class in the set corresponds to a state in the reduced state table. Unfortunately the process of selecting the set of compatibility classes which meets the three conditions must be done by trial and error. Hence, it would be helpful to at least bound the number of states K required in the realization of the minimal-state circuit.

The upper bound U on the number of states in the minimal circuit is given by the expression

$$U = \text{minimum}\{\text{NSMC}, \text{NSOC}\}$$

where

$$\text{NSMC} = \text{number of sets of maximal compatibles}$$

$$\text{NSOC} = \text{number of states in the original circuit}$$

The above equation simply states that we should need no more states in the minimal circuit than the number of states in the original circuit unless there exists some compatibility among states such that NSMC < NSOC, in which case we should require fewer states than NSOC.

The lower bound L on the number of states in the minimal circuit is given by the expression

$$L = \text{maximum}\{\text{NSMI}_1, \text{NSMI}_2, \cdots, \text{NSMI}_i, \cdots\}$$

where

$$\text{NSMI}_i = \text{number of states in the } i\text{th group of the set of}$$
$$\text{maximal incompatibles of the original circuit}$$

The reasonableness of this condition is illustrated by the fact that if there exist two states in the original circuit that are incompatible, then the minimal circuit will have to have at least two states in order to distinguish these incompatible ones.

At this point we may specify the algorithm for state reduction for incompletely specified sequential machines.

State Reduction Algorithm.

STEP 1. Find the maximal compatibles using an implication table and merger diagram.

STEP 2. Find the maximal incompatibles using the implication table of step 1 and another merger diagram.

STEP 3. Find the bounds on the number of required states, U and L.

STEP 4. Find, by trial and error, a set of compatibility classes that satisfy completeness, consistency, and minimality.

STEP 5. Produce the minimum state table. In general it may still contain unspecified next states and outputs.

The trial and error selection of compatibility classes may begin by considering only the maximal compatibles. The set of maximal compatibles is always *complete* and *consistent*. However, the set may not be minimal. We may begin the search for a minimal set of compatibility classes by considering the maximal compatibles taken in groups of L, the lower bound.

Example.

In this example we shall find a reduced state table for the incompletely specified machine of Fig. 7.49(a). First we construct a *closure table* by treating the maximal compatibles as states and finding their sets of next states, as shown in Fig. 7.52(a). Each entry in the table is obtained from the original table by recording the next state of each state within a maximal compatible.

Since NSMC = 5 and NSOC = 8, the upper bound on the number of states is

$$U = \min\{5, 8\} = 5$$

The lower bound is determined from the maximal incompatibles. The set of maximal incompatibles has been derived in Fig. 7.51(b) and is listed below:

$$(ABDF)(BDEF)(BDFH)(AC)(CH)$$

Therefore,

$$L = \max\{4, 4, 4, 2, 2\} = 4$$

The number of states in the reduced machine is bounded by

$$4 \leq K \leq 5$$

Since we want a minimal circuit, we begin with the lower bound to see if we can find four maximal compatibles that satisfy the conditions of completeness

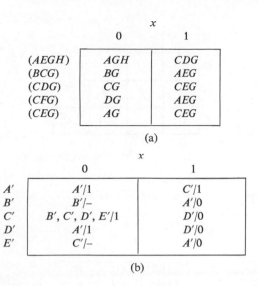

Fig. 7.52 State reduction: (a) closure table; (b) reduced state table.

and consistency. By trial and error we find, using the closure table of Fig. 7.52(a), that no set of four maximal compatibles will satisfy both completeness and consistency. Hence, all five maximal compatibles are required. By definition, the set of maximal compatibles is complete and consistent. Hence, the reduced machine will contain five states:

$$A' = (AEGH) \qquad D' = (CEG)$$
$$B' = (BCG) \qquad E' = (CFG)$$
$$C' = (CDG)$$

The reduced state table which duplicates the performance of Fig. 7.49(a) is given by Fig. 7.52(b).

The multiple next-state entry in Fig. 7.52(b) requires an explanation. Note that if the circuit is in state C' and $x = 0$, then the next state can be any of B', C', D', or E'. This multiple next-state entry exists because the closure table indicates that for $x = 0$, $(CDG) \rightarrow CG$, and hence the next state could be (BCG), (CDG), (CEG), or (CFG).

For the previous example all maximal compatibles had to be used as states of the reduced machine. In some cases, only a subset of the maximal compatibles can be chosen for reducing the machine, as is illustrated in the next example.

Example.

We shall determine the reduced state table corresponding to the one given in Fig. 7.53(a). Steps 1 and 2 of the state reduction algorithm are per-

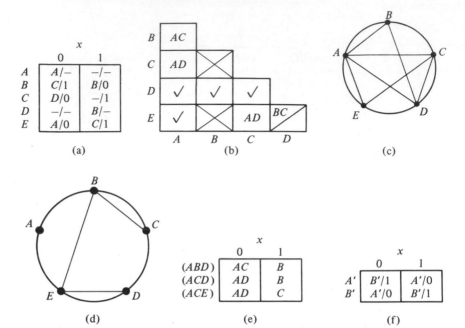

Fig. 7.53   State reduction example: (a) state table; (b) implication table; (c) maximal compatibles; (d) maximal incompatibles; (e) closure table; (f) reduced state table.

formed in Fig. 7.53(b), (c), and (d). From the implication table the compatible pairs are

$$(AB)(AC)(AD)(AE)(BD)(CD)(CE)$$

These compatible pairs are processed on the merger diagram of Fig. 7.53(c) to yield the maximal compatibles

$$(ABD)(ACD)(ACE)$$

In a similar manner the incompatible pairs are found from the implication table to be

$$(BC)(BE)(DE)$$

The merger diagram of Fig. 7.53(d) demonstrates that these pairs are the maximal incompatibles.

Step 3 of the state reduction algorithm calculates the bounds on the number of reduced states. The calculations follow:

$$\text{NSMC} = 3$$

$$\text{NSOC} = 5$$

$$\text{NSMI}_1 = 2$$

$$\text{NSMI}_2 = 2$$

$$\text{NSMI}_3 = 2$$

Hence,

$$U = \min\{3, 5\} = 3$$
$$L = \max\{2, 2, 2\} = 2$$

and

$$2 \leq K \leq 3$$

Step 4 of the algorithm is centered around the closure table of Fig. 7.53(e). We begin our search for two compatibility classes which are complete and consistent by examining the maximal compatibles. Choosing the maximal compatibles (ABD) and (ACE) as trial states we see that they satisfy completeness since the union of all the states contained in these two maximal compatibles contains all the states in the original circuit. They satisfy consistency, as shown in Fig. 7.53(e), and also minimality, as indicated by the lower bound. Therefore, under the definitions,

$$A' = (ABD)$$
$$B' = (ACE)$$

the final minimal circuit for step 5 of the algorithm is shown in Fig. 7.53(f).

Example.

We shall now derive the minimal circuit for the sequential machine shown in Fig. 7.54(a). The implication table for this state table is shown in Fig. 7.54(b). The compatible pairs obtained from the table are

$$(AB)(AD)(BC)(BD)$$

Figure 7.54(c) is the corresponding merger diagram, and the maximal compatibles obtained from the diagram are

$$(ABD)(BC)(E)(F)$$

These maximal compatibles form the closure table shown in Fig. 7.54(d). The upper and lower bounds on the number of states in the minimal circuit are obtained as follows:

$$\text{NSMC} = 4$$
$$\text{NSOC} = 6$$
$$U = \min\{4, 6\}$$
$$U = 4$$

The incompatible pairs are

$$(AC)(AE)(AF)(BE)(BF)(CD)(CE)(CF)(DE)(DF)(EF)$$

A merger diagram for the maximal incompatibles is given in Fig. 7.54(e). From this figure, the maximal incompatibles are derived as

$$(CDEF)(ACEF)(BEF)$$

Now since $\text{NSMI}_1 = 4$, $\text{NSMI}_2 = 4$, and $\text{NSMI}_3 = 3$, then

$$L = \max\{4, 4, 3\}$$
$$L = 4$$

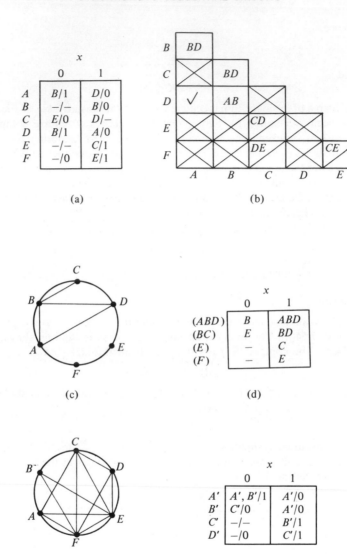

Fig. 7.54 Another example: (a) state table; (b) implication table; (c) maximal compatibles; (d) closure table; (e) maximal incompatibles; (f) reduced state table.

Now note that the bound conditions specify that

$$4 \leq K \leq 4$$

Hence, all the maximal compatibles may be chosen as states of the minimal circuit. Using the symbols

$$A' = (ABD)$$
$$B' = (BC)$$
$$C' = (E)$$
$$D' = (F)$$

the resulting minimal state table is shown in Fig. 7.54(f).

Note that the resultant state table has considerable flexibility. When the circuit is in state A' and the input $x = 0$ is applied the next state can be either A' or B'. This property will serve to simplify the hardware realization, as is shown below.

In the last three examples, step 4 of the state reduction algorithm was approached as a search through a very restricted set of compatibility classes, the set of maximal compatibles. While the consideration of only maximal compatibles is computationally desirable, a minimal reduced state table is not always obtained. If the compatibility classes are not required to be maximal, then a better reduction is often obtained. An algorithm for making such a selection for step 4 which always leads to a minimal reduced table will be presented in Chapter 9. For now, this case will be illustrated only by example.

Example.

Examine the incompletely specified sequential circuit of Fig. 7.55(a). If we apply the state reduction algorithm, we find

STEP 1. Figure 7.55(b) and (c). Maximal compatibles are

$$(ABC)(ACD)(ADE)$$

STEP 2. Figure 7.55(b) and (d). Maximal incompatibles are

$$(BD)(BE)(CE)$$

STEP 3.

$$NSMC = 3$$
$$NSOC = 5$$
$$NSMI_1 = 2$$
$$NSMI_2 = 2$$
$$NSMI_3 = 2$$
$$U = \min\{3, 5\} = 3$$
$$L = \max\{2, 2, 2\} = 2$$
$$2 \leq K \leq 3$$

STEP 4. Consider the closure tables of Fig. 7.55(e) and (f). No set of two maximal compatibles can be found which is complete and consistent. Hence, if we restrict ourselves to maximal compatibility classes, we must choose three states in the reduced machine. However, if we choose compatibility classes (ABC) and (DE), we find that this set is complete, consistent, and minimal.

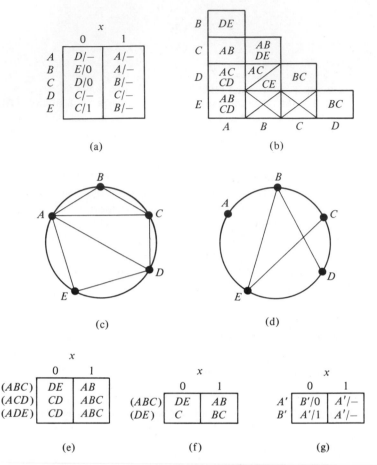

Fig. 7.55   A counter example: (a) state table; (b) implication table; (c) maximal compatibles; (d) maximal incompatibles; (e) closure table for maximal compatibles; (f) closure table for two compatibility classes; (g) reduced state table.

STEP 5. $A' = (ABC)$, $B' = (DE)$.

The minimal reduced state table is shown in Fig. 7.55 (g).

   This completes our discussion of state reduction of incompletely specified sequential circuits. In general, a *near-minimal* reduced machine is produced by using maximal compatibles as states for the reduced machine. However, to guarantee a *minimal* machine, the algorithm developed in Chapter 9 should be applied to find a minimal, complete, and consistent set of compatibility classes to act as states for the reduced machine.

State Assignment and Circuit Realization

Once a reduced state table has been determined, the state assignment and circuit logic equations may be produced using exactly the same rules employed in the completely specified case. However, since certain entries in the state table are unspecified, there is usually a larger number of don't cares in the generated K-maps resulting in better logic minimization.

Example.

For the reduced state table of Fig. 7.54(f), let us complete the realization using D, clocked T, and clocked JK flip-flops. First we must choose a state assignment. Applying rules 1, 2, and 3 to the machine yields

RULE 1. A adj B.

RULE 2. A adj B, A adj C.

RULE 3. A adj B and A adj C, or A adj B and B adj C.

Hence, the following state assignment is chosen:

$$y_2 \; y_1$$

	y_2	y_1
A:	0	0
B:	0	1
C:	1	0
D:	1	1

Substituting these values into Fig. 7.54(f) produces the binary state table (transition table) in Fig. 7.56(a). From this table the K-maps for each realization are derived and the corresponding Boolean logic equations are listed below:

$$D_2 = \bar{x}y_1 + y_2y_1$$
$$D_1 = y_2\bar{y}_1$$
$$------------$$
$$T_{c2} = \bar{x}y_1 + y_2\bar{y}_1$$
$$T_{c1} = y_2 + y_1$$
$$------------$$
$$J_2 = \bar{x}y_1$$
$$K_2 = \bar{y}_1$$
$$J_1 = y_2$$
$$K_1 = 1$$
$$------------$$
$$z = xy_2 + \bar{x}\bar{y}_1$$

Notice that the D and clocked T realizations require eight inputs to gates, and the clocked JK, two. In general the clocked JK flip-flop gives better logic reduction because it has more control logic internal to the device itself.

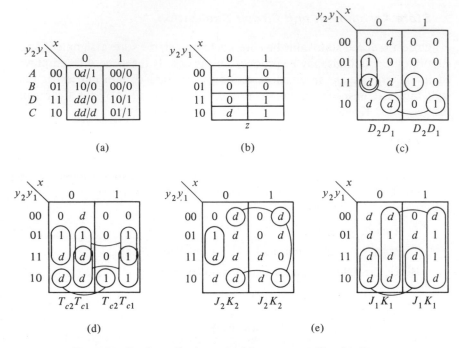

Fig. 7.56 Logic realizations: (a) binary state table; (b) K-map for z; (c) D flip-flops; (d) clocked T flip-flops; (e) clocked JK flip-flops.

Summary

In this chapter we have presented synthesis procedures to realize both completely and incompletely specified logic circuits. State reduction by inspection, partitioning, and the implication table was demonstrated. The concepts of state equivalence for completely specified circuits and state compatibility for incompletely specified circuits were contrasted. Flip-flop input tables and the generation of excitation maps received attention, as did the state assignment problem. Many design examples were completed to illustrate the synthesis techniques. The reader should now have a good grasp of the synchronous sequential circuit synthesis problem. For more detailed information on the synthesis problem the reader is encouraged to pursue further reading from the selected references presented below.

REFERENCES

1. McCluskey, E. J., *Introduction to the Theory of Switching Circuits.* New York: McGraw-Hill Book Company, 1965.

2. KOHAVI, ZVI, *Switching and Finite Automata Theory*. New York: McGraw-Hill Book Company, 1970.

3. BOOTH, TAYLOR L., *Digital Networks and Computer Systems*. New York: John Wiley & Sons, Inc., 1971.

4. HILL, F. J., and G. R. PETERSON, *Introduction to Switching Theory and Logical Design*. New York: John Wiley & Sons, Inc., 1968.

5. MENLY, G. H., "A Method for Synthesizing Sequential Circuits," *Bell Sys. Tech. J.*, Vol. 34, September 1955, pp. 1045–1079.

6. KRIEGER, M., *Basic Switching Circuit Theory*. New York: The Macmillan Company, 1967.

7. HARTMANIS, J., "On the State Assignment Problem for Sequential Machines I," *IRE Trans. Electronic Computers*, June 1961, pp. 157–165.

8. STEARNS, R. E., and J. HARTMANIS, "On the State Assignment Problem for Sequential Machines II," *IRE Trans. Electronic Computers*, December 1961, pp. 593–603.

9. PAULL, M. C., and S. H. UNGER, "Minimizing the Number of States in Incompletely Specified Sequential Switching Functions," *IRE Trans. Electronic Computers*, EC-8, No. 3, September 1959, pp. 356–357.

10. McCLUSKEY, E. J., and S. H. UNGER, "A Note on the Number of Internal Variable Assignments for Sequential Switching Circuits," *IRE Trans. Electronic Computers*, EC-8, No. 4, December 1959, pp. 439–440.

11. KARP, R. M., "Some Techniques of State Assignment for Synchronous Sequential Machines," *IEEE Trans. Electronic Computers*, EC-13, No. 5, October 1964, pp. 507–518.

12. DOLOTTA, T. A., and E. J. McCLUSKEY, "The Coding of Internal States of Sequential Circuits," *IEEE Trans. Electronic Computers*, EC-13, No. 5, October 1964, pp. 549–562.

13. WEINER, P., and E. J. SMITH, "Optimization of Reduced Dependences for Synchronous Sequential Machines," *IEEE Trans. Electronic Computers*, EC-16, No. 6, December 1967, pp. 835–847.

14. TORNG, H. C., "An Algorithm for Finding Secondary Assignments of Synchronous Sequential Circuits," *IEEE Trans. Computers*, C-17, No. 5, May 1968, pp. 461–469.

15. CURTIS, H. A., "Systematic Procedures for Realizing Synchronous Sequential Machines Using Flip-Flop Memory: Part I," *IEEE Trans. Computers*, C-18, No. 12, December 1969, pp. 1121–1127.

16. STORY, J. R., H. J. HARRISON, and E. A. REINHARD, "Optimum State Assignment for Synchronous Sequential Circuits," *IEEE Trans. Computers*, C-21, No. 12, December 1972, pp. 1365–1373.

17. HARING, D. R., *Sequential Circuit Synthesis: State Assignment Aspects*, M.I.T. Research Monograph No. 31. Cambridge, Mass.: The M.I.T. Press, 1966.

PROBLEMS

7.1.   Find the D flip-flop implementation for the sequential machine in Fig. 7.44.

7.2.   Obtain a D flip-flop realization for the synchronous sequential circuit specified by the state table below. Use the indicated state assignment. Write the combinational logic equations.

y_3 y_2 y_1		x 0	1
0 0 0	A	$B/0$	$E/0$
0 0 1	B	$A/1$	$C/1$
0 1 0	C	$B/0$	$C/1$
0 1 1	D	$C/0$	$E/0$
1 0 0	E	$D/1$	$A/0$

7.3.   Find a minimized state table for the synchronous sequential circuit below by
(a) Inspection.
(b) Partitioning.
(c) Implication table.

	I	J
A	$B/0$	$A/1$
B	$C/0$	$A/0$
C	$C/0$	$B/0$
D	$E/0$	$D/1$
E	$C/0$	$D/0$

7.4.   Reduce the following state tables by inspection:

(a)

	I	J
A	$B/1$	$C/0$
B	$A/1$	$C/0$
C	$D/1$	$A/0$
D	$C/1$	$A/1$

(b)

	I	J
A	$A/0$	$E/1$
B	$E/1$	$C/0$
C	$A/1$	$D/1$
D	$F/0$	$G/1$
E	$B/1$	$C/0$
F	$F/0$	$E/1$
G	$A/1$	$D/1$

(c)

	I	J	K
A	A/0	B/1	E/1
B	B/0	A/1	F/1
C	A/1	D/0	E/0
D	F/0	C/1	A/0
E	A/0	D/1	E/1
F	B/0	D/1	F/1

7.5. Reduce the state tables of Problem 7.4 by partitioning.

7.6. Reduce the state tables of Problem 7.4 using implication tables.

7.7. Find a reduced state table for the following synchronous sequential circuit:

	x	
	0	1
A	B/0	C/0
B	D/0	E/0
C	F/0	G/0
D	A/1	B/1
E	C/0	D/0
F	F/0	G/0
G	B/0	F/0

7.8. Using an implication table, reduce the following sequential circuit to a minimum number of states:

	x	
	0	1
A	A/0	C/0
B	D/1	A/0
C	F/0	F/0
D	E/1	B/0
E	G/1	G/0
F	C/0	C/0
G	B/1	H/0
H	H/0	C/0

7.9. Reduce the number of states of the following sequential circuit
(a) By partitioning.
(b) Using an implication table.

	I	J	K
A	D/1	C/0	E/1
B	D/0	E/0	C/1
C	A/0	E/0	B/1
D	A/1	B/0	E/1
E	A/1	C/0	B/1

7.10.   Determine four state diagrams for synchronous sequential circuits as specified by the following requirements. Each circuit has a single input line x and a single output line z.

(a) The first circuit must produce an output $z = 1$ when two consecutive logic 1 inputs x have occurred. The next input after the two logic 1's resets the output to logic 0. For example,

$$x = 01100111110$$

$$z = 00100010100$$

(b) The second circuit must detect the input sequence 101 by producing $z = 1$ as the last 1 occurs. The output z is reset to 0 on the next clock pulse. Two 101 sequences may overlap. For example,

$$x = 010101101$$

$$z = 000101001$$

(c) Repeat Problem 7.10(b) but do not permit overlapping sequences. For example,

$$x = 010101101$$

$$z = 000100001$$

(d) The fourth circuit detects a 01 sequence. The sequence sets $z = 1$, which is reset only by a 00 input sequence. For all other cases, $z = 0$. For example,

$$x = 010100100$$

$$z = 011110110$$

7.11.   Derive the minimum state diagram of a clocked sequential circuit which recognizes the input sequence 1010. Sequences may overlap. For example,

$$x = 00101001010101110$$

$$z = 00000100001010000$$

7.12.   Find the state table of a synchronous sequential circuit which detects the input sequence 0101. The sequences may overlap as shown below:

$$x = 010101001101011$$

$$z = 000101000000010$$

7.13.   Obtain a minimum state diagram for a clocked sequential circuit which recognizes the input sequence 1001 including overlap. For example,

$$x = 0101001000110010010$$

$$z = 0000001000000010010$$

7.14.   Derive the logic equations to implement the four-state sequential circuit in Fig. 7.39 for each unique state assignment using

(a) D flip-flops.
(b) Clocked JK flip-flops.
(c) Clocked SR flip-flops.

7.15.   For the machine below with the given state assignment, find a clocked JK flip-flop implementation. Write the Boolean logic equations and sketch the logic diagram.

$y_2\ y_1$		0	1
		x	
0 0	A	$B/0$	$D/0$
0 1	B	$C/0$	$A/0$
1 0	C	$D/0$	$B/0$
1 1	D	$A/1$	$C/1$

7.16.   Implement the sequential circuit of Problem 7.8 using clocked T flip-flops.

7.17.   Repeat Problem 7.16 using D flip-flops.

7.18.   For the state table of Fig. 7.34, find implementations with each of the three unique state assignments for four-state machines and memory elements of
(a) Clocked T flip-flops.
(b) Clocked JK flip-flops.
(c) Clocked SR flip-flops.

7.19.   Find a clocked D flip-flop realization for the sequential circuit below using each of the three unique assignments for four-state machines:

		0	1
		x	
A		$B/0$	$D/0$
B		$C/0$	$A/0$
C		$D/0$	$A/0$
D		$B/1$	$C/1$

7.20.   Given the following reduced state table and assignment, find the logic equations and logic diagram
(a) Using D flip-flops.
(b) Using clocked JK flip-flops.

$y_2\ y_1$		0	1
		x	
0 0	A	$A/0$	$B/0$
0 1	B	$C/0$	$B/0$
1 1	C	$D/0$	$B/0$
1 0	D	$A/1$	$B/0$

7.21.   Find the logic diagram of an implementation of the following sequential circuit, given the state assignment and
(a) D flip-flops.
(b) Clocked JK flip-flops.
(c) Clocked T flip-flops.

		x	
$y_2\ y_1$		0	1
0 0	A	A/0	B/0
0 1	B	C/0	B/0
1 1	C	D/0	B/0
1 0	D	B/1	A/0

7.22. Find a clocked JK flip-flop realization for the reduced state table and assignment below:

		x	
$y_3\ y_2\ y_1$		0	1
0 0 0	A	B/0	D/0
1 0 1	B	A/0	C/1
1 0 0	C	D/1	C/0
0 0 1	D	B/1	E/1
0 1 0	E	C/0	A/0
1 1 0	F	E/0	F/1

7.23. Verify that the solutions in the text for the sequential circuit of Fig. 7.31 are correct.

7.24. Prove that the logic equations for the BCD counter of Fig. 7.30 are correct.

7.25. Find a state assignment for the following synchronous sequential circuit using the state assignment procedure presented in this chapter:

	x	
	0	1
A	B/0	E/0
B	D/0	A/1
C	D/1	A/0
D	B/1	C/1
E	A/0	A/0

7.26. Find a state assignment for the following sequential circuit. Choose the assignment for state A to be $y_3 = y_2 = y_1 = 0$.

	x	
	0	1
A	B/0	E/0
B	A/1	C/1
C	B/0	C/1
D	C/0	E/0
E	D/1	A/0

7.27. Find a state assignment for the following machine:

	x	
	0	1
A	*B*/0	*D*/1
B	*A*/1	*C*/0
C	*D*/0	*A*/0
D	*C*/1	*B*/1

7.28. Find a state assignment for the following machine:

$y_3\ y_2\ y_1$		x	
		0	1
0 0 0	*A*	*B*/1	*C*/0
	B	*A*/1	*D*/1
	C	*E*/0	*F*/1
	D	*A*/1	*F*/0
	E	*C*/0	*B*/1
	F	*F*/0	*A*/0

7.29. Consider the state assignment problem for the following sequential machine. Set $A = (000)_2$ and generate a good state assignment.

	x	
	0	1
A	*D*/0	*E*/0
B	*C*/0	*F*/1
C	*A*/1	*D*/0
D	*B*/1	*C*/1
E	*A*/0	*D*/1
F	*B*/1	*C*/0

7.30. Find a state assignment for the state table below:

	x	
	0	1
A	*E*/0	*C*/1
B	*E*/0	*A*/0
C	*B*/1	*A*/1
D	*E*/1	*C*/0
E	*B*/0	*F*/1
F	*D*/0	*A*/0

7.31. Use the state assignment procedure to find a binary state assignment for this machine:

	x	
	0	1
A	$B/0$	$D/0$
B	$A/0$	$C/1$
C	$D/1$	$C/0$
D	$B/1$	$E/1$
E	$C/0$	$A/0$
F	$E/0$	$F/1$

7.32. Use the state assignment procedure outlined in this chapter with the closed partition

$$P_1 = (ACG)(BDEF)$$

to find a clocked JK flip-flop implementation for the sequential circuit of Fig. 7.31. Assign a block bit y_1 to the partition. Contrast your design with the text's solution.

7.33. Determine the circuit realization of the state table below. The inputs to the circuit will be voltage levels, and the memory will be clocked D flip-flops. Assume AND, OR, and NOT gates are available for the combinational logic. Draw the logic diagram for your solution.

	x	
	0	1
A	$A/0$	$B/0$
B	$B/0$	$C/1$
C	$C/0$	$D/0$
D	$A/0$	$D/1$

7.34. Repeat Problem 7.19 using clocked JK flip-flops for memory elements.

7.35. A synchronous sequential circuit is to be designed which satisfies the following requirements. The circuit has one input line x and one output line z. These signals are voltage levels. An output $z = 1$ is produced only when three consecutive logic 0 inputs occur or when two consecutive logic 1 inputs occur. A fourth 0 or a third 1 returns the output to logic 0. For example,

$$x = 010000111110$$

$$z = 000010010100$$

(a) Determine a state table for the circuit.
(b) Realize the circuit using clocked T flip-flops.

7.36. Find a minimal logic realization with clocked D flip-flops for the sequential circuit of Fig. P7.1. (*Hint:* Use analysis and synthesis.)

7.37. Find a minimal logic realization with clocked JK flip-flops for the sequential circuit of Fig. P7.1.

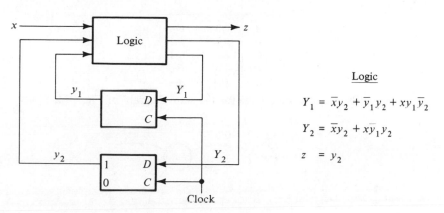

$$Y_1 = \bar{x}y_2 + \bar{y}_1 y_2 + xy_1 \bar{y}_2$$

$$Y_2 = \bar{x}y_2 + x\bar{y}_1 y_2$$

$$z = y_2$$

Fig. P7.1 A sequential circuit.

7.38. For each sequential circuit below, find the maximal compatibles and maximal incompatibles using implication tables and merger diagrams:

(a)

	x	
	0	1
A	$D/$	$C/0$
B	$D/1$	$E/-$
C	$-/-$	$E/1$
D	$A/0$	$C/-$
E	$B/1$	$C/-$

(b)

	x	
	0	1
A	$A/0$	$D/-$
B	$C/-$	$E/1$
C	$A/-$	$B/0$
D	$D/1$	$A/0$
E	$B/-$	$B/0$

(c)

	I	J	K
A	$B/-$	$D/1$	$-/-$
B	$A/-$	$E/-$	$D/0$
C	$A/1$	$B/0$	$C/-$
D	$-/-$	$-/-$	$A/0$
E	$D/0$	$A/1$	$-/-$

7.39. Find a reduced state table for the following incompletely specified sequential circuit:

	x	
	0	1
A	$-/0$	$E/-$
B	$A/-$	$C/1$
C	$B/0$	$C/1$
D	$-/0$	$E/0$
E	$D/1$	$A/-$

7.40. Derive the reduced state table for the state diagram of Fig. P7.2.

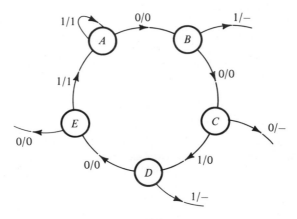

Fig. P7.2

7.41. Find a reduced state table for the following incompletely specified sequential circuit:

	$x_1 x_2$			
	00	01	11	10
A	$A/0$	$B/-$	$A/0$	$C/-$
B	$B/0$	$D/-$	$C/-$	$A/-$
C	$C/0$	$B/1$	$C/0$	$E/-$
D	$D/0$	$E/0$	$E/-$	$A/-$
E	$E/0$	$D/-$	$C/1$	$E/-$

7.42. Obtain the reduced state table for the sequential circuit shown below:

	$x_1 x_2$		
	00	01	10
A	$B/-$	$F/-$	$-/1$
B	$C/0$	$E/-$	$A/-$
C	$B/-$	$C/1$	$-/-$
D	$A/1$	$F/-$	$-/0$
E	$D/-$	$B/0$	$-/-$
F	$C/-$	$E/-$	$A/-$

7.43. Design a clocked sequential circuit for the minimum state table shown below. Use clocked JK flip-flops and the given state assignment for your realization.

y_1 y_2		x	
		0	1
0 0	A	D/1	C/–
0 1	B	–/–	A/0
1 0	C	–/0	B/1
1 1	D	B/1	C/1

7.44. Given the following synchronous sequential circuit
(a) Find the reduced machine.
(b) Find a state assignment.
(c) Find a D flip-flop realization.

	x	
	0	1
A	–/–	A/0
B	B/1	C/–
C	E/1	–/0
D	–/–	A/1
E	B/0	C/–

7.45. Find a realization of the following sequential circuit using clocked JK flip-flops:

	x	
	0	1
A	B/0	–/0
B	A/0	E/0
C	–/–	D/–
D	C/0	A/–
E	B/1	–/1

7.46. Find a realization of the following sequential circuit using clocked JK flip-flops. Note the resemblence to Problem 7.45.

	x	
	0	1
A	B/0	–/0
B	A/0	E/0
C	–/–	D/–
D	C/0	A/–
E	B/–	–/1

7.47. Find the complete implication graph for the following sequential machine. Find a closed two-block partition and make a corresponding state assignment.

	x 0	1
A	C/0	D/0
B	A/0	D/0
C	B/1	E/1
D	E/0	A/0
E	D/1	C/1

7.48. Find a closed partition for the following sequential machine. Find the corresponding state assignment and D flip-flop implementation.

	x 0	1
A	B/0	F/0
B	C/0	D/0
C	A/0	E/0
D	E/0	C/0
E	F/0	A/0
F	D/1	B/1

7.49. Implement the synchronous sequential circuit of Fig. P7.3 using clocked D flip-flops.
  (a) Assume an arbitrary binary state assignment.
  (b) Use the state assignment procedure to find a good assignment.

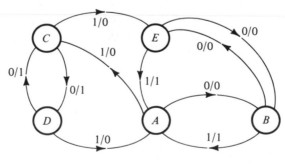

Fig. P7.3

7.50. Find the reduced machines for the following state tables by
  (a) Inspection:

	x	
	0	1
A	*B*/0	*D*/1
B	*B*/0	*C*/0
C	*A*/1	*D*/1
D	*C*/1	*F*/0
E	*B*/0	*D*/0
F	*F*/0	*C*/0

(b) Partitioning:

	x	
	0	1
U	*V*/0	*W*/1
V	*U*/1	*Y*/0
W	*Z*/1	*W*/0
X	*X*/0	*W*/1
Y	*U*/1	*V*/0
Z	*V*/0	*X*/1

(c) Implication table:

	I	*J*	*K*
A	*A*/0	*B*/0	*E*/0
B	*D*/0	*D*/0	*A*/0
C	*C*/0	*C*/0	*E*/1
D	*C*/0	*A*/0	*B*/0
E	*E*/0	*A*/0	*D*/0

8

Asynchronous Sequential Circuits

Many applications require the use of sequential circuits which are not synchronized in any way with a clock signal. These circuits are referred to as asynchronous sequential circuits and will be discussed in the following pages. Asynchronous circuits were discussed briefly in Chapter 6 where they were referred to as type 3 and type 4 circuits.

Types of Asynchronous Circuits

Type 3 circuits have pulse inputs and unclocked memory elements and are often referred to as *pulse mode circuits*. Flip-flops are commonly used for the memory in such circuits. Hence, the model shown in Fig. 8.1 will be adopted as the pulse mode circuit model. Notice the close resemblance to the general sequential circuit model given in Chapter 6. However, restrictions are placed on pulse mode circuits which make them significantly different from the circuits studied in Chapter 7.

Simultaneous input pulses on two or more input lines will not be allowed. This restriction is needed since no clock pulse is present to synchronize state changes. The restriction is also practical since the probability of two pulses occurring at exactly the same time is small. Input pulses should be spaced in time by at least the response time of the slowest memory element. This means

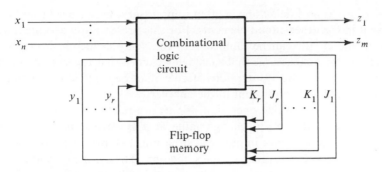

Fig. 8.1   Pulse mode circuit model.†

that no memory element will be in the process of changing state when a new input pulse occurs. Hence, the behavior of the circuit is predictable.

Now consider the information provided by the input pulses to the circuit. It can be argued that since these pulses may occur asynchronously, or, in other words, at random, that no information is provided to the device except when a pulse occurs. Hence, only the uncomplemented form of input pulses are used in the logic realizations of pulse mode circuits.

The analysis of pulse mode circuits closely parallels the analysis of synchronous circuits and was discussed in Chapter 6. Hence, no further discussions will be given here. However, the synthesis of pulse mode circuits will be considered in a later section of this chapter.

Fundamental mode circuits are defined as circuits with level inputs and unclocked memory elements. These were referred to as type 4 circuits in Chapter 6. Figure 8.2 shows the model of a fundamental mode circuit. The memory elements are shown as delay lines in the model. However, in practice,

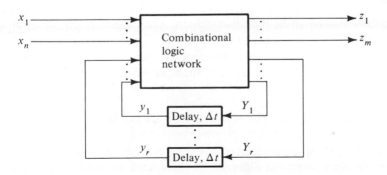

Fig. 8.2   Fundamental mode circuit model.

†Memory inputs are shown for JK flip-flops. However, any type flip-flop can generally be used.

the use of a physical delay line is often unnecessary, because sufficient delay is present in the other circuit elements. For this presentation assume that all delays in the circuit can be lumped into the delay elements shown in the feedback paths. Also assume that each delay element has the same amount of delay Δt. These last two assumptions often cannot be justified in practice and will be removed at a later point in the chapter.

For fundamental mode operation, inputs are restricted so that only one input variable is allowed to change value at a given instant of time. This restriction is required since in practical situations two or more inputs are not likely to change value at precisely the same time. Hence, the second and succeeding changes could occur while the circuit is still responding to the first input change in which case incorrect behavior of the circuit would be likely. A similar situation would exist if the time between two input changes is too small. For predictable operation of fundamental mode circuits, input changes should be spaced in time by at least Δt.

A brief introduction to the analysis of fundamental mode circuits was given in Chapter 6. However, a more thorough look is needed. Both analysis and design of fundamental mode circuits will be considered at length later in this chapter.

Synthesis of Pulse Mode Circuits

The synthesis or design of pulse mode circuits closely parallels the design of synchronous circuits as discussed in Chapter 7. However, when designing pulse mode circuits, remember that no clock pulse is present, that inputs occur on only one line at a time, and that only uncomplemented forms of input signals may be used.

The absence of a clock pulse implies that the circuit timing information must be obtained from the input pulses. Also, flip-flop triggering must be accomplished by the proper utilization of the input signals. Hence, the input pulses not only provide input information but also assume the functions performed by the clock pulse in synchronous circuits.

Design Procedure for Pulse Mode Circuits

This procedure is the same as that given for synchronous circuits. But the details of some steps are different, as illustrated by the two examples that follow the list of steps.

STEP 1. Derive a state diagram and/or state table.

STEP 2. Minimize the state table.

see page 247

STEP 3. Choose a state assignment and generate the transition/output table.

STEP 4. Select the type of flip-flop to be used and determine the excitation equations.

STEP 5. Determine the output equations.

STEP 6. Choose the appropriate logic elements and draw the circuit diagram.

Example.

A pulse mode circuit is to be designed having two input lines, x_1 and x_2, and one output line, z, as shown in Fig. 8.3(a). The circuit should produce an output pulse to coincide with the last input pulse in the sequence x_1-x_2-x_2. No other input sequence will produce an output pulse. Hence the circuit is a sequence detector for the sequence x_1-x_2-x_2.

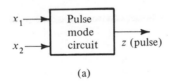

(a)

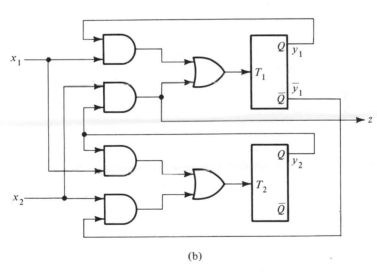

(b)

Fig. 8.3 Pulse mode example.

STEP 1. Define the following three states of the circuit:
A: indicates that the last input was x_1
B: indicates that the sequence x_1-x_2 occurred
C: indicates that the sequence x_1-x_2-x_2 occurred

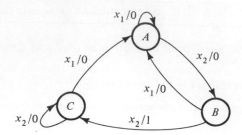

The corresponding state diagram is given above. Note that the format of the state diagram is similar to that used for synchronous circuits. However, the transitions are labeled with the input variable and the output value rather than with both input and output values. Also, remember that the state transitions are triggered by the occurrence of the indicated input pulse and not by a clock pulse.

The state table corresponding to the above state diagram is as follows:

Present State	x_1	x_2
A	$A/0$	$B/0$
B	$A/0$	$C/1$
C	$A/0$	$C/0$

Next State/Output

STEP 2. The state table is minimum as given.

STEP 3. The state assignment A-00, B-01, C-10 produces the following transition/output table:

$y_1 y_2$	x_1	x_2
00	00/0	01/0
01	00/0	10/1
10	00/0	10/0

$Y_1 Y_2 / z$

STEP 4. T flip-flops are chosen as the memory elements. The next state maps and corresponding flip-flop excitation maps are given below:

$y_1 y_2$	x_1	x_2
00	0	0
01	0	1
11	d	d
10	0	1

Y_1

$y_1 y_2$	x_1	x_2
00	0	0
01	0	1
11	d	d
10	1	0

T_1

$$x_1 \quad x_2$$

$y_1 y_2$		
00	0	1
01	0	0
11	d	d
10	0	0

$$Y_2$$

$$x_1 \quad x_2$$

$y_1 y_2$		
00	0	1
01	1	1
11	d	d
10	0	0

$$T_2$$

The above maps can be considered as reduced four-variable Karnaugh maps. Columns corresponding to $x_1 = x_2 = 0$ and $x_1 = x_2 = 1$ are omitted since they contain no pertinent information. The reader should verify that the omitted columns are not needed. Since the columns that remain are not adjacent on the complete map, groupings can be made only within a given column. Hence, the following excitation equations result:

$$T_1 = x_1 y_1 + x_2 y_2$$
$$T_2 = x_1 y_2 + x_2 \bar{y}_1$$

STEP 5. The output map and output equation are given below:

$$x_1 \quad x_2$$

$y_1 y_2$		
00	0	0
01	0	1
11	d	d
10	0	0

$$z = x_2 y_2$$

STEP 6. AND/OR logic can be used to realize the equations. Figure 8.3(b) shows the resulting circuit.

In the above example, the circuit realized took the form of a Mealy-type circuit since the output was a function of both an input and a state variable. A second example will now be presented which describes the realization of a Moore-type circuit. The definition of Mealy and Moore circuits has been presented in Chapter 6.

Example.

Design a pulse mode circuit with inputs x_1, x_2, x_3 and output z. The output must change from 0 to 1 if and only if the input sequence x_1-x_2-x_3 occurs while $z = 0$. The output must change from 1 to 0 only after an x_2 input occurs.

STEP 1. Since the output must remain high between input pulses, a Moore-type circuit is required. Refer to Fig. 8.4(a). The following state diagram and state table satisfies the stated requirements:

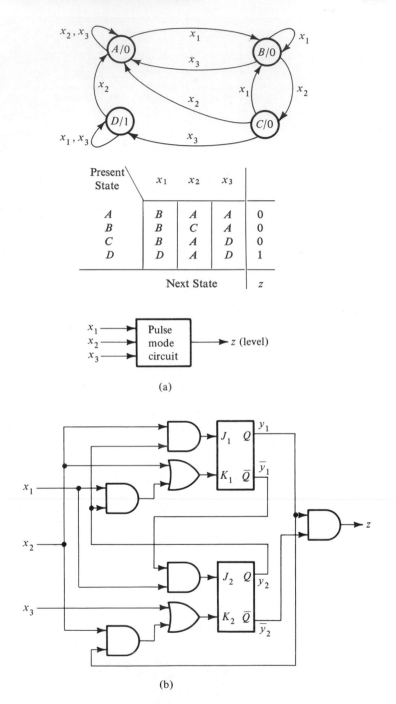

Present State	x_1	x_2	x_3	
A	B	A	A	0
B	B	C	A	0
C	B	A	D	0
D	D	A	D	1
		Next State		z

(a)

(b)

Fig. 8.4   Pulse mode example.

STEP 2. The above table is reduced.

STEP 3. Making the state assignment A-00, B-01, C-11, D-10 yields the following transition/output table:

y_1y_2	x_1	x_2	x_3	
00	01	00	00	0
01	01	11	00	0
11	01	00	10	0
10	10	00	10	1
		Y_1Y_2		z

STEP 4. Next-state maps and the corresponding excitation maps for JK flip-flops are given below:

y_1y_2	x_1	x_2	x_3
00	0	0	0
01	0	1	0
11	0	0	1
10	1	0	1

Y_1

y_1y_2	x_1	x_2	x_3
00	0	0	0
01	0	1	0
11	d	d	d
10	d	d	d

J_1

y_1y_2	x_1	x_2	x_3
00	d	d	d
01	d	d	d
11	1	1	0
10	0	1	0

K_1

y_1y_2	x_1	x_2	x_3
00	1	0	0
01	1	1	0
11	1	0	0
10	0	0	0

Y_2

y_1y_2	x_1	x_2	x_3
00	1	0	0
01	d	d	d
11	d	d	d
10	0	0	0

J_2

y_1y_2	x_1	x_2	x_3
00	d	d	d
01	0	0	1
11	0	1	1
10	d	d	d

K_2

Remember when using the reduced K-maps that groupings must be restricted to within a given column. The following excitation equations result:

$$J_1 = x_2 y_2$$
$$K_1 = x_1 y_2 + x_2$$
$$J_2 = x_1 \bar{y}_1$$
$$K_2 = x_2 y_1 + x_3$$

STEP 5. Since a Moore-type circuit is being realized, z will be a function of state variables only. A 1 output is produced only when the circuit is in state D. Hence,

$$z = y_1 \bar{y}_2$$

STEP 6. Figure 8.4(b) shows the circuit diagram that results when AND/OR logic is used to realize the equations.

This example completes the discussion of pulse mode circuits. Fundamental mode circuits will be the topic of discussion for the remainder of the chapter.

Analysis of Fundamental Mode Circuits

Fundamental mode circuit analysis requires special attention because of the behavioral characteristics of these circuits. Such characteristics are due to the absence of clocked memory and pulse inputs.

The model in Fig. 8.2 can be described by the following set of logic equations at time t:

$$z_i^t = g_i(x_1^t, \ldots, x_n^t, y_1^t, \ldots, y_r^t), \quad i = 1, \ldots, m \tag{8-1}$$

$$Y_j^t = h_j(x_1^t, \ldots, x_n^t, y_1^t, \ldots, y_r^t), \quad j = 1, \ldots, r \tag{8-2}$$

$$y_j^{t+\Delta t} = Y_j^t, \quad j = 1, \ldots, r \tag{8-3}$$

where

$$\mathbf{x} = (x_1, \ldots, x_n) = input\ state,$$
$$\mathbf{y} = (y_1, \ldots, y_r) = secondary\ state,$$
$$\mathbf{z} = (z_1, \ldots, z_m) = output\ state,$$
$$\mathbf{Y} = (Y_1, \ldots, Y_r) = excitation\ state,$$
$$(\mathbf{x}, \mathbf{y}) = total\ state.$$

Alternatively, the equations may be written as

$$\mathbf{z}^t = \mathbf{g}(\mathbf{x}^t, \mathbf{y}^t) \tag{8-4}$$

$$\mathbf{Y}^t = \mathbf{h}(\mathbf{x}^t, \mathbf{y}^t) \tag{8-5}$$

$$\mathbf{y}^{t+\Delta t} = \mathbf{Y}^t \tag{8-6}$$

Changes on various inputs cannot occur simultaneously. However, more than one input can be high at the same time.

Changes in inputs would have to be separated by atleast the time it takes for the device to change states.

Introduction

To introduce the analysis procedure for fundamental mode circuits, consider the circuit shown in Fig. 8.5(a). This circuit is described by the following set of equations:

$$z^t = g(x_1^t, x_2^t, y^t) = x_1^t x_2^t + \bar{x}_2^t y^t$$

$$Y^t = z^t$$

$$y^{t+\Delta t} = Y^t$$

where

$$(x_1, x_2) = \text{input state}$$
$$(y) = \text{secondary state}$$
$$(x_1, x_2, y) = \text{total state}$$
$$(z) = \text{output state}$$
$$(Y) = \text{excitation state}$$

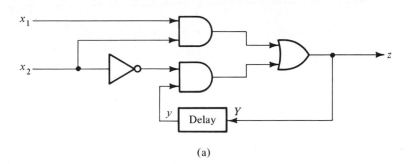

(a)

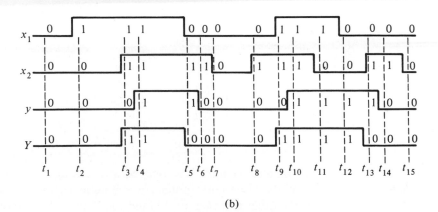

(b)

Fig. 8.5   A fundamental mode circuit: (a) circuit diagram; (b) timing diagram.

Figure 8.5(b) gives the timing diagram of the circuit for a typical input sequence. The construction of timing diagrams has been considered in Chapter 6 and the procedures discussed there remain valid.

A situation of particular interest can be seen at t_3 in Fig. 8.5(b). Observe that Y changes from 0 to 1 in response to the 0 to 1 change in x_2. However, y does not follow with a 0 to 1 change until t_4. This lag in y is due to the delay element included in the feedback path. Since a delay of Δt has been assumed, $t_4 - t_3 = \Delta t$.

An *unstable state* is said to exist at t_3 since $y \neq Y$. Other unstable states exist at t_5, t_9, and t_{13}. When $y = Y$, a *stable state* exists.

It should be noted that the unstable states exist for a period of time equal to Δt and are thus transient in nature. However, the transient behavior of fundamental mode circuits is in general critical to the proper functioning of the device and will be studied in more detail in a later section of the chapter.

In summary, a fundamental mode circuit is in a *stable state* when the following relationship is satisfied:

$$\mathbf{y}^t = \mathbf{Y}^t \tag{8-7}$$

An *unstable state* is given by the relationship below:

$$\mathbf{y}^t \neq \mathbf{Y}^t \tag{8-8}$$

Tabular Representations

It is often convenient to represent fundamental mode circuits in tabular form. The first form to be considered is the *excitation table*. An excitation table presents the excitation state and the output state as functions of the total state. Hence the excitation table is a tabular representation of equations (8-1) and (8-2). The excitation table corresponding to Fig. 8.5(a) is given below:

	$x_1 x_2$			
	00	01	11	10
y = 0	⓪/0	⓪/0	1/1	⓪/0
y = 1	①/1	0/0	①/1	①/1

$$Y/z$$

Note that each column of the table is associated with a unique input state and that each row of the table corresponds to a unique secondary state. Hence, each cell in the table represents a unique total state of the circuit. Contained in each cell is the excitation state and output state specified for the corresponding total state by equations (8-1) and (8-2), respectively. Stable states are indicated by encircling the corresponding excitation state.

Separation of the excitation and output functions into two separate tables is often desired. This has been done below for the example:

	x_1x_2 00	01	11	10	x_1x_2 00	01	11	10
y 0	⓪	⓪	1	⓪	0	0	1	0
1	①	0	①	①	1	0	1	1
		Y				z		

Both formats will be referred to as excitation tables.

The formats illustrated above can be generalized by adding rows and columns as needed to accommodate the necessary states.

A *flow table* is another useful representation of a fundamental mode circuit. Flow tables are similar to excitation tables except that excitation states and secondary states are symbolized by letters or other nonbinary characters. Hence, a flow table specifies the circuit behavior but does not specify the circuit realization. The following table is a flow table for the circuit in Fig. 8.5(a):

	x_1x_2 00	01	11	10
a	ⓐ/0	ⓐ/0	b/1	ⓐ/0
b	ⓑ/1	a/0	ⓑ/1	ⓑ/1

Both flow tables and excitation tables can be used to determine the output response of a circuit to a given input sequence. In addition, secondary and excitation state behavior can be obtained from an excitation table.

The flow table below shows the flow corresponding to the timing diagram in Fig. 8.5(b) for t_1 through t_7. Note the occurrence of unstable states in the flow sequence. Also, observe that an input change causes a horizontal move in the flow table. Vertical moves are produced by changes in secondary states which result because of input changes.

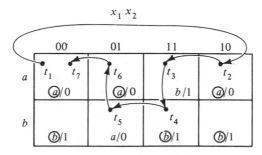

Analysis Procedure

The above example suggests the following analysis procedure.

1. Determine the excitation and the output equations from the circuit diagram.
2. Construct the excitation table.
3. Locate and circle all stable states in the excitation table.
4. Assign a unique nonbinary symbol to each row of the excitation table. Letters or the decimal equivalents of the secondary state codes are often used.
5. Construct the flow table as follows. Replace each stable excitation state in the excitation table with the symbol of the row which has the same secondary state as the unstable excitation state.

This procedure will now be illustrated with the following example.

Example.

Consider the circuit given in Fig. 8.6.

STEP 1. The excitation and output equations are as follows:

$$Y_1 = \bar{x}\bar{y}_2$$
$$Y_2 = x\bar{y}_1$$
$$z = \bar{x}y_1$$

WHAT !? °°

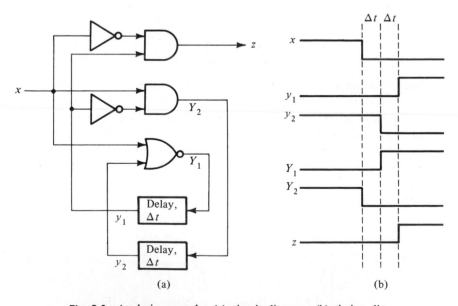

(a) (b)

Fig. 8.6 Analysis example: (a) circuit diagram; (b) timing diagram.

STEP 2. An excitation table is constructed by tabulating the values of Y_1, Y_2, and z for each total state of the circuit. The resulting table is given below:

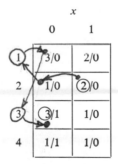

	x	
	0	1
00	10/0	01/0
01	00/0	⑴/0
$y_1 y_2$ 11	00/1	00/0
10	⑽/1	00/0

$$Y_1 Y_2 / z$$

STEP 3. Stable states can be located by the condition $y_1 y_2 = Y_1 Y_2$. These states are encircled as shown.

STEP 4. Decimal equivalents of secondary state codes plus 1 are chosen to represent the corresponding rows in the excitation table.

STEP 5. The flow table that results is given below:

	x	
	0	1
①	3/0	2/0
2	1/0	②/0
③	③/1	1/0
4	1/1	1/0

It is interesting to observe the action of the circuit from stable state 2 when the input changes from 1 to 0. First, the circuit proceeds from stable state 2 to unstable state 1 in row 2. Next, the circuit is taken to unstable state 3 in row 1. Finally, the device is transferred to stable state 3 in row 3. Hence, a state sequence ②-1-3-③ was initiated by the input change. Figure 8.6(b) shows this sequence in the form of a timing diagram. Note that two unstable states are entered before the final stable state is reached.

This concludes the study of fundamental mode circuit analysis. The synthesis of such circuits will be considered in the next section.

Synthesis of Fundamental Mode Circuits

The synthesis of fundamental mode circuits may be accomplished by following a procedure similar to that previously discussed for pulse mode circuits. However, a number of design considerations are unique to the fundamental mode case and will be given special consideration later.

Fundamental mode circuits cannot conveniently be represented by state diagrams or state tables since the total state is determined by both the input state and the secondary state. An alternative representation to the state diagram/state table which is applicable for use with fundamental mode devices is the primitive flow table. A *primitive flow table* is a flow table which contains only one stable state per row.

A synthesis procedure for fundamental mode circuits will now be stated. The procedure will be illustrated by two examples. A third example will be given later in the chapter.

Synthesis Procedure

STEP 1. Construct a primitive flow table from a word description of the circuit to be realized.

STEP 2. Determine a reduced flow table from the primitive flow table.

STEP 3. Make a secondary state assignment.

STEP 4. Construct the excitation table and the output table.

STEP 5. Determine the logic equations for each excitation state variable and for each output state variable.

STEP 6. Realize the logic equations with appropriate logic devices.

Example.

A two-input (x_1, x_2) and one-output (z) asynchronous sequential circuit is to be designed to meet the following specifications. Whenever $x_1 = 0$, $z = 0$. The first change in input x_2 which occurs while $x_1 = 1$ must cause the output to become $z = 1$. A $z = 1$ output must not change to $z = 0$ until $x_1 = 0$. A typical input-output response of the desired circuit is given below:

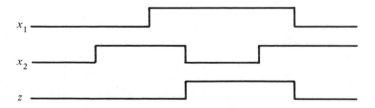

STEP 1. Construct a primitive flow table from a word description of the circuit to be realized.

A primitive flow table which satisfies the requirements of the circuit is given below:

$$x_1 x_2$$

	00	01	11	10
1	①/0	2/–	–/–	6/–
2	1/–	②/0	3/–	–/–
3	–/–	2/–	③/0	4/–
4	1/–	–/–	5/–	④/1
5	–/–	2/–	⑤/1	4/–
6	1/–	–/–	5/–	⑥/0

Several features of the table should be noted. First, there is a unique column for each input combination. Also, each row contains one stable state with a specified output, two unstable states with unspecified outputs, and a column with an unspecified state and an unspecified output. The latter is always two columns away from the column containing the stable state. Since only one input is allowed to change at a given time, this transition will not occur. Hence, no state is specified. Outputs of unstable states will be specified in a later step of the procedure.

The need for each of the specified states will now be explained.

Assume that the device is in state ① and that x_2 changes from 0 to 1. No output change should occur under these conditions. Hence, state ② is entered by way of unstable state 2. A change in x_1 from 0 to 1 while the device is in state ② should not produce an output change either. Therefore, state ③ is entered via unstable state 3. If the circuit is in state ③ and x_2 changes from 1 to 0, an output change from 0 to 1 must take place. This change is produced by creating state ④ with output $z = 1$. Now assume that the device is in state ④ and that x_2 changes from 0 to 1. In this situation, no output change should occur since $x_1 \neq 0$. Therefore, a stable state with $z = 1$ must exist in column 11. State ⑤ satisfies this requirement. State ⑥ is needed since a stable state with $z = 0$ is necessary in column 10 when a 00 to 10 input change is seen. The remaining transitions can be accommodated without defining additional states. For example, if the device is in state ⑥ and x_2 changes from 0 to 1, an output change from 0 to 1 should take place. This can be accomplished by a transition to state ⑤.

STEP 2. Determine a reduced flow table from the primitive flow table. Methods developed for reduction of incompletely specified state tables may be applied to a primitive flow table to obtain a reduced flow table. The absence of present states in a primitive flow table poses no problem in the reduction procedure since each row is identified with a unique stable state. The concept of compatible states is thus replaced by the concept of compatible rows. Two rows are compatible (can be merged) if their states and outputs are compatible in each column of the primitive flow table. Compatibility of stable and unstable states is determined as follows. Stable state (i) and unstable state i are compatible. Stable state (i) and unstable state j are compatible if (i) is compatible with (j). Unstable state i is compatible with unstable state j if (i) is compatible with (j).

The implication table corresponding to the above primitive flow table is given below:

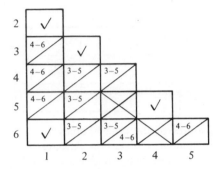

Compatible pairs of rows are seen to be $(1, 2)$, $(1, 6)$, $(2, 3)$, and $(4, 5)$. A merger diagram can be constructed as follows to illustrate the possible mergers:

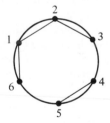

Flow table reduction is completed by selecting a minimal closed cover. For the example, implication requirements are trivial. Hence, the problem simplifies to the selection of a minimal cover. An obvious minimal cover is $\{(1, 6), (2, 3), (4, 5)\}$, which leads to the following reduced flow table:

$x_1 x_2$

	00	01	11	10
(1, 6)	①/0	2/−	5/−	⑥/0
(2, 3)	1/−	②/0	③/0	4/−
(4, 5)	1/−	2/−	⑤/1	④/1

The following equivalent flow table can be produced by relabeling the rows as a, b, and c:

$$x_1 x_2$$

	00	01	11	10
a	ⓐ/0	b/–	c/–	ⓐ/0
b	a/–	ⓑ/0	ⓑ/0	c/–
c	a/-	b/–	ⓒ/1	ⓒ/1

STEP 3. Make a secondary state assignment. Each row in the reduced flow table must be assigned a unique secondary state code. The assignment must meet certain criteria to be discussed in a later section. For now, an arbitrary choice will be assumed acceptable.

In the example, two secondary state variables (y_1, y_2) are needed. The following assignment will be used:

Row	$y_1 y_2$
a	00
b	11
c	01

STEP 4. Construct the excitation table and the output table.

The excitation table is constructed from the reduced flow table by replacing each letter by the corresponding secondary state code as assigned in the previous step. Stable states are encircled. For the example, the following excitation table results:

$$x_1 x_2$$

		00	01	11	10
	00	⑩0	11	01	⑩0
$y_1 y_2$	11	00	⑪	⑪	01
	01	00	11	⑪	⑪

$$Y_1 Y_2$$

The output table is produced by assigning outputs to each unstable state. Rules for making these assignments will now be given.

1. Assign an output of 0 to each unstable state that is a transient state between two stable states each of which has an output of 0 associated with it.

2. Assign an output of 1 to each unstable state that is a transient state between two stable states each of which has an output of 1 associated with it.

3. Assign a don't care condition to each unstable state that is a transient state between two stable states one of which has output 0 and the other output 1.

These rules yield the following output table for the example:

x_1x_2

	00	01	11	10
00	0	0	d	0
y_1y_2 **11**	0	0	0	d
01	d	d	1	1

z

By assigning the outputs in this manner, momentary changes in the output will be avoided when the circuit passes through unstable states.

STEP 5. Determine the logic equations for each excitation state variable and for each output state variable.

This step can be accomplished by transferring the information in the excitation and output tables to K-maps and then by deriving the Boolean logic equations. Maps and equations for the example are shown below:

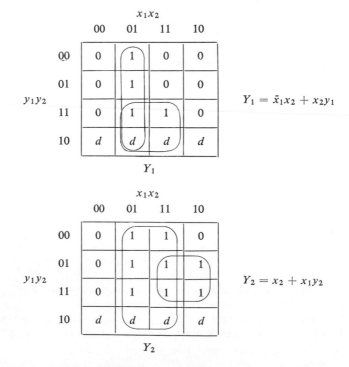

$$Y_1 = \bar{x}_1x_2 + x_2y_1$$

Y_1

$$Y_2 = x_2 + x_1y_2$$

Y_2

$$x_1 x_2$$

	00	01	11	10
00	0	0	d	0
01	d	d	1	1
11	0	0	0	d
10	d	d	d	d

$y_1 y_2$ $z = \bar{y}_1 y_2$

z

STEP 6. Realize the logic equations with appropriate logic devices.

Figure 8.7 shows a realization of the circuit with AND, OR, and NOT gates.

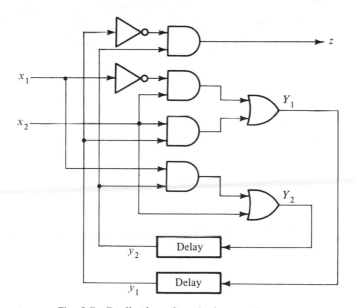

Fig. 8.7   Realization of synthesis example.

Example.

A two-input (x_1, x_2), two-output (z_1, z_2) fundamental mode circuit will be designed which has the following specifications. When $x_1 x_2 = 00$, $z_1 z_2 = 00$. The output 10 will be produced following the occurrence of the input sequence 00-01-11. The output will remain 10 until the input returns to 00 at which time it becomes 00. An output of 01 will be produced following the receipt of the input sequence 00-10-11. Again, the output will remain 01 until a 00 input occurs which returns it to 00.

STEP 1. When constructing the primitive flow table it is helpful to note that at least one stable state must be defined in each column for each possible output that may be produced by the respective inputs. This observation leads to the following partially complete primitive flow table:

	00	01	11	10
1	①/00		–/–	
2		②/00		–/–
3		③/10		–/–
4		④/01		–/–
5	–/–		⑤/10	
6	–/–		⑥/01	
7		–/–		⑦/00
8		–/–		⑧/10
9		–/–		⑨/01

The above table can be completed by establishing the necessary transitions between stable states. Such transitions can be accomplished by specifying the unstable states as shown in the complete primitive flow table below:

x_1x_2

	00	01	11	10
1	①/00	2/–	–/–	7/–
2	1/–	②/00	5/–	–/–
3	1/–	③/10	5/–	–/–
4	1/–	④/01	6/–	–/–
5	–/–	3/–	⑤/10	8/–
6	–/–	4/–	⑥/01	9/–
7	1/–	–/–	6/–	⑦/00
8	1/–	–/–	5/–	⑧/10
9	1/–	–/–	6/–	⑨/01

STEP 2. Flow table reduction is begun by construction of an implication table as shown below:

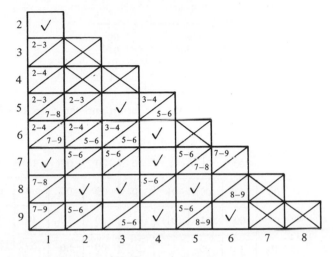

Hence, the compatible pairs of rows are (1, 2), (1, 7), (2, 8), (3, 5), (3, 8), (4, 6), (4, 7), (4, 9), (5, 8), and (6, 9). A merger diagram is helpful when selecting a cover:

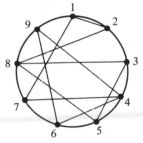

Selection of a minimal closed cover yields the following set:

$$\{(1, 2), (1, 7), (3, 5, 8), (4, 6, 9)\}$$

Note that row 1 has been included in two sets.

The following reduced flow table results from the cover where a is (1, 2), b is (3, 5, 8), c is (1, 7), and d is (4, 6, 9):

	00	01	11	10
		x_1x_2		
a	$\textcircled{a}$/00	$\textcircled{a}$/00	b/–	c/–
b	a/–	$\textcircled{b}$/10	$\textcircled{b}$/10	$\textcircled{b}$/10
c	$\textcircled{c}$/00	a/–	d/–	$\textcircled{c}$/00
d	c/–	$\textcircled{d}$/01	$\textcircled{d}$/01	$\textcircled{d}$/01

STEP 3. The following secondary state assignment will be used:

Row	y_1y_2
a	00
b	01
c	10
d	11

STEP 4. Construction of the excitation and the output tables yields the following:

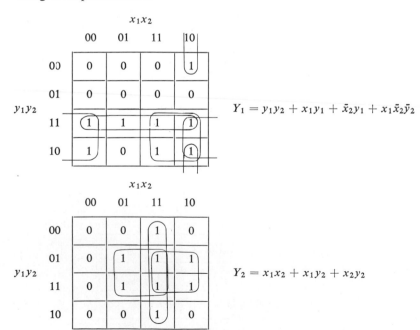

	x_1x_2				x_1x_2			
	00	01	11	10	00	01	11	10
00	⟨00⟩	⟨00⟩	01	10	00	00	d0	00
01	00	⟨01⟩	⟨01⟩	⟨01⟩	d0	10	10	10
10	⟨10⟩	00	11	⟨10⟩	00	00	0d	00
11	10	⟨11⟩	⟨11⟩	⟨11⟩	0d	01	01	01

y_1y_2 (row labels)

Y_1Y_2 z_1z_2

STEP 5. The resulting excitation and output equations can be obtained using K-maps as follows:

$$Y_1 = y_1y_2 + x_1y_1 + \bar{x}_2y_1 + x_1\bar{x}_2\bar{y}_2$$

$$Y_2 = x_1x_2 + x_1y_2 + x_2y_2$$

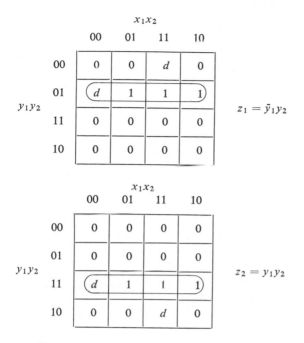

$$z_1 = \bar{y}_1 y_2$$

$$z_2 = y_1 y_2$$

STEP 6. Refer to Fig. 8.8 for the circuit realization.

A third design example will be presented later in the next section. Special requirements must be considered when making the secondary state assignment for a fundamental mode circuit. These requirements will be discussed in the following pages of the chapter.

Introduction to Races, Cycles, and Hazards

The characteristics of individual components from which a logic circuit is constructed influence the performance characteristics of the circuit. In particular, the relative response time of components has a significant effect on the behavior of fundamental mode asynchronous circuits. These effects will now be considered.

Before proceeding, however, the sources of delays in fundamental mode circuits will be briefly discussed. The fundamental mode circuit model given in Fig. 8.2 shows feedback paths with delay elements. Additional delays are present in all physical circuits and are due to the logic elements and the interconnection wires. On the other hand, circuits are often realized without delay elements. In the latter case, delays are due only to the logic and the wires.

The effects of delays on circuit performance will be divided into two categories. The first includes effects due to delays in the feedback paths, while the second considers the effects of delays in the logic and wires.

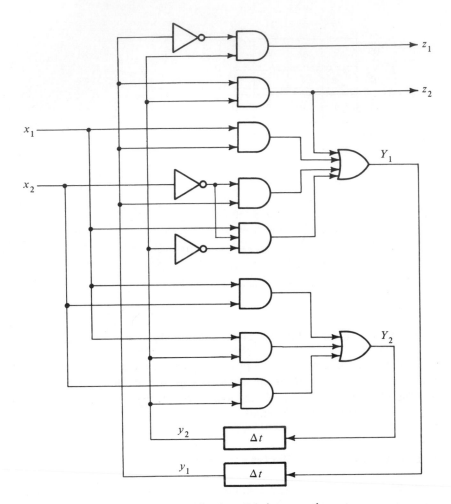

Fig. 8.8 Realization of design example.

Inertial-type devices are often used for the delay elements in feedback paths. An *inertial delay element* is a delay element which responds only to signals that persist for a time equal to or greater than the delay time of the device. To be specific, let ID represent an inertial delay with input Y, output y, and delay Δt, as shown in Fig. 8.9(a). The output y assumes the value of input Y after a time of Δt if the duration of Y is greater than or equal to Δt. An input of duration less than Δt will not propagate to the output. The response of an inertial delay element to a typical input is shown in Fig. 8.9(b).

Inertial delay elements serve to filter out unwanted transients which may occur in the feedback signals. These transients are produced because of the

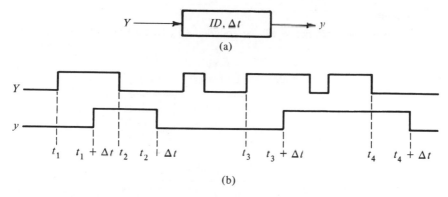

Fig. 8.9   The inertial delay element: (a) inertial delay element;
(b) typical response sequence.

unequal response times of the logic elements and can cause incorrect behavior
by the circuit if not eliminated.

Inertial delay elements are more difficult to realize than are pure delay
elements. However, the advantages provided by their use overcome the
realization complexity. Therefore, for the remainder of the chapter, all delay
elements will be considered as inertial delays.

Races and Cycles

A *race condition* is said to exist in a fundamental mode circuit when two or
more secondary state variables must change value when the circuit is required
to make a transition from one stable state to another stable state. In physical
circuits, the amounts of delay in the different feedback paths are usually not
the same. When unequal delays are possible, a race condition may cause
unexpected or incorrect performance by the circuit. Such conditions will be
illustrated below. Throughout the remainder of the discussion on fundamental
mode circuits, delay elements in one feedback path will not be assumed to
have the same delay as the elements in other feedback paths. A race condition
is said to be *noncritical* if the circuit always operates properly in the presence
of the race. Proper operation refers to the circuit arriving at the correct stable
state. However, in many cases, a race may cause the circuit to reach an
incorrect stable state. The latter case is referred to as a *critical* race condition.

Critical races must always be avoided when designing a circuit. On the
other hand, a designer may often use noncritical races to advantage.

The avoidance of critical race conditions can be accomplished by the
proper assignment of secondary states. This assignment problem is nontrivial
and will be considered in detail later. To more clearly understand the problems
of race conditions, consider the following example.

Example.

The flow table below will be encoded so that race conditions exist:

$$x_1 x_2$$

	00	01	11	10
a	ⓐ/0	b/0	ⓐ/1	b/1
b	a/0	ⓑ/0	c/0	ⓑ/0
c	a/1	©/1	©/0	d/0
d	a/0	c/0	a/1	ⓓ/1

By making the state assignment a-00, b-01, c-10, and d-11, the following excitation table results:

		x_1x_2				x_1x_2		
	00	01	11	10	00	01	11	10
00	⑳	01	⑳	01	0	0	1	1
01	00	⑪	10	⑪	0	0	0	0
y_1y_2 10	00	⑩	⑩	11	1	1	0	0
11	00	10	00	⑪	0	0	1	1
		$Y_1 Y_2$				z		

Both critical and noncritical race conditions exist in this table. A realization of the table is shown in Fig. 8.10.

In the discussion that follows, delay elements will be assumed to be inertial, and delay in logic and wires will be assumed negligible.

An examination of the excitation table shows that a race condition exists when a transition must be made from total state 1011 to total state 0000. This race is noncritical, as will now be shown by an analysis of the circuit for $\Delta_1 t > \Delta_2 t$ and for $\Delta_1 t < \Delta_2 t$. To simplify discussion, let t_0 represent a time when the circuit is in state 1011, let t_1 represent the time when the input state changes from 10 to 00, let t_2 represent the time when the first delay element responds, let t_3 represent the time when the second delay element responds, and let t_4 represent a time after t_3.

Consider the following sequence of events. At t_0, the circuit is in state 1011 with gate outputs as follows: $G1 = 0$, $G2 = 0$, $G3 = 1$, $G4 = 0$, $G5 = 0$, $G6 = 1$, $G7 = 1$, and $G8 = 1$. The input changes from 10 to 00 at t_1. This

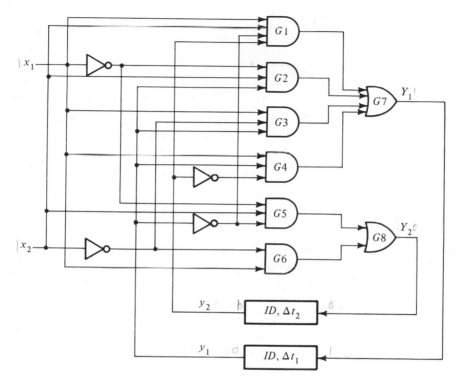

Fig. 8.10 Circuit with races. *Note:* For convenience, the output logic has been omitted.

change makes all gate outputs 0. Hence, $Y_1 Y_2 = 00$. However, $y_1 y_2 = 11$ since they are the outputs of delay elements. Therefore, the circuit is in an unstable state since $y_1 \neq Y_1$, $y_2 \neq Y_2$.

The relative response times of the delay elements influence the remaining analysis. Assume that $\Delta_1 t > \Delta_2 t$. At $t_2 = t_1 + \Delta_2 t$, y_2 becomes 0 in response to the earlier change in Y_2. No further changes in Y_1 or Y_2 are produced by $y_2 = 0$. Hence, at $t_3 = t_1 + \Delta_1 t$, y_1 becomes 0 in response to $Y_1 = 0$. Still no change in $Y_1 Y_2$ is produced, and therefore the circuit has reached a stable state since $y_1 = Y_1$ and $y_2 = Y_2$. The following sequence of total states resulted because of the noncritical race when $\Delta_1 t > \Delta_2 t$:

$$1011\text{-}0011\text{-}0010\text{-}0000$$
$$t_0 \quad\; t_1 \quad\; t_2 \quad\; t_3$$

The reader is encouraged to verify that the following sequence is obtained when $\Delta_1 t < \Delta_2 t$:

$$1011\text{-}0011\text{-}0001\text{-}0000$$
$$t_0 \quad\; t_1 \quad\; t_2 \quad\; t_3$$

Timing diagrams of these changes are given in Fig. 8.11.

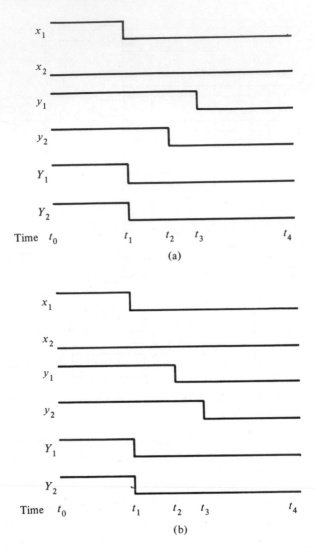

Fig. 8.11 Timing for noncritical races: (a) $\Delta_1 t > \Delta_2 t$; (b) $\Delta_2 t > \Delta_1 t$.

It should be noticed that the circuit response was a function of the relationship between $\Delta_1 t$ and $\Delta_2 t$. However, in each case the final stable state was the state desired. This is characteristic of noncritical races. The sequence of unstable states that a circuit passes through is often unimportant as long as the correct final state is reached.

The occurrence of two or more consecutive unstable states is referred to as a *cycle*. More will be said about cycles in a later discussion.

In contrast to noncritical race conditions, the critical race condition may lead to erroneous behavior by a circuit. Now consider total state 1001 of the example. The circuit response will now be analyzed for the input change 10 to 11. Gates in the circuit have the following outputs when in state 1001: $G1 = 0$, $G2 = 0$, $G3 = 0$, $G4 = 0$, $G5 = 0$, $G6 = 1$, $G7 = 0$, $G8 = 1$. When at t_1, the input changes to 11, gate $G1 = 1$ and $G6 = 0$ and hence $Y_1 = 1$ and $Y_2 = 0$. The remainder of the analysis is influenced by the relation between $\Delta_1 t$ and $\Delta_2 t$. Assume that $\Delta_1 t > \Delta_2 t$. At $t_2 = t_1 + \Delta_2 t$, $y_2 = 0$ due to $Y_2 = 0$. However, y_2 becoming 0 forces $Y_1 = 0$ before ID_1 responds to $Y_1 = 1$. Hence, $y_1 = 0 = Y_1$ and $y_2 = 0 = Y_2$, which implies that the device has reached stability in state 1100. This is an erroneous response, as seen in the excitation table. The transition sequence is given below:

$$1001\text{-}1101\text{-}1100\text{-}1100$$

$$t_0 \quad t_1 \quad t_2 \quad t_3$$

Now consider the case where $\Delta_1 t < \Delta_2 t$. Also assume that $2\Delta_1 t > \Delta_2 t$. At $t_2 = t_1 + \Delta_1 t$, y_1 becomes 1 in response to $Y_1 = 1$. This forces $G1$ to 0, which results in $Y_1 = 0$. At $t_3 = t_1 + \Delta_2 t$, y_2 becomes 0 due to $Y_2 = 0$. When y_2 becomes 0, $G4$ becomes 1, making $Y_1 = 1$ again. By assuming that $2\Delta_1 t > \Delta_2 t$, $t_3 - t_2 < \Delta_1 t$. Hence, the momentary change in Y_1 is not reflected in y_1. The device is now in the stable state 1110 as specified. The state sequence is given below:

$$1001\text{-}1101\text{-}1111\text{-}1110\text{-}1110$$

$$t_0 \quad t_1 \quad t_2 \quad t_3 \quad t_4$$

Refer to Fig. 8.12 for a more detailed timing diagram. The reader should examine the circuit for the other critical race conditions that exist.

The example has shown that a critical race condition can result in erroneous behavior of a circuit. Clearly, such situations should be avoided in all circuits. The problem of avoiding critical races will be considered next.

Avoidance of Race Conditions

Race conditions may be avoided by making the proper secondary state assignment. Stated simply, the secondary state must be assigned so that only one secondary state variable must change at a time for any state transition in the flow table. To accomplish this, it is often necessary to establish cycles between two stable states and to increase the number of state variables used.

Now consider the problem of making a race-free state assignment for the flow table shown above. An examination of the table shows that transitions must be made from row a to row b, from row b to row c, from row c to row d, from row d to row a, and from row c to row a. This information is sum-

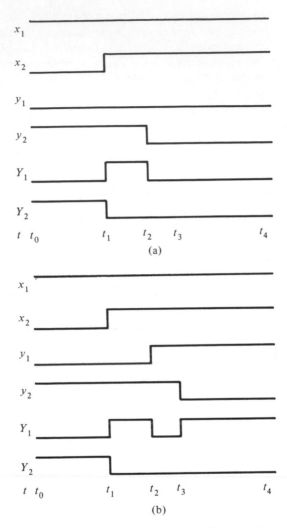

Fig. 8.12 Critical race: (a) $\Delta_1 t > \Delta_2 t$; (b) $\Delta_1 t < \Delta_2 t$.

marized in the transition diagram shown in Fig. 8.13(a). Each node in the diagram corresponds to a row of the flow table. A line connects two nodes when transitions may occur between the corresponding rows. Lines are labeled with the input states that may exist when the transition occurs.

As mentioned earlier, only critical race conditions must be avoided when designing a circuit. Figure 8.13(b) shows a transition diagram including only transitions which may lead to a critical race. Only those transitions which take place in flow table columns containing two or more stable states are critical.

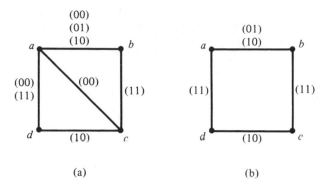

Fig. 8.13 Transition diagrams for Fig. 8.10: (a) complete transition diagram; (b) critical transition diagram.

A critical race-free secondary state assignment exists if the codes corresponding to connected nodes on the transition diagram differ in only 1 bit. The assignment below is clearly critical race-free:

Row	y_1y_2
a	00
b	01
c	11
d	10

Figure 8.14 shows the excitation table and circuit realization for this assignment.

Numerous other critical race-free assignments exist for the above example. A procedure for choosing an assignment is to arbitrarily code a state (c-10), then code one of the connected states by changing 1 bit in the previous code (b-00), and then repeat until all states are coded (a-01, d-11). In general, the state assignment problem is more complex and will be discussed in the following paragraphs.

Race-Free State Assignments

Two methods for making race-free state assignments will be described. The first method is based on the creation of cycles between stable states, while the second method requires the establishment of redundant rows in the flow table. The most economical assignments are usually obtained by the first method, but the second method is more straightforward to use.

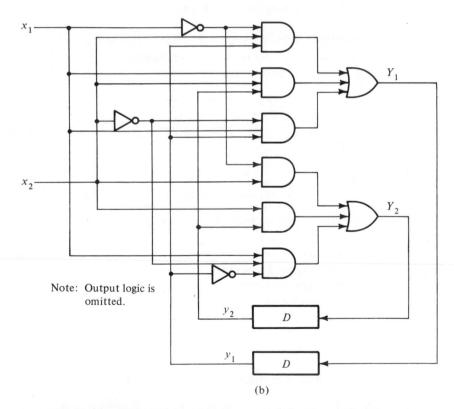

(a)

Note: Output logic is omitted.

(b)

Fig. 8.14 Critical race-free realization: (a) excitation table; (b) circuit realization.

Method 1. Consider the following reduced flow table:

$$x_1x_2$$

	00	01	11	10
a	Ⓐ/0	b/–	c/–	Ⓐ/0
b	a/–	Ⓑ/0	Ⓑ/0	c/–
c	a/–	Ⓒ/1	Ⓒ/1	Ⓒ/1

The critical transition diagram below indicates clearly that no assignment can be made to satisfy the needed adjacencies:

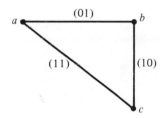

However, if the flow table is modified such that a cycle exists between any two stable states, then a race-free assignment can be made. To illustrate this approach, a cycle will be established between states *a* and *c* in column 11. The modified flow table is given below:

$$x_1x_2$$

	00	01	11	10
a	Ⓐ/0	b/–	d/–	Ⓐ/0
b	a/–	Ⓑ/0	b /0	c/–
c	a/–	Ⓒ/1	Ⓒ/1	Ⓒ/1
d			c/–	

Note that the following sequence of states occurs during the transition from Ⓐ in column 10 to Ⓒ in column 11:

$$Ⓐ - d - c - Ⓒ$$

Hence, the critical transition diagram becomes the following:

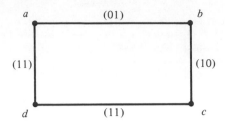

Numerous assignments exist for the modified flow table which are race-free. An example is the following:

Row	$y_1 y_2$
a	00
b	01
c	11
d	10

The resulting excitation table is given below:

$$x_1 x_2$$

$y_1 y_2$	00	01	11	10
00	(00)	01	10	(00)
01	00	(01)	(01)	11
11	00	(11)	(11)	(11)
10	00	dd	11	dd

$$Y_1 Y_2$$

Note the 00 excitation state assigned to state 0010. This was done to avoid the possibility of an unwanted stable state being established in row 10.

In the previous example, a cycle was created without the need to increase the number of state variables above the minimum required. This is not always possible, as will now be illustrated with the following flow table:

x_1x_2

	00	01	11	10
a	$\textcircled{a}$/1	*c*/–	$\textcircled{a}$/0	*b*/–
b	*a*/–	$\textcircled{b}$/1	*c*/–	$\textcircled{b}$/0
c	*d*/–	$\textcircled{c}$/0	$\textcircled{c}$/1	*d*/–
d	$\textcircled{d}$/0	*b*/–	*a*/–	$\textcircled{d}$/1

The critical transition diagram below shows that not all required adjacencies can be met:

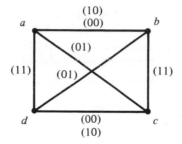

Cycles can be created to yield race-free state assignments only if three secondary state variables are used.

There are numerous ways to establish cycles in the above problem which will avoid critical races. One way is to create a cycle between *a* and *b* in columns 00 and 10 and to create a cycle between *c* and *d* in columns 00 and 10. This is illustrated by the following modified flow table:

x_1x_2

	00	01	11	10
a	$\textcircled{a}$/1	*c*/–	$\textcircled{a}$/0	a^1/–
a^1	*a*/–	–/–	–/–	*b*/–
b	a^1/–	$\textcircled{b}$/1	*c*/–	$\textcircled{b}$/0
c	c^1/–	$\textcircled{c}$/0	$\textcircled{c}$/1	c^1/–
c^1	*d*/–	–/–	–/–	*d*/–
d	$\textcircled{d}$/0	*b*/–	*a*/–	$\textcircled{d}$/1

The transition diagram for the modified flow table is given below:

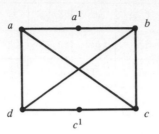

An adjacency map is helpful when selecting the codes to meet the requirements given in the transition diagram. This technique has been used in Chapter 7. The map is similar in format to a K-map except that each cell represents a unique state code. Hence, adjacent cells represent adjacent codes. The three-variable map below shows a state assignment that satisfies all adjacencies. Note that it was necessary to use another transition from d to b.

		y_2y_3			
		00	01	11	10
y_1	0	a	a^1	b	c
	1	d	d^1	d^2	c^1

The corresponding state assignment is as follows:

Row	$y_1y_2y_3$
a	000
a^1	001
b	011
c	010
c^1	110
d	100
d^1	101
d^2	111

An excitation table can then be produced and is shown below:

$y_1y_2y_3$ \ x_1x_2	00	01	11	10
000	(000)	010	(000)	001
001	000	*ddd*	*ddd*	011
011	001	(011)	010	(011)
010	110	(010)	(010)	110
110	100	*ddd*	*ddd*	100
100	(100)	101	000	(100)
101	*ddd*	111	*ddd*	*ddd*
111	*ddd*	011	*ddd*	*ddd*

$Y_1Y_2Y_3$

Method 2. This method is based on the replication of rows in the reduced flow table. States are assigned to the expanded table in such a way that one row in each set of equivalent rows is adjacent to one row in each of the remaining sets of equivalent rows. Also, each row within a set of equivalent rows is adjacent to at least one other row of the same set. Hence, race-free transitions can be made between any two stable states by properly establishing row-to-row transitions.

For four-row flow tables, each row is duplicated in this approach. The state assignments for the expanded table are given in the following table:

y_2y_3 \ y_1	0	1
00	*a*	*a*
01	*b*	*d*
11	*b*	*d*
10	*c*	*c*

For this assignment, $a = 000$ is adjacent to $b = 001$ and $c = 010$ while $a = 100$ is adjacent to $d = 101$. For the above example, the following excitation table results:

x_1x_2

$y_1y_2y_3$			00	01	11	10
a	000		(000)	010	(000)	001
a	100		(100)	000	(100)	000
b	001		000	(001)	011	(001)
b	011		001	(011)	010	(011)
c	010		110	(010)	(010)	110
c	110		111	(110)	(110)	111
d	101		(101)	001	100	(101)
d	111		(111)	101	101	(111)

$$Y_1Y_2Y_3$$

In general, the second method is not as economical as the first since no don't care conditions exist in the final excitation table. However, the second method requires no trial and error selection of codes since the codes have been published for many different-sized tables. Below are the assignment tables for six-row and eight-row tables:

y_1y_2

y_3y_4	00	01	11	10
00	a	b	e	e
01	a	b	f	f
11	c	c	e	f
10	d	d	e	f

y_1y_2

$y_3y_4y_5$	00	01	11	10
000	a	b	c	c
001	a	b	d	d
011	a	a	c	d
010	b	b	c	d
110	e	f	e	e
111	e	f	f	f
101	g	g	g	h
100	h	h	g	h

Example.

Design a two-input (x_1, x_2), one-output (z) fundamental mode circuit which will operate as follows. The output changes from 0 to 1 only on the first x_1 input change which follows an x_2 input change. A 1 to 0 output change occurs only when x_1 changes from 1 to 0 while $x_2 = 1$.

STEP 1. The following primitive flow table statisfies the stated requirements:

$$x_1 x_2$$

00	01	11	10
①/0	2/–	–/–	4/–
1/–	②/0	3/–	–/–
–/–	5/–	③/1	4/–
6/–	–/–	3/–	④/1
1/–	⑤/0	7/–	–/–
⑥/1	8/–	–/–	4/–
–/–	5/–	⑦/0	9/–
6/–	⑧/1	3/–	–/–
6/–	–/–	10/–	⑨/0
–/–	8/–	⑩/0	9/–
⑪/0	2/–	–/–	12/–
11/–	–/–	7/–	⑫/0

Note the presence of two states with output 0 in each of the columns. This condition follows from the requirement that a 0 to 1 output change should occur only on the first x_1 input change which follows an x_2 input change.

STEP 2. The use of an implication table for the primitive flow table shows that (1, 2), (3, 4), (4, 6), (4, 8), (5, 7), (6, 8), (9, 10), and (11, 12) are compatible rows. The corresponding merger diagram is shown below:

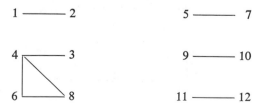

As can be seen, rows 4, 6, and 8 can be merged into a single row. All other rows must be merged in pairs. The minimal reduced flow table which follows from the merger diagram is shown below where $a = (1, 2)$, $b = (3, 4)$, $c = (5, 7)$, $d = (4, 6, 8)$, $e = (9, 10)$, and $f = (11, 12)$:

$$x_1x_2$$

	00	01	11	10
a	$\textcircled{a}/0$	$\textcircled{a}/0$	$b/-$	$b/-$
b	$d/-$	$c/-$	$\textcircled{b}/1$	$\textcircled{b}/1$
c	$a/-$	$\textcircled{c}/0$	$\textcircled{c}/0$	$e/-$
d	$\textcircled{d}/1$	$\textcircled{d}/1$	$b/-$	$\textcircled{d}/1$
e	$d/-$	$d/-$	$\textcircled{e}/0$	$\textcircled{e}/0$
f	$\textcircled{f}/0$	$a/-$	$c/-$	$\textcircled{f}/0$

STEP 3. A minimum of three secondary state variables are required since there are six rows in the reduced flow table. However, no three-variable race-free assignment is possible, because row c must be adjacent to four other rows, as shown in the following transition diagram:

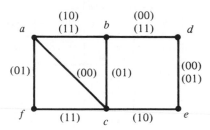

Method 1 described above will be used to obtain a race-free assignment. Intermediate states a^1 and c^1, added as indicated below, allow this to be accomplished:

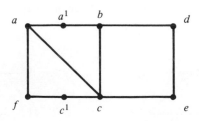

The chosen assignment is given in the following map:

$y_3 y_4$

		00	01	11	10
	00	a	a^1	b	c
$y_1 y_2$	01			d	e
	11				
	10	f			c^1

STEP 4. Excitation and output tables are given below:

$y_1y_2y_3y_4$	x_1x_2 00	01	11	10	x_1x_2 00	01	11	10
a	0000	(0000)	(0000)	0001	0001	0	0	—	—
a^1	0001	—	—	0011	0011	—	—	—	—
c	0010	0000	(0010)	(0010)	0110	—	0	0	—
b	0011	0111	0010	(0011)	(0011)	—	—	1	1
e	0110	0111	0111	(0110)	(0110)	—	—	0	0
d	0111	(0111)	(0111)	0011	(0111)	1	1	—	1
f	1000	(1000)	0000	1010	(1000)	0	—	—	0
c^1	1010	—	—	0010	—	—	—	—	—
			$Y_1 Y_2 Y_3 Y_4$				z	

STEP 5. The corresponding excitation and output equations follow:

$$Y_1 = \bar{x}_2 y_1 + x_1 y_1 \bar{y}_3$$
$$Y_2 = \bar{x}_2 y_2 + y_2 \bar{y}_4 + \bar{x}_1 y_2 + \bar{x}_1 \bar{x}_2 y_4 + x_1 \bar{x}_2 y_3 \bar{y}_4$$
$$Y_3 = y_2 + y_4 + x_1 y_3 + x_2 y_3 + x_1 x_2 y_1$$
$$Y_4 = x_1 y_4 + x_1 \bar{y}_1 \bar{y}_3 + \bar{x}_2 y_4 + \bar{x}_1 y_2$$
$$z = y_4$$

STEP 6. A logic realization of the above equations completes the design process.

Hazards

The subject of hazards was initially discussed in Chapter 3 for combinational logic networks. Static and dynamic hazards can also be present in the combinational logic portion of sequential circuits and should be considered in the design. The previous discussions remain valid, and no further consideration will be given to the subject. Inertial delay elements can be used to filter out transients caused by these hazards.

A third type of hazard is special to the fundamental mode circuit and will be briefly considered. In the discussion that follows, assume that all logic elements have some inherent delay associated with them. This is always true in physical circuits, of course. An *essential hazard* is a hazard caused by unequal delays along two or more paths which originate from the same input line. Such a hazard can cause the circuit to respond incorrectly to input changes. To illustrate this, consider the circuit shown in Fig. 8.15(a). The excitation and output table for the circuit is as follows:

		x		x	
		0	1	0	1
	00	(00)	01	0	0
$y_1 y_2$	01	11	(01)	0	0
	11	(11)	10	1	1
	10	00	(10)	1	1
		$Y_1 Y_2$		z	

Assume that the circuit is in state $x = y_1 = y_2 = 0$. Hence, $Y_1 = Y_2 = 0$. Also assume that NOT gate $N1$ has a delay associated with it which is very large in comparison to the delays of the other elements in the circuit including the feedback delay. Now consider the response of the circuit to a 0 to 1 change in x at time t_1. A timing diagram of the response is shown in Fig. 8.15(b). As can be seen, the circuit becomes stable in state $x = 1, y_1 = 1, y_2 = 0$. This is an incorrect response, as shown in the excitation table.

Critical events occur at times t_5, t_6, t_{10}, and t_{13}. The circuit is in the correct secondary state 01 at t_5. However, since $N1$ has not responded to the input change, $A2$ becomes 1, which forces $Y_1 = 1$ at t_6. This subsequently causes $A3$ to go to zero. At t_{10}, $N1$ becomes 0, forcing $A2$ to 0, which causes $Y_2 = 0$. At t_{13}, y_2 responds to $Y_2 = 0$, and the circuit has reached stability.

Hence, the delay in $N1$ has incorrectly forced $Y_1 = 1$ at t_6 which triggered the sequence of events leading to an incorrect stable state. The effect of such delays can be overcome by providing a sufficient amount of delay in the feedback paths.

Analysis

The analysis procedure given early in the chapter involved the determination of excitation tables, output tables, and flow tables from a circuit diagram. Given these tables, a thorough study is usually warranted to determine if any critical races or hazards exist in the circuit.

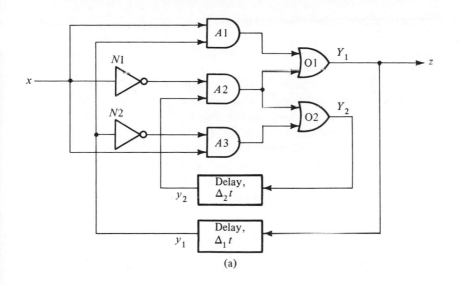

(a)

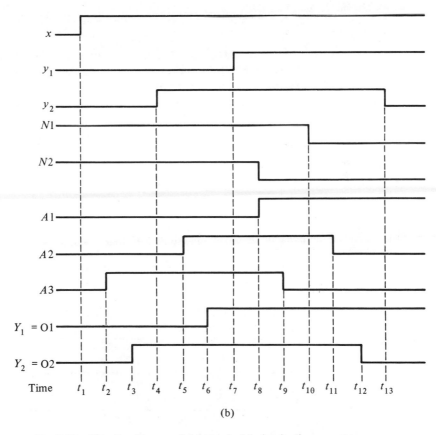

(b)

Fig. 8.15 Circuit with essential hazard: (a) circuit diagram; (b) timing diagram.

Summary

This chapter has been an introduction to the subject of asynchronous sequential circuits. Both pulse mode and fundamental mode circuits were considered. Attention was first given to the design of pulse mode circuits. A design procedure was presented and was illustrated with two examples. The analysis and the design of fundamental mode circuits was considered next. Analysis and design procedures were given and were demonstrated by several examples. Finally, a discussion of races and hazards was undertaken. Procedures for making race-free state assignments were presented and illustrated.

REFERENCES

1. CALDWELL, S. H., *Switching Circuits and Logical Design*. New York: John Wiley & Sons, Inc., 1958.

2. HUFFMAN, D. A., "The Synthesis of Sequential Switching Circuits," *J. Franklin Institute*, Vol. 257, No. 3, March 1954, pp. 161–190, and No. 4, April 1954, pp. 275–303.

3. HUFFMAN, D. A., "A Study of Memory Requirements of Sequential Switching Circuits," *Tech. Report No. 293*, Research Laboratory of Electronics, Massachusetts Institute of Technology, Cambridge, Mass., March 14, 1955.

4. McCLUSKEY, E. J., "Fundamental and Pulse Mode Sequential Circuits," *IFIP Congress Proceedings, 1962*. Amsterdam: North-Holland Publishing Company, 1963.

5. UNGER, S. H., *Asynchronous Sequential Switching Circuits*. New York: John Wiley & Sons, Inc., (Interscience Division), 1969.

PROBLEMS

8.1. Analyze the pulse mode circuit shown in Fig. P8.1:
   (a) Determine a state table.
   (b) Construct a timing diagram for the circuit in response to the following input sequence. Include x_1, x_2, x_3, y_1, y_2, J_1, K_1, J_2, K_2, Y_1, Y_2, and z in your diagram.

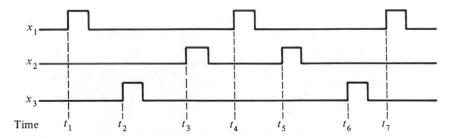

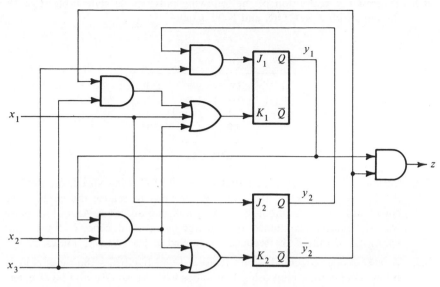

Fig. P8.1

8.2. Analyze the pulse mode circuit shown in Fig. P8.2:
  (a) Determine a state table.
  (b) Determine the output response to the input sequence x_1-x_2-x_1-x_1-x_1-
      x_1-x_2-x_2 if the starting state is 00.
  (c) What form (level or pulse) will an output of $z = 1$ have? Why?

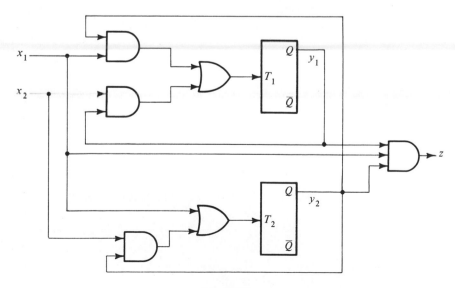

Fig. P8.2

8.3. Determine a realization of the following pulse mode state table. Use JK flip-flops with AND, OR, and NOT gates.

Present State	x_1	x_2	x_3
A	$A/0$	$B/0$	$C/1$
B	$B/0$	$C/0$	$D/0$
C	$C/0$	$D/0$	$A/1$
D	$D/0$	$A/0$	$B/1$

Next State/z

8.4. Design a pulse mode circuit that meets the following specifications. Use AND, OR, and NOT gates with SR flip-flops to realize the circuit. The circuit will have two imputs x_1 and x_2 and one output z. An output pulse will be produced simultaneously with the last of a sequence of three input pulses if and only if the sequence contained at least two x_1 pulses.

8.5. A pulse mode sequential circuit is needed which satisfies the requirements below. Design the circuit using T flip-flops with AND, OR, and NOT gates. Two input lines x_1 and x_2 will be provided along with one output line z. An output transition from 0 to 1 will be produced only on the occurrence of the last x_2 pulse in the sequence x_1-x_2-x_1-x_2. The output will be reset from 1 to 0 only by the first x_1 pulse which occurs following the 0 to 1 output transition. Allow overlapping sequences.

8.6. Analyze the fundamental mode circuit shown in Fig. P8.3:
(a) Determine the excitation and output table.
(b) Construct a flow table.
(c) Use the flow table to determine the output response to the input sequence x_1x_2: 00-01-11-10-00-01-00-10. Assume initially that $x_1 = x_2 = y_1 = y_2 = Y_1 = Y_2 = 0$.

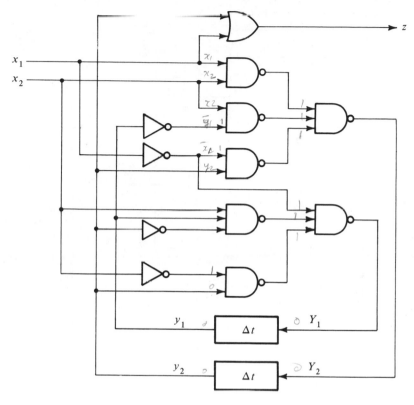

Fig. P8.3

8.7. Consider the circuit in Fig. P8.4. Analyze the circuit as follows:

(a) Construct a timing diagram for the following input sequence. Assume no delay in the logic gates. Also assume that initially $y_1 = Y_1 = 1$ and $y_2 = Y_2 = 0$. Include $x_1, x_2, y_1, y_2, Y_1, Y_2,$ and z in the timing diagram.

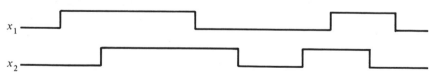

(b) Repeat part (a) assuming that each logic gate has a delay of $\frac{1}{2}\Delta t$.

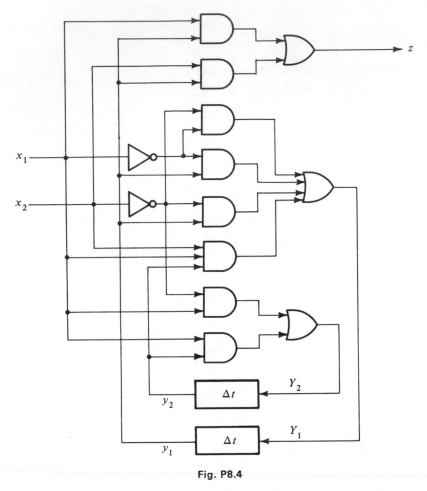

Fig. P8.4

8.8.   Determine a primitive flow table for a fundamental mode circuit which has the following requirements. One input x and one output z are needed. The output should follow the input on every other 0-1-0 transition as indicated below:

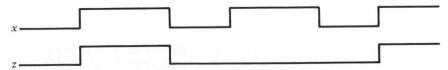

8.9.   A fundamental mode circuit must be designed to satisfy the requirements given below. Determine a primitive flow table for the circuit. Two inputs (x_1, x_2) and one output (z) are required. The output $z = 0$ will always be produced when $x_1 = x_2$. When $x_1 = 0$ and x_2 changes from 0 to 1, an output $z = 1$ must occur. When $x_1 = 1$ and x_2 changes from 1 to 0, an output $z = 1$ must occur. Otherwise, no input change will cause an output change.

8.10. Construct a primitive flow table for a fundamental mode circuit with the following specifications. The circuit must have two inputs (x_1, x_2) and two outputs (z_1, z_2). When $x_1 = x_2 = 0$, the outputs must be $z_1 = z_2 = 0$. If $x_1 = 1$ and x_2 changes from 0 to 1, an output $z_1 = 0$, $z_2 = 1$ will be produced. If $x_2 = 1$ and x_1 changes from 0 to 1, an output $z_1 = 1$, $z_2 = 0$ will be produced. Outputs are reset to $z_1 = z_2 = 0$ only when x_1 and x_2 both equal 0. No output change is produced by any other input change.

8.11. Reduce the primitive flow table given below to a minimum row table:

$x_1 x_2$

	00	01	11	10
1	①/0	2/–	–/–	3/–
2	4/–	②/1	5/–	–/–
3	1/–	–/–	5/–	③/0
4	④/1	2/–	–/–	6/–
5	–/–	2/–	⑤/1	6/–
6	1/–	–/–	5/–	⑥/1

8.12. Repeat Problem 8.11 for the following primitive flow table:

$x_1 x_2$

	00	01	11	10
1	①/0	2/–	–/–	4/–
2	1/–	②/0	3/–	–/–
3	–/–	2/–	③/0	8/–
4	5/–	–/–	7/–	④/1
5	⑤/1	6/–	–/–	4/–
6	5/–	⑥/1	7/–	–/–
7	–/–	6/–	⑦/1	8/–
8	1/–	–/–	3/–	⑧/0

8.13. Determine a minimum row flow table compatible with the following primitive flow table:

$$x_1 x_2$$

	00	01	11	10
1	①/1	6/–	–/–	5/–
2	②/0	4/–	–/–	3/–
3	2/–	–/–	9/–	③/0
4	2/–	④/0	7/–	–/–
5	1/–	–/–	7/–	⑤/1
6	1/–	⑥/1	7/–	–/–
7	–/–	4/–	⑦/0	10/–
8	⑧/0	4/–	–/–	10/–
9	–/–	6/–	⑨/1	3/–
10	1/–	–/–	9/–	⑩/0

8.14. Determine a circuit realization for the following reduced flow table. Use the indicated state assignment. Assume AND, OR, and NOT gates are available for use in the realization.

$$x_1 x_2$$

		00	01	11	10
00	a	ⓐ/0	ⓐ/1	b/–	c/–
01	b	a/–	ⓑ/0	ⓑ/0	d/–
10	c	a/–	a/–	ⓒ/1	ⓒ/1
11	d	a/–	b/–	c/–	ⓓ/0

$y_1 y_2$

8.15. Repeat Problem 8.14 for the flow table below, but assume that only NAND gates are available for use in the circuit:

x_1x_2

		00	01	11	10
00	*a*	ⓐ/00	*b*/–	ⓐ/00	*d*/–
01	*b*	*a*/–	ⓑ/01	ⓑ/01	*c*/–
y_1y_2 11	*c*	*d*/–	ⓒ/10	ⓒ/10	ⓒ/01
10	*d*	ⓓ/00	*c*/–	*c*/–	ⓓ/10

8.16. Repeat Problem 8.14 for the following reduced flow table:

x_1x_2

		00	01	11	10
000	*a*	ⓐ/1	*c*/–	*b*/–	ⓐ/1
001	*b*	ⓑ/0	*d*/–	ⓑ/0	*a*/–
010	*c*	*a*/–	ⓒ/0	*e*/–	ⓒ/0
$y_1y_2y_3$ 101	*d*	*b*/–	ⓓ/1	*f*/–	ⓓ/1
110	*e*	ⓔ/1	*f*/–	ⓔ/1	*c*/–
100	*f*	*a*/–	ⓕ/0	ⓕ/1	*a*/–

8.17. Given the excitation table below,

x_1x_2

	00	01	11	10
00	⟨00⟩	⟨00⟩	11	01
01	11	⟨01⟩	10	⟨01⟩
y_1y_2 10	00	00	⟨10⟩	⟨10⟩
11	⟨11⟩	10	⟨11⟩	10

Y_1Y_2

(a) Find all race conditions in the table.
(b) Are the races critical or noncritical?
(c) Do any cycles exist in the table?

8.18. Analyze the circuit in Fig. P8.5 to determine if the circuit has a critical race. If so, draw a timing diagram to show the effect that the race can have on the circuit response.

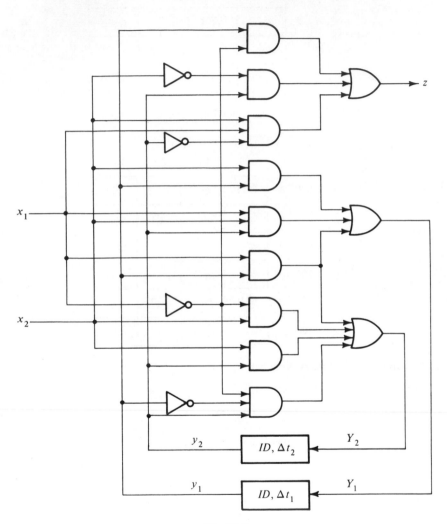

Fig. P8.5

8.19. Repeat Problem 8.18 for the circuit shown in Fig. P8.6.

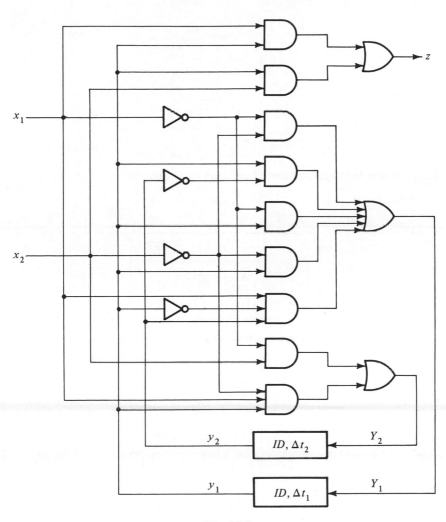

Fig. P8.6

8.20. Determine a critical race-free state assignment for the following reduced flow table. Construct the corresponding excitation table.

x

	0	1
a	$ⓐ/0$	$d/-$
b	$ⓑ/1$	$c/-$
c	$a/0$	$ⓒ/0$
d	$b/1$	$ⓓ/1$

8.21. Repeat Problem 8.20 for the reduced flow table below:

x_1x_2

	00	01	11	10
a	$ⓐ/0$	$b/-$	$c/-$	$ⓐ/0$
b	$ⓑ/1$	$ⓑ/1$	$ⓑ/1$	$c/1$
c	$a/-$	$b/1$	$ⓒ/1$	$ⓒ/1$

8.22. Given the following reduced flow table,

x_1x_2

	00	01	11	10
a	$ⓐ/0$	$d/0$	$ⓐ/1$	$c/0$
b	$ⓑ/0$	$c/-$	$ⓑ/0$	$d/-$
c	$b/0$	$ⓒ/1$	$a/1$	$ⓒ/0$
d	$a/0$	$ⓓ/0$	$b/0$	$ⓓ/1$

(a) Use method 1 to find a critical race-free assignment for the table. Construct the corresponding excitation table.

(b) Repeat part (a) using method 2.

8.23. A fundamental-mode circuit is to be designed to function as part of an electronic lock. The lock has two switch inputs (x_1 and x_2). Design the circuit so that an open signal ($z = 1$) is produced only after the following conditions have been satisfied:

1. Begin with $x_1 = x_2 = 0$.
2. While $x_2 = 0$, x_1 is turned on, then off twice.
3. While x_1 remains off, x_2 is turned on to open the lock.

8.24. A fundamental-mode asynchronous sequential circuit is defined below in Fig. P8.7.

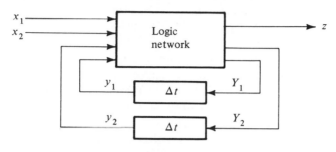

Fig. P8.7

(a) Find a flow table.

(b) Using the flow table, find the output sequence for the input sequence $x_1x_2 = 00, 01, 11, 10, 11, 01, 00, 10$ if the delay lines are initially at zero (stable state $x_1 = x_2 = y_1 = y_2 = 0$).

$$Y_1 = \bar{x}_2 y_2 + x_1 y_1 + x_1 \bar{x}_2$$

$$Y_2 = \bar{x}_1 y_2 + \bar{x}_1 x_2 + x_2 y_1$$

$$z = x_1 \bar{x}_2 + x_2 \bar{y}_1 + \bar{x}_1 y_2$$

8.25. Given the reduced flow table below, find a critical race-free secondary state assignment for this asynchronous sequential circuit. Find a two-level NOR realization using inertial delay elements.

	x_1x_2			
	00	01	11	10
a	ⓐ/0	b/–	ⓐ/1	b/–
b	a/–	ⓑ/0	c/–	ⓑ/0
c	a/–	ⓒ/1	ⓒ/0	b/–

8.26. Find a two-level NAND realization for the following primitive flow table:

a	ⓐ/0	b/–	–/–	c/–
b	a/–	ⓑ/1	d/–	–/–
c	a/–	–/–	d/–	ⓒ/1
d	–/–	b/–	ⓓ/0	e/–
e	a/–	–/–	d/–	ⓔ/0

8.27. Find a two-level NOR implementation for a fundamental mode asynchronous sequential circuit with two inputs (x_1, x_2) and one output (z) which satisfies the following conditions: First, z is always zero when $x_2 = 1$. The output z changes to logic 1 on the first $0 \longrightarrow 1$ transition of x_1 when $x_2 = 0$ and remains logic 1 until x_2 goes to logic 1 and forces z back to logic 0.

8.28. Find a two-level NAND realization of a fundamental mode circuit which has two inputs (x_1, x_2) and one output (z) which satisfies the following conditions: First, $z = 0$ when $x_1 = 0$. The output z goes to logic 1 on the first $1 \longrightarrow 0$ transition on x_2 when $x_1 = 1$. The output remains at logic 1 until x_1 returns to zero.

9

Computer-Aided Design of Sequential Circuits

In Chapters 6, 7, and 8 the theory of sequential circuit analysis and synthesis was developed. Many example sequential circuits were synthesized. In these examples, we noted that as the size of the circuit increases, the more difficult it becomes to find an implementation if all calculations are done manually. In fact, for large problems one sometimes wishes he could find any solution, not just a minimal one.

The process of implementing a digital sequential circuit can be described by the following phases. First, analysis of the particular problem identifies input and output codes and establishes a state table description of the circuit. Second, the design phase of the process reduces the state table, makes a state assignment, and produces the logic diagram of the sequential circuit. The third phase is the construction of the device. Parts must be obtained, physically arranged in a regular manner, mounted on a circuit board, and interconnected in the proper way. The last phase is sometimes called quality control. Here the circuit undergoes testing and modification, if necessary, to guarantee that the final product meets the design goals established in the first phase.

In this chapter we shall discuss a computer-aided-design (CAD) algorithm which automates the second phase of the circuit implementation process. The CAD algorithm finds realizations for *synchronous* sequential circuits when manual solution is impractical. The techniques employed in the algorithm do *not* guarantee a minimal realization. However, the realizations will be "near-minimal" for most cases.

The decision whether to employ the CAD algorithm to a specific sequential machine is not always an easy one to make. In general, sequential circuits which are larger than 16 states or have more than 4 inputs are too large for manual solution; hence, application of the CAD algorithm is indicated. However, if a sequential circuit is to be duplicated many times, the logic designer is duty-bound to attempt a minimal solution if at all feasible. If a sequential circuit is being implemented for a *one-time* application, then by all means apply the CAD procedure to find the logic diagram and proceed with all haste into the construction and quality control phases of the implementation process.

Design Algorithm [1]

In this chapter we shall automate the synthesis of synchronous sequential circuits as presented in Chapter 7. The flow chart for the CAD algorithm is shown in Fig. 9.1. In box 1, the state table for the sequential circuit is entered into the algorithm as data. After examining the state table the algorithm determines if the sequential circuit is completely or incompletely specified. Box 2 is the state minimization subalgorithm for the completely specified case. Boxes 3 and 4 represent the state minimization subalgorithm for the incompletely specified case. Once a reduced state table is found, box 5 is entered to generate a state assignment. Box 6 then uses the reduced state table and chosen state assignment to generate the next-state and output switching functions in the form of equations (6-2) and (6-3) for the sequential circuit model of Fig. 6.1. Once the functions are generated, box 7 applies the CAD algorithm of Chapter 4 to reduce the functions to minimal sum of products form. Box 8 outputs a summary of the design including the reduced state table and switching functions.

Please note that box 6 generates only next-state functions. Hence, this algorithm as presented is applicable only to clocked D flip-flops.

The remainder of this chapter is organized as a discussion of the details of each subalgorithm of Fig. 9.1. Let us begin by examining the state minimization subalgorithms.

State Minimization

For convenience, the state minimization process has been separated into two parts, the completely specified and incompletely specified cases.

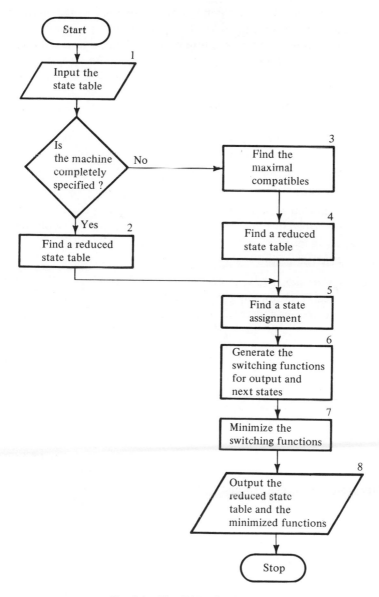

Fig. 9.1 The CAD algorithm.

Completely Specified Circuits

State minimization for completely specified sequential circuits has been presented in Chapter 7. Since state equivalence for completely specified circuits is a well-defined equivalence relation (symmetric, reflexive, and transitive), state reduction is much simpler than for incompletely specified circuits. The CAD algorithm uses the partitioning procedure exactly as developed in Chapter 7. The procedure is fast and guarantees a minimal state circuit each time it is applied.

Incompletely Specified Circuits

The state reduction of incompletely specified circuits may be divided into two parts: the generation of the maximal compatibles and the selection of a complete, consistent, minimal set of compatibility classes. The complete, consistent, minimal set is called the *minimal cover*.

Maximal compatibles. The CAD algorithm employs the implication table method as described in Fig. 7.49. The algorithm sets up the implication table and processes it to generate the compatible pairs. Once the pairs are found, they are merged to form the maximal compatibles.

Reduced state table. In Chapter 7 the technique described for selecting a reduced set of states for a sequential circuit did not guarantee a minimal state table. Here we present a method [2] which does guarantee a minimal machine. Before presenting the method, let us define some new terms.

Let each maximal compatible be represented symbolically as

$$MC_l = (S_1 S_2 \ldots S_j), \quad l = 1, \ldots, m$$

where j is the number of states in MC_l and m is the total number of maximal compatibles. The compatibility classes MC_l have been determined in the previous step of the CAD algorithm. Let $(MC_l)_i$ be the next-state set of MC_l under input I_i. Therefore, each maximal compatible implies s such sets $(MC_l)_i$, $i = 1, \ldots, s$, where s is the total number of inputs to the sequential machine. Note that the next-state sets $(MC_l)_i$ appear as entries in the familiar closure table of Chapter 7. Some of the $(MC_l)_i$ are useful in the state reduction process. In particular, we identify those $(MC_l)_i$ with the following properties:

1. $(MC_l)_i$ has more than one implied state.
2. $(MC_l)_i$ is not contained in MC_l.
3. $(MC_l)_i$ is not contained in $(MC_l)_j$, $j = 1, \ldots, s$ for $i = 1, \ldots, s$.

The resulting set $\{(MC_l)_i, i = 1, \ldots, s\}$ is known as the *class set* for MC_l:

$$CS_{MC_l} = \{(MC_l)_i, i = 1, \ldots, s \,|\, \text{properties } 1\text{–}3\}$$

Example.

Consider the example of Fig. 7.55. The maximal compatibles are (ADE), (ABC), and (ACD). From the closure table of Fig. 7.55(e), the class set for each maximal compatible is

Maximal Compatible	Class Set
(ADE)	CD, ABC
(ABC)	DE
(ACD)	ABC

The definition for class sets above is now extended for any compatibility class CC_l whether it be a maximal compatible or not. We may simply replace each occurrence of MC_l by CC_l in the definitions above:

$$CS_{CC_l} = \{(CC_i)_i, \ i = 1, \ldots, s \mid \text{properties } 1\text{-}3\}$$

In other words, the class set for CC_l consists of those next-state sets which meet properties 1, 2, and 3.

Some additional properties of compatibility classes are also useful in the state reduction method. Suppose that a compatibility class CC_j contains all the states of another compatibility class CC_l and that all the class sets of CC_j are also class sets of CC_l: then class CC_l is said to be *excluded* by CC_j. In other words, CC_l is excluded from consideration by CC_j if $CC_j \supset CC_l$ and $CS_{CC_j} \subseteq CS_{CC_l}$. A *prime compatible* is a compatibility class that is not excluded by any other compatibility class. Note that maximal compatibles will always be prime compatibles. All compatibility classes which are potential candidates for selection in the minimal cover of the original states of the sequential circuit are also prime compatibles.

With these definitions we shall now describe the state reduction process in three phases: the derivation of the prime compatibles, the selection of the minimal cover, and the formation of the reduced state table.

The derivation of the list of prime compatibles begins with the list of maximal compatibles. The maximal compatibles with the largest number of states constitute the initial list of prime compatibles. Suppose they have J states. First generate the class set for each maximal compatible on the initial list. Add to the list of prime compatibles all subsets of order $J - 1$, along with their class sets, of each prime compatible currently on the list. These subsets are also compatibility classes. Check the classes of order $J - 1$ for exclusion by classes of order J. Retain only those classes which are not excluded. At this point we add all maximal compatibles of order $J - 1$, generate their class sets, and check for exclusion. Now we repeat the initial procedure of adding all subsets of order $J - 2$ from the compatibility classes of order $J - 1$ which are on the list. The process continues until subsets of all possible orders are tested, including those of order 1 (the single states of the original circuit).

Although the process seems exhaustive, only prime compatibles are left on the list at each step. When subsets of order K are generated, no set of order $L < K$ is present on the list. Also note that no subsets need be generated for a maximal compatible whose class set is empty. A subset of such a maximal compatible will be excluded by it.

Example.

Consider the sequential machine of Fig. 7.55. The prime compatibles for this machine are derived in Fig. 9.2. All the maximal compatibles of this example are of order 3 so they are all initially entered on the list of prime compatibles. The class sets for the maximal compatibles are then determined. Next all subsets of order 2 of the maximal compatibles are entered on the list of prime compatibles. The test for exclusion indicates that compatibility class (BC) is excluded by (ABC) so it is removed from the list (by a waved

Prime Compatibles	$(CC_l)_0$	$(CC_l)_1$	Class Sets
(ADE)	CD	ABC	CD, ABC
(ABC)	DE		DE
(ACD)		ABC	ABC
(AD)	CD	AC	CD, AC
(DE)		BC	BC
(AE)	CD	AB	CD, AB
~~(AB)~~	~~DE~~	~~~~	~~DE~~
(AC)		AB	AB
~~(BC)~~	~~DE~~	~~AB~~	~~DE, AB~~
(CD)		BC	BC
A			ϕ
B			ϕ
C			ϕ
D			ϕ
E			ϕ

Fig. 9.2 Prime compatibles.

line in Fig. 9.2); (AB) is excluded by (ABC). Last, all compatibility classes of order 1 are listed. For this example none are excluded. This sequential machine has 13 prime compatibles.

Example.

Consider the sequential machine of Fig. 9.3(a). The implication table of Fig. 9.3(b) and the merger diagram of Fig. 9.3(c) produce the maximal compatibles $(ACEF)(CDE)(ABF)(BD)$. The generation of the prime compatibles is shown in Fig. 9.3(d). First the largest maximal compatible $(ACEF)$ is listed as a prime compatible and its class set is found to be empty. Hence, $(ACEF)$ will exclude any of its subsets. Next we list the maximal compatibles of order 3, (CDE) and (ABF), and generate their class sets. For example,

$$\begin{array}{cccc} 00 & 01 & 11 & 10 \\ (ABF) \longrightarrow \;\; DC & AE & F & AF \end{array}$$

We eliminate the single state entry F and the entry AF since $AF \subset (ABF)$,

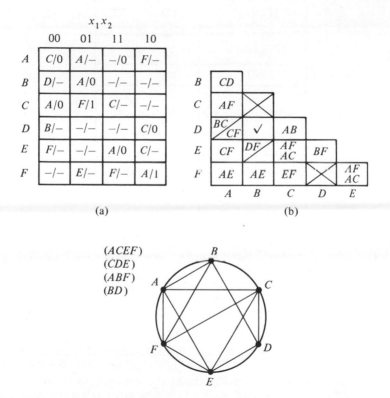

(a)

(b)

(c)

Fig. 9.3 Another example: (a) state table; (b) implication table; (c) maximal compatibles.

Prime Compatibles	Class Sets
$(ACEF)$	ϕ
(CDE)	ABF, AC
(ABF)	CD, AE
(CD)	AB
~~(CE)~~	~~AF, AC~~
(DE)	BF
(AB)	CD
~~(AF)~~	~~AE~~
(BF)	AE
(BD)	ϕ
~~A~~	~~ϕ~~
~~B~~	~~ϕ~~
~~C~~	~~ϕ~~
~~D~~	~~ϕ~~
~~E~~	~~ϕ~~
~~F~~	~~ϕ~~

(d)

Fig. 9.3—*Cont.* (d) prime compatibles.

Hence, the class set of (ABF) is

$$\{CD, AE\}$$

The following step is to generate all second-order subsets of the two third-order prime compatibles, generate their class sets, and test for exclusion. The test indicates that (CE) should be removed from the list because $(ACEF) \supset (CE)$ and $\{AF, AC\} \supset \{\varnothing\}$. Similarly (AF) is removed. The next step adds the only second-order maximal compatible (BD) to this list of prime compatibles. The last step adds all compatibility classes of order 1; however, they are all excluded by (BD) and $(ACEF)$. This sequential machine has eight prime compatibles.

This completes our discussion of the derivation of the list of prime compatibles.

Once the list of prime compatibles has been derived, the search for a complete, consistent, and minimal subset is begun. The definitions for complete, consistent, and minimal compatibility classes have been presented in Chapter 7. If any state of the original machine is covered by only one prime compatible, this prime compatible is said to be *essential*. Let m be the number of maximal compatibles, k be the number of essential prime compatibles, and p be the total number of prime compatibles. The selection of the proper minimal cover is outlined below:

STEP 1. Calculate the bounds U and L on the number of states of the minimal machine as described in Chapter 7.

STEP 2. Eliminate all the k essential prime compatibles from the list. These must be chosen as states in the minimal machine.

STEP 3. Select all combinations of x elements out of the $p - k$ elements remaining on the list from step 2 such that $x + k = L$, the lower bound. Check each combination for completeness and consistency. If a complete and consistent subset is found, $q = 0$, go to step 5; otherwise, go to step 4.

STEP 4. Choose x such that $x + k = L + 1$. If $x + k \geq U$, go to step 6; otherwise, check all combinations of $x + k$ elements for completeness and consistency. If no subset is found, repeat step 4 until for some $x + k = L + q$ a complete and consistent subset is found. Go to step 5.

STEP 5. The minimal machine has $L + q$ states. The process stops.

STEP 6. The minimal machine has U states. The process stops.

Example.

Find a minimal, consistent, complete subset of the prime compatibles shown in Fig. 9.2. For this example, $k = 0$, $U = 3$, $L = 2$, and $p = 9$. The process begins by considering all combinations of $x - L - 2$ prime compatibles. Each combination is formed and tested for completeness and consistency. The combination (ABC) and (DE) meets the stated criteria.

A minimal, consistent, complete subset of the prime compatibles is often called a minimal closed cover.

The last phase of the state reduction process for incompletely specified sequential circuits is the formation of the reduced state table. As the table is being formed, each next-state set for each prime compatible chosen in the minimal cover must be assigned to a prime compatible. Sometimes this assignment can be made with several of the prime compatibles. For the assignment to be made, the prime compatible PC_l must contain the next state set $(PC_j)_i$:

$$PC_l \supset (PC_j)_i$$

Example.

Find the reduced state table for the machine of Fig. 9.3(a). The minimal cover for this machine is $(ACEF)$, (CDE), and (ABF). A closure table is formed as shown in Fig. 9.4(a). Note that the next-state set for (CDE) under input 01 is state F. Since

$$(ACEF) \supset F \longrightarrow PC_1 \supset (PC_2)_{01}$$

$$(ABF) \supset F \longrightarrow PC_3 \supset (PC_2)_{01}$$

Prime compatibles	x_1x_2 00	01	11	10
$PC_1 = (ACEF)$	ACF	AEF	ACF	ACF
$PC_2 = (CDE)$	ABF	F	AC	C
$PC_3 = (ABF)$	CD	AE	F	ACF

(a)

	x_1x_2 00	01	11	10
A'	$A'/0$	$A'/1$	$A'/0$	$A'/1$
B'	$C'/0$	$A', C'/1$	$A'/0$	$A', B'/0$
C'	$B'/0$	$A'/0$	$A', C'/0$	$A'/1$

(b)

Fig. 9.4 Formation of the reduced state table: (a) closure table; (b) reduced state table.

This next-state set can result in two entries in the reduced state table as shown in Fig. 9.4(b). The states are assigned as follows:

$$A' = (ACEF)$$

$$B' = (CDE)$$

$$C' = (ABF)$$

To simplify the handling of these multiple next-state entries, a special procedure has been adopted. Let a particular next-state set $(PC_j)_i$ be contained in r prime compatibles of the minimal closed cover. If $r = 1$, there is only one choice for the next-state entry in the reduced state table. If $r = m - q + 1$, the number of prime compatibles in the minimal closed cover, any prime compatible may be selected so that the next-state entry is a don't care condition. If $1 < r < m - q + 1$, an arbitrary choice of the first prime compatible encountered which contains $(PC_j)_i$ is chosen as the next-state entry. This procedure is computationally efficient; however, for the case $1 < r < m - q + 1$, several don't care minterms for the Boolean switching functions are discarded.

State Assignment

After the state table for the sequential machine has been reduced to a minimal number of states, the next step toward finding an economical realization of a sequential machine is the selection of the number of state variables which will be used; then one must make an assignment of each state of the minimum-state machine to some unique coded combination of these state variables. The number of state variables that may be used to realize a sequential machine has a lower bound but is otherwise arbitrary. The choice of how many state variables to use may depend on several considerations, including facility of implementation, the type of physical elements available for implementation, and cost of implementation.

The cost of implementing a sequential machine is the sum total cost of the storage elements and the combinational elements used to implement the next-state and output functions of the machine. Many types of storage elements and combinational elements are in common use, and each type of element has a different purchase cost. Storage elements, however, are generally more costly and more bulky than combinational elements, and for this reason the CAD algorithm is designed to produce realizations requiring the absolute minimum number of storage elements. This does not imply that there are not cases for which the minimum-state-variable approach is not the cheapest approach. But machines for which an increase in the number of memory elements can reduce total cost occur infrequently, and therefore they will not be considered in this algorithm.

The amount of combinational circuitry needed to realize the next-state and output functions of a sequential machine depends on the input and output coding of the machine, the type of combinational elements to be used in the realization, and the manner in which combinations of state variables are assigned to represent states of the machine. First, it will be assumed that the input coding is given, as is usually the case. Second, since the output interface requirements for a sequential machine may require a specific type of output coding, output circuitry costs are difficult to approximate from a state table representation of a sequential machine. For this reason, output circuitry costs are neglected in the state assignment procedure; only the next-state equations for the state variables are considered. It should be noted that for a machine having many more states than outputs, this neglect of output circuitry is not of great importance, but for a machine having many more outputs than internal states, the output circuitry becomes the dominant cost factor, and the output coding must be known before realization costs can be reasonably evaluated. Since output circuitry costs will be neglected, this design procedure is of greater use in reducing realization costs for machines having small numbers of outputs.

A considerable amount of literature has been written about the state assignment problem, as was demonstrated in Chapter 7. Much of this literature, however, deals with those special classes of machines for which certain state assignments result in *reduced dependency* next-state equations; and while these reduced dependency equations are usually very economical, these special types form but a small class of sequential machines [3]. Also, great difficulty and lengthy calculations are often encountered when one attempts to find a state assignment which results in reduced dependency equations, if such a state assignment exist. For these reasons, reduced dependency techniques have not been considered here. Instead, cost reduction techniques which are applicable to all machines are applied in this procedure.

The state assignment techniques used in this procedure are directed toward producing minimum-cost next-state equations for the state variables used in a sequential machine realization. In particular, the techniques used attempt to make state assignments such that the resulting minterms of the next-state equations can be combined as extensively as possible into simpler Boolean expressions. In particular, state assignment rules 1 and 2 of Chapter 7 have been incorporated into the state assignment portion of the CAD algorithm.

According to rule 1, two states which lead to the same next state under any given input are identified as adjacent states. Adjacent states which produce minterms in the next-state equations are assigned codes differing in only one variable (adjacent codes) whenever possible. The only adjacent states which do not produce minterms in the next-state equations are those adjacent states leading to the state which has the *all-zero* state assignment code. These adjacencies are neglected.

The state assignment subalgorithm of box 5 in Fig. 9.1 is begun by searching through the state table and finding which state appears as a next state most often. This state is assigned the all-zero state assignment in order to reduce the number of minterms contained in the next-state equations. In case two or more states tie for the honor, one of these states in chosen arbitrarily to have the all-zero assignment. This gives a starting point for making further assignments. States adjacent to this *reference* state are assigned codes containing only a single 1 until all codes with a single 1 are used or until all states adjacent to the reference state are assigned. Then, another state having an assigned code is designated as the reference state, and once again unassigned states adjacent to this new reference state are assigned unused codes which are adjacent to the code of the reference state. Each state which has been assigned a code is in turn used as the reference state for making further assignments until all states have been assigned a code. If it happens that some states are left unassigned after this process, rule 2 of the state assignment procedure of Chapter 7 is employed to identify additional adjacencies. Rule 2 states that a next-state pair under logically adjacent inputs (for a single present state) should be assigned adjacent codes. Once these new adjacencies are identified, all states with assigned codes are again processed as the reference state and the process is repeated. If any states are unassigned after this process is completed, an arbitrary assignment is given to an unassigned state and it is made the reference state. A series of arbitrary assignments guarantees that the process will finish the state assignment task.

Example.

Find a state assignment for the sequential machine in Fig. 9.5. Only the next states have been defined for this machine.

Present state	x 0	1	
1	3	4	
2	1	1	
3	2	1	Next
4	3	4	state

Fig. 9.5 State assignment example.

STEP 1. State 1 is transferred to most often; assign the code 00 to state 1.

STEP 2. Rule 1 is used to identify the adjacencies:

$$1 \text{ adj } 4: \quad (14) \xrightarrow{0} 3, \quad 3 \neq 1.$$
$$1 \text{ adj } 4: \quad (14) \xrightarrow{1} 4, \quad 4 \neq 1$$
$$2 \text{ adj } 3: \quad (23) \xrightarrow{1} 1$$

If any next state is state 1, that adjacency is deleted. Delete 2 adj 3.

STEP 3. State 1 is the reference state.

STEP 4. State 4 is adjacent to state 1; assign the code 01 to state 4.

STEP 5. No other adjacencies can be satisfied with state 1 as the reference; state 4 is made the reference.

STEP 6. No other adjacencies can be satisfied with state 4 as the reference. More adjacencies must be identified by rule 2.

STEP 7. Rule 2 identified the adjacencies

3 adj 4:   State 1 under inputs 0, 1

1 adj 2:   State 3 under inputs 0, 1

3 adj 4:   State 4 under inputs 0, 1

STEP 8. State 4 is still the reference. State 3 is adjacent to state 4; assign the code 11 to state 3.

STEP 9. The only remaining code 10 is assigned to state 2.

Under this state assignment, the following next-state equations are produced:

$$Y_2 = \bar{x}\bar{y}_2 + \bar{x}y_1$$
$$Y_1 = \bar{y}_2$$

A binary assignment $(1 \longrightarrow 00, 2 \longrightarrow 01, 3 \longrightarrow 10,$ and $4 \longrightarrow 11)$ yields

$$Y_2 = \bar{x}\bar{y}_1\bar{y}_2 + y_1 y_2$$
$$Y_1 = x\bar{y}_1\bar{y}_2 + xy_1 y_2 + \bar{x}\bar{y}_1 y_2$$

In the above example, the arbitrary binary state assignment requires 19 inputs to gates, whereas the one produced by the algorithm requires but 5. Despite the considerable savings made by the algorithm's assignment, in general, there is little evidence it will find the optimal assignment.

Generation of the Switching Functions

Once the reduced state table and a state assignment have been derived for a given sequential machine, all that remains is to generate the minterms of the next-state and output switching functions and to minimize them. Here we shall describe the process of generating the minterms.

The subalgorithm of box 6 of Fig. 9.1 is illustrated by the example of Fig. 9.6(a). Assume that the state assignment has been specified by box 5 of Fig. 9.1. The first step in generating the switching functions is to rearrange the table according to the following rules:

RULE 1. Inputs, present states, and outputs are assigned numbers which are 1 larger than the binary values of their coded assignments.

RULE 2. Next states and outputs which are don't cares are assigned the values 0.

Applying these rules to Fig. 9.6(a) produces the state table of Fig. 9.6(b).

In generating the state table of Fig. 9.6(b), the state assignment is examined to see if any of the possible combinations are omitted, due to adjacency requirements or other reasons. For example, if state assignments 000, 001, 010, 011, and 110 have been used, then 100, 101, and 111 are assigned as don't care conditions. In the example of Fig. 9.6(a), assignments 101, 110, and 111 are don't care rows, while the input condition 11 represents a don't care column.

Next the expanded transition table of Fig. 9.6(c) is obtained. Here storage arrays are formed for $Y_1, Y_2, Y_3, z_1,$ and z_2 in which 0, 1, or d is stored in each array element. Minterms and don't cares are found for the switching functions Y_i and z_i by testing the elements in the function's storage array. Each time a 1 is found, a minterm is recorded for the function according to the rule

Minterm = (State number of present state -1) $+ 2^{N_{FF}}$ (input number -1)

where N_{FF} is the number of next-state variables (or flip-flops). Each time a d is found, a don't care is recorded for the function according to the rule

Don't care = (State number of present state -1) $+ 2^{N_{FF}}$ (input number -1)

Note that the present state and input numbers correspond to the storage array subscripts.

		Input x_1x_2		
Assignment	Present state	00	01	10
0 1 0	1	3/00	2/00	3/10
0 0 1	2	2/00	4/01	–/–
0 1 1	3	5/–	5/00	–/–
1 0 0	4	5/00	5/01	5/–
0 0 0	5	2/00	5/10	5/–

Next state/Output

(a)

Present state	Input 1	2	3
1	2/1	1/3	1/0
2	2/1	5/2	0/0
3	4/1	2/1	4/3
4	1/0	1/1	0/0
5	1/1	1/2	1/0

(b)

	1	2	3	4
1	001/00	000/10	000/dd	ddd/dd
2	001/00	100/01	ddd/dd	ddd/dd
3	011/00	001/00	011/10	ddd/dd
4	000/dd	000/00	ddd/dd	ddd/dd
5	000/00	000/01	000/dd	ddd/dd
6	ddd/dd	ddd/dd	ddd/dd	ddd/dd
7	ddd/dd	ddd/dd	ddd/dd	ddd/dd
8	ddd/dd	ddd/dd	ddd/dd	ddd/dd

$Y_1 Y_2 Y_3/z_1 z_2$

(c)

Fig. 9.6 Switching function generation: (a) example reduced machine; (b) decimal state table; (c) expanded transition table.

Example.

Find the next-state and output functions for Fig. 9.6(c). Consider Y_1. Under input 2 for present state 2 there is a minterm whose number is

$$\text{Present state} - 1 = 1$$

$$\text{Input number} - 1 = 1$$

$$\text{Minterm} = 1 + 2^3(1) = 9$$

Under input 3 for present state 4 there is a don't care whose number is

$$\text{Don't care} = (4 - 1) + 2^3(3 - 1)$$
$$= 3 + 8(2)$$
$$= 19$$

The resulting switching functions are

$$Y_1 = \sum m(9) + d(5\text{--}7, 13\text{--}15, 17, 19, 21\text{--}31)$$

$$Y_2 = \sum m(2, 18) + d(5\text{--}7, 13\text{--}15, 17, 19, 21\text{--}31)$$

$$Y_3 = \sum m(0\text{--}2, 10, 18) + d(5\text{--}7, 13\text{--}15, 17, 19, 21\text{--}31)$$

$$z_1 = \sum m(8, 18) + d(3, 5\text{--}7, 13\text{--}17, 19\text{--}31)$$

$$z_2 = \sum m(9, 12) + d(3, 5\text{--}7, 13\text{--}17, 19\text{--}31)$$

Switching Function Minimization

Once the switching functions have been generated in box 6 of Fig. 9.1, the last major step in the CAD algorithm is the minimization of the switching functions in box 7. An algorithm suitable for computer-aided function minimization has been developed in Chapter 4 and is employed here to minimize the switching functions in two-level sum of products form. The reader is referred to Chapter 4 for a complete description of this portion of the algorithm.

Design Example

The CAD algorithm of Fig. 9.1 has been implemented in reference [4]. The algorithm is applied to the sequential circuit of Fig. 9.7. The maximal compatibles are listed below:

$$(1567) \ (136) \ (145) \ (12)$$

Present state	Inputs 1	2	3	4
1	5/–	–/–	–/–	6/4
2	4/1	1/–	3/1	2/–
3	–/–	–/1	–/2	2/–
4	6/3	5/2	3/–	–/–
5	–/–	1/–	–/3	7/–
6	–/1	6/–	5/–	–/–
7	7/1	–/2	1/–	–/4

(a)

	1	2	3	4
1	1/1	1/2	1/3	1/4
2	1/1	1/1	1/2	1/4
3	1/3	1/2	2/3	1/4
4	3/1	–/–	2/1	2/4

(b)

Fig. 9.7   Design example: (a) state table; (b) reduced state table.

The prime compatibles are then generated as listed below:

(1567) (136) (145) (12) (14) (36) (45) (2) (4)

For this example, the minimal cover is just the maximal compatibles. Under the definitions

$$1 \longrightarrow (1567)$$
$$2 \longrightarrow (136)$$
$$3 \longrightarrow (145)$$
$$4 \longrightarrow (12)$$

the reduced state table of Fig. 9.7(b) is found.

Next box 5 of the algorithm generates the state assignment:

$$y_1 \; y_2$$

1 $\longrightarrow$ 0	0
2 $\longrightarrow$ 0	1
3 $\longrightarrow$ 1	0
4 $\longrightarrow$ 1	1

Using the following coding for the input symbols

$$x_1 \; x_2$$

1 $\longrightarrow$ 0	0
2 $\longrightarrow$ 0	1
3 $\longrightarrow$ 1	0
4 $\longrightarrow$ 1	1

and the output coding

$$z_1 \; z_2$$

1 $\longrightarrow$ 0	0
2 $\longrightarrow$ 0	1
3 $\longrightarrow$ 1	0
4 $\longrightarrow$ 1	1

box 6 generates the following switching functions:

$$Y_1 = \sum m(3) + d(7)$$
$$Y_2 = \sum m(10, 11, 15) + d(7)$$
$$z_1 = \sum m(2, 8, 10, 12\text{--}15) + d(7)$$
$$z_2 = \sum m(4, 6, 9, 12\text{--}15) + d(7)$$

Last, box 7 minimizes the functions as follows:

$$Y_1 = \bar{x}_1 y_1 y_2$$
$$Y_2 = x_1 \bar{x}_2 y_1 + x_1 y_1 y_2$$
$$z_1 = \bar{x}_2 y_1 \bar{y}_2 + x_1 \bar{y}_2 + x_1 x_2$$
$$z_2 = x_2 \bar{y}_2 + x_1 \bar{y}_1 y_2 + x_1 x_2$$

This completes the design example. The reader is encouraged to attempt this design process by hand.

Summary

In this chapter we have presented a computer-aided-design (CAD) algorithm which generates the logic equations for a sequential circuit given the state table of the circuit. The design is *not* optimal for the following reasons:

1. The state assignment problem has been greatly simplified. State assignments produced by the algorithm for reduced dependency machines can require twice as much circuitry as the optimal assignment under worst case conditions. However, in general, most machines are not of the reduced dependency type and the algorithm produces assignments which average only 10% above the cost of the optimal assignment for typical sequential machines not of the reduced dependency class.
2. No multiple output minimization is attempted in minimizing the switching functions for the next-state and output variables.
3. Only clocked D flip-flops are allowed in the design.
4. Don't care conditions may be lost in the algorithm which produces the reduced state table for incompletely specified machines. In the case of multiple entries where the number of possible compatibility classes for the next-state transition is greater than 1 and less than the number of sets in the minimal cover, the first class in the list is arbitrarily chosen.

Even with these limitations, the CAD algorithm does produce a solution for many practical problems in which a manual solution would be impractical.

REFERENCES

1. SHIVA, S. G., and H. T. NAGLE, JR., "Computer-Aided-Design of Sequential Circuits," *Fifth Annual Southeastern Symposium on System Theory, Raleigh, N.C.*, March 22–23, 1973.
2. GRASSELLI, A., and F. LUCCIO, "A Method for Minimizing the Number of Internal States in Incompletely Specified Sequential Networks," *IEEETEC*, Vol. EC-14, June 1965, pp. 350–359.

3. DOLOTTA, T. A., and E. J. MCCLUSKEY, "The Coding of Internal States of Sequential Circuits," *IEEETEC*, Vol. EC-13, October 1964, pp. 549–562.

4. SHIVA, S. G., and H. T. NAGLE, JR., "Computer-Aided Design of Digital Networks," Parts 1, 2, and 3, *Electronic Design*, Vol. 22, 1974 (submitted for publication).

PROBLEMS

9.1. Find a near-minimal set of next-state and output equations for the completely specified synchronous sequential circuit of Fig. P9.1.

	0	1
1	1/1	2/1
2	3/0	8/1
3	5/1	1/0
4	6/0	1/0
5	8/1	1/0
6	2/1	3/0
7	2/1	5/0
8	7/1	1/1
9	9/0	4/1
10	13/0	12/1
11	17/0	17/0
12	5/1	13/1
13	2/1	9/1
14	10/1	10/0
15	16/0	6/1
16	10/0	6/1
17	16/1	7/1

Fig. P9.1

9.2. Find a reduced realization using clocked D flip-flops for the sequential circuit of Fig. P9.2.

	1	2	3	4
1	4/0	5/1	7/0	6/1
2	2/0	3/0	5/0	7/0
3	1/0	2/1	3/0	4/0
4	2/1	5/0	7/0	6/1
5	3/0	6/1	9/0	10/1
6	4/0	5/1	7/0	6/1
7	7/1	8/0	10/1	9/0
8	2/0	3/0	5/0	7/0
9	9/1	2/1	3/1	4/1
10	4/0	5/1	7/0	6/1

Fig. P9.2

9.3. List a set of near-minimal next-state and output equations for the synchronous sequential circuit of Fig. P9.3.

	1	2	3	4	5	6	7	8
1	2/1	3/2	4/3	5/4	16/15	15/14	14/13	13/12
2	3/2	4/3	5/4	6/5	1/0	16/15	15/14	14/13
3	4/3	5/4	6/5	7/6	2/1	1/0	16/15	15/14
4	5/4	6/5	7/6	8/7	3/2	2/1	1/0	16/15
5	6/5	7/6	8/7	9/8	4/3	3/2	2/1	1/0
6	7/6	8/7	9/8	10/9	5/4	4/3	3/2	2/1
7	8/7	9/8	10/9	11/10	6/5	5/4	4/3	3/2
8	9/8	10/9	11/10	12/11	7/6	6/5	5/4	4/3
9	10/9	11/10	12/11	13/12	8/7	7/6	6/5	5/4
10	11/10	12/11	13/12	14/13	9/8	8/7	7/6	6/5
11	12/11	13/12	14/13	15/14	10/9	9/8	8/7	7/6
12	13/12	14/13	15/14	16/15	11/10	10/9	9/8	8/7
13	14/13	15/14	16/15	1/0	12/11	11/10	10/9	9/8
14	15/14	16/15	1/0	2/1	13/12	12/11	11/10	10/9
15	16/15	1/0	2/1	3/2	14/13	13/12	12/11	11/10
16	1/0	2/1	3/2	4/3	15/14	14/13	13/12	12/11

Fig. P9.3

9.4. Find a realization using clocked D flip-flops for the incompletely specified sequential circuit of Fig. P9.4.

	1	2	3
1	1/10	3/9	4/–
2	3/4	5/–	7/1
3	6/6	8/7	9/2
4	5/–	–/–	2/–
5	2/1	3/2	4/9
6	10/0	9/2	7/3
7	3/4	4/3	2/6
8	1/2	2/–	4/–
9	8/–	6/–	7/6
10	–/–	2/3	1/1

Fig. P9.4

9.5. Find a near-minimal set of next-state and output equations for the incompletely specified, synchronous, sequential circuit of Fig. P9.5.

	1	2	3	4
1	3/–	2/0	7/6	2/0
2	6/2	4/2	8/7	3/1
3	9/4	–/–	9/8	4/3
4	12/0	6/5	–/–	5/2
5	–/–	8/7	10/9	–/–
6	2/5	10/9	11/10	–/–
7	7/6	–/–	12/11	8/6
8	10/–	14/2	–/–	7/–
9	13/–	12/1	13/12	–/–
10	2/3	13/12	14/13	6/5
11	5/–	7/0	–/–	4/–
12	8/–	–/–	–/–	5/–
13	11/2	6/–	1/0	–/–
14	–/–	2/1	–/–	–/–

Fig. P9.5

10

Special
Topics
in
Sequential
Devices

The material presented in this chapter is a continuation of our previous discussions on sequential logic circuits. In particular, we shall consider the decomposition of sequential circuits, linear sequential circuits, and iterative arrays. These topics build on the fundamentals of sequential circuits presented in Chapters 6, 7, and 8. However, each topic is described independently of the others in this chapter.

Decomposition of Sequential Machines [1]

Some sequential machines may be decomposed into a collection of smaller machines called *submachines*. For example, consider the machine M shown in Fig. 10.1(a). A *serial decomposition* of M would have the structure given in Fig. 10.1(b). Machines M_1' and M_2' are submachines of M. Submachine M_1' is called an *independent submachine* because it does not have an input from M_2'. On the other hand, M_2' is a *dependent submachine* because one of its inputs is provided by M_1'. Figure 10.1(c) shows the structure of a *parallel decomposition* of M. In this structure, both M_1^* and M_2^* are independent submachines.

The general model of M given in Fig. 10.1(a) implies the following func-

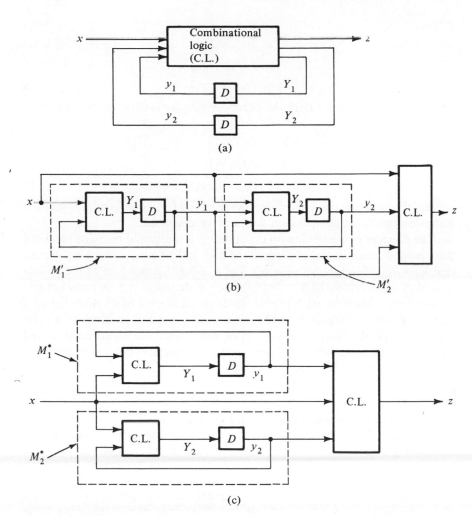

Fig. 10.1 Serial and parallel decomposition: (a) general model; (b) serial decomposition; (c) parallel decomposition.

tional dependencies of Y_1, Y_2, and z:

$$Y_1 = f_1(x, y_1, y_2)$$
$$Y_2 = f_2(x, y_1, y_2)$$
$$z = f_3(x, y_1, y_2)$$

These dependencies can be restated in more specific terms for decomposed machines. In the serial case, the following functional dependencies are evident:

$$Y_1 = f_1(x, y_1)$$
$$Y_2 = f_2(x, y_1, y_2)$$
$$z = f_3(x, y_1, y_2)$$

For a parallel decomposition, the dependencies are further restricted as follows:

$$Y_1 = f_1(x, y_1)$$
$$Y_2 = f_2(x, y_2)$$
$$z = f_3(x, y_1, y_2)$$

Serial or parallel decompositions do not exist for all sequential machines. Requirements for decomposition will now be discussed.

The concept of a partition on the states of a sequential machine has been used several times in earlier discussions and will be used again here. Recall that a *partition* π on the set of states S of a sequential machine M is a collection of disjoint subsets of S, called blocks, whose union is S. A partition π is *closed* if and only if for each pair of states in a common block of π, the next states implied by the pair, for each input, are in a common block of π. The symbol π_i, where i is any integer, will be used to denote a particular closed partition, while the symbol τ_j, where j is any integer, will be used to denote a particular arbitrary partition.

Example.

Consider the machine defined in Fig. 10.2.

$\pi_1 = \{(AB), (CDE)\}$ is a closed partition on the states of the machine. The partition $\tau_2 = \{(AB), (CD), (E)\}$ is a partition that is not closed.

Let τ_i and τ_j be partitions on the states of a machine M. The *product* of τ_i and τ_j, denoted $\tau_i \cdot \tau_j$, is defined as the partition on M such that two states are in the same block of $\tau_i \cdot \tau_j$ if and only if the two states are in the same

	\multicolumn{2}{c}{x}
	0	1
A	$C/0$	$E/0$
B	$D/0$	$E/0$
C	$D/0$	$B/0$
D	$E/0$	$A/0$
E	$C/1$	$B/1$

Fig. 10.2 Example machine.

block of τ_i and are in the same block of τ_j. If τ_i and τ_j are both closed, then $\tau_i \cdot \tau_j$ is closed.

Example.

From Fig. 10.2, let

$$\tau_1 = \{(AB), (CDE)\}$$
$$\tau_2 = \{(AB), (CD), (E)\}$$
$$\tau_3 = \{(ACE), (BD)\}$$
$$\tau_4 = \{(AC), (BD), (E)\}$$

Then

$$\tau_1 \cdot \tau_2 = \{(AB), (CD), (E)\}$$
$$\tau_1 \cdot \tau_3 = \{(A), (B), (CE), (D)\}$$
$$\tau_1 \cdot \tau_4 = \{(A), (B), (C), (D), (E)\}$$

A block of τ_i and a block of τ_j are said to be *connected* if and only if they contain at least one common state. The *sum* of τ_i and τ_j, denoted $\tau_i + \tau_j$, is defined as the partition on M such that two states are in the same block of $\tau_i + \tau_j$ if and only if they are in connected blocks of τ_i and τ_j. If τ_i and τ_j are both closed, then $\tau_i + \tau_j$ is closed.

Example.

From the previous example, block (AB) from τ_2 and block (AC) from τ_4 are connected. Observing other connected blocks yields

$$\tau_2 + \tau_4 = \{(ABCD), (E)\}$$

Also,

$$\tau_1 + \tau_4 = \{(ABCDE)\}$$

The partition on M containing only a single block is called the *identity partition* and is denoted $\pi(I)$. The partition on M with only one state per block is called the *zero partition* and is denoted $\pi(0)$.

Example.

For the previous example,

$$\pi(I) = \{(ABCDE)\}$$
$$\pi(0) = \{(A), (B), (C), (D), (E)\}$$

A machine M can be decomposed into two submachines M_1' and M_2' operating in series if and only if there exists a closed partition π_i on M and a partition τ_j on M such that $\pi_i \cdot \tau_j = \pi(0)$. The corresponding realization of M can be obtained by assigning the states of M according to π_i and τ_j.

Example.

Consider the machine defined by the state table given in Fig. 10.3(a):

$$\pi_1 = \{(AB), (CD)\}$$
$$\tau_2 = \{(AC), (BD)\}$$
$$\pi_1 \cdot \tau_2 = \pi(0)$$

Define the following state assignment:

	y_1	y_2
A	0	0
B	0	1
C	1	0
D	1	1

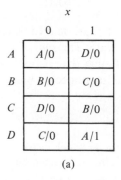

	x	
	0	1
A	A/0	D/0
B	B/0	C/0
C	D/0	B/0
D	C/0	A/1

(a)

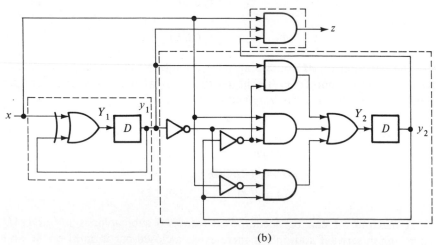

(b)

Fig. 10.3 Serial decomposition: (a) state table; (b) logic diagram.

Note that states in the same block of π_1 are assigned like values of y_1 and that states in the same block of π_2 are assigned like values of y_2. By using the realization procedure given in Chapter 7, a realization of the machine can be obtained. This realization is shown in Fig. 10.3(b).

A machine M can be decomposed into two submachines M_1^* and M_2^* operating in parallel if and only if there exist two closed partitions π_i and π_j on M such that $\pi_i \cdot \pi_j = \pi(0)$. Again, the corresponding realization of M can be obtained by making a state assignment for the states of M according to π_i and π_j.

Example.

Consider the machine defined in Fig. 10.4(a):

$$\pi_1 = \{(AB), (CD)\}$$
$$\pi_2 = \{(AC), (BD)\}$$
$$\pi_1 \cdot \pi_2 = \pi(0)$$

By assigning the states according to blocks of π_1 and π_2, the following state assignment is obtained:

	y_1	y_2
A	0	0
B	0	1
C	1	0
D	1	1

Figure 10.4(b) gives the corresponding realization.

It is interesting to note that the independent machines in the decomposed realizations can be specified by the blocks of the corresponding closed partitions.

Example.

Consider the previous example. The state tables which define M_1^* and M_2^* can be obtained from π_1 and π_2 and the original state table given in Fig. 10.4(a). Let α and β represent block (AB) and block (CD), respectively, of π_1. Also, let γ and δ represent blocks (AC) and (BD), respectively, of partition π_2. The resulting state tables are presented in Fig. 10.4(c) and (d).

The following examples illustrate extensions of the above results. Other, more general, decomposition structures exist but are beyond the scope of this text.

$$x$$

	0	1
A	$A/0$	$C/0$
B	$A/0$	$D/0$
C	$C/0$	$A/1$
D	$C/1$	$B/1$

(a)

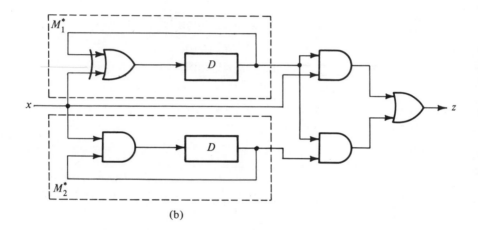

(b)

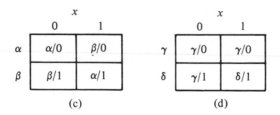

$$x$$

	0	1
α	$\alpha/0$	$\beta/0$
β	$\beta/1$	$\alpha/1$

(c)

$$x$$

	0	1
γ	$\gamma/0$	$\gamma/0$
δ	$\gamma/1$	$\delta/1$

(d)

Fig. 10.4 Parallel realization: (a) state table; (b) logic diagram;
(c) state table for M_1^*; (d) state table for M_2^*.

Example.

See the state table given in Fig. 10.5(a). The following are closed partitions:

$$\pi_1 = \{(ABCD), (EFGH)\}$$
$$\pi_2 = \{(ABEF), (CDGH)\}$$
$$\pi_3 = \{(ACEG), (BDFH)\}$$

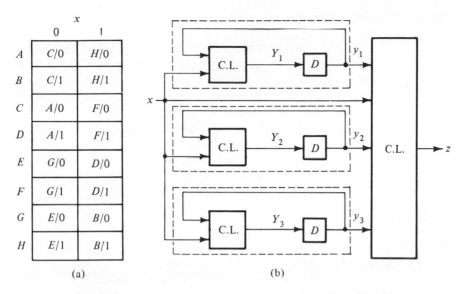

| | x | |
	0	1
A	$C/0$	$H/0$
B	$C/1$	$H/1$
C	$A/0$	$F/0$
D	$A/1$	$F/1$
E	$G/0$	$D/0$
F	$G/1$	$D/1$
G	$E/0$	$B/0$
H	$E/1$	$B/1$

(a)   (b)

Fig. 10.5 A parallel decomposition example: (a) state table; (b) realization.

Also, $\pi_1 \cdot \pi_2 \cdot \pi_3 = \pi(0)$. Hence, a realization consisting of three independent submachines can be obtained.

See Fig. 10.5(b) for a diagram of the realization.

Example.

Let M be a machine with closed partitions π_1 and π_2 and with a non-closed partition τ_3. If $\pi_1 \cdot \pi_2 \cdot \tau_3 = \pi(0)$, then M can be realized with a structure as shown in Fig. 10.6.

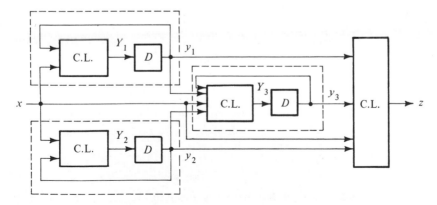

Fig. 10.6 Combination of serial and parallel decomposition.

Linear Sequential Machines

In this section we shall present an introduction to linear sequential machines. We shall first illustrate what they are and then we shall show some of the ways in which they are used. The linear sequential machine will not be treated here in depth, and hence the reader is referred to references [2] and [3] for a much more complete discussion of the subject.

It is important to note that although the discussion here will be confined to the single input-single output case in which the signals are elements of the set $\{0, 1\}$, the analysis can easily be extended to the multiple input-multiple output case where the signals are elements of the set $\{0, 1, 2, \ldots, p - 1\}$.

Definition

We define a binary linear sequential machine (BLSM), shown in Fig. 10.7, as a single input-single output network composed of interconnections of unit delays and modulo 2 adders in which the inputs and outputs are elements of the set $\{0, 1\}$. Although there are many ways in which the elements may be interconnected, we restrict our definition to the cases in which every closed loop contains a unit delay element.

The model shown in Fig. 10.7 is basically that of a finite state machine. Note, however, that the logic block contains only mod 2 adders (EXCLUSIVE-OR gates) and that the memory elements are simple delay units. It is assumed that the mod 2 additions are performed instantly and that the unit delays are synchronized with an external clock. The mod 2 multiplier as shown in Fig. 10.7(d) can be implemented using an AND gate and is sometimes used to build a general-purpose BLSM.

Models

Because of the nature of the BLSM it is normally implemented using shift registers (see Chapter 11). Some of the most convenient models for these BLSM's will be considered here.

Feedforward model. The feedforward model is a two-terminal network in which the output is a mod 2 sum of certain input bits. The output z can be expressed mathematically as a function of D, where D is the unit delay operator and D^i is used to represent an i-unit delay.

Example.

A simple feedforward shift register is shown in Fig. 10.8. Using the delay operator and the notation of Fig. 10.7 we can derive the equations which

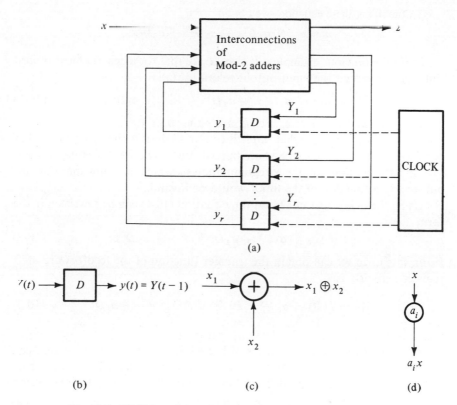

(a)

(b)   (c)   (d)

Fig. 10.7 BLSM model and component: (a) basic model of a single-input, single-output BLSM; (b) unit delay element; (c) mod 2 adder symbol; (d) mod 2 multiplier.

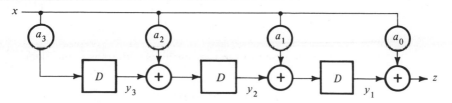

Fig. 10.8 A simple feedforward shift register.

relate the output to the input:

$$y_3 = a_3 Dx$$
$$y_2 = D(a_2 x \oplus y_3)$$
$$y_1 = D(a_1 x \oplus y_2)$$
$$z = a_0 x \oplus y_1$$

Combining these equations we obtain

$$z = a_0 x \oplus a_1 D^1 x \oplus a_2 D^2 x \oplus a_3 D^3 x$$

From the previous example it is easy to see that for a general feedforward shift register circuit the input-output relationship is

$$z = a_0 x \oplus a_1 D^1 x \oplus a_2 D^2 x \oplus \cdots \oplus a_k D^k x \qquad (10\text{-}1)$$

where all the a_i's, $i = 0, 1, 2, \ldots, k$, are either 0 or 1.

It is important to note that implicit in our analysis is the assumption that the delay elements in our BLSM are initially quiescent, i.e., set equal to zero. Without this assumption the foregoing analysis which indicates that the output is only a function of the input would be invalid.

Using the delay operator notation, equation (10-1) can be rewritten in the form

$$z = (a_0 \oplus a_1 D^1 \oplus a_2 D^2 \oplus \cdots \oplus a_k D^k)x \qquad (10\text{-}2)$$

From this form we can obtain the transfer function of the feedforward shift register network as

$$\frac{z}{x} = T(D) = a_0 \oplus a_1 D^1 \oplus a_2 D^2 \oplus \cdots \oplus a_k D^k \qquad (10\text{-}3)$$

which is a polynomial in the delay operator D.

Because of the linear properties of the BLSM's their interconnection can be handled very easily. The transfer function for the machine resulting from the serial interconnection of two machines T_1 and T_2 is given by the expression

$$T_3 = T_1 \cdot T_2 \qquad (10\text{-}4)$$

where all arithmetic is modulo 2. For parallel interconnection the resulting transfer function is

$$T_3 = T_1 \oplus T_2 \qquad (10\text{-}5)$$

Example.

The serial interconnection of the two machines with transfer functions

$$T_1 = 1 \oplus D^2$$
$$T_2 = 1 \oplus D^2 \oplus D^3$$

is shown in Fig. 10.9(a). The resultant machine with transfer function

$$\begin{aligned}
T_3 &= (1 \oplus D^2) \cdot (1 \oplus D^2 \oplus D^3) \\
&= [1 \cdot (1 \oplus D^2 \oplus D^3)] \oplus [D^2 \cdot (1 \oplus D^2 \oplus D^3)] \\
&= 1 \oplus D^2 \oplus D^3 \oplus D^2 \oplus D^4 \oplus D^5 = 1 \oplus D^3 \oplus D^4 \oplus D^5
\end{aligned}$$

is given in Fig. 10.9(b).

Feedback model. Once again in this and subsequent analyses we assume that the BLSM is quiescent. The following example illustrates the manner

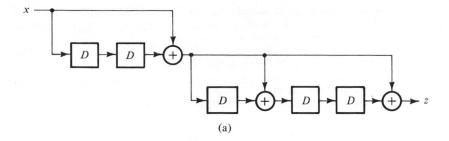

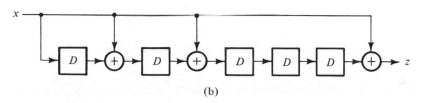

Fig. 10.9   Serial interconnection of two machines: (a) serial interconnection; (b) resultant machine.

in which to derive a transfer function for the feedback shift register arrangement.

Example.

The equations which describe the simple feedback shift register network shown in Fig. 10.10 are given below:

$$y_2 = D(x \oplus b_3 z)$$
$$y_1 = D(y_2 \oplus b_2 z)$$
$$z = D(y_1 \oplus b_1 z)$$

By combining the equations we obtain the transfer function

$$\frac{z}{x} = T(D) = \frac{D^3}{1 \oplus b_1 D \oplus b_2 D^2 \oplus b_3 D^3}$$

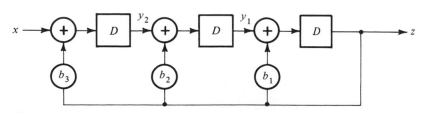

Fig. 10.10   A simple feedback shift register.

The transfer function for a general feedback shift register network, obtained by extrapolating the results described in the previous example, is

$$\frac{z}{x} = T(D) = \frac{D^k}{1 \oplus b_1 D^1 \oplus \cdots \oplus b_k D^k} \tag{10-6}$$

Feedforward-feedback model. By combining the two models above we obtain the model shown in Fig. 10.11. Note that in this case the output is dependent on not only the present and past inputs but also a finite number of past outputs. The transfer function for this model, which is expressed as the ratio of two polynomials in D, is

$$T(D) = \frac{a_0 \oplus a_1 D^1 \oplus \cdots \oplus a_k D^k}{1 \oplus b_1 D^1 \oplus b_2 D^2 \oplus \cdots \oplus b_k D^k} \tag{10-7}$$

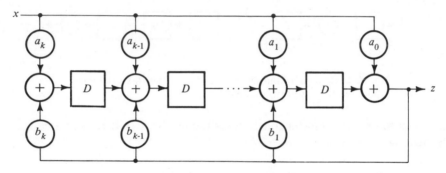

Fig. 10.11 A general network for the feedforward-feedback model.

This combined model allows us to realize transfer functions which are the ratio of two polynomials in D by employing the fewest number of shift register elements.

Polynomial Multiplication and Division [4]

BLSM's can also be used to multiply and divide polynomials. For example, the feedforward network can be used for polynomial multiplication, the feedback network can be used for polynomial division, and finally, multiplication and division can be combined into one network by using the feedforward-feedback model.

Applications

Generating cyclic codes. One of the important uses of a BLSM is that of generating cyclic codes. Although the BLSM is used for both encoding and decoding of cyclic codes, only the former application will be presented here.

Suppose that we want to generate an (N, L) cyclic code, where N is the length of the code words and L is the number of *information bits*. If the code words are N bits long and only L of these bits are used for information, then $N - L$ bits of the code word are redundant and these are called the *check bits*. Since L bits are used for information, then there are 2^L code words N bits in length.

The encoding operation described below generates a systematic parity check code, i.e., a code in which the first L bits are information and the last $N - L$ bits are parity checks.

The steps employed in generating the codewords for an (N, L) binary cyclic code are briefly summarized below:

STEP 1. Choose a generator polynomial $g(x)$ for the code. The polynomial should be a primitive polynomial with period N. A primitive polymomial is one which cannot be factored. The actual polynomial chosen will depend on the error detection/correction capability required. These polynomials have been tabulated and appear in numerous references; see, for example, reference [4].

STEP 2. Write the information word as a polynomial in x, which we call $M(x)$.

STEP 3. Multiply the information polynomial $M(x)$ by x^{N-L} to obtain $x^{N-L}M(x)$. This is equivalent to annexing $N - L$ zeroes to the information word.

STEP 4. $x^{N-L}M(x)$ is then divided by the generator polynomial $g(x)$ to obtain a remainder $R(x)$.

STEP 5. Add the remainder $R(x)$ to $x^{N-L}M(x)$, using mod 2 arithmetic to obtain the code polynomial $x^{N-L}M(x) \oplus R(x)$, which represents the code word.

It is important to note that in the code word, $x^{N-L}M(x) \oplus R(x)$, the information bits correspond to $x^{N-L}M(x)$ and are the L highest-order coefficients of the code polynomial. The check bits correspond to $R(x)$ and are the $N - L$ lowest coefficients of the code polynomial. The following example will serve to illustrate the encoding procedure.

Example.

From the indicated reference [4] we find that one of the possible generator polynomials for a (7, 4) cyclic single error correcting code is

$$g(x) = 1 \oplus x^2 \oplus x^3$$

Since $N = 7$ and $L = 4$, the cyclic code contains $2^4 = 16$ code words, 7 bits in length. The information words range from 0000 to 1111. Suppose, for example, that we wish to encode the information word 1010. This information word corresponds to the information polynomial $M(x) = x^3 \oplus x$. Then $x^{N-L}M(x) = x^3(x^3 \oplus x) = x^6 \oplus x^4$. Dividing $x^{N-L}M(x)$ by $g(x)$ yields the remainder $R(x) = 1$. Hence, the code polynomial $x^{N-L}M(x) \oplus R(x) = x^6 \oplus x^4 \oplus 1$, where $x^6 \oplus x^4 \oplus 1$ corresponds to the code word (1010001). Note that this code word is in the form

1010   001

Information   Check

Bits   Bits

The hardware used to implement this encoding process is shown in Fig. 10.12. The feedback shift register performs the division by $g(x)$. The encoding is performed by annexing $N - L$ zeroes to the low-order end of the message bits and shifting this augmented message through the registers, most significant bit first. Initially sw 1 is open and sw 2 is closed. An open switch supplies a logic 0. When the last zero is shifted into the register the remainder $R(x)$ resides in the registers. At this point sw 1 closes and sw 2 opens. The remainder is shifted out at precisely the proper time to follow the information bits which were delayed $N - L$ shift times while the remainder was being calculated.

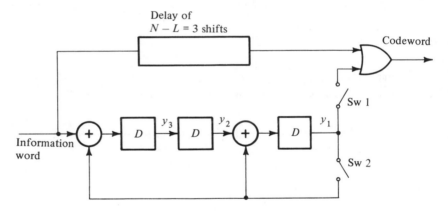

Fig. 10.12 Network for deriving the codewords of a cyclic code.

In this example the information bits are 1010. Annexing $N - L = 3$ zeroes yields the augmented message 1010000. As this message is shifted through, most significant bit first, the contents of the shift registers change in the following manner:

Input	y_3 y_2 y_1	Output	
1	0 0 0		
0	1 0 0		
1	0 1 0		
0	1 0 1	1	sw 2 closed
0	1 1 1	0	
0	1 1 0	1	
0	0 1 1	0	
	1 0 0	0	
		0	sw 1 closed
		1	

The last row is the remainder, and hence the code word obtained at the output is 1010001.

Generation of binary sequences. The BLSM can be used to generate various bit streams which are useful in many applications. Two such applications are presented here: test sequences and random number sequences.

Suppose that in testing some logic circuit it is necessary to generate all possible nonzero input sequences of a specified length. One method of accomplishing this is demonstrated in the following example.

Example.

Consider the feedback shift register network shown in Fig. 10.13. Suppose that the initial state of the machine is 111. Then if the input is a string of 0's, the output will cycle through the following set of states: $111 \rightarrow 110 \rightarrow 011 \rightarrow 100 \rightarrow 010 \rightarrow 001 \rightarrow 101 \rightarrow 111 \rightarrow$ etc. Note that because the states cycle, the initial state could have been any one of the elements in the string. This set of states is called a cycle set. The only other cycle set for this BLSM is the trivial one, $000 \rightarrow 000$.

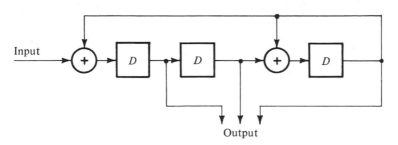

Fig. 10.13   A test sequence generator.

It is important to note that for a BLSM with k shift registers the maximum number of states in a cycle set is $2^k - 1$. If the polynomial which generates the feedback shift register is primitive, then the BLSM will have two cycle sets, one that is trivial and one that is maximal.

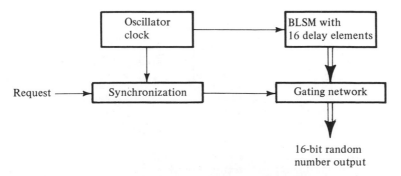

Fig. 10.14   Sixteen-bit random number generator.

Quite often in system applications we have need of a random or pseudo-random number generator. Suppose, for example, that a 16-bit random number was required upon request. A network such as that shown in Fig. 10.14 could be used to generate the required numbers where the BLSM is a feedback shift register derived from a primitive polynomial of order 16.

Iterative Networks

Introduction

An iterative network is composed of a set of identical subnetworks connected in tandem. In general, the network itself can be bilateral, and each subnetwork, called a cell, can contain sequential as well as combinational logic. However, we shall restrict the discussion here to the case in which the network is unilateral and only combinational logic is used in each cell.

The iterative network is comparable to the sequential machine, and the reader is encouraged to watch for this connection as he progresses through the material in this section.

Model

The general form of the iterative network is shown in Fig. 10.15(a). However, with one important exception, we shall employ the model shown in Fig. 10.15(b). Note that all the important parameters are defined in the figure.

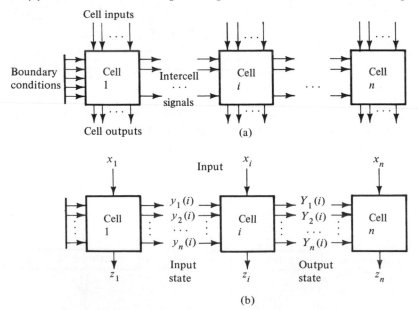

Fig. 10.15 Model for an iterative network: (a) general iterative network; (b) restricted iterative network.

A comparison of the iterative network with the sequential machine indicates that the boundary condition in the iterative network corresponds to the initial state in a sequential machine, the information transmitted via the intercell signals corresponds to a state change in a sequential machine, and the input string which is applied to all cells simultaneously in the iterative network is applied one at a time in succession as a discrete time sequence to the sequential machine.

Since all the cells in the iterative network are identical, the complete network is specified once the type of subnetwork and the number of subnetworks are known. The cell structure is, of course, dependent on the function to be performed, and the number of cells depends on the length of the input string.

The cell structure is defined by a cell table which is analogous to the state table in the sequential machine. Our basic approach to the design of an iterative network is the specification of a typical cell in the network. The form of the typical cell i is dependent on its input x_i, its output z_i, the information which it receives from the previous cell $y_1(i) \cdots y_n(i)$, and the information which cell i must pass on to the next cell $Y_1(i) \cdots Y_n(i)$. Note that the intercell signals $y_1(i) \cdots y_n(i)$ describe the operation of all previous cells $1, 2, 3, \ldots, i - 1$ in the chain.

Iterative Network Design

Some typical problems for which the iterative network is a viable solution will now be presented.

Example.

In Chapter 1 we discussed the use of a parity bit on magnetic tape for error detection. Here we want to design an iterative network which will check the information as it comes off the nine-track tape to see if an error has occurred.

The form of the iterative network is shown in Fig. 10.16(a). Since the input is 9 bits in length (8 bits for information and 1 bit for parity), the iterative network contains 9 cells. Only a single output is needed to indicate the presence or absence of an error. We assume even parity coding, i.e., that the word on the tape contains an even number of 1's.

Since the only information we seek concerning the word on tape is whether the number of 1's in the entire word is odd or even, the intercell signals incoming to cell i need only indicate whether the number of 1's in the input string $x_1 \cdots x_{i-1}$ is odd or even. Hence, only a single line is required between cells.

Suppose now that the intercell signal $y(i)$ is to be 1 if the number of 1's contained in all preceding cells is odd. Then at each cell we want the output to be 1 if and only if either the incoming intercell signal or the cell input, but not both, is a 1. From our previous work in earlier chapters we know that the element which produces an output of 1 if and only if one of its inputs is a 1 is an EXCLUSIVE-OR gate. Therefore the iterative network in Fig. 10.16(b) with a boundary condition of zero is the desired circuit.

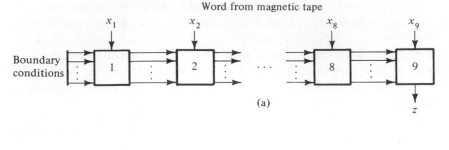

(a)

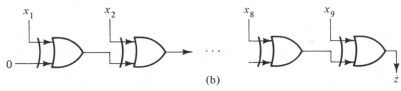

(b)

Fig. 10.16 Iterative network for parity check circuit: (a) basic iterative network; (b) final iterative network.

Example.

We want to design an iterative network for a circuit with n inputs. The network is to provide a two 1's indication by producing an output of $z = 1$ if and only if at least two of the n inputs are equal to 1.

The iterative network will consist of n cells since the length of the input string is n. The cell table for the iterative network, which is the same as the corresponding state table for a sequential machine which would recognize input sequences of length n in which two of the n inputs are equal to 1, is derived in Fig. 10.17(a) and (b).

Note that state A corresponds to no inputs equal to 1, state B corresponds to one input equal to 1, and state C corresponds to two or more inputs equal to 1. This state information is the intercell signal which provides each cell with all the necessary information about the previous cells.

Using the following state assignment

$$A = 00$$
$$B = 01$$
$$C = 11$$

we obtain the K-maps shown in Fig. 10.17(c). From these maps we obtain the logic equations:

$$Y_1(i) = y_1(i) + y_2(i)x_i$$
$$Y_2(i) = y_2(i) + x_i$$

The output z generated by the n cell is given by the expression

$$z = Y_1(n)$$

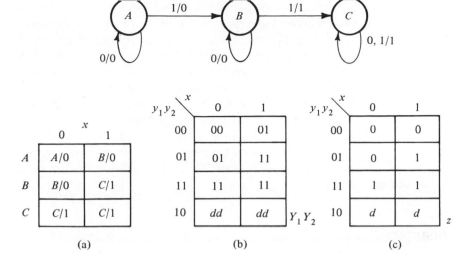

Fig. 10.17   Development of a two 1's indicator iterative network:
(a) state diagram; (b) state table; (c) K-maps for intercell and output signals.

The equations above for $Y_1(i)$ and $Y_2(i)$ describe the typical cell. In general the first and last cells are much simpler than the typical cell. For example, the boundary conditions on the first cell are

$$y_1(1) = y_2(1) = 0$$

Therefore,

$$Y_1(1) = 0$$

$$Y_2(1) = x_1$$

In the last cell, no intercell signal need be generated—only the output is required. Hence, the complete iterative network is shown in Fig. 10.18.

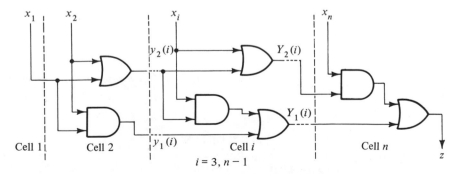

Fig. 10.18   Iterative network for indicating two 1's.

Practical Considerations

When considering whether to employ an iterative network or a sequential machine to solve a particular problem, there are a number of features which from a physical standpoint are very important. For example, the input to an iterative network must be a fixed, finite length, input string. Delay time also becomes a consideration because of the multilevel nature of the system. If the system has a large number of cells, cost becomes a factor, and, in addition, external amplification may be required due to the deterioration of signals over a long span. Nevertheless, iterative networks appear to simplify the design of many large digital systems by allowing the designer to create a small subnetwork and then cascade many of these subnetworks to form the larger system.

Summary

A brief introduction to three special topics in the theory of sequential devices was given. The topics were decomposition, linear sequential machines, and iterative arrays.

For a more complete coverage of the topics, the reader should consult the listed references. In particular, see [1] for decomposition, [2], [3], and [4] for linear sequential circuits; and [5] for iterative arrays.

REFERENCES

1. HARTMANIS, J., and R. E. STEARNS, *Algebraic Structure Theory of Sequential Machines.* Englewood Cliffs, N.J.: Prentice-Hall, Inc., 1966.

2. GILL, ARTHUR, *Linear Sequential Circuits.* New York: McGraw-Hill Book Company, 1966.

3. KAUTZ, WILLIAM H., ed., *Linear Sequential Switching Circuits.* San Francisco: Holden-Day, Inc., 1965.

4. PETERSON, W. W., *Error Correcting Codes.* Cambridge, Mass.: The M.I.T. Press, 1961.

5. HENNIE, FREDERICK C., *Iterative Arrays of Logical Circuits.* Cambridge, Mass.: The M.I.T. Press, 1961.

PROBLEMS

10.1. Determine a realization of the following state table such that the realization consists of two machines in series:

	x	
	0	1
A	A/0	D/0
B	D/1	A/1
C	C/1	B/0
D	B/0	C/1

10.2. Determine a realization of the following state table such that the machine consists of two machines operating in parallel:

	x	
	0	1
A	C/0	B/0
B	D/1	A/1
C	A/0	D/0
D	B/1	C/1

10.3. Find a realization of the following state table which has the structure shown in Fig. P10.1:

	x	
	0	1
A	A/0	E/0
B	B/1	D/1
C	C/0	D/1
D	A/0	E/1
E	C/0	D/0

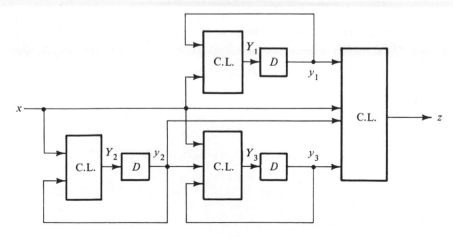

Fig. P10.1

10.4.   Find the transfer function of the machine resulting from the serial inter-connection of two identical machines shown in Fig. P10.2.

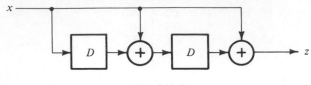

Fig. P10.2

10.5.   Draw a shift register network with the fewest number of elements that will realize the transfer function

$$T(D) = \frac{1 \oplus D \oplus D^4}{1 \oplus D^2 \oplus D^3}$$

10.6.   Derive the feedforward shift register network which can be used to multiply any polynomial $d(x)$ by a fixed polynomial $c(x) = 1 \oplus x \oplus x^3$. Illustrate the operation of the network by multiplying $c(x)$ by the polynomial $d(x) = 1 \oplus x^2$.

10.7.   Derive a feedback shift register network that will divide any polynomial by $c(x) = 1 \oplus x \oplus x^3$. Then use this network to divide the polynomial $x^5 \oplus x^2 \oplus x \oplus 1$ by $c(x)$.

10.8.   The generator polynomial for a (7, 4) single error correcting cyclic code is $g(x) = 1 \oplus x \oplus x^3$. Derive a feedback shift register network for encoding the 16 information words $0000, 0001, \ldots, 1111$. Illustrate the use of this circuit by encoding the information word 0110.

10.9.   Design an iterative network that will produce an output of $z = 1$ if all elements of an input string of length 4 are 1's.

10.10.   Design an iterative network that will recognize the input string 100.

10.11.   An iterative network is to be designed which will accept an input string of length 4 and produce an output of $z = 1$ if the number of 1's in the input string is odd.

11

Applications of Digital Logic

In previous chapters we have developed the theory of design for both combinational and sequential digital logic circuits. Many examples have been presented to emphasize techniques in logic design at the moment they were introduced. The purpose of this chapter is to weld many of these design techniques together and apply them to larger, practical design problems. First we shall introduce a number of digital subsystems and modules, including counters. The remainder of this chapter is organized as a series of independent case studies. The reader may concentrate only on those which interest him, omitting the others without loss of continuity.

Digital Modules and Subsystems

In previous chapters the reader has encountered many combinational logic and sequential circuit synthesis techniques. In general, they were all based on logic gates (AND, OR, NOT, NAND, NOR, etc.) and memory elements (flip-flops, delay lines, inertial delays, etc.) as the fundamental building blocks. However, in addition to these digital logic elements, the computer logic designer has many other basic elements at his disposal which can be classified as logic modules or subsystems. In other words, the designer does not have to begin each digital system design from "ground zero" using only logic gates and memory elements. In many applications he may merely interconnect certain digital modules or subsystems which have already been designed and constructed by the logic component manufacturers. In this section we shall introduce several such modules.

n-to-2ⁿ Decoders

An n-to-2^n decoder is a multiple output combinational logic network with n input lines and 2^n output signals. For each possible input condition one and only one output signal will be at logic 1. Therefore, one may consider the n-to-2^n decoder as simply a minterm generator.

The logic structure of the decoder is shown in Fig. 11.1. Figure 11.1(a) and (b) illustrates two 2-to-4 decoders. The first is constructed of AND gates and inverters, while the second uses only NAND gates. Using the NAND gate design, an output 0 indicates the presence of the corresponding minterm. Hence, the signals may be considered in complemented form. Signals in complemented form are suitable for further processing using NAND logic. For example, if

$$f(A, B, \ldots, Z) = m_i + m_j + \cdots + m_k \qquad (11\text{-}1)$$

then

$$f(A, B, C, \ldots, Z) = \overline{\overline{m}_i \cdot \overline{m}_j \cdot \ \cdots \ \overline{m}_k}$$

Figure 11.1(c) illustrates a *tree* structure for a 3-to-8 decoder. Note that in a tree structure, only *two-input* AND gates are required, no matter how many input lines are present.

A final structure called the *dual tree* is demonstrated in Fig. 11.1(d) for a 4-to-16 decoder. In the dual-tree structure the n input lines are divided into k and l groups ($k + l = n$) and then two smaller decoders k to 2^k and l to 2^l are used to generate 2^k and 2^l internal signals. Then two-input AND gates are used to combine these signals to form the 2^n output lines for the total decoder network.

The n-to-2^n decoders find many applications in the synthesis of digital switching networks. The logic designer can assume that a decoder module is available as shown in Fig. 11.1(e), even if he must build it himself.

Shift Registers

A *shift register* is a digital module constructed from memory elements which serves to manipulate bit positions of binary data. An example shift register is illustrated in Fig. 11.2(a). This n-bit shift register is constructed using master-slave flip-flops. The shift pulse signal is normally low and experiences a low-high-low ($0 \rightarrow 1 \rightarrow 0$) transition to shift the data one bit position to the left. Data normally reside in the slave flip-flops. On the rising,

or positive, edge ($0 \rightarrow 1$), data from the slave flip-flop of shift-register stage
(or cell) X_{i-1} are transferred to the master flip-flop of stage X_i. On the falling,
or negative, edge ($1 \rightarrow 0$), the master flip-flop of each stage sends the data to
its slave. Hence, each shift pulse ($0 \rightarrow 1 \rightarrow 0$) causes all data bits to shift

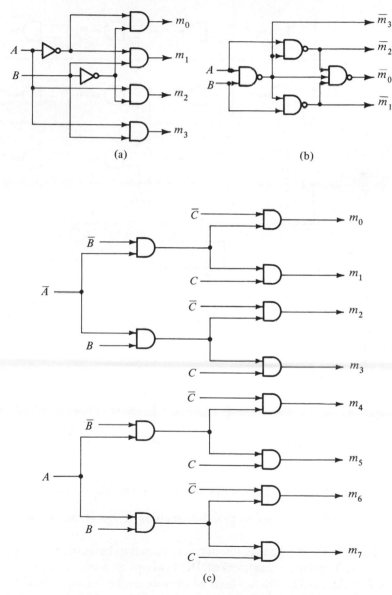

Fig. 11.1 *n*-to-2^n decoders: (a) 2-to-4 decoder; (b) 2-to-4 decoder;
(c) 3-to-8 tree decoder.

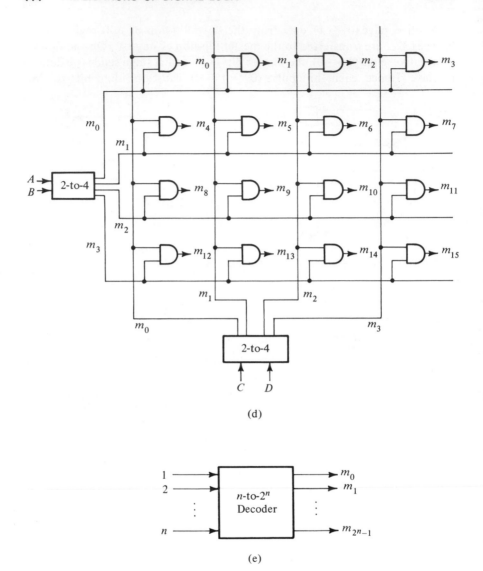

(d)

(e)

Fig. 11.1—*Cont.* (d) 4-16 dual-tree decoder; (e) decoder module.

left one bit position. The key to this shift-register design is the master-slave flip-flop.

In Chapter 6 the clocked JK flip-flop was shown to be of the master-slave variety. A shift register using clocked JK flip-flops is demonstrated in Fig. 11.2(b). For the clocked JK flip-flops to operate in the shifting mode, the *J* and *K* inputs must have complementary signals. This condition is satisfied in the design.

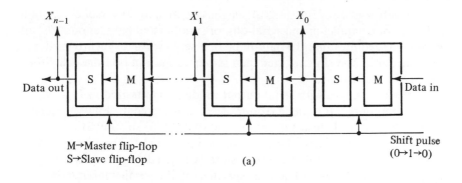

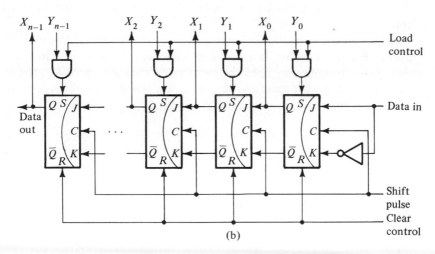

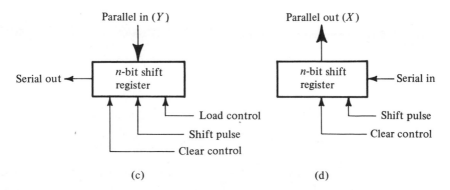

Fig. 11.2 The shift register: (a) shift register with master-slave flip-flops; (b) shift register with clocked JK flip-flops; (c) parallel-to-serial; (d) serial-to-parallel.

The shift register of Fig. 11.2(b) may be operated in three modes: serial-in and serial-out, parallel-in and serial-out, or serial-in and parallel-out. The all-serial mode requires that the data-in be in a serial format synchronized with the shift pulse. The shift register then serves as an n-pulse time delay for a stream of serial data.

The parallel-input with serial-output mode is emphasized in Fig. 11.2(c). Proper operation in this mode requires the following control pulse sequence. First, a clear control pulse must be applied to drive all shift-register stages to logic 0. Second, the parallel data must be connected to the input lines Y_i, $i = 0$, $n - 1$. Then a load control pulse is applied to drive certain shift-register stages to the logic 1 state as specified by the parallel input data. Last, n shift pulses are furnished to the network to generate a serial stream of output data.

The last mode of operation is the serial input with parallel output. For proper operation in this mode a clear control pulse may be applied to zero all stages of the shift register. Then the serial input data are applied to the register synchronized with n shift pulses. After the last shift pulse has returned to zero, the parallel data are available at the flip-flop outputs X_i, $i = 0$, $n - 1$.

The shift register module depicted in Fig. 11.2(c) and (d) finds very widespread usage in digital systems design. For example, see linear sequential circuits and iterative networks in Chapter 10.

Adders

In many computer logic applications it is necessary to add binary numbers. In Chapter 1 it was demonstrated that addition of binary numbers in the radix complement number system is sufficient to perform the normal addition, subtraction, multiplication, and division operations of the digital computer. Of course, the adder circuits must be accompanied by the proper complementing network and arithmetic registers. Here we shall design several serial and parallel adder circuits.

Half-adder. A *half-adder* (HA) is a multiple output combinational logic network which adds 2 bits of binary data producing sum-bit and carry-bit output signals. See Fig. 11.3(a). The input bits x_i and y_i are added mathematically in binary as shown in the truth table of Fig. 11.3(b). From the truth table we observe

$$s_i = x_i \oplus y_i$$
$$c_{i+1} = x_i y_i$$

(11-2)

A two-input NAND gate realization of these Boolean functions is presented in Fig. 11.3(c).

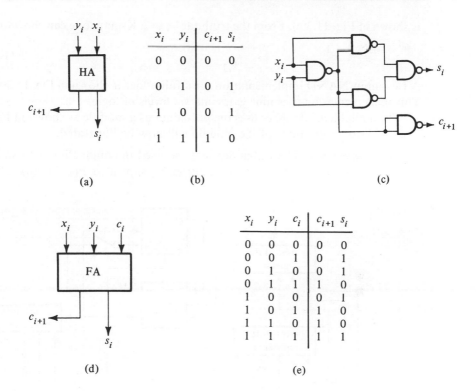

	x_i	y_i	c_{i+1}	s_i
	0	0	0	0
	0	1	0	1
	1	0	0	1
	1	1	1	0

(a)   (b)   (c)

x_i	y_i	c_i	c_{i+1}	s_i
0	0	0	0	0
0	0	1	0	1
0	1	0	0	1
0	1	1	1	0
1	0	0	0	1
1	0	1	1	0
1	1	0	1	0
1	1	1	1	1

(d)   (e)

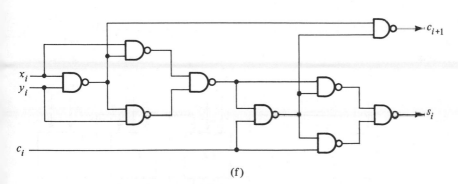

(f)

Fig. 11.3 Adder circuits: (a) half-adder; (b) HA truth table; (c) NAND gate HA; (d) full-adder; (e) FA truth table; (f) NAND gate FA.

Full-adder. In performing binary addition it was shown in Chapter 1 that at each bit position we, in general, shall be adding two data bits and one carry bit. Hence, a *full-adder* (FA) is a multiple output combinational logic network which adds 3 binary bits. See Fig. 11.3(d). The truth table for the full-adder is shown in Fig. 11.3(e). From the truth table, or a K-map, one can show that

$$s_i = x_i \oplus y_i \oplus c_i$$
$$c_{i+1} = x_i y_i + x_i c_i + y_i c_i \qquad (11\text{-}3)$$

A two-input NAND implementation for a full-adder is shown in Fig. 11.3(f). This implementation uses nine gates and six levels of logic.

The digital logic designer uses the full-adder as a module as shown in Fig. 11.3(d). Two applications of the module will now be illustrated.

Serial adder unit. The full-adder may be used in conjunction with shift-register modules to perform serial addition, as shown in Fig. 11.4(a). This

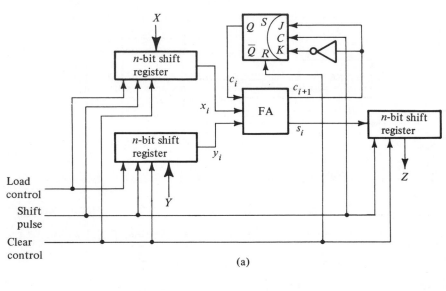

(a)

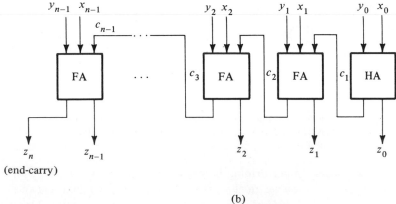

(b)

Fig. 11.4 Adder units: (a) serial adder unit; (b) pseudo-parallel adder unit.

configuration uses two parallel-to-serial shift registers to hold the X and Y data words, and one serial-to-parallel shift register to hold the sum Z of X and Y. One clocked JK flip-flop is employed to time-delay the carry bits. For proper operation, a clear control pulse is applied first to clear all flip-flops to logic 0. Then a load control pulse enters the binary data for X and Y into the full-adder input shift registers. Since the carry-delay flip-flop is at logic 0, the sum of the two least significant bits is now residing at the serial data input of the register Z. Now n shift pulses are applied to the three shift registers and the carry-delay flip-flop. With each pulse the addition of another bit position is performed. After the completion of the last shift pulse, the sum is available at the parallel data output lines of the register Z.

Although the serial adder requires but one full-adder, it uses three shift registers and is relatively slow. Parallel connection of several adder circuits can greatly increase the speed performance of an adder unit.

Pseudoparallel adder unit. An adder unit which employs $n - 1$ full-adders and one half-adder is illustrated in Fig. 11.4(b). This configuration uses one adder circuit for each bit position of the two-input data words. The operation to be performed is shown below:

$$
\begin{array}{r}
X \longrightarrow \quad (x_{n-1}x_{n-2} \ldots x_1 x_0)_2 \\
+ \, Y \longrightarrow + \, (y_{n-1}y_{n-2} \ldots y_1 y_0)_2 \\
\hline
Z \longrightarrow \quad (z_n z_{n-1} z_{n-2} \ldots z_1 z_0)_2
\end{array}
$$

The configuration is called *pseudoparallel* because carries must propagate, or ripple, through the length of the adder unit. In general, the worst case propagation path is through one half-adder and $n - 1$ full-adders from the inputs x_0 and y_0 to the end-carry position z_n.

The pseudoparallel adder unit is much faster than the serial one. However, this design is unsatisfactory in some high-speed applications as n becomes large.

High-speed adder units. The fastest adder design would be strictly parallel. That is, all the inputs would be applied simultaneously and propagate through two levels of logic to obtain the result. However, this approach would require an enormous amount of logic circuitry and is not practical to employ. Several compromises are employed between the pseudoparallel and strictly parallel alternatives.

Carry-look-ahead adders divide the full-adders into groups and employ carry bypass logic to speed up the carry propagation. This technique is a reasonable one to employ when numerical data are to be added at high-speed fixed intervals.

For asynchronous applications a carry-completion-detection adding scheme can speed up the adding process remarkably. This scheme adds logic circuitry to each full-adder, which signals to a control circuit when it has finished adding. On the average the carries will propagate only about one-fifth the length of the adder unit; so, rather than wait for the worst case propagation delay each time two numbers are added, the carry completion signal allows new additions to be begun as soon as the last addition is finished, in an asynchronous manner.

Still another speed-up technique is useful when a string of numbers are to be totaled, or accumulated. A carry-save technique inhibits carry propagation by saving the carries between stages in storage flip-flops. Then, on the last addition, the carries are allowed to propagate in the pseudoparallel manner.

Complete details on these techniques are available in references [1]–[3] and are beyond the scope of this chapter.

Accumulators

An accumulator is an adder unit which totals a series of binary data. It functions like a cash register in that any number of binary data items may be added while the accumulator keeps the current total sum. Just as with the cash register one can exceed the operating range of the accumulator and produce overflow.

A serial accumulator may be designed from the serial adder unit of Fig. 11.4 by eliminating one of the shift registers as shown in Fig. 11.5(a). For proper operation the following control sequence should be employed. First, pulse the clear accumulator control line to initialize all flip-flops to logic 0. Then a load pulse occurs followed by n shift pulses. Now the first piece of binary data is in register Z, and register X will again be in the all-zero state. At this point new data are supplied to the parallel input lines of register X and another load pulse is applied. After n shift pulses, the sum of two data items appears in register Z. Any number of data items may be added as long as the n-bit range is not exceeded by the total sum. A serial accumulator is satisfactory for many low-speed digital system designs.

For higher-speed operation, the parallel accumulator design of Fig. 11.5 (b) is more suitable. This design is based on a pseudoparallel adder unit with a feedback storage register Z. The proper operation of this circuit requires that the clear control be pulsed to initialize the circuit. Afterwards one accumulate pulse is necessary to add each new data item. This unit is faster than the serial design and is much less complicated to operate. Accumulator modules find frequent application in digital logic design.

One-shots

A *one-shot* is an edge-triggered logic element which generates an output pulse from an input signal transition. See Fig. 11.6(a). From the truth table in Fig. 11.6(b) the set and reset terminals (S and R) may be used to hold the

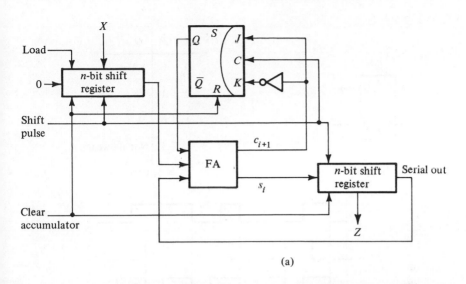

(a)

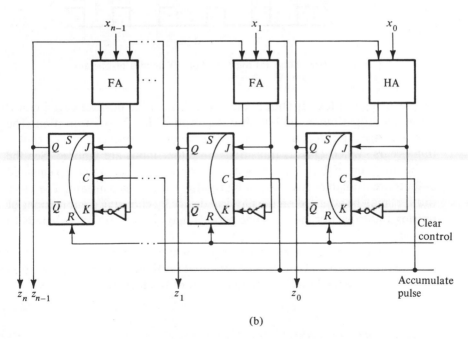

(b)

Fig. 11.5 Accumulators: (a) serial binary accumulator; (b) parallel binary accumulator.

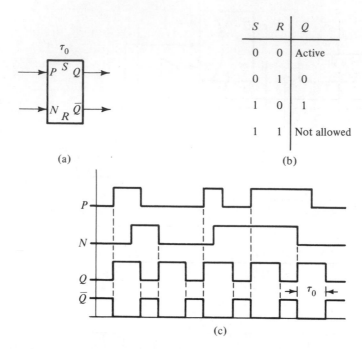

(a)

S	R	Q
0	0	Active
0	1	0
1	0	1
1	1	Not allowed

(b)

(c)

Fig. 11.6 One-shots: (a) logic symbol; (b) modes of operation; (c) timing diagram ($S = R = 0$).

output Q high or low. If both S and R are 0, then the positive edge input P causes an output pulse on Q when P is excited with a $0 \rightarrow 1$ transition. The negative edge input N causes an output pulse on Q whenever a $1 \rightarrow 0$ transition occurs. When $Q = 1$, transitions on either input are ignored. See the timing diagram of Fig. 11.6(c). Note that both the true and complemented outputs are available. Also, the output pulse width τ_0 is constant. The pulse width τ_0 may be adjusted on the physical device by choosing combinations of resistor and capacitor values. Time periods may range from nanoseconds to seconds.

One-shots may be connected in cascade, in parallel, or in a variety of other ways to generate special effects. They are used for timing and pulse generation purposes and depend much on the intuition of the logic designer for proper application.

Counters

Counters are a class of sequential logic circuits which tally a series of input pulses; the input pulses may be regular or irregular in nature. The counter is a fundamental part of most digital logic applications. It is used in timing units, control circuits, signal generators, and a host of other devices. Its utility is demonstrated in the case studies which follow.

Counters may be categorized as binary/nonbinary or asynchronous/synchronous. Several example counter designs are described below. Throughout this chapter counter flip-flops have been labeled X_i because they normally serve as inputs to some other digital device.

Binary Counters

Synchronous design. A synchronous n-bit binary counter constructed of clocked JK flip-flops is illustrated in Fig. 11.7(a). This design is suggested by the state sequence listed in Fig. 11.7(b). Note that each bit X_i should be complemented on the next count pulse if all bits X_k for $k = 0, 1, \ldots, i - 1$ are at logic 1; bit X_0 is always complemented on each count pulse. Hence, a

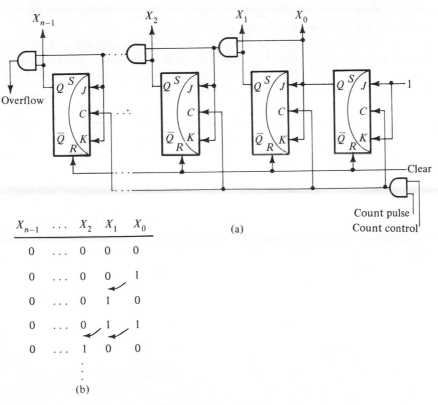

(a)

X_{n-1}		X_2	X_1	X_0
0	...	0	0	0
0	...	0	0	1
0	...	0	1	0
0	...	0	1	1
0	...	1	0	0

(b)

Fig. 11.7 (a) Synchronous binary counter $(S = 0)$; (b) binary counter states.

two-input AND gate is associated with each counter flip-flop. A counter flip-flop and its associated control circuitry is sometimes called a *counter stage*.

Under normal operating conditions the J and K inputs to each flip-flop should remain stable at either logic 1 or 0 while the count pulse undergoes its $0 \rightarrow 1 \rightarrow 0$ transitions. A logic 1 on the clear control line will force all counter outputs to logic 0 and hold them there until the clear is returned to logic 0, its normal logic value. The count control signal is used to inhibit the count pulses and leave the counter in some nonzero state, if such behavior is required for a particular application.

Asynchronous design. One may eliminate the AND gates in the synchronous design by observing the counter state transitions from another viewpoint; see Fig. 11.8(a). Counter stage X_i is complemented each time state X_{i-1} makes a $1 \rightarrow 0$ transition; stage X_0 is always complemented. A counter based on these observations is demonstrated in Fig. 11.8(b). A common clear command may be used to initialize the counter to the 0 state, and the count control command is held at logic 1 for counting; logic 0 inhibits all counting and can leave the counter in some nonzero state.

Let us examine the behavior of this asynchronous binary counter as overflow occurs. All stages are at logic 1 as shown in Fig. 11.8(c). After the count pulse falls, the slave flip-flop of counter stage X_0 responds in t_{sl} seconds. Each stage then follows in a similar manner until the entire counter has reached the logic 0 state. It is important that the reader note the transient condition produced by this count sequence. Instead of the desired state change $(2^n - 1)_{10}$ to $(0)_{10}$, the counter has passed through the following state sequence:

$$(2^n - 1)_{10} \longrightarrow (2^n - 2)_{10} \longrightarrow (2^n - 4)_{10}$$
$$\longrightarrow (2^n - 8)_{10} \longrightarrow \cdots \longrightarrow (2^{n-1})_{10} \longrightarrow (0)_{10} \qquad (11\text{-}4)$$

Although these transitions are rapid, they can generate unwanted transient conditions if the counter outputs are used to drive a combinational logic circuit. See the discussions of hazards in Chapter 3. Because of the transient behavior described in equation (11-4), an asynchronous binary counter is sometimes called a *ripple* counter.

Up/Down Counters

Down counter design. A down, or backward, counter is one whose state transitions are reversed from those of the standard binary counter, which is also known as an *up*, or *forward*, counter. Examine the state tables of Fig. 11.9(a). The down counter behaves as a complemented up counter; hence, an asynchronous down counter may be constructed using clocked JK flip-flops, as indicated in Fig. 11.9(b). The clear control signal drives the counter to the

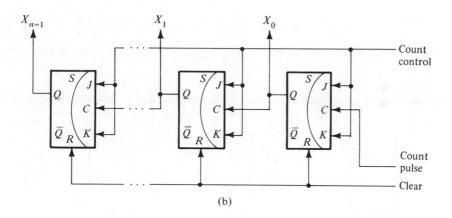

(a)

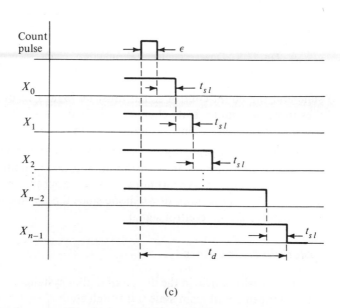

Fig. 11.8 (a) Binary counter states; (b) asynchronous binary counter ($S = 0$); (c) timing diagram (asynchronous).

Up counter					Down counter				
X_{n-1}	$\cdots$	X_2	X_1	X_0	X_{n-1}	$\cdots$	X_2	X_1	X_0
1	$\cdots$	1	1	1	0	$\cdots$	0	0	0
0		0	0	0	1		1	1	1
0		0	0	1	1		1	1	0
0		0	1	0	1		1	0	1
0		0	1	1	1		1	0	0
0	$\cdots$	1	0	0	1	$\cdots$	0	1	1

(a)

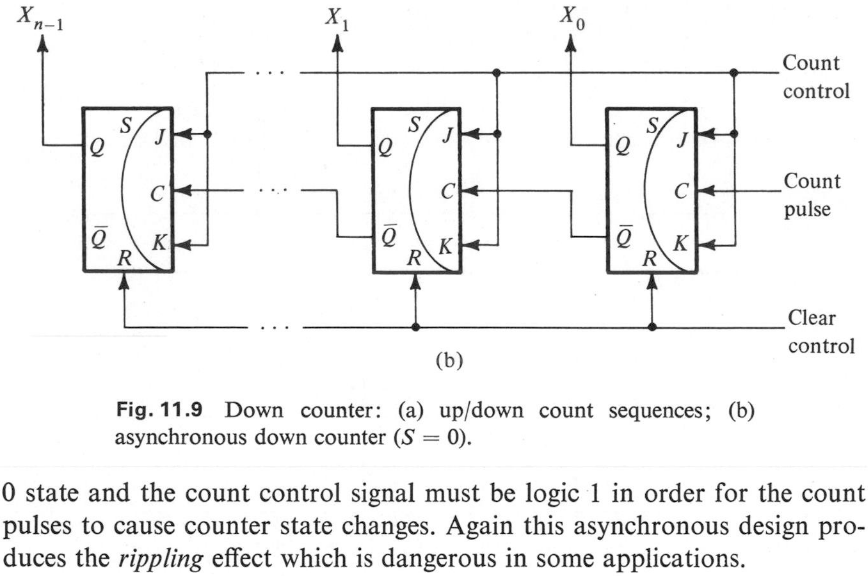

Fig. 11.9 Down counter: (a) up/down count sequences; (b) asynchronous down counter ($S = 0$).

0 state and the count control signal must be logic 1 in order for the count pulses to cause counter state changes. Again this asynchronous design produces the *rippling* effect which is dangerous in some applications.

Combination up/down design. Many digital systems require a counter design which can function in both the up and down modes of operation. A combination up/down synchronous counter appears in Fig. 11.10. This counter is either in the up or down mode since the down control signal is the complement of the up control signal.

Modulo N Counters

Many occasions arise in the design of digital systems in which a counter is needed that can count from state 0 through state $N - 1$ and then cycle back to state 0; such counters are said to be *modulo N* counters. The most common

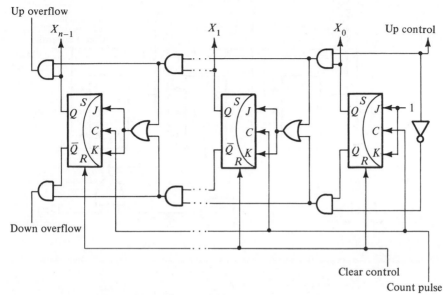

Fig. 11.10 Synchronous up/down counter ($S = 0$).

modulo N counters are the binary ones previously discussed. For binary counters, N is equal to 2^n, where n is the number of counter stages. Counters with other values for N are also very useful.

Synchronous BCD design. A synchronous BCD (binary coded decimal) counter is a modulo 10 counter. The BCD counter must behave like a binary one until state 9 is reached. At this point we must force the counter back to the state (0000) instead of allowing the 10 state (1010) to be reached. A synchronous BCD counter design appears in Fig. 7.30; the reader is referred to Chapter 7 for the design details.

Asynchronous BCD design. An asynchronous, or ripple, counter can be designed by modifying the binary counter of Fig. 11.8(b). Suppose we add a two-input AND gate to detect $X_3 = X_1 = 1$ (the state ten) and use this signal to drive the counter immediately to 0 via the common reset line. See Fig. 11.11(a). Let us now examine the transient behavior of this ripple counter design.

In Fig. 11.8(c) and equation (11-4) the transient behavior of the counter from states 0 through 9 has been defined. A state diagram is presented in Fig. 11.11(b). In this figure the smaller circles represent transient states. The worst case transient condition occurs on the transition from state 7 to state 8. Due to the rippling effect three intermediate states are observed. Consider the transition from state 9 to state 0. The ripple effect will cause the counter to enter state 8 and then state 10. However, the feedback circuit will cause a

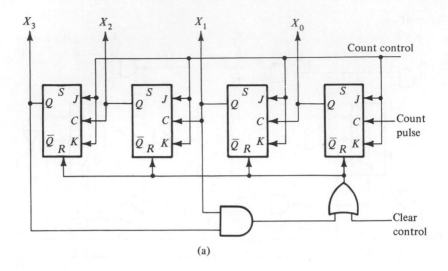

(a)

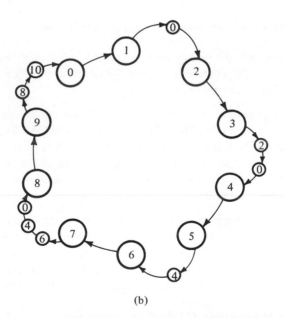

(b)

Fig. 11.11 BCD counter: (a) asynchronous BCD counter; (b) state diagram for the asynchronous counter.

clear signal to reset all the counter stages to logic 0. Several comments about this transient behavior are in order. First, if the count pulses are much slower than the time delay of the clocked JK flip-flops, the counter will pass through the transient states rapidly and reside in the desired states most of the time. A second observation is that only even-numbered states appear more than

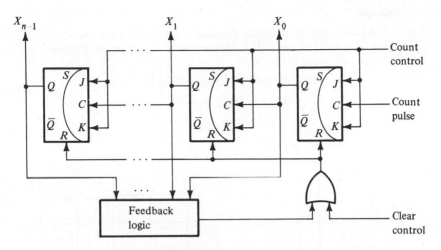

Fig. 11.12　General modulo N asynchronous counter.

once on the state diagram; therefore, the *odd*-numbered states exhibit stable behavior even in ripple-type counters.

General feedback design. The design technique used above in the asychronous BCD counter may be generalized for exploitation in any general modulo N counter, as shown in Fig. 11.12. The feedback logic consists of an AND gate with appropriate inputs to detect the state N, the modulus of the counter. The number n of counter states needed is determined by the relation

$$2^{n-1} < N \le 2^n \qquad (11\text{-}5)$$

Now let us examine another class of counters.

Special Sequence Counters

Occasionally a digital system requires a counter which possesses the ability to count in several ways under the command of some input control signal. Methods for synthesizing a general synchronous sequential circuit have been presented in detail in Chapter 7. Here we shall demonstrate another method, the *application equation technique*, which is especially useful for synthesizing counters from clocked JK flip-flops.

As the first step in presenting the method, let us review the operation of the clocked JK flip-flop with $S = R = 0$ and $C = 0 \rightarrow 1 \rightarrow 0$; see Fig. 11.13(a). In Fig. 11.13(b) the simplified state equation for the clocked JK flip-flop is derived:

$$Q^{k+1} = J^k \bar{Q}^k + \bar{K}^k Q^k \qquad (11\text{-}6)$$

The design method matches equation (11-6) to a particular application, which is shown by example below. Equation (11-6) may be derived from (6-14) by setting $C = 1$, $S = 0$, and $R = 0$ in the latter.

Example.

Consider the special sequence counter specified in Fig. 11.13(c) and (d). If one places X_1^{k+1} and X_0^{k+1}, the next-state variables, on K-maps [see Fig. 11.13(e)], one finds

$$X_1^{k+1} = (\bar{x}X_0)\bar{X}_1 + (\bar{X}_0)X_1$$
$$X_0^{k+1} = (1)\bar{X}_0 + (0)X_0 \tag{11-7}$$

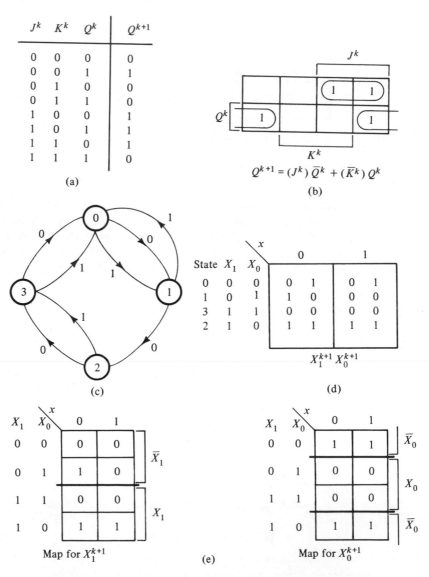

Fig. 11.13 Application equation method: (a) state table for clocked JK flip-flop; (b) K-map for Q^{k+1}; (c) special sequence counter; (d) state table for counter; (e) next-state K-maps.

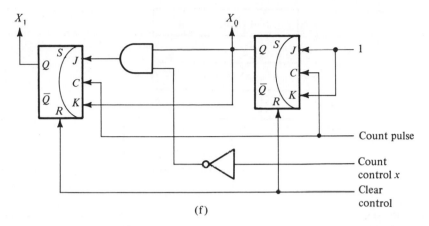

(f)

Fig. 11.13—Cont. (f) Logic diagram.

Note the special form in which these equations are written. Taking them off a K-map in this form means that the map for bit X_i^{k+1} must be separated into halves, one for $\bar{X}_i^k$ and the other for X_i^k. Minterm (or maxterm) groupings must not cross this imposed map separation boundary. Comparing (11-7) with (11-6) one discovers that

$$J_1 = \bar{x}X_0, \quad K_1 = X_0$$
$$J_0 = 1, \quad K_0 = 1$$

(11-8)

The resulting special sequence counter is presented in Fig. 11.13(f).

Case Studies in Digital Design

Digital Fractional Multipliers

A digital fractional multiplier is a device which transforms a stream of input pulses x into a controlled stream of output pulses z. Let N_x be the number of input pulses for a particular time period, and let N_z be the number of output pulses; then

$$N_z = \frac{C}{2^n} N_x$$

where

$$C = (c_0 c_1 c_2 \ldots c_n)_2$$

In other words, any number of the incoming pulses may be transferred to the output because

$$0 \leq C \leq 2^n$$

A block diagram for the digital fractional multiplier (DFM) is shown in Fig. 11.14(a). The incoming pulses drive an n-bit binary counter whose outputs are ANDed with the incoming pulses to selectively form the inter-

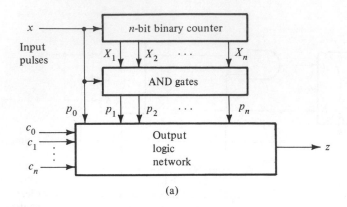

(a)

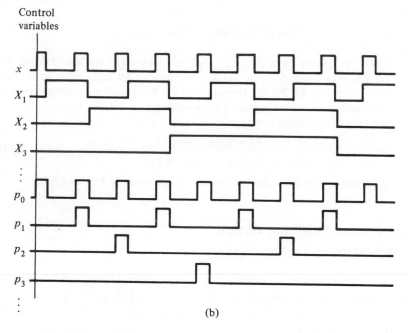

(b)

Fig. 11.14   Digital fractional multipliers: (a) block diagram; (b) timing diagram.

mediate pulses p_i, as shown in Fig. 11.14(b):

$$p_0 = x$$
$$p_1 = X_1 x$$
$$p_2 = \bar{X}_1 X_2 x$$
$$p_3 = \bar{X}_1 \bar{X}_2 X_3 x$$
$$\vdots$$
$$p_i = \bar{X}_1 \bar{X}_2 \ldots \bar{X}_{i-1} X_i x$$

The output logic network consists of the following switching function:

$$z = \sum_{i=0}^{n} c_i p_i$$

where the series sum represents the logic OR. When c_0 is logic 1, all input pulses reach the output. When $c_0 = 0$, only a fraction of the input pulses reaches the output, the number of which is a function of the control variables $c_1, c_2, \ldots, c_n$. The DFM finds application in timing generators, code generators, pulse generators, control units, and many other similar devices.

Video-Telephone Sync-Pulse Detector

This case study is concerned with the video-telephone system shown in Fig. 11.15(a). Each video-telephone set contains a cathode ray tube (CRT) for displaying the received picture from another video-telephone, and a vidicon camera for generating the picture to be transmitted. The channel may be a cable, microwave link, or some similar transmission facility. In fact, quite often the channel will consist of a combination of these transmission facilities connected in tandem.

The vidicon sweeps across the head and shoulders view of the person talking, starting at the upper left of the picture and moving right as shown in Fig. 11.15(b). The dots shown in the figure represent samples taken by the vidicon. The vidicon produces a voltage that is proportional to the light intensity for each sample taken. The voltage then is quantized into seven levels. These seven levels correspond to light levels from white to black with intermediate levels of gray. Because there are seven quantized levels, a 3-bit quantizer is employed. These seven levels could then be channel-encoded such that

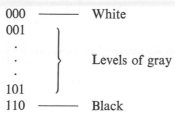

where the code 111 is reserved for the line sync pulse. The data are transmitted in a bit serial manner. When the sync pulse is detected, the receiver camera flies back to start a new line, as shown in Fig. 11.15(b). The use of the line sync pulse ensures that all the lines start at a well-defined left edge. This prevents the occurrence of skewed lines which distort the picture.

The problem in this case study then is to design a sync-pulse detector which will trigger the flyback circuit. The state diagram and state table for the circuit that will detect a sync pulse 111 are shown in Fig. 11.15(c) and (d).

This circuit must be designed so that it automatically resets after three input pulses. This reset procedure will ensure that no false output occurs due to consecutive sequences which produce an overlapping 111 sequence. Note

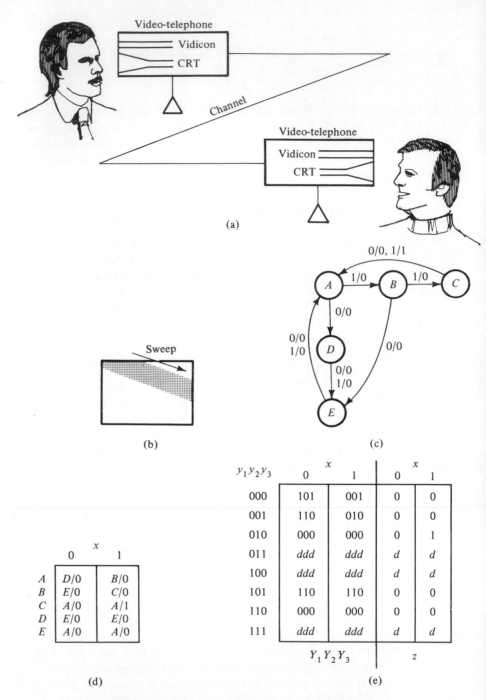

Fig. 11.15 Video-telephone case study: (a) system description; (b) sweep generation; (c) state diagram; (d) state table; (e) transition table.

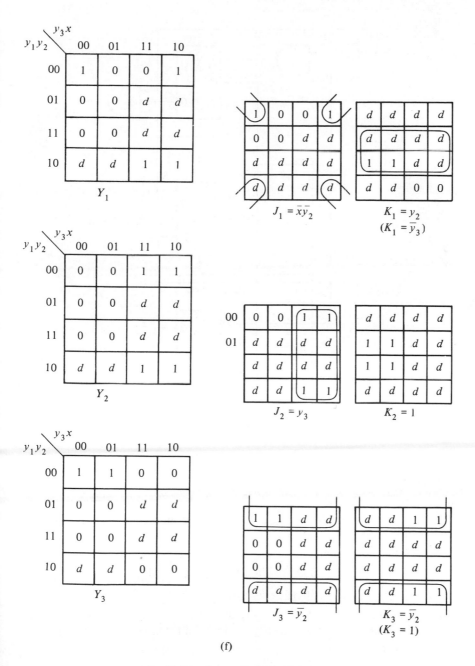

Fig. 11.15—*Cont.*   (f) Excitation maps.

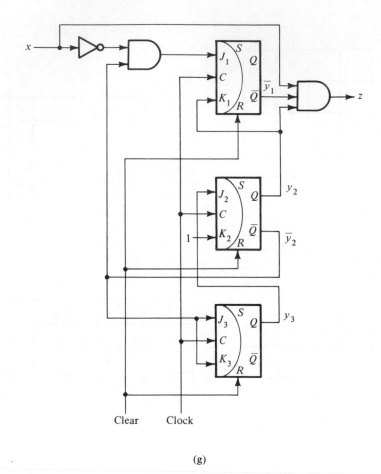

(g)

Fig. 11.15—*Cont.* (g) Logic diagram.

that the state diagram is arranged so that every input sequence of length 3 returns the machine to the starting state A.

Using the assignment

$$A = 000, \quad B = 001, \quad C = 010,$$
$$D = 101, \quad E = 110$$

and assuming a clocked JK flip-flop realization of the detector, the pertinent tables and K-maps are shown in Fig. 11.15(e) and (f). The flip-flop excitation functions are

$$J_1 = \bar{y}_2\bar{x}, \quad I_2 = y_3, \quad J_3 = \bar{y}_2, \quad z = x\bar{y}_1y_2,$$
$$K_1 = y_2, \quad K_2 = 1, \quad K_3 = \bar{y}_2$$

The logic diagram is shown in Fig. 11.15(g).

Parking Lot Controller

A manufacturing company furnishes a free parking lot for its employees. The parking lot is located near the factory and is not large enough to accommodate all the employees of the firm. Hence, to avoid congestion and double parking, a control system must be designed for the lot. The lot configuration is shown in Fig. 11.16(a).

The control circuit must count cars as they enter and leave the lot. Normally the exit gate is closed and a pressure sensor located just inside the lot sends a signal which opens it. Hence, cars may not enter the exit gate. The entrance gate, on the other hand, remains open until the lot is full. The digital

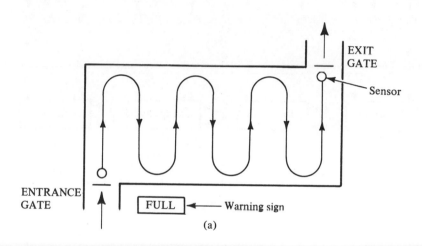

(a)

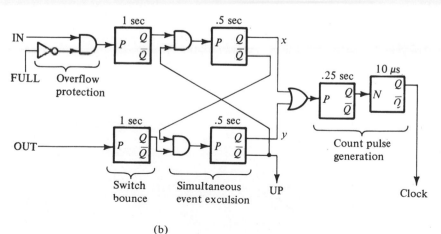

(b)

Fig. 11.16 Parking lot controller: (a) parking lot configuration; (b) counter control signals.

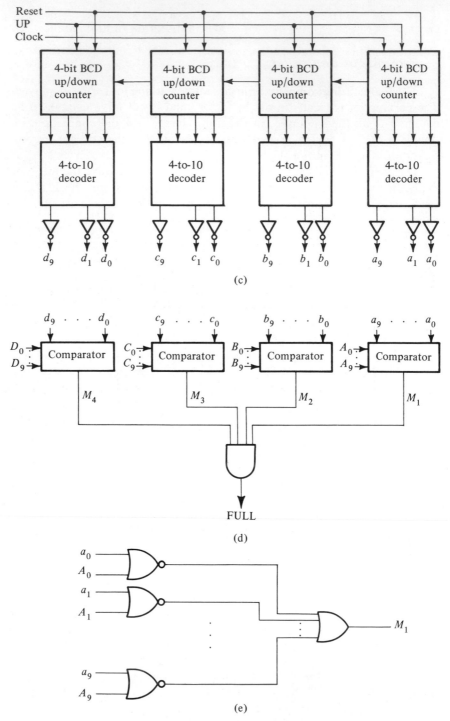

Fig. 11.16—*Cont.* (c) Counters and decoders; (d) comparator section; (e) example comparator.

controller must furnish a signal to close this gate and light the FULL warning sign. The entrance gate once closed remains in this state until a car passes the exit sensor. A pressure sensor is also located just inside the entrance gate to provide a count pulse for the controller.

The controller will consist of three parts; the counter control section, an up/down BCD counter, and a comparator section. The counter control section is displayed in Fig. 11.16(b). The signals IN and OUT come from the pressure sensors. These signals are first filtered to eliminate mechanical switch bounce by two 1-second one-shots. Then they pass through an exclusion circuit which prevents simultaneous IN and OUT pulses from adversely affecting the control sequence. Since the two signals cannot occur at exactly the same time, the one arriving first "locks out" the other until it has completed its counting action. Since the signals x and y can never be logic 1 at the same time, an OR gate is used to drive two one-shots that generate the count pulse for the clock input to the up/down BCD counters.

The BCD up/down counters are connected to a series of 4-to-10 decoders, as shown in Fig. 11.16(c), to transform the counter's outputs into a decimal format. The use of four counter modules restricts the parking lot size to a maximum of 9999 automobiles.

To provide a flexible design, four rotary switches, each having 10 positions, are used to set the maximum number of cars allowed in the parking lot. The switches are positioned on a control panel in a secure location. The switches provide a logic 1 on 9 of its output lines while the tenth is grounded to logic 0. For example, label the switches $DCBA$ and set the automobile limit to 1532. If the switches are coded

$$D = (D_9 D_8 \cdots D_0)$$
$$C = (C_9 C_8 \cdots C_0)$$
$$B = (B_9 B_8 \cdots B_0)$$
$$A = (A_9 A_8 \cdots A_0)$$

then $D_1 = 0, C_5 = 0, B_3 = 0$, and $A_2 = 0$. All other lines D_i, C_i, B_i, and A_i (36 of them) are at logic 1.

The last section of the controller compares the switch settings to the counter outputs, as shown in Fig. 11.16(d). The comparator matches each BCD digit, and if they all match, the lot is full. An example comparator is illustrated in Fig. 11.16(e). Since only one of the a_i and A_i can be logic 0 at one time, the two-input NOR gates perform the comparison with the 10-input OR gate combining the NOR outputs to form M_1, the matching output signal.

When the lot is filled, the FULL signal goes to logic 1, which closes the entrance gate and illuminates the warning sign. The FULL signal is NOTed and ANDed with the IN signal in the counter control section. This prevents a devious factory worker from pressing the entrance pressure sensor when the lot is filled to drive the counters past the switch settings thus opening the entrance gate so that he can double park.

Light Beam Counter

Consider the design of a sequential circuit that counts the number of persons entering a bank each day. The input sensors are two light beams separated by a distance of 6 inches. A corridor with light beams is sketched in Fig. 11.17(a). A person should be counted only if the first beam x_1 is broken and then the second beam x_2 is broken. The light sensors are designed so that when broken the output x_i is logic 1. Persons leaving the bank break beam x_2 then x_1 and are to be ignored, as well as those who hesitate and break only one beam.

The counter design has two parts, an asynchronous count pulse generator and an asynchronous ripple BCD counter. The primitive flow table for the count pulse generator is shown in Fig. 11.17(b). An implication table and merger diagram are illustrated in Fig. 11.17(c) and (d). A minimal cover for the compatible rows is

$$a = (124)$$

$$b = (35)$$

The reduced flow table is presented in Fig. 11.17(e). Choosing the state assignment

$$a \longrightarrow 0$$

$$b \longrightarrow 1$$

the switching functions become

$$Y = x_1 \bar{x}_2 + x_1 y$$

$$z = x_1 x_2 y$$

and the final logic design is shown in Fig. 11.17(f).

For proper operation, the counter reset is pulsed each morning to clear the counter to 0. At the end of the day the digit displays will show the total number of persons who have entered the bank since that morning. (Perhaps the bank president could be persuaded to purchase a second system to count those leaving to ensure the bank is empty when he closes his doors!)

Digital Combination Lock

A digital lock is to be used for controlling pedestrian traffic into a large computer installation. The lock has a keyboard consisting of 10 push buttons labeled 0, 1, . . . , 9 and 1 push button labeled RESET. The logic diagram for

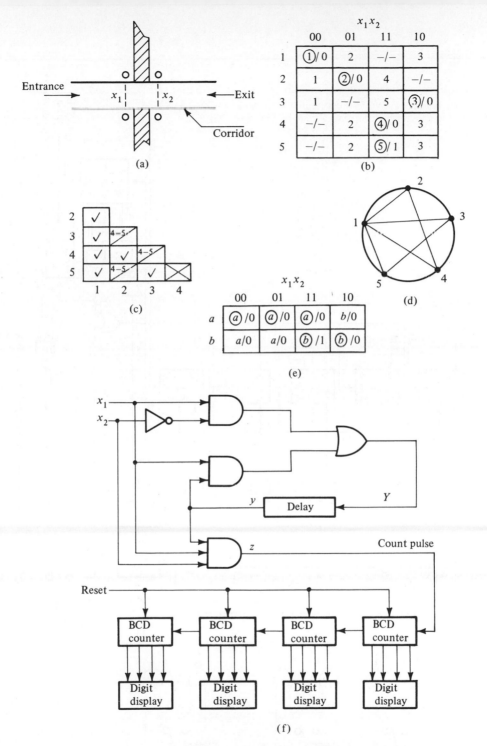

Fig. 11.17 Light beam counter: (a) light beams; (b) primitive flow table; (c) implication table; (d) merger diagram; (e) reduced flow table; (f) logic diagram.

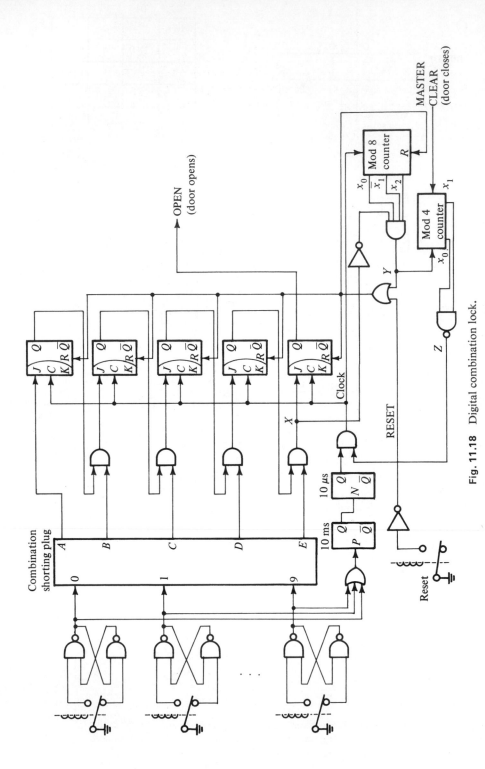

Fig. 11.18 Digital combination lock.

the lock is shown in Fig. 11.18. The buttons $0, 1, \ldots, 9$ are connected to cross-coupled NAND gates which serve as switch-bounce filters. The switch-bounce filters provide, for each pressed digit button, a single pulse to a combination shorting plug. The purpose of the shorting plug is to connect the 5 output signals $A, B, \ldots, E$ to the 10 input digits in a prescribed secret order. The shorting plug determines the combination of the lock and the combination is changed by exchanging plugs. For example, if the combination is 85223, then

$$A = 8$$
$$B = 5$$
$$C = 2$$
$$D = 2$$
$$E = 3$$

The combination is a five-digit number whose proper sequence causes the five clocked JK flip-flops to sequentially change to the logic 1 state. Upon receipt of the fifth correct digit, the OPEN signal releases the locked entrance door.

Each time a digit button is pushed, two one-shots generate a clock pulse which drives a modulo 8 binary counter and five clocked JK flip-flops. The modulo 8 counter is decoded on count 5 if the signal X is not logic 1. In other words, if the fifth digit is not going to generate the OPEN signal, the modulo 8 counter and decode logic generate the signal Y, which resets the clocked JK flip-flops and the modulo 8 counter to the 0 state. The signal Y is pulsed on each incorrect five-digit input combination. On the third incorrect attempt the signal Z goes to logic 0 and inhibits any further attempts at opening the digital lock. The third incorrect attempt "freezes up" the whole device and the MASTER CLEAR signal must be generated from inside the computer room to return the digital combinational lock to the operational state. The signal $\bar{Z}$ can be used to sound an alarm if desired.

Under normal circumstances, a correct five digit combination is applied, after initially pressing the RESET signal, and the door lock is released by the OPEN signal. As the door closes a mechnical switch generates a MASTER CLEAR pulse which resets the mod 4 counter; this allows the next user three new attempts at the combination.

Asynchronous Data Converter

An automated test station is to be designed for testing various digital subsystems. One device to be tested generates a serial data stream in an irregular asynchronous manner. The automated test system must be interfaced to the device under test, as shown in Fig. 11.19(a). The serial data format is specified in Fig. 11.19(b). Figure 11.19(b) also illustrates the clock signal, which must be produced by the interface clock generator.

The nature of the serial data is important and determines the interface design. The first bit of the serial data is always logic 0 and is called the *start bit*. This means a new data word always begins with a $1 \rightarrow 0$ transition. The

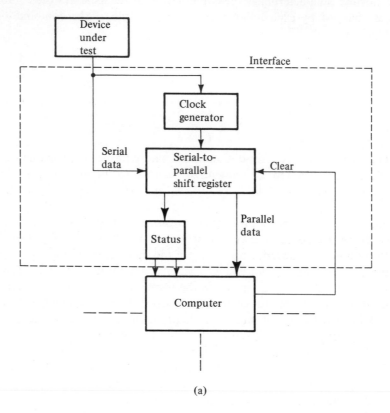

(a)

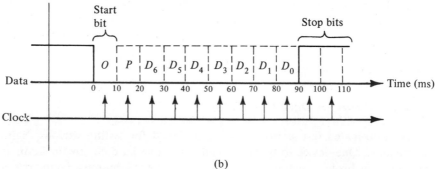

(b)

Fig. 11.19 Asynchronous data converter: (a) system description; (b) serial data format.

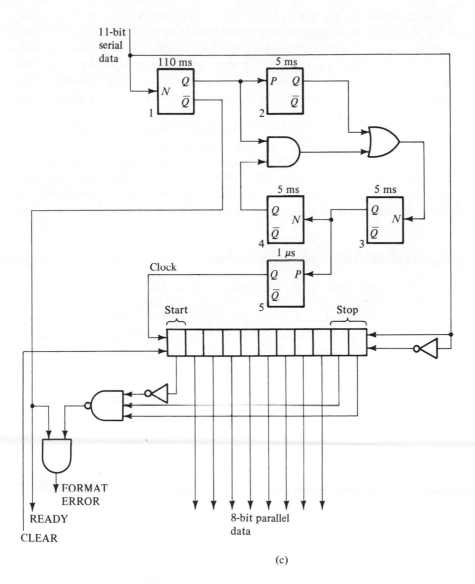

(c)

Fig. 11.19—*Cont.* (c) Logic diagram.

last two data bits are always logic 1 and are named *stop bits*. Hence, we may use these 3 bits to test for an incorrect data format. Please note that an 11-bit serial data word always has a fixed, or synchronous, spacing between bits. However, the entire word may occur at any time in an asynchronous manner.

The logic diagram for the asynchronous serial-to-parallel data converter is shown in Fig. 11.19(c). The clock generator consists of five one-shots, one AND gate, and one OR gate. The start bit triggers one-shot 1, which generates a pulse which is 110 milliseconds long. The complement of this signal (READY) tells the computer that the data are not available during this time period. One-shot 1 also closes (by the AND gate) the loop formed by one-shots 3 and 4. These two one-shots alternately trigger one another until one-shot 1 breaks the loop. The purpose of one-shot 2 is to initiate the loop at the proper time, while one-shot 5 actually generates the narrow clock pulse which shifts the data register.

After the eleventh serial data bit has been entered into the shift register, the READY signal goes high and the computer may take the 8-bit, parallel data. If a stop bit is logic 0 and/or the start bit is logic 1, the computer receives a warning by a logic 1 on the FORMAT ERROR line. Once the computer receives the data, it pulses the CLEAR line and destroys the parallel data. Note that the cleared register will signal a format error to the computer.

Adaptive Traffic Light Controller

A busy street corner in a metropolitan area poses a traffic congestion problem. The traffic light runs on a 100-second cycle. The traffic count distribution fluctuates continuously and deviates markedly from any fixed average number. Therefore, the city has designed an adaptive traffic light controller for installation at the corner of Sequential Street and Combinational Avenue, as shown in Fig. 11.20(a). The controller can change cycles every 5 minutes, allowing the street with the larger traffic count a larger share of the 100-second timing cycle. The cycle consists of a 50-second green dwell, a 10-second yellow dwell, and a 40-second red dwell on the busier street.

The pressure sensors A and B supply control signals to an asynchronous n-bit up/down counter through two one-shots, an EXCLUSIVE-OR, and an NAND gate. The size of the counter is chosen so that 2^{n-1} is greater than the largest number of cars that can pass a sensor in 5 minutes. The counter bit X_{n-1} always indicates which street has more traffic. Every 5 minutes the clock generator pulses the counter reset and stores the current value of X_{n-1} in the clocked JK flip-flop x. The signal x controls a synchronous sequential circuit, which provides the actual control signals for the traffic light.

The state diagram of the sequential circuit is shown in Fig. 11.20(b). Assuming the state assignment of Fig. 11.20(c), the following switching functions may be derived:

$$Y_4 = \bar{y}_1\bar{y}_2\bar{y}_4 + \bar{x}\bar{y}_3\bar{y}_4 + x\bar{y}_1 y_3 y_4 + \bar{y}_1\bar{y}_3\bar{y}_4$$

$$Y_3 = \bar{y}_1\bar{y}_2 y_3 y_4 + \bar{x}\bar{y}_3 y_4 + x y_1 y_4$$

$$Y_2 = y_2\bar{y}_3 + \bar{y}_2 y_3 y_4 + \bar{x}y_3 y_4$$

$$Y_1 = y_2 y_3\bar{y}_4 + \bar{x}y_1\bar{y}_3 + x y_2 y_3$$

$$z_4 = y_2\bar{y}_3 + y_2\bar{y}_4 + \bar{x}y_1\bar{y}_3$$

$$z_3 = \bar{y}_1\bar{y}_2\bar{y}_3 + \bar{y}_1\bar{y}_2\bar{y}_4 + x\bar{y}_1 y_3 y_4$$

$$z_2 = y_1 y_3 \bar{y}_4 + xy_1\bar{y}_3$$

$$z_1 = \bar{x}y_3 y_4 + y_1 y_3 y_4$$

The sequential circuit logic diagram is shown in Fig. 11.20(d).

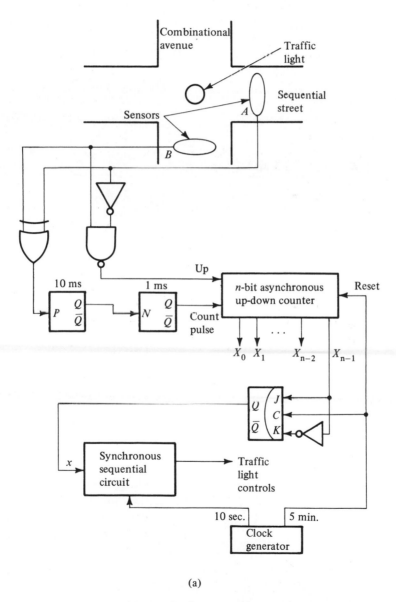

(a)

Fig. 11.20 Adaptive traffic light controller: (a) block diagram.

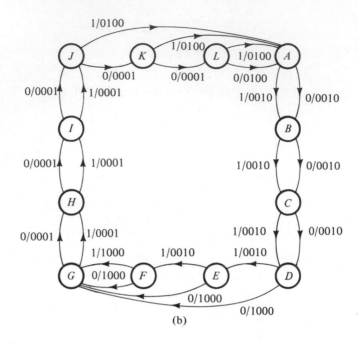

(b)

y_3y_4 \ y_1y_2	00	01	11	10
00	A	G		J
01	B	H		K
11	D	E		F
10	C	I		L

(c)

Fig. 11.20—*Cont.*   (b) State diagram; (c) state assignment map.

This completes the design of the adaptive traffic light controller. Although it was designed around a fixed timing cycle, the number of states can be altered and the same design procedure is applicable to other traffic situations.

Summary

This chapter has been oriented toward the practical aspects of digital systems design. The fundamental concepts of decoders, adders, shift registers,

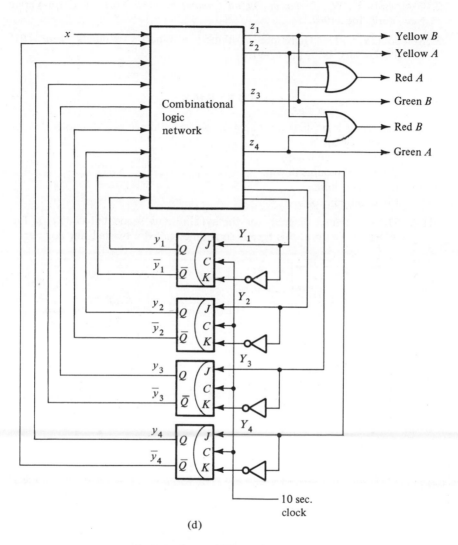

Fig. 11.20—*Cont.* (d) Logic diagram.

one-shots, and counters were first developed. These fundamental concepts were then applied to a series of disjoint case studies in digital design. After consuming the contents of this chapter the reader should be able to solve independently a design problem of his own.

REFERENCES

1. FLORES, I., *The Logic of Computer Arithmetic*. Englewood Cliffs, N.J.: Prentice-Hall, Inc., 1963.

2. GSCHWIND, H. W., *Design of Digital Computers*. New York: Springer-Verlag New York, Inc., 1967.

3. MACSORLEY, O. L., "High Speed Arithmetic in Binary Computers," *Proc. IRE*. Vol. 49, January 1971, pp. 67–91.

PROBLEMS

11.1. Sketch the logic diagram for a 4-bit binary up/down ripple counter. Let the control signals be
(a) $U = 1$ (counts up).
(b) $U = 0$ (counts down).
(c) Count pulse.
(d) Clear control.

11.2. Draw a timing diagram for the synchronous sequential circuit of Fig. P11.1. A circuit of this type is sometimes called a twisted ring counter.

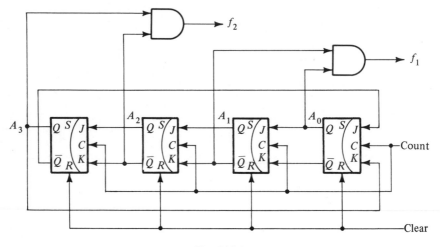

Fig. P11.1

11.3. Use clocked JK flip-flops and the application equation technique to find the logic diagram for the following special sequence counter; label the sequence control signal x and the flip-flops A_0 and A_1:

$$x$$

	0	1
0	1	2
1	2	3
2	3	0
3	0	1

11.4. Design a special sequence counter to count as shown below:

$$x$$

	0	1
0	1	1
1	2	3
2	3	3
3	0	0

11.5. Find the state sequences for the counter shown in Fig. P11.2.

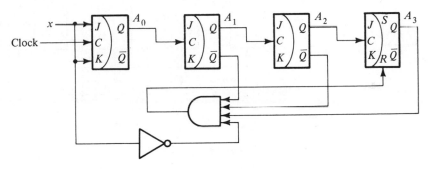

Fig. P11.2

11.6. Use the application equation technique to derive a clocked JK flip-flop implementation for the sequential circuit of Fig. 7.31.

11.7. Draw a timing diagram for the clock generator circuit of Fig. 11.19(c). Show on your diagram a typical serial data word and the outputs of all five one-shots in the circuit.

11.8. Draw a timing diagram for the count pulse generator of Fig. 11.20(a). Show the signals A, B and the output of the EXCLUSIVE-OR gate, the two one-shots, and the count pulse.

11.9. Examine the light beam counter circuit of Fig. 11.17(f). Analyze the circuit to determine what happens when a person leaves the bank, changes his mind at the door, and returns to the teller's cage, producing the following input sequence:

x_1	x_2
0	0
0	1
1	1
1	0
1	1
0	1
0	0

11.10. Design two logic circuits for subtraction. Make them counterparts to the half-adder and full-adder circuits.

11.11. Design a synchronous modulo 5 counter using clocked JK flip-flops.

11.12. Draw a timing diagram for the sequential circuit in Fig. P11.3.

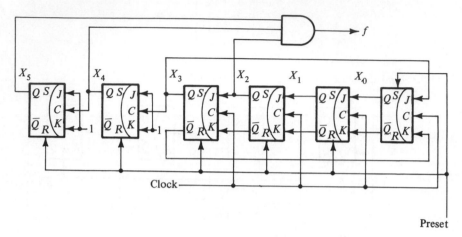

Fig. P11.3

11.13. Design an accumulator circuit for totaling 10 4-bit binary numbers. Use full-adders and do not allow overflow. Assume all 10 numbers enter the accumulator on the same four input lines.

11.14. Design an arithmetic unit which will add and subtract two binary numbers as shown in Fig. P11.4. Given

$$A = (a_4a_3a_2a_1a_0)_2, \qquad B = (b_4b_3b_2b_1b_0)_2$$

when

$$x = 0 \longrightarrow Z = A \text{ plus } B$$

$$x = 1 \longrightarrow Z = A \text{ minus } B = A \text{ plus } [B]_2$$

You may use clocked JK flip-flops for the registers.

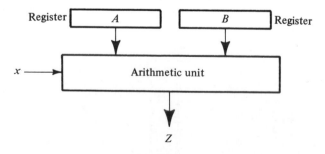

Fig. P11.4

12

Fault
Diagnosis
of
Logic
Circuits

The determination of whether or not a device is capable of functioning properly is an important practical problem. *Fault diagnosis* or *fault testing* is the process used in making such a determination. The process of fault diagnosis consists of both the collection of the necessary data and the analysis of the data which leads to a conclusion about the device under test.

This chapter provides an introduction to the subject of fault diagnosis of logic circuits. We will begin by giving some general terminology and then follow with discussions of fault models, test generation, test selection, and fault dictionaries. Both combinational and sequential circuits are considered.

Introduction

Fault testing begins with the application of a sequence of inputs to a circuit under test and the observation of the corresponding output sequence. The process is completed with an analysis of the output sequence that leads to a conclusion about the condition of the circuit under test. All or part of the process may be carried out by automation.

A *fault* will be defined informally as any condition that causes a device to function improperly.

The two primary objectives of testing are fault detection and fault location. *Fault detection testing* is the process of determining whether or not a fault is present in a given device. A set of inputs to a logic circuit that can be used to detect a fault in the circuit is a *fault detection test set* (FDTS). *Fault location testing* is the process of determining which fault is present in a faulty device. A *fault location test set* (FLTS) is a set of inputs which can be used to locate a fault. Testing for both detection and location of faults is referred to as *fault diagnosis testing*. The term *diagnostic test set* (DTS) will refer to a set of inputs used for fault diagnosis.

Fault Models

We will now consider the concept of a fault in more detail. Logic networks may contain faults caused by broken or shorted interconnections, bad logic elements, improper power voltage, poor noise immunity, and others. Faults may be categorized in several ways. A faulty condition which does not change with time is referred to as a *solid* or *permanent* fault. On the other hand, a fault which appears and disappears with time is called an *intermittent* fault. Other categories of faults specify the effect of a fault on the device. In this context, *logical faults* are faults which cause a given logic device to function as an entirely different logic device. *Nonlogical* faults include all faults other than logical faults. We will be concerned only with solid, logical faults.

In order to study the effect of faults on a logic circuit, a fault model must be established. A popular and useful model for representing faults in logic circuits is the *stuck-at fault model*. In this model, a fault in a circuit is represented as a wire in the circuit either stuck-at logic 0 (s-a-0) or stuck-at logic 1 (s-a-1). Figure 12.1 shows a circuit with a s-a-0 fault. The fault can be identified as wire (lead) ③ s-a-0. An abbreviated notation for the fault is 3/0. A faulty circuit can be considered as a logic circuit which realizes a function different from that realized by the fault-free circuit. A standard functional notation will be adopted for the representation of faulty circuits. If $f(\mathbf{x}_n) = f(x_1, x_2, \ldots, x_n)$ represents a fault-free circuit, $f^{p/d}(\mathbf{x}_n)$ represents the same circuit with fault p/d where p is a wire label, d can be 0 or 1 as appropriate for

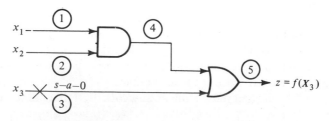

Fig. 12.1   "Struck at" fault model for ③ s-a-0.

s-a-0 or s-a-1, and n is the number of input variables. The faulty circuit of Fig. 12.1 has the following representation.

$$f^{3/0}(\mathbf{x}_3) = x_1\, x_2$$

Fault 2/1 would yield the function below.

$$f^{2/1}(\mathbf{x}_3) = x_1 + x_3$$

A *single fault* exists when one and only one wire is stuck. When more than one wire is stuck, a *multiple fault* exists. Circuits with r wires have $2r$ possible single faults based on the stuck-at model. When multiple faults are considered $3^r - 1$ faults can be enumerated. The latter number includes single faults as a special case of multiple faults.

The stuck-at model is justified by its simplicity and by its accurate representation of a large class of faults which occur in practical circuits. Open or shorted components such as transistors and diodes can be described as causing stuck-at faults in a circuit. Broken wires and wires shorted to ground or to high voltage can be represented as stuck-at faults. On the other hand, wires shorted together are not represented by the stuck-at model.

We will focus our attention strictly on single, stuck-at faults. However, the techniques presented are fundamental to other fault models as well.

Combinational Logic Networks

We will now consider the problem of fault diagnosis for combinational logic networks. The following discussion serves to introduce the topics covered later.

Let $f(\mathbf{x}_n)$ represent the output of a logic network which is being tested for a possible fault. Clearly, the set of all 2^n possible inputs to the network could be used as a FDTS. The use of all possible inputs for testing is referred to as *exhaustive testing* and is impractical for networks with a large number of input wires. However, the method is straightforward as seen by the following example.

Consider the network shown in Fig. 12.1. Two copies of the network were tested by applying all eight possible input combinations to each copy and by observing the resulting network responses. Table 12.1 shows the results of the test. Copy 1 is seen to contain a fault since some incorrect responses were obtained. On the other hand, copy 2 is judged to be fault-free.

Most networks can be adequately tested without the use of the exhaustive approach as will be seen on the following pages where the determination of efficient FDTS's for combinational logic networks will be discussed. An efficient FDTS is a set of input combinations which test for any possible fault

TABLE 12.1. Exhaustive Testing

Tests,	Responses	
$x_1\ x_2\ x_3$	Copy 1	Copy 2
0 0 0	0	0
0 0 1	0	1
0 1 0	0	0
0 1 1	0	1
1 0 0	0	0
1 0 1	0	1
1 1 0	1	1
1 1 1	1	1

in a specified set of faults. The test set contains a minimum or near-minimum number of input combinations.

Test Generation

Test generation can be described as the process of determining a test for a given fault in a given network. When more than one such test exists, all tests which can be used to detect the fault are usually determined. This section contains a discussion of test generation for single stuck-at faults in combinational logic networks. Two methods for test generation are described: the EXCLUSIVE OR method and the path-sensitizing method. Also included are discussions of untestable faults and test generation for multiple output networks.

Let $f(\mathbf{x}_n)$ represent a fault-free logic network. A *test* T_i for fault p/d is any input $\mathbf{x}_n^j$ to the network for which the following relationship is satisfied:

$$f(\mathbf{x}_n^j) = \bar{f}^{p/d}(\mathbf{x}_n^j) \tag{12-1}$$

where the superscript j is the decimal value of the n binary inputs. For example, from Fig. 12.1, $\mathbf{x}_3^1 = (001)$ is a test for 3/0 since $f(\mathbf{x}_3^1) = 1 = \bar{0} = \bar{f}^{3/0}(\mathbf{x}_3^1)$. This definition is justified by observing that a test for a given fault must produce a different response when the fault is present than when the fault is not present. A given fault may have more than one test, and a given test may test for more than one fault.

The previous condition, which must be satisfied by an input in order to be a fault test, may be restated in terms of the EXCLUSIVE-OR operation as follows:

$$f(\mathbf{x}_n^j) \oplus f^{p/d}(\mathbf{x}_n^j) = 1 \tag{12-2}$$

This alternative description forms the basis of the first test generation procedure presented later.

A *fault table* is a table which displays a set of faults and a set of test inputs. Table 12.2 shows a fault table containing all single faults and all

TABLE 12.2 Fault Table

Tests, x_1 x_2 x_3 \ Faults	1/0	1/1	2/0	2/1	3/0	3/1	4/0	4/1	5/0	5/1
0 0 0	0	0	0	0	0	1	0	1	0	1
0 0 1	0	0	0	0	1	0	0	0	1	0
0 1 0	0	1	0	0	0	1	0	1	0	1
0 1 1	0	0	0	0	1	0	0	0	1	0
1 0 0	0	0	0	1	0	1	0	1	0	1
1 0 1	0	0	0	0	1	0	0	0	1	0
1 1 0	1	0	1	0	0	0	1	0	1	0
1 1 1	0	0	0	0	0	0	0	0	1	0

inputs for the network in Fig. 12.1. A 1 in row i, column j, (i, j), indicates that the input listed in row i is a test for the fault listed in column j. On the other hand, a 0 in (i, j) indicates that input i is not a test for fault j. For example, input 010 is a test for faults 1/1, 3/1, 4/1, and 5/1 but is not a test for 1/0, 2/0, 2/1, 3/0, 4/0 or 5/0.

EXCLUSIVE-OR method. A straightforward method for generating all possible tests for a given fault in a network will now be described. Let $f(\mathbf{x}_n)$ represent a fault-free network, and let p/d be a fault for which tests are to be derived. The method starts with the construction of the truth tables of f and of $f^{p/d}$. Next, compute and record $f \oplus f^{p/d}$ for each row of the truth tables. These steps are illustrated in Table 12.3 for faults 1/0, 2/1, and 3/0 in the network of Fig. 12.1.

TABLE 12.3. EXCLUSIVE-OR Method

x_1 x_2 x_3	f	$f^{1/0}$	$f^{2/1}$	$f^{3/0}$	$f \oplus f^{1/0}$	$f \oplus f^{2/1}$	$f \oplus f^{3/0}$
0 0 0	0	0	0	0	0	0	0
0 0 1	1	1	1	0	0	0	1
0 1 0	0	0	0	0	0	0	0
0 1 1	1	1	1	0	0	0	1
1 0 0	0	0	1	0	0	1	0
1 0 1	1	1	1	0	0	0	1
1 1 0	1	0	1	1	1	0	0
1 1 1	1	1	1	1	0	0	0

From the definition of a fault test, equation (12-2), it follows that tests for fault p/d are indicated by the 1's in the column corresponding to $f \oplus f^{p/d}$.

For example, fault 1/0 can be tested for only by input 110, whereas fault 3/0 can be tested for by either 001, 011, or 101.

Tests for fault p/d are minterms of the Boolean function $f \oplus f^{p/d}$. Hence, by expressing f and $f^{p/d}$ algebraically, an expression which gives all tests for p/d can be determined by application of Boolean algebra without the use of truth tables. If $F^{p/d}$ represents all tests for fault p/d, then $F^{p/d} = f \oplus f^{p/d}$. For fault 1/0 in Fig. 12.1,

$$F^{1/0} = (x_1 x_2 + x_3) \oplus (x_3) = x_1 x_2 \bar{x}_3$$

The minterm $x_1 x_2 \bar{x}_3$ implies test 110. For 3/0,

$$\begin{aligned} F^{3/0} &= (x_1 x_2 + x_3) \oplus (x_1 x_2) \\ &= (\bar{x}_1 + \bar{x}_2) x_3 \\ &= \bar{x}_1 x_3 + \bar{x}_2 x_3 \end{aligned}$$

which has minterms $\bar{x}_1 \bar{x}_2 x_3$, $x_1 \bar{x}_2 x_3$, and $\bar{x}_1 x_2 x_3$, implying tests 001, 101, and 011.

The algebraic approach is especially beneficial when functions of a large number of variables are involved. For example, consider the six-variable function which corresponds to the network in Fig. 12.2:

$$g(\mathbf{x}_6) = (x_1 + x_2)(x_3 + \bar{x}_4) + (x_3 + \bar{x}_4)(x_5 + x_6)$$

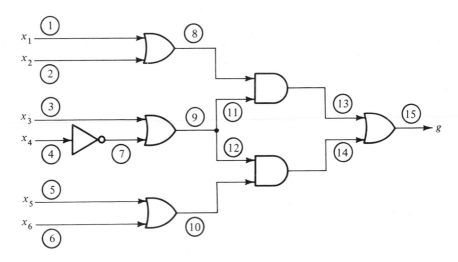

Fig. 12.2   Network with fanout.

Consider the generation of tests for 4/0. The truth table approach would require the formation of three tables of 64 entries each. Clearly, this requires more effort than the algebraic approach illustrated below for the same case:

$$G^{4/0} = g(\mathbf{x}_6) \oplus g^{4/0}(\mathbf{x}_6)$$
$$= [(x_1 + x_2)(x_3 + \bar{x}_4) + (x_3 + \bar{x}_4)(x_5 + x_6)]$$
$$\oplus [(x_1 + x_2) + (x_5 + x_6)]$$
$$= (x_1 + x_2 + x_5 + x_6)\bar{x}_3 x_4$$
$$= x_1\bar{x}_3 x_4 + x_2\bar{x}_3 x_4 + \bar{x}_3 x_4 x_5 + \bar{x}_3 x_4 x_6$$

Many tests for 4/0 are seen to exist.

Tests for internal faults such as 11/0 can also be determined by the above method as follows:

$$G^{11/0} = g(\mathbf{x}_6) \oplus g^{11/0}(\mathbf{x}_6)$$
$$= [(x_1 + x_2)(x_3 + \bar{x}_4) + (x_3 + \bar{x}_4)(x_5 + x_6)]$$
$$\oplus [(x_3 + \bar{x}_4)(x_5 + x_6)]$$
$$= (x_1 + x_2)(x_3 + \bar{x}_4)x_5 x_6$$
$$= x_1 x_3\bar{x}_5\bar{x}_6 + x_1\bar{x}_4\bar{x}_5\bar{x}_6 + x_2 x_3\bar{x}_5\bar{x}_6 + x_2\bar{x}_4\bar{x}_5\bar{x}_6$$

One test implied by $G^{11/0}$ is $x_1 = x_2 = x_3 = 1$, $x_4 = x_5 = x_6 = 0$.

While the EXCLUSIVE-OR method is straightforward, computation is often lengthy for the truth table approach and tedious for the algebraic approach. This is especially true when tests must be derived for all $2r$ single faults in a network. A test generation method that overcomes some of these computational difficulties is presented in the next section.

Path-sensitizing method. The approach taken in the path-sensitizing method is to first select a path from the fault site to the network output. Inputs are then chosen so that the logic value of lines in the path are a function of the fault. A path has been *sensitized* from the fault site to the output when this condition has been established. Consider the OR gate in Fig. 12.3(a) for an

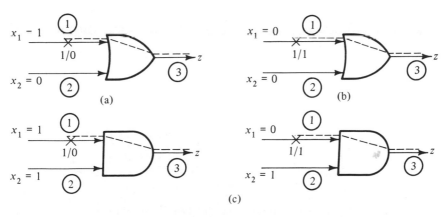

Fig. 12.3 Path sensitizing for gates: (a) OR gate with 1/0; (b) OR gate with 1/1; (c) faulty AND gates.

example. Output z is dependent on the logic value at line ① when the logic value at line ② is 0. Let 1/0 be the fault for which a test is being derived. The input $x_1 = 1$, $x_2 = 0$ makes the output $z = 1$ when 1/0 is not present and $z = 0$ when the fault is present. Hence, $x_1 = 1$, $x_2 = 0$ sensitizes a path from the potential fault 1/0 to the output and is therefore a test for 1/0. The input $x_1 = x_2 = 0$ sensitizes a path for fault 1/1 as shown in Fig. 12.3(b) and is a test for 1/1. Paths can be sensitized in an AND gate, as shown in Fig. 12.3(c). In general, paths are sensitized through the basic logic gates, as shown in Fig. 12.4.

Path sensitizing can be extended for use in networks of logic gates. This extension will now be described for the fanout-free network shown in Fig. 12.5. First, a test will be determined for fault 1/0. Only one path from lead ① to the network output exists and will be sensitized as shown in Fig. 12.5(a). The input $x_1 = 1$ is required to establish the proper logic value at line ① to test for a stuck-at-0 fault, while the value $x_2 = 1$ is necessary for sensitizing the path through the AND gate. To extend the path through the OR gate to the output, input $x_3 = 0$ is needed. The test 110 has therefore been established for fault 1/0.

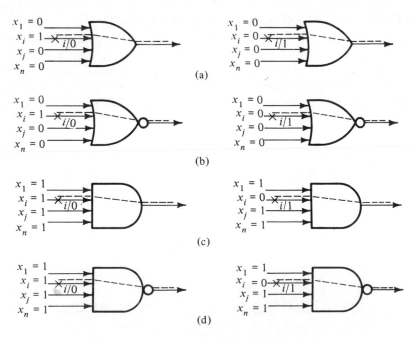

Fig. 12.4   Path sensitizing in popular logic gates: (a) OR gate; (b) NOR gate; (c) AND gate; (d) NAND gate.

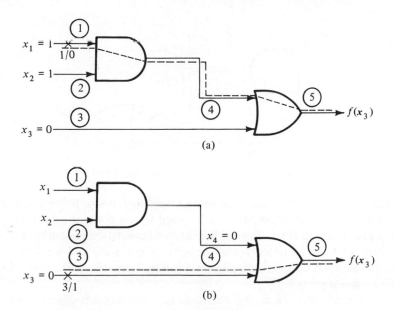

Fig. 12.5 Path sensitizing for networks: (a) path for 1/0; (b) path for 3/1.

Now consider the test determination for fault 3/1. The input $x_3 = 0$ is required to initialize the path since a s-a-1 fault is being considered. A path is sensitized to the output by establishing logic value 0 at lead ④. This lead is labeled x_4 as shown in Fig. 12.5(b). Setting $x_3 = x_4 = 0$ sensitizes the necessary path and is referred to as the *forward trace* step in the path-sensitizing method. To make $x_4 = 0$, x_1 and x_2 must be either 00, 01, or 10. Fixing x_1 and x_2 is referred to as the *backward trace* step in the method. The three tests 000, 010, or 100 have been found for 3/1.

The path-sensitizing method can be summarized as follows:

1. Select the fault for which tests are to be determined and select a path from the fault site to the network output.
2. Sensitize the path (forward trace).
3. Establish network inputs as required by 2 above (backward trace).

A useful application of path sensitizing besides test generation is the determination of the set of faults tested for by a given input. Again consider the network in Fig. 12.5 with input 110. For clarity, the network has been redrawn in Fig. 12.6. Lines along the path from input x_1 to the network output are labeled $1 \rightarrow 0$, which has the following meaning: Logic value with *no* fault $\rightarrow$ logic value with fault. Hence, faults 1/0, 4/0, and 5/0 are all tested for by input 110. The path from ② to ④ is also sensitized by $x_1 = 1$. Therefore, the input 110 tests for 2/0 also.

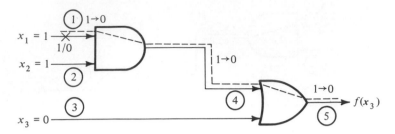

Fig. 12.6   Propagation along sensitized path.

The previous discussion can be summarized as follows. For a given sensitized path, each lead along the path is tested for an s-a-0 or s-a-1 fault. The above also leads to the following fact about fanout-free networks. Fanout-free networks can be tested for all possible single s-a-0 and s-a-1 faults by testing each input lead for s-a-0 and s-a-1 faults. Networks with fanout do not exhibit this property.

The use of path sensitizing on networks with fanout will now be considered. Care must be taken for this case. Three examples involving networks with fanout will be presented to illustrate the potential problems. After identification of the problems, guidelines will be given for avoiding the problems.

A simple network with fanout is shown in Fig. 12.7. Consider the derivation of a test for fault 2/0 in the network. Since line ② fans out, there are two paths from the fault site to the network output. Hence, there are two single paths and one double path which can be sensitized. These three cases are illustrated in Fig. 12.7(a), (b), and (c), respectively. The notation $1 \rightarrow 0$ is again used to show that each case produces a test for 2/0. Hence, 110, 011, and 111 are all tests for 2/0.

Tests will now be derived for fault 2/0 in the fanout network of Fig. 12.8. Again, two single paths and one double path exist for the fault. Notice, however, that when the double path is sensitized the network output is 1 whether or not the fault 2/0 is present. Hence, the input 111 is not a test for the fault. But inputs 110 and 011 are both tests.

The last two examples illustrate that in one case a multiple path produced a test but in another case a multiple path did not produce a test. Single paths produced tests for both examples. A generalization which might be considered after seeing these examples is that only single paths should be sensitized when deriving tests. However, the network shown in Fig. 12.9 provides a counterexample to such a generalization. The attempt to obtain a test for $\alpha/0$ by sensitizing a single path is shown in Fig. 12.9(a). Contradictory requirements for network inputs are indicated. Similar results are obtained when the other

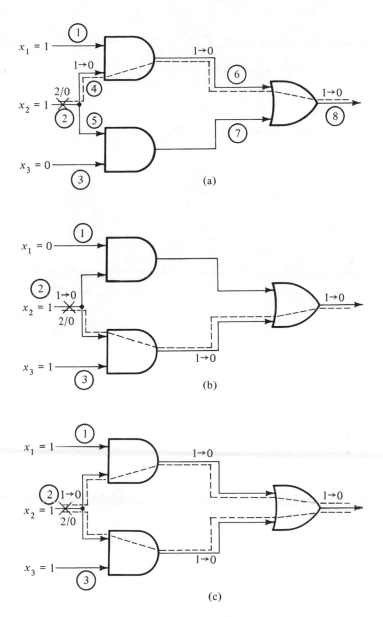

Fig. 12.7   Path sensitizing in network with fanout: (a) single path produced by 110; (b) single path produced by 011; (c) double paths produced by 111.

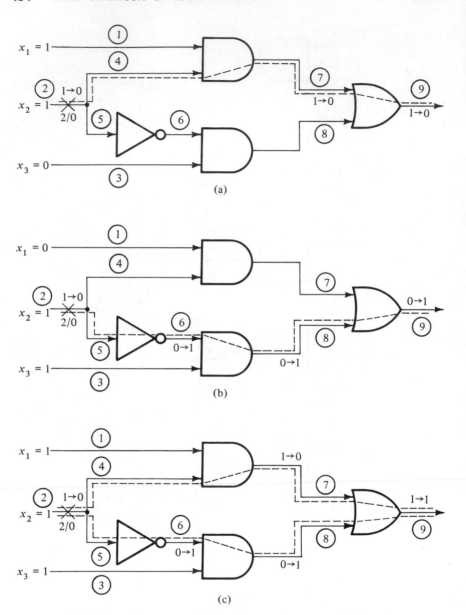

Fig. 12.8   Path sensitizing-network with unequal parity: (a) single path produced by 110; (b) single path produced by 011; (c) double path produced by 111 is not a test.

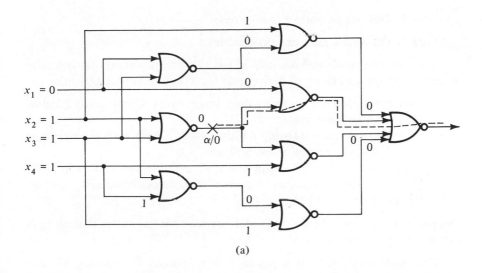

(a)

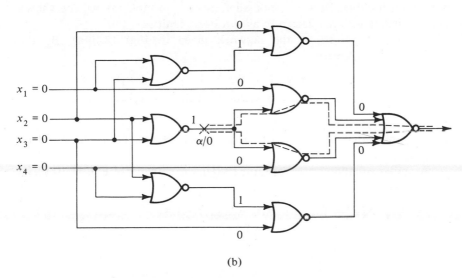

(b)

Fig. 12.9 Schneider's counterexample to single path sensitizing:
(a) single path does not produce test; (b) double path produces
test.

single path is sensitized. Figure 12.9(b) gives the successful derivation of a
test when the double path is sensitized.

The effect of fanout on path sensitizing can be summarized by the following three cases:

CASE 1. Both single and multiple paths produce tests.

CASE 2. Only single paths produce tests.

CASE 3. Only multiple paths produce tests.

The following guidelines are helpful for avoiding problems that can arise when using path sensitizing to derive tests for a fault in fanout networks:

1. Attempt to derive tests using only single paths. Continue to 2 below only if no tests are found.
2. Attempt to derive tests using multiple paths. Check each potential test for validity. Stop when a test is found.
3. If there are m possible single paths, all possible multiple paths of 2, 3, ..., m combinations must be examined before concluding that no test exists.

A procedure based on the above guidelines does not guarantee that all tests for a given fault will be found.

Untestable faults. A fault p/d is said to be *testable* if and only if there exists at least one test for the fault. All faults considered in previous examples have been testable. However, not all faults are testable, as will be shown below. Such faults are referred to as *untestable* faults.

Consider fault 8/1 in the network given in Fig. 12.10(a). By the EXCLUSIVE-OR method,

$$
\begin{aligned}
F_a^{8/1} &= (x_1\bar{x}_2 + x_1x_2x_3) \oplus (x_1\bar{x}_2 + x_1x_3) \\
&= (x_1\bar{x}_2 + x_1x_3) \oplus (x_1\bar{x}_2 + x_1x_3) \\
&= 0
\end{aligned}
$$

which implies that no tests exist for fault 8/1. Hence, fault 8/1 would be untestable.

A similar situation arises for fault 13/0 in the network of Fig. 12.10(b), as seen below:

$$
\begin{aligned}
F_b^{13/0} &= (x_1x_2 + \bar{x}_1x_3 + x_2x_3) \oplus (x_1x_2 + \bar{x}_1x_3) \\
&= (x_1x_2 + \bar{x}_1x_3) \oplus (x_1x_2 + \bar{x}_1x_3) \\
&= 0
\end{aligned}
$$

Fault 13/0 is untestable.

Note, however, that $F_a^{8/0}$ and $F_b^{13/1}$ are nonzero, as shown below:

$$
\begin{aligned}
F_a^{8/0} &= (x_1\bar{x}_2 + x_1x_2x_3) \oplus (x_1\bar{x}_2) \\
&= x_1x_2x_3 \\
F_b^{13/1} &= (x_1x_2 + \bar{x}_1x_3 + x_2x_3) \oplus (1) \\
&= x_1\bar{x}_2 + \bar{x}_1\bar{x}_3
\end{aligned}
$$

Hence, 8/0 in f_a and 13/1 in f_b are testable.

The question of how to identify untestable faults thus arises. An answer to the question can be found in a study of redundancy in logic networks. A

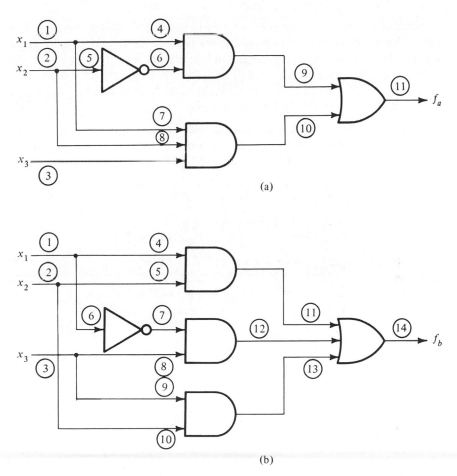

Fig. 12.10 Networks with redundancy: (a) literal redundancy;
(b) term redundancy.

network contains *redundancy* if and only if there exists a line in the network which can be cut and replaced by an appropriate logical constant (0 or 1) without changing the function realized by the network. A network without redundancy is referred to as a *nonredundant* network. The networks in Fig. 12.10 both contain redundancy, as demonstrated below.

Line ⑧ of the network in Fig. 12.10(a) can be cut and replaced with a constant 1 input to the AND gate without modifying the logic function f_a. This can be easily justified with Boolean algebra. Hence, the literal x_2 is not needed in the expression and therefore indicates a redundancy in the network.

In Fig. 12.10(b), line ⑬ can be cut and replaced by logic 0 without changing the function realized by the network. Therefore, the line is redundant.

Untestable single faults can occur only in networks with redundancy. The untestable faults correspond to redundant lines in the network and can be identified as follows. Let i be a redundant line in a network. If i can be cut and replaced by the logical constant d (0 or 1, but not both), then the fault i/d is untestable. However, fault $i/\bar{d}$ is testable. If i can be replaced by both d and $\bar{d}$, then faults i/d and $i/\bar{d}$ are both untestable.

Multiple output networks. Most logic networks which occur in practice have more than one output terminal. In other words, more than one logic function is realized by the network. Figure 12.11 shows a network with two

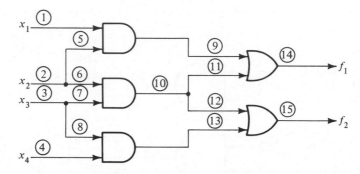

Fig. 12.11   Multiple output network.

output terminals. When generating tests for a fault in this network both output functions must be considered. Let $F^{p/d}$ represent the Boolean function which describes all possible tests for fault p/d. Then

$$F^{p/d} = F_1^{p/d} + F_2^{p/d}$$

where $F_1^{p/d}$ and $F_2^{p/d}$ represent all tests for fault p/d at terminals f_1 and f_2, respectively.

For example, consider faults 1/0 and 3/1:

$$
\begin{aligned}
F^{1/0} &= F_1^{1/0} + F_2^{1/0} \\
&= [(x_1x_2 + x_2x_3) \oplus (x_2x_3)] + [(x_2x_3 + x_3x_4) \oplus (x_2x_3 + x_3x_4)] \\
&= [x_1x_2\bar{x}_3] + [0] \\
&= x_1x_2\bar{x}_3
\end{aligned}
$$

$F_2^{1/0} = 0$ since fault 1/0 cannot be observed at f_2.

$$
\begin{aligned}
F^{3/1} &= F_1^{3/1} + F_2^{3/1} \\
&= [(x_1x_2 + x_2x_3) \oplus (x_1x_2 + x_2)] + [(x_2x_3 + x_3x_4) \oplus (x_2 + x_4)] \\
&= [\bar{x}_1x_2\bar{x}_3] + [x_2\bar{x}_3 + \bar{x}_3x_4] \\
&= x_2\bar{x}_3 + \bar{x}_3x_4
\end{aligned}
$$

Fault 3/1 can be observed at both f_1 and f_2.

In general for a network with m output terminals, the tests for fault p/d are given by the following:

$$F^{p/d} = F_1^{p/d} + F_2^{p/d} + \cdots + F_m^{p/d}$$

Fault Detection

Two methods for determining tests for a given single, testable s-a-0 or s-a-1 fault were presented in the previous section. The problem of selecting an FDTS for a given network will be considered in this section. An FDTS for a given network is said to be *complete* if there is at least one test in the set for every possible fault in the network. A *minimum* FDTS is a complete FDTS which contains the fewest number of tests of any complete FDTS. The network in Fig. 12.7 has the following minimum FDTS:

$$\text{FDTS}_m = \{010, 011, 101, 110\}$$

In the following paragraphs, methods for selecting minimum FDTS's will be considered. The selection of near-minimum FDTS's will also be described. The fault table of a network is assumed to be known before selection of a FDTS is begun. Any one of the methods presented in the previous section can be used to produce the fault table. However, the table need not contain all possible faults of a network when used in the selection process. Only faults at network checkpoints must be considered. The *checkpoints of a network* are the wires of the network which satisfy either of the following descriptions:

1. All input wires which are not fanout stems.
2. All wires in the network which are fanout branches.

The term *fanout stem* refers to the wire preceding the fanout point, and the term *fanout branches* refers to the wires beyond the fanout point. The checkpoints for the network in Fig. 12.7 are 1, 3, 4, and 5. Table 12.4 shows the corresponding fault table.

A minimum fault detection test set can be selected from a fault table by choosing the fewest number of inputs that cover all faults. This process is equivalent to the prime implicant selection step of the Quine-McCluskey procedure where the fewest number of prime implicants is chosen that cover all minterms. The selection procedure described in Chapter 3 for the Quine-McCluskey procedure is directly applicable here and will not be repeated. Applying the procedure to Table 12.4 yields $\{110, 010, 101, 011\}$ as a minimum test set.

The selection of a minimum test set can become lengthy for fault tables of moderate to large size. Hence, the use of procedures for selecting test sets that are not necessarily minimum is often more practical. As will be seen, such procedures often yield a minimum set. The near-minimum procedure described here is based on the computation of a weight for each input in the

TABLE 12.4.   Fault Table with Checkpoint Faults Only

Tests, $x_1\ x_2\ x_3$ \ Faults	1/0	1/1	3/0	3/1	4/0	4/1	5/0	5/1
0 0 0								
0 0 1								1
0 1 0		1		1				
0 1 1			1				1	
1 0 0						1		
1 0 1						1		1
1 1 0	1				1			
1 1 1								

fault table. The *weight* of a given input is defined as the number of faults tested by the input. Inputs for the near-minimum test set are selected by the following procedure:

STEP 1. Compute the weight of each input in the fault table.

STEP 2. Select the input with the largest weight. Make an arbitrary choice if more than one input has the largest weight.

STEP 3. Reduce the fault table by deleting the input selected and all of the faults covered by this input.

STEP 4. Recompute the weight of each input in the reduced fault table.

STEP 5. Terminate the procedure when all inputs in the reduced table have weight 0. Otherwise, repeat steps 2–5.

Example.

The above procedure will now be illustrated for Table 12.5:

STEP 1. The inputs are weighted as follows: $T_1, 2$; $T_2, 2$; $T_3, 2$; $T_4, 3$; $T_5, 4$; $T_6, 4$.

TABLE 12.5

Tests \ Faults	1	2	3	4	5	6	7	8	9	Weights
T_1				1			1			2
T_2							1	1		2
T_3				1	1					2
T_4	1				1	1				3
T_5	1		1			1			1	4
T_6		1	1					1	1	4

STEP 2. Select T_5.

STEP 3. The reduced fault table is given below.

Tests \ Faults	2	4	5	7	8	Weights
T_1		1		1		2
T_2				1	1	2
T_3		1	1			2
T_4			1			1
T_6	1				1	2

STEP 4. New weights are shown on the reduced table above:

STEP 5. Repeat steps 2–5.

STEP 2. Select T_1.

STEP 3. The reduced table is shown below:

Tests \ Faults	2	5	8	Weights
T_2			1	1
T_3		1		1
T_4		1		1
T_6	1		1	2

STEP 4. Weights are shown in the table above.

STEP 5. Repeat steps 2–5.

STEP 2. Select T_6.

STEPS 3 and 4. See the table below:

Tests \ Faults	5	Weights
T_2		0
T_3	1	1
T_4	1	1

STEP 5. Repeat steps 2–5.

STEP 2. Select T_3.

STEPS 3 and 4. See the table below:

Tests \ Faults		Weights
T_2		0
T_4		0

STEP 5. Stop. Test set $= \{T_1, T_3, T_5, T_6\}$.

The choice of whether to find a minimum test set or to find a near-minimum test set will vary with the situation. When the most efficient test set is a necessity in order to minimize testing time, then a minimum test set should be found. But when test selection time is more important than testing time, then a near-minimum test set should be the objective.

Fault Location and Diagnosis

The problem of locating a given fault in a network can be described as the ability to distinguish the given fault from all other possible faults that may occur in the network. Two faults are *distinguishable* if and only if there exists at least one fault detection test for one of the faults that is not a test for the other fault. From Fig. 12.5, faults 1/1 and 2/1 are distinguishable. Among other distinguishable faults in Fig. 12.5 are 3/0 and 5/0. Two or more faults are *indistinguishable* or *equivalent* if and only if they have the exact same set of fault detection tests. In Fig. 12.5, {1/0, 2/0, 4/0} and {3/1, 4/1, 5/1} are seen to be two sets of indistinguishable faults.

Let $F^{i/d_i - j/d_j}$ be a Boolean function which represents all tests which distinguish between faults i/d_i and j/d_j in a network realizing $f(\mathbf{x}_n)$. Then

$$F^{i/d_i - j/d_j} = F^{i/d_i} \oplus F^{j/d_j} \tag{12-3}$$

where F^{i/d_i} and F^{j/d_j} describe all tests for i/d_i and j/d_j, respectively. If i/d_i and j/d_j are indistinguishable, then $F^{i/d_i - j/d_j} = 0$.

For an illustration of Equation (12-3), consider Fig. 12.5:

$$F^{1/1 - 2/1} = F^{1/1} \oplus F^{2/1}$$
$$= \bar{x}_1 x_2 \bar{x}_3 \oplus x_1 \bar{x}_2 \bar{x}_3$$
$$= \bar{x}_1 x_2 \bar{x}_3 + x_1 \bar{x}_2 \bar{x}_3$$

Therefore, tests 010 and 100 can distinguish between faults 1/1 and 2/1.

$$F^{1/0 - 2/0} = F^{1/0} \oplus F^{2/0}$$
$$= x_1 x_2 \bar{x}_3 \oplus x_1 x_2 \bar{x}_3$$
$$= 0$$

Hence, faults 1/0 and 2/0 are indistinguishable.

Faults which are distinguishable from all other faults can be precisely located by the use of a complete fault location test set. However, a fault which is indistinguishable from other faults can be located only to within the set of equivalent faults. The precision to which an FLTS can locate a fault is called the *fault resolution* of the set.

A test set is a fault location test set if and only if the response of the network to the test input sequence uniquely identifies the fault with the desired resolution. A DTS must produce a response that identifies the network as fault-free or that identifies the fault with the desired resolution. The set {001, 010, 011, 100, 110} is a DTS for the network in Fig. 12.7.

The meanings of the responses that can be produced by a test set can be conveniently displayed in a *fault dictionary*. Table 12.6 shows a maximum resolution fault dictionary for the network in Fig. 12.7. Such a dictionary is constructed by determining the network responses to each input in the test set in the presence of each unique single fault condition.

TABLE 12.6. Fault Dictionary

Test Sequence	$x_1 x_2 x_3$ 001	—	010	—	011	—	100	—	110	Condition
	0		0		0		0		0	2/0
	0		0		0		0		1	3/0
	0		0		1		0		0	1/0
Response	0		0		1		0		1	Fault-free
Sequence,	0		0		1		1		1	4/1
z	0		1		1		0		1	1/1
	1		0		1		0		1	5/1
	1		0		1		1		1	2/1
	1		1		1		1		1	6/1

Sequential Logic Circuits

We will now turn our attention to the problem of fault diagnosis of sequential logic circuits. In particular, we will look at a method of test generation and a procedure for test application.

Synchronous sequential circuits that can be represented by the finite state machine model given in Chapter 6 will be considered. A block diagram of the model is given in Fig. 6.1. The equations which describe the model are repeated below.

$$z_i = g_i(x_1, \ldots, x_n, y_1, \ldots, y_r), \quad i = 1, \ldots, m$$

$$Y_j = h_j(x_1, \ldots, x_n, y_1, \ldots, y_r), \quad j = 1, \ldots, r$$

$$y_j^{k+1} = Y_j^k, \qquad\qquad j = 1, \ldots, r.$$

In discussions that follow, the circuit inputs $x_1, \ldots, x_n$ will be referred to as *primary inputs* to the combinational logic in the model. Circuit outputs $z_1, \ldots, z_m$ will be called *primary outputs*. The states $y_1, \ldots, y_r$ and next states $Y_1, \ldots, Y_r$ will be called *secondary inputs* and *secondary outputs*, respectively.

It will be assumed that in general only primary inputs can be independently controlled and that only primary outputs can be observed during testing. In other words, tests can only be applied at the $x_1, \ldots, x_n$ inputs, and test responses can only be observed at the $z_1, \ldots, z_m$ outputs. Hence the states of the circuit cannot in general be observed.

The circuit description will be assumed to be given in the form of a circuit diagram. It will also be assumed that no redundancy exists in the circuit and that the memory elements are D type flip-flops. Additionally, it will be assumed that the fault-free circuit is a realization of a reduced state table. In other words, the state table that corresponds to the fault-free circuit contains no equivalent states. Finally, it will be assumed that the fault-free circuits are strongly connected. A circuit is *strongly connected* if and only if there exists for each ordered pair of states (S_i, S_j) of the circuit an input sequence that will transfer the circuit from state S_i to state S_j.

Test Generation

We will use an extension of path sensitizing as a test generation method. In a previous section, it was shown that a combinational logic circuit could be tested for the presence of a specified stuck-at fault by the application of a single combination of input values. Later it will be shown that a sequence of input combinations is generally required to test for a specified stuck-at fault in a sequential logic circuit.

Consider the generation of a test for fault 2/0 in the circuit shown in Fig. 12.12(a). Path sensitizing concepts can be used to show that if $x = 1$ and $y = 0$ then the fault 2/0 could be observed at the primary output z. Therefore a test for 2/0 is the application of the input $x = 1$ while the circuit is in state $y = 0$. If the circuit starts in state $y = 1$, the input $x = 1$ will take the circuit to state $y = 0$. Hence the input sequence 11 constitutes a test for the fault 2/0 regardless of the starting state of the circuit. These results are summarized below.

Starting state $y = 1$

x:	1	1
Fault-free z:	0	1
Faulty z:	0	0

Starting state $y = 0$

x:	1	1
Fault-free z:	1	0
Faulty z:	0	0

It should be noted that if the circuit is known to be in state $y = 0$, then a single $x = 1$ input provides a test for fault 2/0. But if the starting state is unknown, the 11 sequence is required.

Generally, the test sequence for a specified fault will consist of two disjoint subsequences called the *initialization sequence* (IS) and the *observation sequence* (OS). The initialization sequence takes the circuit from an unknown starting state to a state needed by the observation sequence. Then, the observation sequence completes the sensitization of a path from the fault site to a primary output of the circuit.

Circuit initialization will be considered in more detail later. For now, the discussion will be centered on the determination of the necessary initial state and the OS for a specified fault.

Consider the case of fault 4/0 in the circuit of Fig. 12.12(a). It is easily seen that no path exists from the fault site to a primary output of the circuit. However, if $y = 1$ and $x = 0$, a path is sensitized from the fault site to secondary output Y. When a clock pulse occurs, the sensitized path will be extended through the memory element. Hence, the fault 4/0 will appear at the output of the memory element. If $x = 1$ is then applied, the sensitized path will be extended to the primary output z.

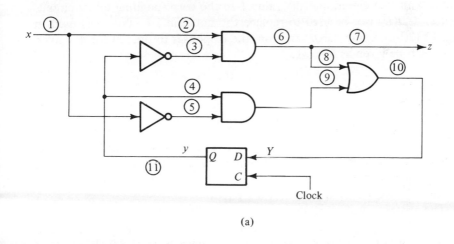

(a)

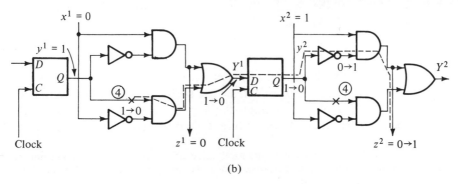

(b)

Fig. 12.12 Test generation: (a) circuit diagram; (b) iterative model.

The events described above are summarized in Fig. 12.12(b). Note that the iterative model represents, simultaneously, the original circuit for two consecutive periods of time. The iterative model is convenient for this purpose and will be utilized in the discussions that follow. A summary of the test is given below:

$$
\begin{aligned}
x&: \quad 0\ 1 \\
\text{Fault-free } y&: \quad 1\ 1 \\
\text{Faulty } y&: \quad 1\ 0 \\
\text{Fault-free } z&: \quad 0\ 0 \\
\text{Faulty } z&: \quad 0\ 1 \\
\text{Time}&: \quad 1\ 2
\end{aligned}
$$

The logic values along a sensitized path can be conveniently denoted by the symbols D or $\bar{D}$. A D implies the value 1 in a fault-free circuit and the value 0 in the corresponding faulty circuit. On the other hand, a $\bar{D}$ implies the value 0 in a fault-free circuit and the value 1 in the corresponding faulty circuit. Hence, a $D(\bar{D})$ can be used to replace the notation $1 \rightarrow 0(0 \rightarrow 1)$ used in Fig. 12.12(b).† Using the D notation, the responses to the test for 4/0 given above can be given as follows:

$$
\begin{aligned}
x&: \quad 0\ 1 \\
y&: \quad 1\ D \\
z&: \quad 0\ \bar{D} \\
\text{Time}&: \quad 1\ 2
\end{aligned}
$$

When a D or a $\bar{D}$ has been propagated to the output of a memory element, a *virtual fault* is said to exist on the corresponding line of the circuit. The concept of a virtual fault will be used when discussing the generation of observation sequences in the following pages.

The generation of an observation sequence for a specified fault in a given sequential circuit proceeds as follows. Determine an initial state and a sequence of primary inputs that sensitize a path from the fault site to a primary output of the circuit. This process can also be considered as the propagation of a $D(\bar{D})$ from the fault site to a primary output of the circuit.

A procedure for generating an observation sequence is given below for a specified fault.

STEP 1. Using path-sensitizing concepts, choose an initial state $\mathbf{y}^k$ and an input $\mathbf{x}^k$ that propagates a D or $\bar{D}$ from the fault site to a primary output $\mathbf{z}^k$. If this can be accomplished, compute the response of the circuit to the chosen $\mathbf{y}^k$ and $\mathbf{x}^k$, and terminate the procedure. Otherwise, go to step 2.

---

†The symbol $D(\bar{D})$ representing the logic value of a sensitized path should not be confused with the symbol D that represents the data input terminal of a D flip-flop. Both notations are in common use.

STEP 2. Using path-sensitizing concepts, choose an initial state and an input that propagates a D or $\bar{D}$ from the fault site to a secondary output $\mathbf{Y}^k$. If more than one choice exists, make an arbitrary selection. Compute the response of the circuit to the selected $\mathbf{y}^k$ and $\mathbf{x}^k$. Go to step 3.

STEP 3. Choose an input $\mathbf{x}^{k+1}$ that will propagate the virtual fault reflected in $\mathbf{y}^{k+1}$ to a primary output $\mathbf{z}^{k+1}$. If this can be accomplished, compute the response of the circuit to the chosen $\mathbf{x}^{k+1}$ and terminate the procedure. Otherwise, go to step 4.

STEP 4. Choose an input $\mathbf{x}^{k+1}$ that will propagate the virtual fault in $\mathbf{y}^{k+1}$ to a secondary output $\mathbf{Y}^{k+1}$. If more than one choice exists, make an arbitrary selection and compute the circuit response. If no choice exists, go to step 5. Otherwise, return to step 3, replacing k with $k + 1$.

STEP 5. Return to the last step (k') of the procedure where an arbitrary choice was made. Delete this selection and all succeeding selections. Make a new selection and go to step 3, replacing k with $k' + 1$.

Example.

The procedure outlined above will be used to generate observation sequences for the faults 7/0 and 8/1 in the circuit given in Fig. 12.13(a). Iterative models of the circuit are shown in Fig. 12.13(b) and (c) for faults 7/0 and 8/1, respectively.

Consider fault 7/0.

STEP 1. No path exists from line 7 to z. Therefore, go to step 2.

STEP 2. A path exists from line 7 to secondary output Y_1. The path can be sensitized to the output by choosing $\mathbf{y}^1 = 10$ and $\mathbf{x}^1 = 1$. Responses to this input combination are $\mathbf{Y}^1 = D0$ and $z^1 = 1$. Go to step 3.

STEP 3. Since $\mathbf{Y}^1 = D0$, $\mathbf{y}^2 = D0$. The virtual fault $y_1 = D$ can be propagated to z by choosing $\mathbf{x}^2 = 1$. The circuit response will be $\mathbf{Y}^2 = D\bar{D}$ and $z = D$. Terminate the procedure.

In summary, a test for fault 7/0 in the circuit can be accomplished by setting the circuit to state 10 and then applying the input $x = 1$ for the next two consecutive clock pulses. The corresponding output response will be $0D$. In other words, a 01 response will be obtained when 7/0 is not present, and a 00 response will be obtained if 7/0 is present.

Consider fault 8/1.

STEP 1. Cannot be accomplished. Go to step 2.

STEP 2. Choose $\mathbf{y}^1 = 00$ and $\mathbf{x}^1 = 1$. The circuit response is $\mathbf{Y}^1 = \bar{D}1$ and $\mathbf{z}^1 = 0$. Go to step 3.

STEP 3. Note that a path exists from the virtual fault $y_1^2 = \bar{D}$ to the output z^2. However, the path cannot be sensitized since $y_2^2 = 1$. Therefore, the virtual fault must be propagated to a secondary output. Go to step 4.

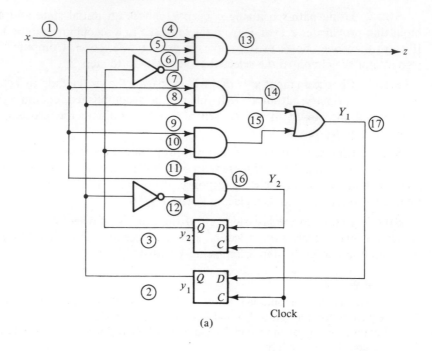

(a)

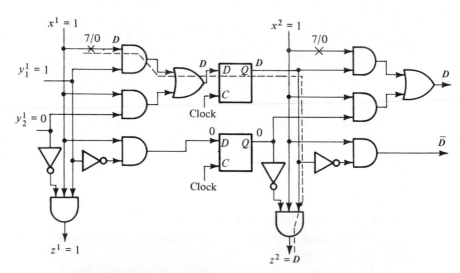

Fig. 12.13 Observation sequence generation: (a) circuit diagram; (b) observation sequence for 7/0.

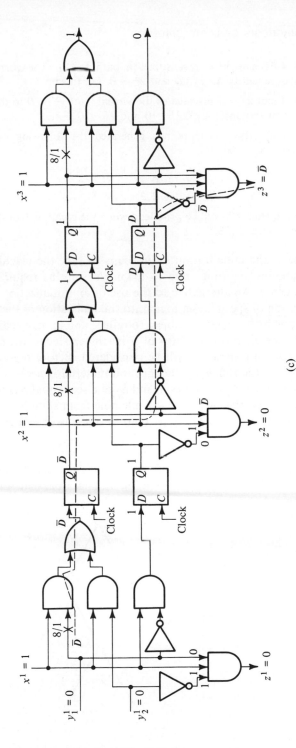

Fig. 12.13—*Cont.* (c) Observation sequence for 8/1.

STEP 4. Choosing $x^2 = 1$ sensitizes a path to Y_2. The corresponding circuit response will be $Y^2 = 1D$ and $z^2 = 0$. Go to step 3.

STEP 3. Input $x^3 = 1$ propagates the virtual fault $y_2^3 = D$ to the primary output. Circuit responses are $Y^3 = 10$ and $z^3 = \bar{D}$.

In summary, the procedure has generated the following observation sequence given $y^1 = 00$:

$$\begin{array}{llll} x: & 1 & 1 & 1 \\ z: & 0 & 0 & \bar{D} \\ t: & 1 & 2 & 3 \end{array}$$

An output sequence 000 will be produced when the circuit is fault-free, while 001 will be produced if 8/1.

The purpose of the initialization sequence is to take the machine under test from an unknown starting state to a known state as required by the observation sequence. An alternative to the use of an initialization sequence is the incorporation of special reset logic into the realization of the machine. However, the reset logic would be subject to failure and in many cases would not be practical for all possible states of a machine. Hence, the subject of initialization sequence generation will be considered. Before presenting this discussion, however, the following background material is necessary.

A *transfer sequence* (TS) for states S_i and S_j of a sequential machine is the shortest input sequence that will take the machine from state S_i to state S_j. The following example illustrates the derivation of transfer sequences.

Example.

We want to derive the minimum input sequence that will take the sequential circuit described by the state table in Fig. 12.14(a) from state A to state B.

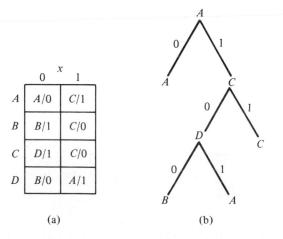

	x	
	0	1
A	A/0	C/1
B	B/1	C/0
C	D/1	C/0
D	B/0	A/1

(a)   (b)

Fig. 12.14 Deriving a transfer sequence: (a) state table; (b) transfer tree.

To accomplish this, we assume the circuit is in state A and we form the tree shown in Fig. 12.14(b). The tree, which is derived from the state table, indicates that an input of 0 or 1 when applied to the circuit in state A will transfer the circuit to state A or state C, respectively. The complete tree is generated by following this procedure and terminating a branch whenever a state is duplicated.

Figure 12.14(b) shows that the shortest transfer sequence that will drive the circuit from state A to state B is $x = 100$.

A *homing sequence* (HS) is an input sequence that produces an output response that indicates the state of a machine after the homing sequence has been applied. A *preset homing sequence* is a homing sequence that does not employ the output response to determine subsequent inputs in the sequence. In other words, the symbols in the sequence are independent of the response to the sequence. The derivation of preset homing sequences will be illustrated by the following example.

Example.

The sequential circuit for which we will obtain a homing sequence is defined by the state table in Fig. 12.15(a). The homing sequence is derived via the homing tree shown in Fig. 12.15(b). Each node of the tree represents

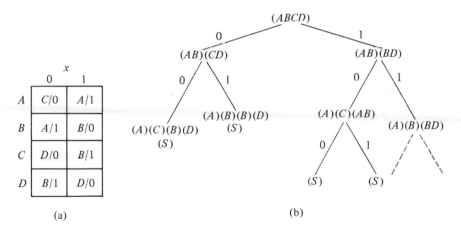

(a)   (b)

Initial State	Input	Output	Final State
A	00	00	D
B	00	10	C
C	00	01	B
D	00	11	A

(c)

Fig. 12.15   A preset homing sequence: (a) state table; (b) homing tree; (c) homing sequence 00.

a set of states referred to as an *ambiguity* since it indicates a lack of knowledge about the actual state of the circuit. A branch is drawn from each node for each possible input to the circuit. The tree is constructed as follows. Assume the ambiguity (ABCD) which indicates that the state of the circuit is unknown. Determine the ambiguity (AB) (CD) for a 0 input. Note that the component (AB) corresponds to an output of 1, and the component (CD) corresponds to an output of 0. The complete homing tree is derived by generating the branches in this manner. A branch is terminated whenever all components of an ambiguity contain only a single state or when an ambiguity is repeated. The ambiguities containing only single state components are labeled with an (S) as shown in Fig. 12.15(b). The input sequences which lead from the initial ambiguity (ABCD) to an ambiguity containing only single state components are homing sequences.

An analysis of the homing sequence 00 is shown in Fig. 12.15(c). Note that every output sequence can be identified with a unique final state.

All reduced sequential machines possess at least one homing sequence. By definition, a strongly connected machine has at least one transfer sequence for each ordered pair of states. Hence, a reduced, strongly connected machine M can be initialized to any desired state S_i by the method described below.

1. Select a homing sequence (HS) for M.
2. Apply HS to M and observe the output response.
3. Determine state of M after applying HS. Call this state S_j.
4. If $S_i \neq S_j$, apply a transfer sequence TS(S_j, S_i).

The generation of initialization sequences as described above pertains to fault-free circuits. Hence, if an initialization sequence so generated is applied to a faulty circuit then the desired initialization may or may not occur. This suggests two questions. First, if the proper initialization does not occur, can the fault be detected by the method described here? Second, can initialization sequences be generated that are independent of the fault? Answers to these questions are beyond the scope of this text. Hence, it will be assumed that initialization to the proper state can be accomplished by some means.

Testing Procedures

A testing procedure for sequential circuits will now be described that is based on the above approach to test generation. The procedure will be followed by an illustrative example.

STEP 1. Generate an observation sequence for each possible single fault in the circuit.

STEP 2. Construct a test table.

STEP 3. Identify observation sequences covered by another observation sequence. A sequence OS_1 covers a sequence OS_2 if OS_1 and OS_2 require the same initial state and if each element in OS_2 is the same as the corresponding element in OS_1. For example, the sequence 11 with initial state 10 covers the sequence 1 with initial state 10.

STEP 4. Reduce the test table by merging observation sequences that are covered into the covering sequence.

STEP 5. Assign a weight to each observation sequence in the reduced table. The weight of a given OS is equal to the number of faults tested by the sequence.

STEP 6. Initialize the circuit to a state required by an observation sequence with the largest weight.

STEP 7. Apply the corresponding observation sequence. If a fault-free response is obtained, go to step 8. Otherwise, terminate the test procedure.

STEP 8. Identify an observation sequence that satisfies the following criteria. The OS requires as an initial state the final state produced by the previous OS. The sequence has the largest weight of all such OS's. If such a sequence exists, go to step 7. Otherwise, go to step 9.

STEP 9. Identify the observation sequence with the largest weight that has not been applied to the circuit. If all sequences have been applied, terminate the test. Otherwise, go to step 10.

STEP 10. Initialize the circuit to the initial state required by the OS chosen in step 9. Go to step 7.

The procedure outlined above will test for all single faults in the circuit. However, the test sequence generated by the procedure may not be minimum in length.

Example.

Consider the circuit given in Fig. 12.13(a). The above procedure will be used to generate a test sequence for the circuit.

STEP 1. Follow the observation sequence generation procedure described earlier for each possible fault in the circuit.

STEP 2. A test table for the circuit is given in Table 12.7.

STEP 3. OS_1 is covered by OS_5. OS_2 is covered by OS_7, etc.

STEP 4. Table 12.8 shows the reduced test table. Note that output sequences are modified to reflect the mergers of observation sequences. Also, the corresponding fault sets are separated by a semicolon.

STEP 5. The weights of each OS are given in Table 12.8.

STEP 6. OS_6 of the reduced table has the largest weight. Therefore initialize the circuit to state 10.

STEP 7. Apply the input sequence 11. The circuit is left in state 10.

TABLE 12.7. Test Table

	Required Initial State, y_1 y_2	Observation Sequence, x	Output Sequence, z	Final State, y_1 y_2	Faults Tested
1	1 0	1	D	1 0	1/0, 2/0, 3/1, 4/0, 5/0, 6/0, 13/0
2	1 0	0	$\bar{D}$	0 0	1/1, 4/1, 13/1
3	0 0	1	$\bar{D}$	0 1	2/1, 5/1, 13/1
4	1 1	1	$\bar{D}$	1 0	3/0, 6/1, 13/1
5	1 0	1 1	1 D	1 0	7/0, 8/0
6	0 0	1 1 1	0 0 $\bar{D}$	1 0	8/1, 10/1
7	1 0	0 1	0 $\bar{D}$	0 1	7/1
8	0 1	1 1 1	0 0 D	1 0	9/0, 10/0
9	0 1	0 1	0 $\bar{D}$	0 1	9/1
10	0 1	1 1	0 $\bar{D}$	1 0	11/0, 12/0, 16/0
11	0 0	0 1 1 1	0 0 0 $\bar{D}$	1 0	11/1
12	1 1	1 1	0 D	1 0	12/1, 16/1, 17/0
13	0 0	0 1	0 $\bar{D}$	0 1	17/1

TABLE 12.8. Reduced Test Table

	Initial State, y_1 y_2	Observation Sequence, x	Output Sequence, z	Final State	Faults Tested	Weight
1	0 0	1 1 1	$\bar{D}$ 0 $\bar{D}$	1 0	2/1, 5/1, 13/1; 8/1, 10/ 1	5
2	0 0	0 1 1 1	0 $\bar{D}$ 0 $\bar{D}$	1 0	17/1; 11/1	2
3	0 1	0 1	0 $\bar{D}$	0 1	9/1	1
4	0 1	1 1 1	0 $\bar{D}$ $\bar{D}$	1 0	11/0, 12/0, 16/0; 9/0, 10/0	5
5	1 0	0 1	$\bar{D}$ $\bar{D}$	0 1	1/1, 4/1, 13/1; 7/1	4
6	1 0	1 1	D D	1 0	1/0, 2/0, 3/1, 4/0, 5/0, 6/0, 13/0; 7/0, 8/0	9
7	1 1	1 1	$\bar{D}$ D	1 0	3/0, 6/1, 13/1; 12/1, 16/1, 17/0	6

STEP 8. OS_5 requires 10 as an initial state.

STEP 7. Apply the input sequence 01. The circuit is left in state 01.

STEP 8. OS_3 and OS_4 require an initial state 01. OS_4 has a larger weight than OS_3.

STEP 7. Apply input sequence 111. The circuit is left in state 10.

STEP 8. No remaining OS requires 10 as the initial state. Go to step 9.

STEP 9. OS_7 has the largest weight of all sequences not yet applied.

STEP 10. Initialize the circuit to state 11. Go to step 7.

STEP 7. Apply input sequence 11. The circuit is left in state 10.

STEP 8. No remaining sequence requires the initial state 10.

STEP 9. OS_1 has the largest weight of the remaining tests.

STEP 10. Initialize the circuit to state 00. Go to step 7.

STEP 7. Apply the input sequence 111. The final state is 10.

STEP 8. No remaining observation sequences require 10 as the initial state.

STEP 9. OS_2 has the largest weight of the remaining tests.

STEP 10. Set the circuit to state 00. Go to step 7.

STEP 7. Apply the input sequence 0111. The circuit is left in state 10.

STEP 8. No remaining sequences require initial state 10.

STEP 9. OS_3 has the largest weight of the remaining sequences.

STEP 10. Set the circuit to state 01. Go to step 7.

STEP 7. Apply the input sequence 01. The circuit is left in state 01.

STEP 8. No remaining sequences required initial state 01.

STEP 9. All sequences have been used. Terminate the procedure. The following input-output sequence has been generated:

	OS_6		OS_5		OS_4			OS_7		OS_1			OS_2				OS_3

$$x: \; 1 \;\; 1 \;\; 0 \;\; 1 \;\; 1 \;\; 1 \;\; 1 -1 \;\; 1 -1 \;\; 1 \;\; 1 -0 \;\; 1 \;\; 1 \;\; 1 -0 \;\; 1$$
$$z: \; D \;\; D \;\; \bar{D} \;\; \bar{D} \;\; 0 \;\; \bar{D} \;\; \bar{D} -\bar{D} \;\; D -\bar{D} \;\; 0 \;\; \bar{D} -0 \;\; \bar{D} \;\; 0 \;\; \bar{D} -0 \;\; \bar{D}$$

A dash indicates a point in the test where the circuit must be reset to a state as required by the OS to follow.

Consider for a moment the question of fault location. The circuit testing approach is suited for use in testing for fault location to a set of indistinguishable faults. For the previous example, assume that the following results are obtained when the test sequence is applied:

	OS_6		OS_5		OS_4	

$$x: \; 1 \;\; 1 \;\; 0 \;\; 0 \;\; 1 \;\; 1 \; \ldots$$
$$z: \; 1 \;\; 1 \;\; 0 \;\; 0 \;\; 0 \;\; 1 \; \ldots$$

These results indicate that an incorrect response was obtained for the second input of OS_4. Hence, from the reduced test table, Table 12.8, it can be concluded that the fault is either 11/0, 12/0, or 16/0.

Summary

This chapter has introduced the subject of fault diagnosis of logic circuits. First, a general discussion of fault diagnosis was presented. Next, fault diagnosis for combinational logic networks was discussed. Methods for generating tests and for making a diagnosis were considered. Finally, test generation and application procedures were described for sequential logic circuits.

REFERENCES

1. ARMSTRONG, D. B., "On Finding a Nearly Minimal Set of Fault Detection Tests for Combinational Logic Nets," *IEEETEC*, Vol. EC-15, No. 1, February 1966, pp. 66–73.

2. AVIZIENIS, A., "Fault Tolerant Computing: An Overview," *Computer*, Vol. 5, No. 1, January–February 1971, pp. 5–7.

3. BOSSEN, D. C., and S. J. HONG, "Cause-Effect Analysis for Multiple Fault Detection in Combinational Networks," *IEEETC*, Vol. C-20, No. 11, November 1971, pp. 1252–1257.

4. BOURICIUS, W. G., E. P. HSIEH, G. R. PUTZOLU, J. P. ROTH, P. R. SCHNEIDER, and C. J. TAN, "Algorithms for Detection of Faults in Logic Circuits," *IEEETC*, Vol. C-20, No. 11, November 1971, pp. 1258–1264.

5. BREUER, M. A., "A Random and an Algorithmic Technique for Fault Detection Test Generation for Sequential Circuits," *IEEETC*, Vol. C-20, No. 11, November 1971, pp. 1364–1371.

6. CHANG, H. Y., E. G. MANNING, and G. METZE, *Fault Diagnosis of Digital Systems*. New York: John Wiley & Sons, Inc. (Interscience Division), 1970.

7. FRIEDMAN, A. D., and P. R. MENON, *Fault Detection in Digital Circuits*. Englewood Cliffs, N.J.: Prentice-Hall, Inc., 1971.

8. HENNIE, F. C., *Finite-State Models for Logical Machines*. New York: John Wiley & Sons, Inc., 1968.

9. KAUTZ, W. H., "Fault Testing and Diagnosis in Combinational Digital Circuits," *IEEETC*, Vol. C-17, No. 4, April 1968, pp. 352–367.

10. KOHAVI, Z., and P. LAVALLEE, "Design of Sequential Machines with Fault Detection Capabilities," *IEEETEC*, Vol. EC-16, No. 4, August 1967, pp. 473–484.

11. MOORE, E. F., "Gedanken-Experiments on Sequential Machines," in *Automata Studies*, ed. by C. E. Shannon. Princeton, N.J.: Princeton University Press, 1956.

12. ROTH, J. P., W. G. BOURICIUS, and P. R. SCHNEIDER, "Programmed Algorithms to Compute Tests to Detect and Distinguish Between Failures in Logic Circuits," *IEEETEC*, Vol. EC-16, No. 5, October 1967, pp. 567–580.

PROBLEMS

12.1. Determine the function realized by the network in Fig. P12.1 for each of the following faults:
  (a) 1/0.
  (b) 1/1.
  (c) 3/0.
  (d) 4/1.

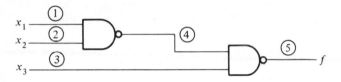

Fig. P12.1

12.2. Repeat Problem 12.1 for faults
  (a) 2/0.
  (b) 8/1.
  (c) 9/0.
  (d) 5/0.
  in the network in Fig. P12.2.

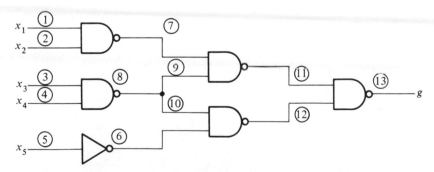

Fig. P12.2

12.3. Use the EXCULSIVE-OR method to determine all tests for all faults listed in Problem 12.1.

12.4. Repeat Problem 12.3 using the path-sensitizing method.

12.5.   Use the EXCULSIVE-OR method to determine all tests for all faults listed in Problem 12.2.

12.6.   Repeat Problem 12.5 using the path-sensitizing method.

12.7.   List all faults which can be detected by each of the following tests for the network in Fig. P12.2:
(a) 10101.
(b) 10100.
(c) 11011.
(d) 11010.

12.8.   Construct a fault table containing all possible faults and all possible input combinations for the network in Fig. P12.1.

12.9.   Construct a fault table containing only checkpoint faults for the network in Fig. P12.3.

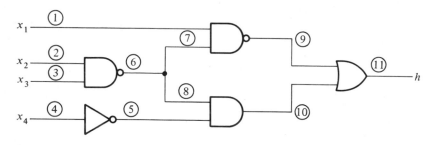

Fig. P12.3

12.10.   Find a minimum FDTS from the fault table below:

Tests \ Faults	a	b	c	d	e	f	g	h
000	1							1
001		1				1		
010	1		1				1	
011				1		1		
100	1							1
101		1			1		1	
110							1	1
111	1			1			1	1

12.11.   Find a FDTS from the table in Problem 12.10 using the near-minimum selection procedure.

12.12. Repeat Problems 12.10 and 12.11 for the following table:

Tests \ Faults	a	b	c	d	e	f	g	h	i
1	1		1						
2		1		1		1			
3			1		1				
4				1					1
5					1		1		
6		1							1
7							1	1	
8	1							1	

12.13. Determine all tests which can be used to distinguish each of the following
pairs of faults:
(a) 1/0–4/1.
(b) 2/0–3/0.
(c) 7/0–8/0.
(d) 1/1–7/1.
Refer to Fig. P12.3.

12.14. Given the circuit in Fig. P12.4, determine an initialization sequence and

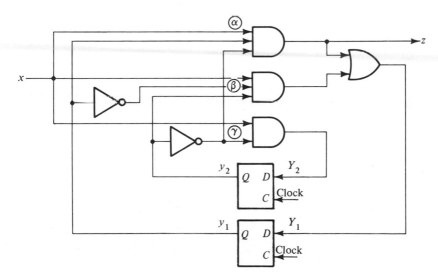

Fig. P12.4

an observation sequence for each of the following faults:
(a) $\alpha/1$.
(b) $\beta/0$.
(c) $\gamma/1$.

12.15. Repeat Problem 12.14 for the circuit given in Fig. P12.5 and the following faults:
(a) $\alpha/1$.
(b) $\beta/0$.
(c) $\gamma/0$.
(d) $\delta/1$.

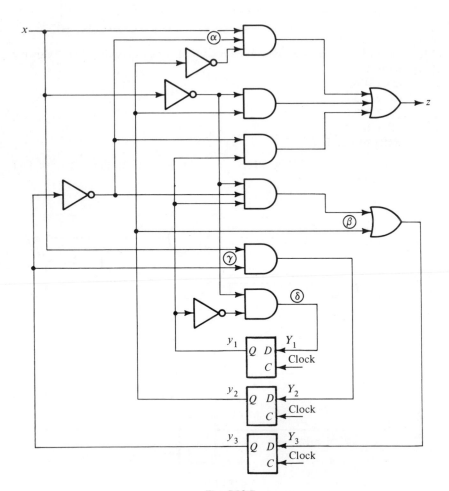

Fig. P12.5

12.16   Reduce the hypothetical test table shown below by taking advantage of test coverage:

	Initial State	Observation Sequence	Output Sequence	Final State	Faults Covered	
1	S_1	1	$\bar{D}$	S_2	$a_0,$	c_1
2	S_2	0	$\bar{D}$	S_2	$b_0,$	i_0
3	S_3	1	$\bar{D}$	S_3	$g_0,$	f_0
4	S_4	0	D	S_1	$h_1,$	b_1
5	S_2	1	$\bar{D}$	S_3	$l_0,$	e_0
6	S_1	11	$0\bar{D}$	S_3	$j_0,$	g_1
7	S_3	10	$0\bar{D}$	S_4	$n_0,$	j_1
8	S_3	00	$0D$	S_1	$p_0,$	m_0
9	S_2	10	$0\bar{D}$	S_4	$f_1,$	h_0
10	S_4	011	$10\bar{D}$	S_3	$a_1,$	i_1
11	S_2	100	$00D$	S_1	$n_1,$	k_0
12	S_3	100	$00D$	S_1	$p_1,$	l_1
13	S_1	101	$00\bar{D}$	S_3	$d_0,$	k_1
14	S_2	1001	$001\bar{D}$	S_2	$m_1,$	d_1
15	S_4	0111	$100\bar{D}$	S_3	$e_1,$	c_0

12.17.   Develop a test procedure for a circuit with the following reduced test table:

	Initial State	Observation Sequence	Output Sequence	Final State	Faults Covered
1	S_1	011	$0\bar{D}\bar{D}$	S_3	$a_0, d_1; e_1, h_0$
2	S_2	111	$\bar{D}1D$	S_1	$b_1; e_0$
3	S_3	010	$01\bar{D}$	S_4	c_0, f_0
4	S_4	001	$0\bar{D}D$	S_1	$a_1, c_1, f_1; g_0, h_1$
5	S_1	100	$0\bar{D}$	S_2	b_0, d_0, g_1

12.18.   The circuit whose test table is given in Problem 12.17 is initialized to state S_1. An input sequence 011010 is applied to the circuit and the output response 001010 is observed. Is the circuit faulty? If yes, what fault is present?

12.19.   The circuit shown in Fig. P12.6 is initialized to state $y_1 = 0, y_2 = 1$, and the
input sequence $x = 010111$ is applied. Determine all single faults that would
be detected by this sequence.

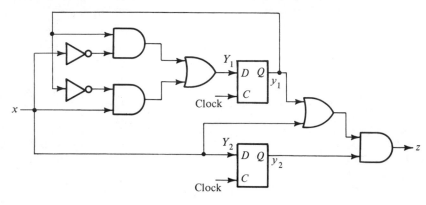

Fig. P12.6

Index